30.00

ROMAN HISTORY

THE THEORY OF
THE MIXED CONSTITUTION
IN ANTIQUITY

KURT VON FRITZ

ARNO PRESS
A New York Times Company
New York — 1975

Editorial Supervision: MARIE STARECK

————◆————

Reprint Edition 1975 by Arno Press Inc.

Copyright © 1954 Columbia University Press,
  New York
Reprinted by permission of
  Columbia University Press

ROMAN HISTORY
ISBN for complete set: 0-405-07177-9
See last pages of this volume for titles.

Manufactured in the United States of America

————◆————

Library of Congress Cataloging in Publication Data

Fritz, Kurt von, 1900-
    The theory of the mixed constitution in antiquity.

    (Roman history)
    Reprint of the ed. published by Columbia University
Press, New York.
    Bibliography: p.
    1. Polybius. 2. State, The. I. Title. II. Series.
[JC81.P767F7 1975]   320.1'5   75-7318
ISBN 0-405-07082-9

The Theory of the
Mixed Constitution in Antiquity

KURT VON FRITZ

The Theory of
the Mixed Constitution
in Antiquity

A CRITICAL ANALYSIS OF
POLYBIUS' POLITICAL IDEAS

NEW YORK

COLUMBIA UNIVERSITY PRESS

The Stanwood Cockey Lodge Foundation has generously provided funds to assist in the publication of this volume.

PUBLISHED IN GREAT BRITAIN, CANADA, INDIA, AND PAKISTAN
BY THE OXFORD UNIVERSITY PRESS
LONDON, TORONTO, BOMBAY, AND KARACHI

LIBRARY OF CONGRESS CATALOG CARD NUMBER: 54-10329

MANUFACTURED IN THE UNITED STATES OF AMERICA

PREFACE AND INTRODUCTION

No PART of ancient political theory has had a greater influence on political theory and practice in modern times than the theory of the mixed constitution.

This theory is for the first time found in Plato's *Laws*. It appears first in the story told in the third book of that work: The three Peloponnesian kingdoms of Argos, Lacedaemon, and Messene entered into a compact providing that, if ever in any one of them the king should try to exceed the limits of his power under the law, or the people should try to deprive the king of his legitimate powers, the two other nations would come to the help of the party that had been wronged. The theory appears for the second time, and in a more elaborate form, in the same book in an analysis of the Spartan constitution.

This second analysis, which follows closely upon the first one, is preceded by the statement that the soul of a mortal is not able to wield sovereign power, the greatest among men, without being filled with unreasonableness, the greatest disease, and so incurring hatred. A god who saw this, so Plato continues, gave the Spartans a double kingship in order to bring the power of each of the kings nearer to the right measure. Then a man who had within him the divine spark, when he saw that the sovereign power was still "boiling over," mixed it with the power of a council of elders, and finally, when even after this the royal power was still not without insolence, the ephors were added as an additional fetter.

It is clear that in both cases Plato is concerned with the danger inherent in absolute political power, and that he is of the opinion that there must be a check to all political power, and that this must be done by distributing power over several governmental agencies which counterbalance one another. On the other hand, he speaks of a mixture of these various agencies and devices. So in a way what he says includes the notions of a mixed political order and of a system of checks and balances, though these two terms are not used explicitly.

After Plato the same fundamental idea recurs in Aristotle, Dicaearchus, and other ancient writers. But it is in the form which it was given by Polybius that it has had its greatest influence on modern political theory and practice. Polybius' theory was taken up, discussed and, with some modifications, adopted by Cicero in his *De re publica,* and though this work is supposed to have been lost until a palimpsest with a large part of it was discovered in 1821, there can hardly be any doubt that St. Thomas had some knowledge of it and was to some extent influenced by it. Machiavelli, who, according to a very widely accepted opinion, stands on the threshold of modern political philosophy, in his *Discorsi* (Chapter VI) repeats several pages of Polybius' sixth book in a paraphrase sometimes approaching a literal translation without mentioning Polybius' name. From then on the theory in its Polybian form, or in various forms strongly influenced by Polybius either directly or indirectly, remained an important thread in modern European political thought, a development which in a way culminated in Montesquieu's *De l'esprit des lois.* It is true that for Montesquieu the English constitution played a similar role to that of the Roman constitution for Polybius. But just as Polybius' analysis of the Roman constitution was prompted by the observation that this political order, though it had not been molded according to a preconceived theory, but had come into being through a long and natural development, appeared to present a perfect illustration of the truth of theories elaborated by his predecessors, so Montesquieu also would hardly have arrived at his theory on the basis of an observation of the English constitution alone if there had not been earlier, similar theories, of which that of Polybius was undoubtedly the most influential.

As everybody knows, the theory in the new form which it was given by Montesquieu has had a dominating influence on the shaping of the constitution of the United States. But beyond that one can say that, though there have been various cross-currents, the great majority of the many constitutions that have been made and adopted in Western Europe in the nineteenth and twentieth centuries have been decisively influenced by the related, though by no means identical, theories of the mixed constitution, of the system of checks and balances, and of the separation of powers. There has of course been no period in history in which the theory was not opposed by some political writers, but generally speaking one may say that the theory was dominant in the Western world in the latter half of the eighteenth and the first half of the nineteenth centuries. The theoretical controversy at that time turned rather around the question of whether a system of checks and balances could and should be based on a written constitution consciously elaborated according to certain principles of reason, or whether such a system can function only when it is based on precedent and custom as they developed through the centuries. Since then criticism of the theory has been steadily on the increase, not only in the so-called totalitarian countries but also in the so-called democracies. In the Anglo-Saxon countries this criticism has mainly assumed the form of a revival of Hobbes's theory of sovereignty.

Polybius himself had offered his theory not as a purely theoretical construction, but as the result of historical studies. Specifically he believed that the two examples of Sparta and Rome proved beyond doubt the superiority of what he called mixed constitutions over any other kind of constitution, and he had therefore supplemented his purely theoretical chapters by an analysis of the constitutions of these two countries, especially the constitution of Rome. But the validity of his historical analysis has also been questioned. Mommsen in the second volume of his Roman history expressed the opinion that nothing could be more absurd than Polybius' attempt to explain the excellent political order of the Roman Republic as an even mixture of monarchy, oligarchy, and democracy. E. Schwartz, on the other hand, who, though better known as a philologist, was also a historian of high rank, spoke of Polybius' deep understanding for the essence of the Roman state. Yet these scholars were among the highest-ranking experts in the field of ancient history. If one takes up the ordinary textbooks on the history of political theory or ancient political theory, he will find the whole scale of possible judgments, ranging from the highest admiration for the brilliance of Polybius' analysis to its complete depreciation as a purely theoretical construction which has little, if any, relation to political reality.

There have been several attempts to determine in what way Polybius was influenced by his predecessors and by various philosophical doctrines, especially the doctrines of the Stoics. But no major attempt seems ever to have been made to show in detail how far Polybius'

analysis of the historical phenomena on which his theory, according
to his own testimony, is based, is correct or what its deficiencies are,
if any. Nor has any attempt ever been made to show clearly and in
detail in what way Polybius was influenced by his own experience as a
statesman in the Achaean League, or in what way he tried to apply
whatever theories or ideas he may have taken over from his predecessors to the historical reality which he tried to analyze, how far his
analysis was influenced by such preconceived ideas, or how far his
theory was actually the result of concrete historical observation. Yet it
would seem obvious that it is not possible to arrive at sound and
reliable conclusions in the welter of conflicting opinions found in modern books except through a thorough and objective investigation of
this kind. To fill this gap, at least to some extent, is the purpose of
the present book.

An investigation of this kind is by no means an easy task. This is
especially true of its most important part, the comparison of Polybius'
theory with the actual development and functioning of the Roman
constitution. Our knowledge of and insight into the history of the
Roman constitution have made very considerable progress since the
time when Mommsen wrote his two monumental works, his *Römische
Geschichte* and his *Römisches Staatsrecht;* and quite a number of problems which he had left unsolved have been solved in the meantime.
But as is always the case in the progress of science and scholarship, the
solution of some problems has led to new problems, and a number of
questions to which definite answers apparently had been given were
opened again, since the answers had once more become uncertain. This
is an endless process. Everywhere specialization turns to ever more
minute problems and investigations, and so frequently becomes farther
and farther removed from the great issues. Yet specialization loses its
meaning if it is not again and again related to greater problems. There
is no perfect solution of this difficulty. But the attempt must always
be made to bridge the ever-widening gap.

In the present case nothing would be more helpful and convenient
than if all the major relevant problems of the history of the Roman
constitution had been solved definitely and if such firmly established
factual historical knowledge could be used to test the accuracy of
Polybius' theoretical analysis. Consequently nothing has been farther

from the desire of the author of the present book than to make new contributions in this connection to the history of the Roman constitution. Unfortunately the actual situation is very different. It is completely impossible to test the accuracy of Polybius' theory against its historical background without touching almost constantly on controversial points of Roman constitutional history. It was therefore necessary to find a way of dealing with such questions. I have dealt with two questions which are of fundamental importance for the present inquiry in two special papers which were written in preparation for the present book and published elsewhere (see list on pp. 475 ff.), and I may therefore perhaps be excused for citing these papers frequently where this is necessary. But if I had tried to write special papers on every controversial point that has to be touched in this book, it would never have been written. Most of the controversial questions, therefore, had somehow to be dealt with within the book. When dealing with such matters it is of course desirable to present the whole material and to discuss it thoroughly. But if I had tried to do this, the result would have been a book of several volumes unusable for the reader for whom it is mainly destined. I therefore had to find an abbreviated method of dealing with such problems. It seems to me that to a rather considerable degree this is quite possible. To take an example, not from constitutional history but from the investigation of Polybius' philosophical background: The attempt has been made several times to show that Polybius was a Stoic because he often uses Stoic terms and because he sometimes appears to advocate a "Stoic" attitude, especially in military and political leaders. It certainly would be desirable to collect and present all the evidence. Yet it seems to me that if it can be shown in a few pages with a few striking examples that Polybius uses Stoic terms in so un-Stoic a fashion that he cannot possibly have been a Stoic in a technical sense, though as an educated man he knew Stoicism and though he was obviously impressed by it, this is a more pertinent contribution to the question than a collection of all Stoic terms in Polybius' work, with the added conclusion that on the basis of such statistics he must have been a Stoic.

In regard to the history of the Roman constitution it was, in addition, necessary to concentrate strictly on those points which are of the greatest relevance for the problem under discussion and to leave many problems untouched which are either of only secondary importance or too complicated to be dealt with, even in an abbreviated form, within the context of the present book. Thus, when in the seventh chapter I had to show that most of the powers which Polybius attributed to the Senate had no firm legal basis, I have adduced the most striking pieces of evidence in four of the five fields of power mentioned by Polybius, but have merely referred to the fifth, i.e., the powers of the Senate in regard to the "allied" communities in Italy, since the problems in regard to this field are so complicated that it would have required a book on that subject alone to deal with them in any adequate way. However, though it would have been desirable to carry through the demonstration for all five fields if this had been possible within the framework of the present book, it was sufficient to demonstrate the point in four of the five fields in order to show conclusively that the powers attributed to the Senate were of a somewhat different nature from those of the consuls and of the popular assemblies, and also that there had been very considerable shifts of power within the period during which, according to Polybius, the balance of power between consuls, Senate, and people continued to be almost perfect.

It is hardly necessary to say that everything which is not strictly relevant to the subject had to be excluded. Thus I made only the shortest possible reference to the importance of alliances between noble families in Roman politics, not because I am unaware of the very great value of the numerous books which have been written on this subject in recent years, but because it seems to me that this aspect of Roman political life, however interesting in itself, has only a remote connection at best with the problem of the mixed constitution. Likewise, to take an example from a different context, when I pointed out that the term "tyrant" in the seventh to fifth centuries B.C. in Greece designated not merely a bad monarch, but acquired a technical meaning which makes it very useful in designating a political phenomenon generally neglected in political theory, I did not discuss the Oriental origin and pre-Greek meaning of this term. The reader therefore should not look for this kind of information.

A difficulty of composition arose from the fact that the book, though a large part of it is concerned with ancient history, is addressed not only to ancient historians but also to political theorists. If the assumption could have been made that all or most of its readers will have a fairly detailed knowledge of Roman history, about one third of the ninth and tenth chapters could have been omitted. Since this could not be expected, it was necessary to describe in these chapters as briefly as possible some aspects of the composition of the population of the Roman empire and some events of the last century of the Republic with which the expert in ancient history is quite familiar. I have tried to connect the presentation of facts with the theoretical analysis in such a way that there are no long passages containing anything but known facts, but it was not possible to eliminate such passages altogether if the less well-prepared reader was not to be left in the dark concerning the concrete historical foundations of the general analysis.

While the expert in ancient history may find in the ninth and tenth chapters of the present book some pages that do not tell him anything new, the political scientist may perhaps consider some of the first chapters, which deal with Polybius' personal background and with his general methods and studies, unnecessarily detailed. I do not believe that such a judgment would be justified. It is true that in a sense the validity of Polybius' theory can be tested on the basis of the historical evidence alone. The reader who is interested only in this aspect of the question may begin the book with the fifth chapter, or, if he wishes, he may even begin with the last chapter and read the book backwards. I am convinced that anyone who concerns himself seriously with the problems which it poses will ultimately come to ask most of the questions which the first four chapters try to answer, for it is not sufficient to show that one part of a political theory is supported by the historical evidence while another part is proved to be unsound. It is also necessary to find the source of the errors, and this is not possible without investigating the personal background of the author of the theory, his personal experiences, his position in life, the influence of the ideas of others on him, and also his particular native gifts and deficiencies. For this reason the first chapters could not be omitted, but they need not be read first, though it is obvious why they have to be at the beginning of the book.

In testing Polybius' theory against historical reality and in comparing it with other political theories, I have, on the whole, confined myself to the ancient world, because this is the world from which the theory originated, because it is the part of history with which I am most familiar, and because an attempt to extend the inquiry to medieval and modern history would require several more volumes. It is true that under modern conditions many problems have become more complicated, but the most fundamental factors have not changed essentially. There is much material in ancient history by which Polybius' theory can be tested in such a way that the results *mutatis mutandis* are still valid in our day. In addition, ancient history has the great advantage that it can be surveyed from the beginning to the end so that the ultimate results of all actions and institutions can be observed, which is not the case with modern history. In regard to political theories that can be compared with the theory of Polybius, I have made one exception to the general rule adopted. I have, in the last chapter, discussed Hobbes's theory of sovereignty in its relation to Polybius' theory of the mixed constitution, both because the theory of Hobbes constitutes the most radical criticism of any theory that advocates any kind of divided sovereignty—and all the interrelated theories of the mixed constitution, of the system of checks and balances, and of the separation of powers come essentially under this head—and because the theory of Hobbes is finding so many adherents in our time. No critical appraisal of Polybius' theory would have been adequate which neglected the most radical criticism which has, at least implicitly, been directed against it. Apart from this a discussion of the main features of Hobbes's theory seems all the more justified in the present context, since Hobbes himself not infrequently refers to examples from Greek and Roman history to support various points in his arguments.

In conclusion I have to thank Professor K. Ziegler of Göttingen for having made accessible to me in galley proof his excellent and thorough article on Polybius in Pauly-Wissowa, thus enabling me to refer to it for a fuller discussion of various problems concerning Polybius' life and concerning the composition of his work. I wish to thank Professor E. Kapp for having read the whole manuscript and Professor A. Schiller for having read the seventh chapter, and both colleagues for a number of valuable suggestions. Finally, I am under great obligation to Professor M. Ostwald, who kindly helped in reading the proofs and also checked the index.

KURT VON FRITZ

Columbia University
in the City of New York
June 1, 1954

Contents

Appendices

THE THEORY OF THE
MIXED CONSTITUTION IN ANTIQUITY

I

POLYBIUS' LIFE AND POLITICAL BACKGROUND

POLYBIUS was born in the Arcadian city of Megalopolis about 200 B.C.[1] Soon after his birth his father Lycortas became one of the leading statesmen of the so-called Achaean League, so that Polybius, from his earliest childhood, grew up amidst the most intense political activity, in which, at a very early age, he began to participate.

Though Polybius himself makes it clear that his political theory was essentially determined by his conviction that the enormous success of Rome, which within his own lifetime conquered the greater part of the world then known, was due to the excellence of the Roman constitution, there can be hardly any doubt that his basic political philosophy was also influenced by the political environment in which he grew up. The outstanding factors in this environment were the political structure of the Achaean League and the two great figures of Aratus of Sicyon and Philopoemen. Aratus died about a decade before Polybius' birth but continued to be revered as the founder of the League in the form in which it existed at Polybius' time. Philopoemen, the great general and political leader, died when Polybius was about seventeen years old but had been the hero of his boyhood, and Polybius retained a vivid memory of him.

THE ACHAEAN LEAGUE

It is, of course, impossible within this introductory chapter to discuss all the many difficult problems connected with the details of the constitution of the Achaean League.[2] It must therefore suffice to discuss those of its features which are emphasized by Polybius himself or, though not directly emphasized by him, can be shown to have had an influence on his political attitude.

In trying to describe the essential characteristics of this constitution one has to distinguish between the laws and rules regulating the relation of the cities belonging to the League to one another and the political order or orders prevailing in the various member cities individually. In regard to the first point, Polybius himself stresses above all the fact that, unlike the Attic Sea Confederacy and the Peloponnesian Confederacy of the fifth century, there was no dominating or even leading city. All the members, whether they had belonged to the original confederacy or had joined it only recently, and whether they had joined it of their own free will or under some initial pressure, were entirely on the same footing. At the same time he points out that the members of the League formed a very closely knit unit having the same laws, weights, measures, and monetary system, and, in addition, even a common government, a common deliberative assembly, and a common law court, so that in a way the whole territory of the League could be considered as belonging to one state.[3]

The latter part of Polybius' remarks shows clearly that the so-called Achaean League was less a simple confederacy or league than what in modern times would be called a federal state. The most essential features of the political organization of this federal state were, as far as can be established, the following: The executive or administrative branch of the government was headed by the strategos, who was at the same time the actual, not merely nominal, commander-in-chief of the federal military forces and the president of the League. In addition to this president there was a college of ten damiurgs, who seem to have had a position similar to that of the Athenian archons. All questions of major importance, however, had to be referred to two types of political assemblies, one of which, the synodos, assembled at regular intervals, probably four times every year, while the other, the synkletos, was convoked at irregular times and when the need arose, in order to make the most important decisions, those, for instance, concerning war and peace, treaties with other nations, and the like. The annual elections for the federal government took place in one of the regular synodes. Whether these synodes were representative bodies consisting of elected representatives of the cities in numbers proportionate to the size of these cities, or whether they were primary assemblies, is a question that has not yet been solved with certainty. However, there can be hardly any doubt that the extraordinary assemblies or synkletoi were primary assemblies in which every citizen of voting age from any of the cities belonging to the League could participate and cast his vote, though the final counting was by cities, not by individual votes.

Since, furthermore, the available evidence seems to indicate that the right to vote in these assemblies did not depend on property qualifications, the constitution of the federal state appears extremely democratic. There were, however, several factors which modified in fact, if not in law, the democratic character of the federal constitution. Since the regular assemblies met only four times a year for a few days, and since the extraordinary assemblies, because of their very character as primary assemblies, could not be convoked very often, the president, either by himself or together with the damiurgs, had to make a great many decisions without placing them before the assemblies for deliberation; and the history of the League presents many examples of decisions which, in the ordinary course of things, had to be made by the assemblies but were sometimes made by the president alone if he could reasonably assume that he would obtain the approval of the assembly later. Hence the actual, if not the legal, freedom of action of the chief executive was very considerable. In order to guard against the danger that a president might become too powerful, a provision had been inserted into the federal constitution to the effect that no president could be re-elected for the year immediately following his one-year term of office. Nevertheless the great political leaders of the League often succeeded in retaining their dominating influence, though not their official power, during the years in which the constitution prevented them from holding the supreme office.

The most important political issues, as mentioned before, had to be brought before the extraordinary assemblies for decision. But the fact that the synkletoi were primary assemblies, together with the increasing size of the Achaean League, made it undoubtedly impossible for a great number of the poorer citizens to make use of their voting rights. For since the historical evidence seems to indicate clearly that, in contrast to Athens, the League did not pay any compensation to the citizens attending the popular assemblies, it was naturally much easier for wealthy people to pay the traveling expenses and the costs of their stay in the city in which the assembly took place (and to accept the loss of income caused by their being away from home) than it was for the poorer people. This difference cannot have failed to express itself in the proportionate numbers of people from each class who actually made use of their right to vote. Thus the strictly democratic character of the federal constitution was tempered by a rather strong oligarchic or plutocratic factor. This factor, however, was of rather indefinite weight. The assemblies met sometimes in one place, sometimes in another. But wherever they met the poorer population in and near the meeting place always had a better opportunity to participate in the vote than did the population of the more distant member cities. And, perhaps even more important, if a question of great consequence to the poorer classes was to be decided, they might make a special effort to participate in the vote and so make their influence felt or even impose their will on the wealthy. Thus there was a safety valve. Nevertheless the League as a whole remained socially and politically conservative, as can be seen from the fact that, at least until the time of Polybius' exile in 169 B.C., its official policy was consistently opposed to social reformers such as Agis, Cleomenes, and Nabis of Sparta.

Apart from the military, political, and economic decisions concerning the League as a whole, the individual cities belonging to it naturally had their own independent local administrations and, as we would say, states' rights. To what extent local constitutions were under federal control cannot be exactly determined on the basis of the available evidence. But it is clear that the League did not admit tyrannical regimes or absolute monarchies. In this sense all the cities belonging to the League had to be "democracies." Apart from this there seem to have been no hard and fast rules. In 192 Sparta appears to have become a member of the League "under its ancient constitution." But because of the tumultuous conditions which prevailed in Sparta before this event and the defective state of the ancient tradition, it is difficult to know exactly what this meant.[4] At any rate, after Sparta in 189 had revolted against the League and been brought back by force, the Spartans were ordered to abandon the laws and institutions of Lycurgus and "to get accustomed" to Achaean institutional traditions.

This then was the political and constitutional tradition in which Polybius grew up. His attitude towards this system and the role which it plays, or rather does not play, in his political theory is most revealing in several respects. In that section of his work in which he begins to tell the history of the Achaean League,[5] Polybius praises the constitution of the League most highly and says that it would hardly be possible to find anywhere a system more favorable to political equality and liberty, or, in other words, a more perfect example of "true democracy" than the Achaean League. In the history of the first phase of the League's development, which follows upon this passage, Polybius especially emphasizes its struggle against foreign kings and native tyrants, a struggle so successful that in the end a number of tyrants voluntarily gave up their tyrannies in order to take their cities into the League and enter upon political careers under its elective system. This, together with the analysis of the main features of the federal constitution given above, shows what "true democracy" means to Polybius in this connection: negatively and above all, the absence of "tyranny" or any other kind of absolute one-man rule; positively, a federal state in which all member states have equal rights; and finally, a system in which the government is elected and controlled by "the people," but in which the "good and substantial" people have a greater share in expressing and formulating "the will of the people" than has the common crowd. Obviously in such a system there will be found a complicated balancing and counterbalancing of various political forces and influences, and there can hardly be any doubt that Polybius' aversion to any kind of political system in which one of the elements constituting the body politic completely dominates the others is closely related to his experience with and approval of the political system of the Achaean League.

It is all the more remarkable that in spite of this no reference to the Achaean League is found anywhere in the extensive extant parts of the sixth book of Polybius' work, in which he discusses his theory of the superiority of mixed constitutions or systems of checks and balances over any other kind of political system. The League, it would seem, along with Sparta, Carthage, and Rome, could have been used as an example of the kind of constitution that Polybius advocates. What is more, in his account of the early history of the Achaean League, Polybius expressly says that the excellent political system of the League contributed greatly to its success in expanding over an ever-increasing part of the Peloponnesus.[6] Thus there seems to be a close parallel to Rome, whose success and expansion in Polybius' opinion was also due to the excellence of its constitution. Why then the complete silence in regard to the Achaean League in that part of Polybius' work in which he systematically sets forth his political theory?[7]

As mentioned before, Polybius praised the political system of the League as that of a "true democracy." In the sixth book democracy is not praised; it is identified as one of the simple political systems which are bound to disintegrate and are definitely inferior to the more stable mixed constitutions. Obviously the seeming discrepancy is due to a difference in the use of the term *democracy*. In the sixth book Polybius uses this word in the sense in which it was used by Plato and Aristotle, who designated by it political systems such as the Athenian democracy of the late fifth century which were characterized by rather unlimited majority rule and consequently by a strong political influence of the poorer classes. In the second book, on the other hand, Polybius employs the word democracy in a sense widely accepted in his time and in ours—to mean freedom from arbitrary power exercised by an individual or a group—and perhaps even to mean something approaching what we today call a system of checks and balances. It seems odd that Polybius should not have realized that the term *democracy*, as used of the Achaean League, meant something entirely different from the same term as applied to Athens, and that thus, by an apparently purely terminological difficulty, he should have been prevented from mentioning the Achaean League in his political theory.

In fact, however, the difficulty was not purely terminological. When Polybius analyzes the structure of the Roman Republic, the consuls represent to him the monarchic element, the Senate the oligarchic element, and the tribunes of the plebs and the assemblies of the people the democratic element in the state. When he weighs the powers of these elements against one another, he tries in every way to describe these powers in terms of well-defined competences, though such an attempt, as will be shown later, encounters very serious difficulties. Within the political structure of the Achaean League, on the other hand, there existed, as pointed out above, a many-sided, shifting, and adjustable balance of powers. But this balance of powers was due to a combination of constitutional provisions and extraconstitutional circumstances which could not be described in terms of definite political agencies and their official competences. It would have been ridiculous to consider the damiurgs or the synodos as the oligarchic elements in the state, similar to the Senate in Polybius' analysis of the Roman constitution or to the gerousia in his account of Sparta, even if the synodos were a representative rather than a primary assembly. Thus the Achaean League, in order to be brought into Polybius' general scheme, would have required a different and deeper analysis. But no such deeper analysis can be found in Polybius' political theory, though extraconstitutional elements, as will be shown later, played a very important, in fact a decisive, part in the shifting balance of powers within the Roman Republic no less than in the League. That Polybius paid no attention to such elements in this theoretical analysis, though he grew up in and admired a system in which such factors played a very important role, is very characteristic of his whole way of thinking and indicative of one of the greatest shortcomings of his political philosophy.

ARATUS OF SICYON

The first origins of a confederacy of the cities of Achaea cannot be traced, since they go back to a time of which there is no historical record. But the Achaean League in the form in which it existed at the time of Polybius was a product of the fourth century, and it was in the fifty years preceding Polybius' birth that it gradually rose to considerable influence and power. As a result of the conquest of Greece by Philip after the battle of Chaeronea, and then again by Philip's son, Alexander the Great, the territory of the original confederacy had come under Macedonian domination, and in the wars among Alexander's successors, which were partly fought out in the Peloponnesus, even the remnants of the League seem to have been completely broken up. It was only in 280 B.C., when Macedonian power had been

weakened by continuous warfare, that four of the Achaean cities revolted and by concluding an alliance with one another formed the
nucleus of a new confederacy. In the following years other Achaean
cities freed themselves from Macedonian domination, and in 275 the
renewed League already comprised nine cities—the majority of the
larger cities of Achaea proper, i.e., of the district along the north coast
of the Peloponnesus in which the Achaean dialect was spoken.

The decisive event in the history of the new League, however, was
the accession in 250 B.C. of the non-Achaean city of Sicyon, and with it
the Sicyonian Aratus, who by a sudden coup had overthrown the
tyranny of Nicocles in his native city and established a republican
regime. Despite his youth, Aratus at once began to exert a very strong
influence on the general policy of the League, and after he had, in
245, become for the first time its president and commander-in-chief,
he continued, until his death in 213, to be the leading statesman of
this political body, though according to the provisions of the constitution he could hold the highest office only every second year. From the
beginning it was, according to Polybius,[8] Aratus' aim to make the
cities of the League, and if possible the whole Peloponnesus, independent of the Hellenistic kings, the successors of Alexander, and
to replace by republican regimes the indigenous tyrannies still to be
found in the Peloponnesus, thereby restoring external and internal
liberty and freedom in the whole peninsula. In the pursuit of this
policy Aratus not infrequently gave military support to antimonarchic
groups in their attempts to overthrow native tyrants in Peloponnesian
cities, especially if such cities promised to become members of the
League after their liberation. Furthermore, in the wars of the Achaean
League against the Aetolian Confederacy and against Sparta, Aratus
on various occasions conquered Greek cities, which then received an
Achaean garrison so that they would not again fall into the hands of
the enemy, even though the citizens did not wish to join the League.
But with the exception of such cases, in which there seemed to be a
compelling reason, Aratus seems to have refrained from forcing cities
to become members of the League against the outspoken will of the
majority of the populace, and even when external circumstances forced
him to deviate from this principle he made, according to Polybius,
every effort to win over by friendly treatment a large part, if not the

majority, of the citizens.[9] He appears to have been convinced that an unwilling ally or subject was a liability rather than an asset, and consequently it was his constant policy to hold the League together by demonstrating to its member states that it was profitable for them to belong to it.

As a military leader Aratus was extremely successful in preparing and conducting nocturnal surprise attacks on cities but, as Polybius himself points out again and again, he was a rather bad general in the field, since he apparently lost his confidence regularly in the face of an enemy army in battle array. As a result of this weakness he lost many important battles which might have been won by a better commander, but, if we can trust Polybius, he not only always managed to retain his power and influence within the League in spite of these failures, but was also a master in the art of turning defeat into victory by diplomatic negotiations and by persuading other powers that it was in their interest to come to the support of the League when it was in distress. In summary one may say that he was a man to whom statesmanship meant above all proficiency in a game of power politics, but a game in which diplomatic skill and sound policy in the handling of human beings in general were infinitely more important than brute force.

That the Aratean tradition in which he grew up had a profound influence on Polybius' political thinking cannot be denied. In his political theory the problem of power is much more dominant—to the exclusion of other no less important factors of political life—than it is in the political philosophy of Plato or Aristotle. But he does not, like other political theorists who pride themselves on being realists, identify power politics with a policy of brute force. On the contrary, he emphasizes repeatedly that a policy of brute force, of cruelty and intimidation, is a bad policy even from the point of view of power politics. Thus, when he speaks of the actions of Philip V of Macedon after the victory of the Achaeans and the Macedonians over the Aetolian League, he blames him most severely for the wanton cruelty with which he treated the defeated enemy.[10] And though the Aetolians appear as the very prototype of barbarism and political wickedness throughout almost the whole of Polybius' work, he here expresses the opinion that even these wicked Aetolians, if Philip had treated them with unexpected leniency and decency, would have become his sincere admirers and friends. Polybius concludes with the observation that it is much more *profitable* to conquer an enemy by generosity and decency than to have the greatest successes in the field for, he says, "to arms the vanquished yield from necessity but to decency from conviction." Since Polybius is at the same time convinced that the possession of too much power, especially if unchallenged over a long period, is apt to produce arrogance and disregard of others, his fundamental beliefs lead to the paradox that a restriction of power is good from the very point of view of power politics. But this paradox and its implications may be discussed later. For the present it will suffice to have pointed out that Polybius' inclination to consider everything from the point of view of power relations as well as his awareness of the fact that political power is by no means identical with the exercise of brute force are both in perfect agreement with the tradition established by Aratus.

There is, however, still another factor in Polybius' relations to Aratus that is of some importance. Down to the year 228 B.C. Aratus, according to Polybius' report, had been able to follow with remarkable success the policy outlined above. Especially since the death of the Macedonian king Demetrius II in 229 B.C. had everything been going exceedingly well, one city after the other joining the League of its own accord and a whole group of tyrants giving up their rule voluntarily in order to enter upon political careers within the League. In the following year, however, Aratus, so Polybius says,[11] saw the first forebodings of a great danger arising on the political horizon. During the lifetime of Demetrius the Aetolian League had been allied with the Achaean League against Macedon, and the mutual antagonism between the two Leagues had for some time given way to understanding and friendship. But after the death of Demetrius the Aetolian League made peace with the new regent of Macedon, Antigonus Doson, and, according to Polybius, tried to bring about an alliance with Sparta and Macedon against the Achaean League, of whose extraordinary successes it had become jealous. If the Aetolians had been successful in this attempt it would have been disastrous for the Achaeans. But fortunately, so Polybius tells us, Aratus, with the acumen of a great statesman, saw the danger before it was too late and took up secret negotiations with the Macedonian regent (who later made himself king), thus forestalling the coalition and laying the groundwork for a later alliance with Macedon, which, for a long time after 224 B.C., remained a cornerstone of the foreign policy of the Achaean League.

The accuracy of Polybius' interpretation of these events has been the subject of much controversy among modern scholars. There cannot be much uncertainty concerning the main events on the Achaean side, though they are complicated enough.[12] In the winter of 227/26 the government of Megalopolis, one of the members of the League, with the permission of "the Achaeans," (Polybius does not name the body that granted this permission), sent an embassy to Antigonus asking for his help against the Lacedaemonians, who had made repeated inroads on their territory. The ambassadors obtained from Antigonus a letter addressed to the government of Megalopolis promising his succor subject to the approval of the Achaean League. The Megalopolitans submitted the letter to an assembly of the Achaeans, asking that Antigonus be called upon immediately by the League to make good his promise. The assembly appeared to be favorably inclined towards this demand, but Aratus persuaded them to make an attempt first to defend themselves by their own means and to call upon the support of the Macedonians only if and when they should prove to be unsuccessful. This proposal was approved by the assembly and an alliance between the League and Macedon was not concluded until the year 224 B.C. when the Achaeans had suffered a number of signal defeats at the hands of the Spartans.

This is what happened openly, and there is no serious reason to question Polybius' report so far. There were also, however, according to him,[13] some secret transactions. In the first place, the embassy to Antigonus had been instigated by Aratus himself. Secondly, in addition to calling on Antigonus for help for their own city, the Megalopolitan ambassadors, on the special instructions of Aratus, entered on secret negotiations concerning a possible future alliance between Macedon and the Achaean League. Antigonus' answer to these secret advances, which were communicated by the Megalopolitan ambassadors to Aratus, was also favorable. Yet Aratus did not at that time dare advocate an alliance between the League and Macedon openly, for two reasons. First, he knew that the ultimate price to be paid for such an alliance would be Corinth, which some years before had been snatched from the Macedonians in a sudden night attack, and that there would be a general outcry against the proposal to hand over one of the member cities of the League to the traditional enemy from which it had been liberated. In the second place, he did not wish to bear the blame if the alliance with the great power of the North, which had been the traditional enemy of the Achaeans, should turn out to have its dangers. He therefore wanted to wait until a situation arose in which the majority of the Achaeans would demand such an alliance. For these reasons Aratus carefully concealed his role in the negotiations between the Megalopolitans and Antigonus, and even spoke against immediate acceptance of Antigonus' offer to Megalopolis when the question was discussed in the Achaean assembly.

This is a complicated story, and, according to Polybius,[14] Aratus did not dare reveal everything in his memoirs, which he wrote and published several years later, after the alliance had been in effect for some time. On the other hand it seems that in these memoirs Aratus boasted of his foresight in having taken up secret negotiations with Macedon at a time when no one else had recognized the danger threatening from a possible alliance of that northern power with the Aetolian League and Sparta. It would therefore appear that the only fact mentioned by Polybius not revealed by Aratus in his memoirs is that it was Aratus who induced the Megalopolitans to send an embassy to Antigonus for help so that he could use this embassy for his secret negotiations, though, in the assembly, he acted as if he had no part whatever in this transaction and actually dissuaded the Achaean League from allowing the Megalopolitans to make use of Antigonus' offer.[15]

Though it is rather extraordinary that Aratus' role as instigator of the Megalopolitan embassy should have been so well hidden, the main facts concerning his secret negotiations with Antigonus are probably correct. It is rather in regard to the motives of Aratus that serious doubts may arise, and many modern scholars have contended that Aratus' fear of an alliance between the Aetolian League and Macedon was a pretense by which he tried to justify his policy, which otherwise might have caused strong antagonism among his fellow countrymen.

In support of Polybius' version it has been said that Aratus could have had no other motive since the Spartan policy of wholesale expansion under the leadership of Cleomenes had not yet started at the time when Aratus began his secret negotiations with Antigonus.[16] This argument, however, is not very strong; for, according to Polybius' own account, the Megalopolitans asked for help against Sparta, not against the Aetolians. The Aetolians, on the other hand, again according to Polybius' own report,[17] did not begin hostilities against the Achaean League until the alliance between the League and Macedon had become effective several years later. The only reason that Polybius can adduce for Aratus' suspicion against the Aetolians is the fact that they did not defend some Peloponnesian cities belonging to their League against the Spartans, an argument which is not very convincing considering the fact that Aratus himself had made movements against some of the same cities without encountering opposition from the Aetolians either.

It is not possible, nor is it necessary, to take up this complicated question in detail within the present context. For even if Aratus' motives were not quite what Polybius says they were, the only thing of which Polybius can be accused in regard to this part of his report is to have given too ready credence to Aratus' own explanation of his policy. But it was necessary to discuss this matter briefly because of its importance for a just evaluation of Polybius' presentation of subsequent events.

The preliminary secret negotiations between Aratus and Antigonus through the Megalopolitan embassy laid the ground for the actual alliance with Macedon which was concluded two years later in the winter of 225/24. By that time the Achaeans had suffered one defeat after another at the hands of the Spartan king Cleomenes, who by then had openly started on a career of conquest. According to Polybius [18] these defeats "compelled" the Achaeans to turn "with one accord" for help to Antigonus. Aratus sent his own son to conduct the negotiations. Antigonus accepted; and the problem of Corinth, according to Polybius, solved itself. For, after Corinth had been taken by Cleomenes, it became possible for the Achaeans to hand over the Corinthian citadel to Antigonus without incurring the blame of ceding a free member of the League to a foreign king.

This is what Polybius tells about the events. The same story is also related by Plutarch in his biographies of Cleomenes and Aratus, but with an extremely important addition. According to Plutarch,[19] Cleomenes, after the crushing defeat which he had inflicted on the Achaeans near the Hecatombaeum in the neighborhood of Dyme, offered to return to the Achaeans all the territory and prisoners he had taken on the condition that he be granted the "hegemony" by the Achaeans. What this demand meant can probably be inferred from analogy with an earlier event. In 243/42, after the liberation of Corinth from Macedon, the Achaeans had concluded an alliance with Ptolemy Euergetes and had given him the "hegemony," that is, the supreme command, over the Achaean armies. If this analogy is correct, there was a precedent, and if what Plutarch says subsequently is true,[20] the Achaeans did not "with one accord" turn to Antigonus, but, on the contrary, the majority were ready to grant Cleomenes' demand in return for what he had offered. In fact, according to Plutarch, the Achaean assembly did accede to his demands, and a date was set for the ratification of the agreement and the official appointment of Cleomenes as supreme commander of the League. It was only in consequence of a sudden illness of the king, which prevented his appearing on the date which had been set, that Aratus was able to prevent the execution of the agreement. When, some time later, Cleomenes appeared with a Spartan detachment before Lerna, he was told that he must enter the city alone or conduct further negotiations outside the city. This, according to Plutarch, so incensed the Spartan king, who had believed that everything had been settled, that he withdrew at once and declared war on the Achaeans. Only now were the Achaeans ready to follow Aratus' advice and turn for help to Antigonus.

There can be hardly any doubt that this part of Plutarch's narrative is based on the historical work of Phylarchus. Because of his highly oratorical style and the violent attacks Polybius made on him, Phylarchus does not enjoy the reputation of a very trustworthy historian. But the story of Cleomenes' offer and the reaction of the Achaeans to it can hardly be pure invention, and it has therefore, in its main parts, been almost universally accepted by modern scholars.

It is clear then that the Achaeans and their political leader Aratus were faced with a tremendous decision. For decades it had been the aim of Aratus to bring together an ever greater part of the Greeks in a grand league which would make them independent of the constantly encroaching Hellenistic kings. Now an occasion offered itself to conclude an alliance which would have united the whole Peloponnesus and which, through a union of the Achaean with the superior Spartan army, would probably for the first time have enabled a Greek power to withstand successfully the attacks of any individual Hellenistic king. On the other hand, the supreme command of a Spartan king over the Achaean armies was bound, by force of geographical circumstances, to be something very different from an Egyptian king having the supreme command over the same armies. The result would doubtless have been the complete supremacy of Sparta over the Peloponnesus. For Aratus himself, above all, it would have meant that he would have had to turn over the results of his labors to the young Spartan king and to cede the first place to him. In addition this Spartan king was the promoter of social reforms which must have been utterly distasteful to the conservative Achaean leader.

The alternative for Aratus was to give up largely what had been the main aim of all his political activities up to now and bring the Macedonians again into Greece, even handing over to them some Greek cities which he himself had liberated from them. There was no doubt either that in this way the Achaean League would become dependent on Macedon. Yet as compensation it was certain that this dependence would be less close than the dependence on Sparta, that there would be much more room left for Aratus' own political leadership, and that there would certainly be no pressure in favor of social reforms. Faced with this alternative Aratus obviously did not hesitate to join the Macedonians, though the majority of the Achaean cities appear to have favored acceptance of Cleomenes' offer; and through clever manipulations he was successful.

Modern historians generally have expressed the opinion that Aratus was right, or at least that he did what was the natural thing for him to do in the circumstances. Yet even if one agrees with this judgment, one cannot find it astonishing that many Greeks considered the complete reversal of his previous policy a betrayal of the Greek cause, and Phylarchus has given violent expression to this opinion.[21] It is in no way surprising and no reflection on Polybius' historical objectivity that he sided with Aratus on this question. But that he passed over the offer made by Cleomenes with complete silence is a somewhat different matter.[22] There can hardly be any explanation for his silence, except his desire to avoid the disagreeable question of whether Aratus had been right from the Hellenic point of view, especially since his decision had very far-reaching consequences in the future. This arouses again the suspicions voiced earlier concerning the accuracy of Polybius' explanation of Aratus' motives when he first took up negotiations with Antigonus through the intermediary of the Megalopolitans.[23] At any rate one can hardly avoid the conclusion that the objectivity of Polybius was not quite so great as his unrhetorical—in fact very pedestrian—style and his violent attacks on other historians whom he accuses of a lack of veracity have made most of his readers believe. The recent discovery of a papyrus fragment [24] dealing with events of the year 203 B.C. has led some modern commentators to suspect that here too Polybius has somewhat obscured the facts, this time not for the greater glory of the founder of the Achaean League, but of Scipio Africanus, the ancestor by adoption of his Roman friend, the younger Scipio.

But even if it is admitted that Polybius was not always and in all respects as objective a historian as he often has been believed to be,[25] one must not draw any wrong conclusions concerning his analysis of the Roman constitution, which plays such a decisive part in his political theory. The two instances mentioned do not show Polybius as a deliberate political propagandist; and for reasons which will reveal themselves presently, it would have been absurd for him to make propaganda for the Roman constitution. If Polybius' personal predilections and prejudices affected his constitutional theory and his analysis of the Roman political order, it was in a far more subtle way.

PHILOPOEMEN, LYCORTAS, AND ROME

Since the political activities of Philopoemen fall almost exclusively, and those of Polybius' father Lycortas exclusively, within the period when the Achaean League had come into contact with Rome and when its relations to Rome assumed increasingly dominant importance, it seems expedient to consider Polybius' relations to these men and to Rome together.

Until the last years of Aratus' life Rome had remained almost completely beyond the political horizon of the Achaean League. In 219/18, however, the relations between Macedon, which since 224/23 had remained closely allied with the Achaean League, and Rome became very strained, and in 215 Philip V, the successor of Antigonus Doson, concluded an alliance with Hannibal against the Romans. The League, under the leadership of Aratus, refused to give any help to Philip in this war. Nevertheless, when in 212 the Romans concluded a counteralliance with the Aetolian League, which by then had become very hostile to the Achaeans, the Achaean League was dragged into the war very much against its will. This was the first serious encounter of the Achaean League with Rome, and though, in 205, a peace was concluded between Macedon and Rome, in which their mutual allies were included, it was clear that in any future conflict the overwhelming power of Rome would have to be reckoned with.

A decisive turning point in the relations between the League and Rome occurred in the year 198. The war against Carthage had hardly been brought to a successful conclusion when the Senate, in spite of the war-weariness of the Roman people, contrived to start a new war against Philip V. The Achaeans, though officially still in close alliance with Macedon, again tried to remain neutral. However, they were soon compelled to make their choice. In 198, two years after the outbreak of the war, a Roman embassy appeared at one of the popular assemblies demanding that the Achaeans join Rome as active military allies against the Macedonian power, to which they were still tied by a most solemn treaty, which had even been incorporated in the constitution of the League. On the advice of Aristaenus, then president of the League, the majority, impressed by the overwhelming strength of the Romans, after a long and heated discussion voted to accede to this demand, though some cities, among them Megalopolis, the native city of Polybius, refused to participate in the vote.

In the following decade the League reaped enormous territorial benefits from this breach of faith. By 191 B.C. it extended over the whole Peloponnesian peninsula, and in 189 it was even increased by the accession of some cities outside the Peloponnesus. Nevertheless, by the end of this period, the relations between the League and Rome had not improved. Both the military alliance of 198 against Macedon and a more comprehensive alliance with Rome, by which the original alliance was replaced, probably in the winter 194/93, were officially concluded on terms of equality between the two contracting parties. But the enormous difference in power could not fail to make itself felt politically, especially since in this period the League was no longer, as in former times, satisfied with the voluntary accession of cities seeking protection from tyrants or foreign enemies, but was embarked on a policy of conquest.

In the first years after 198 the League had been militarily weak, and the territorial gains which it obtained were the direct result of Roman efforts rather than of its own military exertions. In the following years, however, and especially after Philopoemen, a dashing general, had become its military and political leader, the Achaean League began to make conquests of its own in which the Romans had no direct part. Nevertheless, on some occasions the Romans interfered in favor of one or another of the common enemies, claiming that, since they had made by far the greater contribution to the over-all effort, even if not to the specific battle by which the conquest had been effected, they should also be consulted in the final peace settlement. When faced with direct Roman interference of this kind the Achaeans always gave in immediately, but in the course of time Philopoemen began to embark upon a new policy. By a combination of force and diplomacy he attempted, wherever possible, to create a *fait accompli*, which made it difficult for the Romans to find a reason for direct interference. If the Romans, however, tried to interfere, he finally even ventured to disregard their friendly advice, at the same time, nevertheless, demonstrating the loyalty of the League to Rome by Achaean participation in campaigns conducted in regions in which the Achaeans had no territorial interests of their own.

The Roman Senate for a long time obviously did not consider these incidents sufficiently serious for a show of force or even a threat of force. But there can hardly be any doubt that the Romans resented this show of independence on the part of their little ally, while the Achaeans in their turn, in spite of the great benefits which the alliance had brought to them, resented Roman interference in what they considered their well-earned rights and were naturally apprehensive of the future when, after further victories, there would be no power left that could check the omnipotence of the Romans. The difficulty was increased by the fact that in 198, after their first victory over Macedon, the Romans had made much of their disinterestedness and had promised freedom to all Greeks who were under Macedonian domination, thus enabling those Greek cities which had since been conquered by the Achaeans to appeal to the noble sentiments of the Romans and ask for help and protection against Rome's Achaean allies.

This was the situation when Polybius was a young boy and his father for the first time assumed a prominent role in the conduct of Achaean foreign policy. When, in 189, the Spartans tried to revolt against the League and sent an embassy to Rome to ask for Roman mediation, Lycortas headed an Achaean embassy to plead against Roman interference with what the League considered its internal affairs.[26] This time, however, Philopoemen's method of settling the matter evoked the outspoken displeasure of the Senate, and three years later, in 186, Lycortas, who was then president of the League for the first time, was compelled at an assembly of the League to defend the policy of Philopoemen in front of the Roman envoy Appius Claudius.[27] Finally, after Philopoemen's death in 183, Lycortas became for a short time his political heir, stubbornly trying, by diplomacy and legal argument, to defend Achaean independence against Roman interference. This task, however, became ever more difficult.

After having been president of the League—probably three times, in 187/86, 184/83, and 182/81—Lycortas suffered for the first time a major political setback in 180 when, in the elections for the presidency, he was defeated by Callicrates, who advocated a policy of complete submissiveness to Rome. His party did not win the upper hand again until Archon, a close political associate of Lycortas, who in 174 had even pleaded for a reconciliation of the League with Macedon, was elected president for 172/71,[28] and then again for 170/69, this second time with Polybius as hipparch or vice-president of the League.[29]

The events of these years and of those immediately following are very complicated, and even Polybius' own account of the policy and opinions of his father and himself is not always quite clear. Not very long before Polybius' election to the vice-presidency it seems there was a rumor that a Roman envoy, C. Popilius, was going to accuse Archon, Lycortas, and Polybius before the assembly of the Achaean League of being enemies of Rome.[30] But nothing came of it at the time, and the political influence of Lycortas and Polybius does not seem to have been affected by the rumor. However, a short time later, when a new war between Rome and Macedon broke out, a slight disagreement between Lycortas and Archon seems to have developed.[31] Lycortas advocated absolute neutrality in the coming war and wished the Achaean government to assume a rather stern attitude towards those Achaeans who tried to win favor with the Romans by advocating complete submissiveness to their wishes. Archon agreed with him as far as neutrality at that moment was concerned, but stressed the overwhelming strength of the Romans and the consequent necessity of avoiding anything that was likely to arouse their displeasure. Though Polybius does not express himself very clearly on this point, it appears that on this occasion he found himself more in agreement with Archon than with his father Lycortas.

Some months later, when a decisive battle between Romans and Macedonians in Thessaly was expected, Archon came to the conclusion that it would no longer be safe to continue a policy of neutrality, and he induced the Achaean assembly to vote unreserved support of the Romans with the full military force of the League. It was also voted that Polybius, as head of an embassy, should go to Thessaly to ask the Roman consul Marcius when and where he wished the Achaean army to join him. But when Polybius arrived at his destination he postponed the interview with the consul "because of the unfavorable circumstances," and delivered his message only after Marcius had accomplished the greater part of his task, "since this seemed to him a good time for the interview." [32] In other words, Polybius, according to his own report, presented the Achaean offer only when it was no longer needed; and he seems to have been very much gratified when the consul thanked him, saying that he was not in need of Achaean assistance, "since this," as Polybius is eager to point out, "saved the League an enormous expense."

The story of this embassy, in the course of which Polybius appears to have deviated from his instructions, is followed by a still stranger story. While the other members of the embassy returned home, Polybius remained for some time in the camp of the consul, and when, a little later, another Roman general, Appius Centho, who was stationed in Epirus, asked for an Achaean auxiliary corps of five thousand men, the consul asked Polybius to return home and prevent the Achaeans from acceding to the demands of his fellow general. Polybius points out that this demand placed him in a somewhat embarrassing situation, since he did not consider it possible to reveal openly in the Achaean assembly that the Roman consul himself had asked him to oppose the request of another Roman general. But he succeeded in obtaining a negative vote on purely technical grounds.[33]

Obviously some points in this story are not quite clear. Especially do the motives of the consul in making his strange demand remain in the dark, though one may say that jealousy between Roman generals at the time in question was not exactly uncommon. But one thing is perfectly clear, that Polybius tried to give to the Romans as little as was possible if their open and direct displeasure was to be avoided. He certainly was not enthusiastically pro-Roman at this period when he was slightly over thirty years old, and he obviously still approved of the way in which he had acted then when he wrote about these events some twenty years later.[34]

The events of the following years were to show that Polybius' policy had not been quite successful. Though all Greek states hurried to send congratulatory embassies to Rome after the decisive victory of the Romans at Pydna, the Romans now embarked on a much sterner policy and demanded the surrender of all those leading men in Greece whose "loyalty" to the Romans was suspect. More than one thousand Achaeans were brought to Italy, mostly to Etruria, on the pretext that they had been exiled by the Achaeans themselves,[35] but in reality in order to make any revival of an anti-Roman party impossible. None of them was permitted to return home before the end of seventeen years, and Polybius was one of these.

There is an interesting chapter among the fragments of Polybius' work [36] in which he discusses critically the attitude of different groups of anti-Roman statesmen in Greece. Roughly speaking, he says, there were three groups. The first group was not pleased to see the whole world come under the domination of one power, but supported neither the Romans nor their enemies, leaving the outcome to fate. The men belonging to the second group were glad to see the struggle approach a decision and worked for a victory of the Macedonians over the Romans, but were not able to win the support of their countries for this policy. The men of the third group finally were successful in persuading their countries to ally themselves with the Macedonians. After the defeat this third group, he says, behaved on the whole as decent and self-respecting men should. They faced the situation squarely and perished bravely. Among the second group, on the other hand, there were many who tried to save their lives by lying or abject supplications, thus destroying their reputations both with their contemporaries and with posterity. The men of the first group, Polybius contends, were, however, in an entirely different position. Since they had never taken up negotiations with the Macedonian kings and had not advocated an alliance with Macedon but had merely stood for neutrality, they had every right to defend themselves against the accusation of having been enemies of the Romans and to save their lives.

These chapters are very revealing in several respects. Polybius accepted the policy of demanding the death of political leaders solely because they had worked to bring about an alliance between their countries and the enemy of the victor. He obviously considered this a more or less natural and customary occurrence in the game of power politics. A decent man will suffer the consequences of the failure of his policy without flinching, and if, even in defeat, he does not abandon the principles for which he has fought, he deserves praise and admiration. However, one who tries to save his life by abject submission to the victor will earn only contempt. This is a simple philosophy which some will be inclined to call Stoic. But while this attitude is quite in agreement with the precepts of Stoic philosophy, one should not forget that such notions of correct conduct had been widely accepted in ancient Greece long before Zeno founded his school, so that there is no reason to believe that a man expressing these views must have been an adherent of the more elaborate doctrines of Zeno and his successors. Above all, however, it is obvious that the discussion of the second and third groups of anti-Roman statesmen serves largely as a background for the discussion of the first group, in which Polybius is especially interested. Nor can there be any doubt that Polybius himself belonged to that group, for though there is no evidence that his life was ever in direct danger,[37] we learn from both his own reports and those of other writers that party politicians everywhere tried to rid themselves of their political opponents by denouncing them to the Roman victors. What is most characteristic of Polybius, then, is a caution and reasonableness which combine love of independence with a certain readiness to give in to the inevitable, even to the extent of submitting to foreign domination as long as this was possible without a serious loss of personal dignity. But his disgust with the servility of many Greeks and of some Oriental rulers was sincere, and his later relations with the Romans show clearly that he tried to live up to his principles.

While most of the other Greek hostages were distributed over the little country towns of Italy, mostly in Etruria, Polybius had the good fortune to become acquainted with Aemilius Paullus, the victor of Pydna and one of the leading generals and statesmen of the time, and was permitted, through Paullus' influence, to stay at his house in Rome. Of still greater importance to his later life was his acquaintance with Aemilius Paullus' very young son, P. Cornelius Scipio Aemilianus, later conqueror and destroyer of Carthage. In the thirty-first book of his historical work Polybius himself has told how this lifelong friendship with the younger Scipio was first begun.[38] He used to have long conversations with the two young sons of Aemilius Paullus, Q. Fabius Maximus Aemilianus and P. Cornelius Scipio, but had addressed himself mainly to the elder brother until one day, when they happened to be alone, Scipio blushingly took his hand and asked him whether, like some other people, he considered him too quiet and slow-minded a fellow, not worthy of the great family into which he was born, since he never talked to him. "No, by no means," answered Polybius, "do not let any such idea enter your head. I have addressed your brother only because he is the elder of you two and because I believed that in this way you would have your share in the conversation also. But I shall be very glad to help you to become worthy of your forefathers." Upon this, Polybius relates, the young Scipio grasped his hands and said, "May I see the day when you will consider everything else of secondary importance and live entirely with me."

This was the beginning of a lasting friendship which was to be of equal importance to both men, though in different ways. Through Polybius the influence of Greek ideas on the younger Scipio became very strong, both in his private [39] and public life. For Polybius the friendship with Scipio meant a unique opportunity of becoming acquainted with the whole machinery of the Roman state in its actual functioning. Later it also offered the possibility of obtaining from the Romans better conditions for his home country, which in the meantime had come entirely under Roman domination. But what is most important is that Polybius, in the years of his enforced sojourn in Rome, became convinced of the superiority of the Roman constitution over all other existing constitutions, a conviction which became fundamental to his whole political philosophy.

Not very many details are known about the seventeen years of Polybius' involuntary stay in Italy beyond his friendship with Scipio. But there is one incident which Polybius tells himself and which is of some significance. Through the younger Scipio, Polybius had become acquainted with Demetrius, the son of Seleucus IV Philopator, whom his father in 175 had sent to Italy as a hostage. When, in 164, Antiochus IV Epiphanes, who had ruled in his stead, died, Demetrius asked for permission to return home and claim the crown of the kingdom of his father. After the Senate had declined to give this permission he asked Polybius for his advice,[40] and Polybius advised him "to take a risk well worth taking for the sake of a crown." Demetrius nevertheless asked the Senate a second time for permission to return to his kingdom, but when he again received a negative answer he followed Polybius' advice, and Polybius helped him in its execution. Since Demetrius was acquainted with the younger Scipio and since, as Polybius tells [41] it, at a later occasion "the sensible people" in the Senate—obviously the Scipionic party—favored the cause of Demetrius, there can hardly be any doubt that Polybius acted with the knowledge and approval of his high-ranking Roman friends. This shows that as early as 163 B.C. he was, at least as far as questions of foreign policy were concerned, occasionally admitted to the councils of his protectors and was not limited to discussing general problems of ethical and political theory when he was in their company. Especially significant, however, in regard to the composition of his work, is the fact that he tells the whole story so openly and at such detail.

In 150 B.C. the Achaean exiles finally were permitted to go home because, as Cato said caustically, it mattered little whether some tottering old Greeks were going to be carried to their graves by Greek or by Roman pallbearers. Polybius, who was not a tottering old man, did not return to spend the rest of his life in Megalopolis or to assume again a leading position in the Achaean League, which at that time still enjoyed some semblance of independence. He stayed in Megalopolis for only a very short time. In 149 he was sent, at the request of the consul M. Manilius, to Lilybaeum, possibly in order to participate in the Roman negotiations with Carthage, but more likely as an engineering expert for the impending siege of that city. But he returned to Megalopolis before having reached his destination when he learned in Corcyra that the Carthaginians had accepted the conditions set by the Romans and that therefore his services were probably no longer needed.[42] Not very much later, however, when war with Carthage did break out, Polybius appears to have received a second summons, which he heeded, for he must have been in Africa in 149 since, according to his own report,[43] he had a conversation with the Numidian king Massinissa shortly before the latter's death at the beginning of 148. Probably in the following year Scipio entrusted him with the task of exploring the northwest coast of Africa,[44] and in 146 he was, in the company of Scipio, present at the destruction of Carthage and heard his Roman friend express the fear that some day the same fate might befall Rome.[45]

In the meantime, affairs in Greece had taken a turn for the worse. After a long period of submissiveness to Roman "advice," the leaders of the Achaean League had, in 150, again begun to embark on an independent policy in settling the affairs of the Peloponnesus. After four years of increasingly strained relations the president of the League, Critolaus, encouraged by similar tendencies elsewhere, bluntly told the Roman envoys at one of the federal assemblies that the Achaeans wished to have the Romans as their friends but not as their masters. This time the Romans declared war. The Greek armies, as was to be expected, were quickly defeated, and now the Romans took brutal measures to prevent similar troubles in the future. The various Greek leagues, confederacies, or federal states were dissolved. The individual cities retained their local self-government but were forbidden to enter into alliances with one another or with foreign powers and were subjected to a great many regulations imposed by Rome. Thebes and Chalkis were partly destroyed, and Corinth was looted of its art treasures and then burnt down.

Though Polybius had been violently opposed to the policy of Critolaus, which he considered utter folly, he was still very much attached to his country, and this sudden outburst of brutality on the part of the Romans must have been a severe blow to him. Nevertheless he accompanied the Roman commission which was appointed to regulate the affairs of Greece, and after the commission had returned to Rome he was entrusted with the task of settling points of dispute that arose from the new regulations.[46] In carrying out this task he tried to convince his fellow countrymen that submission to the Roman regulations was the only sensible course that they could follow, while at the same time he exerted all his influence at Rome to mitigate undue hardships and to moderate the conditions imposed. In both respects he appears to have been eminently successful, and after having completed his task, he was feted and received official honors all over Greece.

The later years of Polybius' life are less well known, and most of the few details that we have or can infer are not of very great importance for an evaluation of his political views. So a few data may suffice.[47] He traveled to Alexandria, possibly about 139, though he apparently did not, like the Stoic philosopher Panaetius, belong to the official entourage of Scipio Aemilianus, who traveled in Egypt and the Orient at that time. He appears to have been present at the siege of Numantia in 134/33, and it was probably on his way back that he visited such points of geographical and historical interest as the passes of the Alps through which Hannibal had passed when he invaded Italy. Polybius died at the age of 82 (not earlier than 120 B.C.), from injuries suffered through a fall of his horse.[48]

Polybius' life and political background, from what can be determined about them, show that in many respects he was very well fitted for the task of giving an objective and adequate account of the Roman political system. His father Lycortas had doubtless seen to it that he received the very best education available,[49] and it will be noted that he was very well acquainted with Greek philosophy and political theory in general. As one of the leading men of the Achaean League he had an intimate knowledge of its political structure and administration and of its individual member states, and so was enabled to see the influence of political institutions on the success or failure of foreign policy and war. He was almost equally well acquainted with the political structure of other Peloponnesian communities, especially Sparta, with its unique constitution. Above all he was afforded a unique opportunity, for a Greek, to see the working of the Roman constitution from the inside, so to speak. When he began his work, this constitution may have seemed to function very smoothly, but he lived to see the first cracks in the wonderful edifice and the first signs of a brewing revolution which, some seventy years after his death, was to lead to the destruction of the Roman Republic and to the establishment of an increasingly absolutist monarchic regime.

His historical work, it is true, is undoubtedly colored by his Hellenic as well as by his Achaean patriotism, and it has been shown that where these two patriotisms clash, he is not able to give a straight account of the historical facts. But he was not brought up to be a friend and admirer of Rome. And though he later became convinced that the only reasonable course for the Greeks was to submit to the overwhelming power of the Romans and tried to convince his fellow countrymen of this necessity, his historical work as a whole is certainly not a piece of pro-Roman propaganda. In contrast to Roman historians such as Livy and his annalistic models, he repeatedly defends Hannibal against Roman aspersions on his character [50] and also gives a favorable account of Hannibal's father Hamilcar.[51] He sets forth all the arguments of those who accused the Romans of the basest treachery and perfidy in their dealings with Carthage before the outbreak of the Third Punic War and also mentions those who tried to defend the Roman actions, apparently without taking sides in this dispute.[52] He also criticizes the Romans severely for their brutal policy in Greece in and after 146 B.C.[53] Though Polybius' friendship for the younger Scipio was undoubtedly strong and sincere, and though, as far as the struggle of various factions within Rome is concerned, he may have been biased in favor of Scipio and his friends, there is no indication whatever that he ever developed a Roman patriotism comparable to his deep feelings for Greece and the Achaean League.

Thus it is quite clear that Polybius' enthusiastic praise of the Roman constitution is not due to any purpose of propaganda—the Romans, by the way, unlike the Athenians, the Spartans, and many modern governments, never tried to induce other cities or nations to adopt constitutions similar to their own—nor to any innate or acquired prejudice in favor of Rome. On the contrary, it appears that Polybius, faced with the painful experience that the Greeks were quite helpless in the face of organized Roman power, looked for an explanation of this phenomenon which hurt his native pride as a Greek, and it came as a revelation to him when he thought he had discovered that the reason for this superiority was the excellence of the Roman constitution—a constitution which, without being the conscious work of one man or a group of men, had somehow naturally developed according to the precepts of the best Greek political theory. This is the reason why the analysis of the Roman constitution has become the central piece in his whole work.

Though from all these points of view Polybius appears extremely well qualified for this task, he has also considerable shortcomings as an analyst of the Roman constitution. Perhaps in consequence of the Aratean tradition in which he was brought up, he has a tendency to interpret all events as nothing but the results of power struggles neglecting other factors in social and political life which, though they may have a decisive effect on the power structure in the state, are not in themselves a result of the struggle for power but have an entirely different origin. He is generally inclined to oversimplify and over-rationalize what he sees, and he is apt to overlook whatever cannot be easily described in terms of the traditional political terminology and does not manifest itself in well-defined and clearly recognizable political institutions. Because of these shortcomings it is necessary in a just evaluation of his general theory of the mixed constitution to revise his analysis of the political system of republican Rome, on which his general theory is based.

II

THE COMPOSITION OF POLYBIUS' WORK

AND ITS PRESENT STATE OF PRESERVATION

THE GREAT HISTORICAL WORK of Polybius comprised forty books and, in its main part, covered the period from 220 B.C., that is, from the time immediately preceding the outbreak of the so-called Second Punic War, to the year 146 B.C., which is the year of the destruction of Carthage and Corinth and of the definite end of Greek independence. Only the first five books of the work have been preserved in their entirety or almost in their entirety, for even in these books there are some minor lacunae in the manuscripts that are extant. These first books contain the general introduction, a survey of the history of the five decades preceding the Second Punic War, and a very detailed discussion of the causes and the beginnings of this war down to the defeat of the Romans in the battle of Cannae in 216 B.C.

All the other books, including the sixth, which contains Polybius' political theory and his analysis of the Roman constitution, have to be reconstructed from fragments, which in their turn must be brought together from various sources. The most important of these sources is a manuscript codex of Urbino of the 11th or 12th century,[1] which contains extensive extracts from the first eighteen books of Polybius' work and from which are derived by far the greater part of the fragments of the sixth book which have come down to us. A second major source is the collection of extracts from ancient historical works which the emperor Constantinus Porphyrogenitus caused to be made in the first half of the tenth century of our era. In this collection the excerpts are arranged in fifty-three sections according to topics. Unfortunately, however, only one of these, the section *De legationibus* [on embassies], has been preserved almost completely. Of the section *De virtutibus et vitiis* [on virtues and vices] about one half has come down to us. Of

the section *De sententiis* [on general judgments or opinions], the only
one in which fragments of the sixth book pertinent to Polybius' political theory can be found, rather extensive fragments have been discovered in a Vatican palimpsest.[2] There are also fragments of the
section *De insidiis* [on secret plots or ambushes].

In addition to these systematic excerpts there are also a considerable
number of more or less literal quotations from the work of Polybius,
including the sixth book, in later Greek or Latin authors, who cite
him by name. Finally, there have been attempts by modern scholars
to reconstruct some of the lost parts of Polybius' work, especially of
the sixth book, from works of other ancient authors, particularly from
Cicero's *De re publica*,[3] though these authors either do not name
Polybius at all or mention him only in a general way as a man whose
ideas they have used. Such reconstructions are of course precarious
and can be used in a discussion of Polybius' political theory only with
the greatest caution.

The fragmentary state of preservation of Polybius' historical work
obviously renders difficult any analysis of its composition. Yet this
problem cannot be entirely neglected. For, considering the fact that
Polybius lived to the age of eighty-two but must have begun his
historical work when he was well under forty, it is clearly necessary
to reckon with the possibility that, in the course of this enormously
eventful period of over forty years, he may have changed his views
on some matters and thus his work may show traces of later revisions.
That there are, in fact, unmistakable traces of such revisions has always been evident to anyone who has read the whole work with close
attention, and in modern times a rather extensive philological literature on this problem has sprung up. Within the framework of the
present study it is clearly impossible to discuss in detail all the observations that can be found in this literature and all the many, often
contradictory, conclusions that have been drawn from them. On the
other hand, it is certainly relevant for an adequate understanding of
Polybius' political philosophy to know whether two opinions which
he expresses in different fragments of the sixth book are part and
parcel of the same systematically elaborated theory, or whether they
represent different viewpoints which Polybius took at different times.
I shall try, therefore, in the present chapter, to give a brief outline

of the general problem as an introduction to the more specific questions that may arise later in connection with the analysis of Polybius' political theory.

At the beginning of his work Polybius states [4] that it is his main purpose to show how, in a period of slightly less than fifty-three years, the Romans succeeded in subjecting almost the whole inhabited world to their rule. A little later he announces that he will take the 140th Olympiad as his starting point, but that by way of an introduction he will first give a summary of the events since 264 B.C., the year of the outbreak of the First Punic War, since this is necessary for a full understanding of the causes of the Second Punic War. From this announcement it is clear that he intended to write the history of the 52 to 53 years from the beginnings of the Second Punic War (219/18) to the battle of Pydna (167 B.C.). In other words, though it was after the battle of Cannae in 216 B.C. that the Romans reached the lowest point in their political power and territorial expansion since the early fourth century, Polybius naturally began with the outbreak of the war in which Cannae was the greatest but not the first major defeat of the Romans. He intended to carry the narrative down to the crushing victory of Rome over Macedon, by which the Roman supremacy over the whole Mediterranean world was firmly established for the next several hundred years.

This, then, was Polybius' original plan. In the final form of his work, however, the history of the 53 years from the outbreak of the Second Punic War to the battle of Pydna fills only the first twenty-nine books. There are in addition fragments of ten more books in which the narrative was carried down further to the destruction of Carthage and Corinth in 146 B.C. The change of plan which this addition indicates is discussed at some length by Polybius himself at the beginning of his third book, and this discussion, as well as the way in which it is inserted, is of the greatest importance for the composition of the work as a whole.

Since the first two books are devoted to the general introduction and to a summary of the events of the five decades preceding the Second Punic War, the third book marks the beginning of the main narrative. In the first chapters of this book Polybius informs the reader in some detail as to how he is going to tell the history of the period down to the battle of Pydna. He concludes with the remark that this history will enable the reader to see clearly how the Romans handled everything and how they succeeded in subjecting the whole world to their domination. Then he adds some observations of a different nature:

If success and failure were the final criteria on which to base one's judgment of states and individuals in regard to praise and blame, then I could stop at the point indicated and bring my work to an end with the last-mentioned events, *as was my original intention.* For the growth of Roman power was now complete. But . . . since what the common crowd considers the most striking success has, when used improperly, not infrequently led to the greatest catastrophe, while misfortune, when endured with fortitude and manliness, has often been turned into a good, it is necessary to add a description of the subsequent attitude of the victors, of the nature of their rule, and of the way in which this rule was accepted and judged by their subjects. For only in this way will it be possible to see whether the domination of the world by the Romans was a good or an evil. . . .[5]

Following this discussion of the reasons for his change of plan, Polybius gives a brief summary of the events of the years 167 to 146, and then concludes with the words: "This, then, is my plan. But for its execution I shall have to rely on Fortune whether she will grant me a life long enough for its completion." [6]

This explanation shows that the change in plan was prompted not merely by a desire to extend the history a little further down the years after the part originally planned had been concluded, but by a profound change in outlook, and that this changed outlook was certainly not quite unrelated to the author's views of the structure of the Roman state. When Polybius first set out to write his history he wanted to show how it was possible for the Romans to conquer the world so shortly after their most crushing defeat. He had found the solution to this problem in the excellence of their constitution. Thus the analysis of this constitution must, from the outset, have been planned as a central part of the whole work. When Polybius changed his plan he does not appear to have abandoned his conviction that the Roman constitution had been one of the major causes of Rome's success. But success of this kind was no longer to him the ultimate criterion of excellence. He now wanted to determine whether the success of the Romans was a benefit for that major part of mankind that had come under their sway.

Since only a comparatively small part of the later books is preserved, it is, unfortunately, not possible to see how Polybius tried to answer this question in detail, but the general trend of his inquiry is quite recognizable. Obviously he did not come to the conclusion that the apparent success of the Romans turned out to be "the greatest catastrophe" for the world. There are some passages in this part of his work in which he praises the Romans for the high moral principles which they followed in their policy on certain occasions.[7] But the leading figures in most of these instances are either Aemilius Paullus, the father of Polybius' friend Scipio Aemilianus, or Scipio himself. In other passages his opinion of the morality of Roman policy in the later period does not appear very high.[8] Most important, however, in this connection are the chapters in which he gives a survey of various opinions concerning the justice of the Roman cause in the last wars against Carthage and Macedon.[9] As mentioned on an earlier occasion, Polybius at this juncture does not seem to commit himself personally; he merely reports the judgments of others. But it can hardly have been unnoticed by Polybius that the arguments of those who defend the Romans without qualification are by far the weakest. Of the two remaining groups, one condemns the Romans outright, while the other contends that the Romans had always been distinguished by the high principles of their policy but that in more recent times the character of their policy had changed for the worse; they were gradually being corrupted by a lust for power like other nations before them. The views of this last group, as presented by Polybius, appear the most convincing.

There are other indications that this last opinion in all likelihood came nearest to Polybius' own convictions. There would hardly have been much cause to inquire whether the success of the Romans was really a proof of their superior qualities if the events of the third quarter of the second century B.C. had not evoked some doubts in this respect. The attitude of the younger Scipio is contrasted with the much less praiseworthy attitude of the majority of the young Roman nobles.[10] All this seems to indicate that there was not only a change in Polybius' subjective outlook, but that, in his opinion, the Romans themselves had changed, and while in the passages mentioned he discusses mainly the consequences of this change for other nations, it can hardly have escaped his notice that there were analogous changes in the internal fabric of the Roman state. The observation of these changes, which during the last decade of Polybius' life must have become visible even to the eyes of a much less attentive observer than himself, cannot have failed to affect his views concerning the absolute stability of the Roman constitution. The problems of the composition of the sixth book and of the composition of the work as a whole are, therefore, very closely connected with each other.

It is then of some importance to determine the time at which the discussion of Polybius' new plan was written, both in terms of absolute chronology and in relation to other parts of the work. In this connection it appears significant that Polybius, in the relevant chapters of the third book,[11] describes in detail the way in which he is going to deal with the period down to the battle of Pydna, but in regard to the second part of the work gives merely a survey of the main events which he will have to narrate. This seems to indicate that at the time when he wrote these chapters the major part of the first twenty-nine books of his work had already been composed, if not in their final form, at least in their general outline, while he did not yet have a very definite plan for the second part. An attempt to determine the probable absolute date of the second plan leads to the same conclusion. A plan to continue the work down to 146 B.C. cannot have been conceived before that date. Since Polybius, furthermore, soon after the destruction of Corinth, at which he was present, was entrusted with a special mission that must have occupied him for about a year, and about which, after its completion, he undoubtedly had to report to the Senate, the discussion of his revised plan can hardly have been written very long before 140 B.C. Nor can it have been written very much later, for in his old age, as Cicero tells us,[12] Polybius wrote a history of the Numantine War, which ended in 133 B.C. This indicates that his great historical work must have been completed around 130 B.C., though he appears to have made additions and revisions until the very last years of his life.[13] The last ten or eleven books of the work must, therefore, have been written in the decade between 140 and 130, and the discussion of the changed plan must have been inserted at the beginning of this period, since at that time Polybius did not yet have a definite plan of composition for the second part of his work. At the same time it follows that a very large part of the original plan must have been completed by then, since it is hardly conceivable that most of the forty books of which the work consisted were composed within the short compass of the one decade from about 140 to about 130 B.C. Thus there can be no doubt that the introductory chapters of the third book were inserted long after the main part of this and of the succeeding books had been written.

This is not the only instance of later rearrangement or revision. M. Gelzer has tried to show [14] that most of the survey of early Achaean history which is now found in the second book was written during the very first years of Polybius' exile in Rome, when the Achaean League was still in the focus of his interest and when he had not yet acquired an intimate inside knowledge of the Roman state, but that these chapters must have been inserted in the place they now occupy at a much later time. Gelzer concluded that Polybius must first have planned to write a history of the Achaean League, but gave up this plan in favor of the more comprehensive work, and that he inserted some parts of the earlier work, which had already been elaborated in the later one, when he gave this later work its final form. The arguments which Gelzer has set forth in support of his assumption are rather convincing. But even if they are not accepted as conclusive, there can be no doubt that he has proved conclusively that some passages of the second book must have been written before, others after, 146 B.C.

Many sections, demonstrably inserted later into an already existing context, consist of first-hand descriptions of certain geographical localities which Polybius is able to give as a result of his travels. In a famous passage of his third book [15] Polybius says that at a time when, through the domination of the Romans, nearly all regions of the world have become accessible by sea or by land and when Greek statesmen are relieved of all great tasks and so have unlimited leisure for study and inquiry, an attempt should be made to obtain more accurate knowledge of the places that played an important part in history. For that reason, he continues, he himself has undertaken a number of travels to Africa, Spain, and Gaul, with the purpose of correcting the errors of earlier writers. Since Polybius could not leave Italy in the period of his exile from 167 to 151, and since he cannot have been in the West before 167, it is certain that he must have undertaken these travels after 151, some of them probably considerably later.

One of the most important eye-witness accounts in Polybius' work concerns the western approaches to the Alps, through which Hannibal passed on the occasion of his invasion of Italy, and the inquiries that Polybius made on the spot.[16] Yet the history of Hannibal's invasion of Italy must belong to the very earliest parts of Polybius' great work and therefore, in the main, must have been written long before 150 B.C. Another example, of essentially the same kind, is the eye-witness account of Carthago Nova in the tenth book.[17] The latest insertion of a geographical item is obviously the reference to the exact measurement of the Via Domitia,[18] which can hardly have been made before 120 B.C., the year in which this road was built. Since many examples show that Polybius was most eager to collect new bits of geographical information and use them for the improvement of his work, there is no reason to consider this reference as an interpolation by someone else. Finally there is still another section demonstrably inserted rather late into an early book, consisting of a passage in the third book,[19] in which Polybius not only refers to events of the year 146 B.C., but also presupposes that at the time when he wrote these words all the forty books of the final version of his work were completed, at least in a rough draft.

Since, then, there is plenty of evidence which shows that Polybius continued to make additions and corrections in his work down to the very last years of his life and since in one case he himself indicates that his views in regard to one fundamental question changed to some extent after the decisive events of the year 146 B.C., it is natural that a good many attempts have been made to find out whether there are not other discrepancies in Polybius' work which may be due to a change in his viewpoints. The most ambitious of these attempts was undertaken by R. Laqueur who believed himself able to reconstruct from the text as we have it five different and consecutive "editions."[20] It need hardly be said that if there really had been five completely revised "editions" of the work, three of them published before the final and posthumous one as Laqueur assumes, it would require truly superhuman ingenuity to discover traces of the earlier editions, let alone to reconstruct them solely on the basis of the final one, and this while the final edition has not even been preserved in its entirety, but for the most part exists only in a very fragmentary condition. In fact, Laqueur's reconstructions are often based on very forced arguments,[21] and not infrequently on false interpretations of the text.[22] It is not impossible that the first fifteen books of Polybius' work were published before the completion of the work as a whole [23] and then, of course, not in the form in which we now have them, since, as has been shown above, they contain additions that must have been made very late in Polybius' life. But even the existence of this earlier edition cannot be proved conclusively. At any rate everything indicates that the version which has come down to us goes ultimately back to a manuscript which Polybius continued to revise until his death and which was published posthumously, the late annotations of the author being inserted in the text for the most part in a somewhat random fashion.

This state of things is, of course, much more favorable to the possible discovery of traces of changes of opinion or viewpoint in the extant version of Polybius' work than a sequence of revised and published editions would be, since such full-scale revisions in all likelihood would have eliminated, or at least obscured, the remnants of earlier versions. In spite of this it would be quite wrong to start with the assumption that all apparent or real discrepancies or inconsistencies in Polybius' thought or concepts must necessarily be due to changes in his viewpoint, and to the fact that the extant versions of his histories apparently never underwent a thorough revision from beginning to end with the aim of making everything agree with Polybius' latest opinions. There is a good deal of evidence to prove that such inconsistencies may have reasons of a different nature.[24]

III

POLYBIUS' PRINCIPLES OF HISTORIOGRAPHY
AND HIS THEORY OF THE ORIGIN OF THE STATE

IT WAS POLYBIUS who coined the expression "pragmatic history" or "the pragmatic method of historiography,"[1] yet the meaning of "pragmatic," as Polybius uses it, is not quite identical with, though it is closely related to, the meaning which the term has acquired in modern times. In coining the new term Polybius wished to set off his own method against other methods of which he disapproved, and the full meaning of the term as he uses it is, therefore, to some extent determined by this contrast to other prevailing trends in the historiography of Polybius' own time and of the preceding century.

Polybius was strongly opposed to the dramatizing type of historiography[2] which had developed especially since the time of Alexander the Great, though its less pronounced beginnings can be traced back to the early fourth century. This type of historiography fulfilled to some extent the functions of the novel in modern literature. It catered to a public which demanded from history entertainment at least as much as enlightenment.[3] In its later phases this type of historiography was apparently also influenced by Aristotle's famous statement, made in connection with his discussion of tragedy, that poetry is more philosophical than history.[4] By dramatizing history many historians of the Hellenistic age believed that they could raise history to the level of poetry.[5] They also believed, though in varying degrees, that by tampering occasionally with factual, but purely accidental, truth, they could attain that higher and timeless truth which, in Aristotle's opinion, is the domain of poetry.

To all this Polybius was most strongly opposed. History, in his opinion, had above all to tell the truth, the important truth to be sure—Polybius would probably have shaken his head over a modern pragmatist like Cornford, who asserts that to the true historian any ascertainable fact must be equally important as any other ascertainable fact—but important factual truth and nothing but what is true.[6] But if Polybius was opposed to the dramatizing type of historiography, he also despised the scholarly historian [7] who derived all his knowledge exclusively from books and documents, who had never had any personal political experience, and who would not even take the trouble to interrogate the real actors on the political scene, to cross-examine eyewitnesses, to obtain firsthand knowledge of the practical working of political bodies such as the Senate in Rome, or to visit the places in which the historical events about which he wrote had taken place. "Plato," he writes,

has said that human affairs will be well attended when either the kings become philosophers or philosophers become kings, but I would say that everything will be well with history when practical statesmen turn to writing history, and not, as they do now, as an avocation but all through their lives with undivided intention and in the conviction that this is one of the most necessary and noble things they can do, or if those who wish to become historians consider a practical political training a prerequisite for their work.[8]

Thus history, in the opinion of Polybius, should be written by practical statesmen, but it should also be written *for* men who are or wish to become political or military leaders; if other historians have written for entertainment, he wishes above all to write to serve this higher practical purpose. The range of what can be learned from history, he believes, is very wide. Of Jacob Burckhardt's famous dictum concerning the purpose of history, "Wir wollen nicht klüger werden für ein ander Mal, sondern weise für alle Zeiten," Polybius would have emphatically accepted the second and positive part, but violently disagreed with the first and negative one. When a man sees that he cannot change the course of events, then he will draw consolation and fortitude from his knowledge of the past, which has taught him that similar misfortunes have always befallen men.[9] This is the wisdom for all times that a man can learn from history: to brace himself against the sudden onslaughts of fortune, in the knowledge that much is happening in this world that even the keenest and best-trained mind cannot foresee or avert. This is also the reason why Tyche, or

Fortune, plays such an extraordinarily large part throughout Polybius' work, and for the same reason it is unthinkable that he should ever have intended to exclude this concept entirely from his philosophy of history.[10]

But Polybius also and most emphatically believes that history should make the statesman "wiser for another time" by teaching him to avoid the mistakes that others have made in the past. If such lessons are to be learned from history, it is necessary to be aware of what causes, controllable by human beings, produce what effects. This is why Polybius sometimes inveighs against those who explain everything by Tyche, or Fortune. That the statesman should learn from history to brace himself against the unpredictable but also to predict the predictable and to control it whenever this is possible sums up his fundamental philosophy on this problem, though Polybius nowhere expressed it exactly in this way.

The lessons of this second kind that can be learned from history are again manifold and cover a very wide range. They begin with purely technical matters, as for instance in the field of military engineering, where one can learn that a surprise attack on a city may fail simply because the ladders prepared for climbing the walls are not long enough.[11] The lessons extend to military tactics and strategy, a subject on which Polybius has much to say whenever he deals with wars and battles,[12] as well as to discussions on the advantages and disadvantages of citizen armies and armies of mercenaries, and, finally, to the highest problems of sound policy.[13] Not everything, however, is either entirely unpredictable or subject to direct human control. Often the statesman, trained by history, will be able to predict that certain causes will have certain effects,[14] but cannot change the causes. In such cases his ability to foresee the future will enable him to adapt himself to inevitable changes and to avoid catastrophes that would otherwise befall him. In making it possible to predict changes of this kind, history, in Polybius' opinion, has made the greatest progress, "so that those who are eager to learn from history are now able to deal methodically with almost any contingency that may arise." [15]

The historian, therefore, must not be content with presenting the facts truthfully; he must also, and primarily, inquire into causes. In discussing the causes of the Second Punic War, Polybius makes a threefold distinction,[16] which, he believes, every historian ought to make, and which, in fact, historians have very widely accepted. The distinctions are: first, the real and underlying causes of an event, which often may precede the actual event by many years or even decades; second, the reasons or pretexts given by the statesmen or political leaders for their decisions, which, however, are but rarely identical with their real motives, much less with the deeper causes of an event; and, finally the beginning of a great event, that is, those happenings and actions which precede an event directly and which to a superficial observer may appear to be its causes—as for instance, in case of a war, the breach of a treaty, a quarrel over certain rights, or the violation of a boundary. In dealing with the first type of cause, which is of course by far the most important one, Polybius makes a further distinction between what may be called the active or driving motive (as, in the case of the Second Punic War, the dissatisfaction of Hamilcar after the First Punic War and the Carthaginians' indignation over Roman encroachments in Sardinia) and the circumstances which caused the driving motive to result in action at a given moment (as the belief of the Carthaginians that their power had increased sufficiently to give them a chance of success in a renewed war with the Romans).[17]

The relation, then, between Polybius' theory of historical causation and his political theory is quite clear. One of the most important types of primary causes in history, in his opinion, consists in the power constellations existing at any given moment. These power constellations in their turn are greatly influenced by the stability or instability of the internal political structure of the states involved.[18] The degree of stability can be largely determined on the basis of general political theory. Such a theory therefore will benefit the practical statesman in various ways. Polybius believes that, under certain favorable circumstances, a good constitution can be created by a wise statesman; [19] when the opportunity occurs, political theory will then provide such a statesman with a sound theoretical foundation. But political theory will also enable a statesman to evaluate the stability or instability of states in which he has no influence. In fact, it will even make it possible for him, within certain limits, to predict in what way the constitution of a given state may develop in the future [20] and to take his own measures in accordance with this foreknowledge.

Political theory derived from historical experience is thus a very essential part of "pragmatic history," as defined by Polybius, and deserves a central part in any historical work. Polybius expounds his general political philosophy in connection with a detailed analysis of the Roman constitution at the time of the battle of Cannae. Rome at this time appears to him to be the most perfect example of a well-balanced and stable political system that had yet been evolved in history. He inserted this discussion of the Roman constitution immediately after his narrative of the battle because he believed that it was chiefly due to the excellence of the constitution of their republic that the Romans were able to recover so quickly from this crushing defeat and to conquer the greater part of the inhabited world within hardly more than fifty years after Cannae.[21]

Polybius begins [22] the exposition of his political theory by taking issue with those teachers of political science who speak only of three types of constitutions: monarchy, or one-man rule; oligarchy, or minority rule; and democracy, or majority rule. In each of these three cases, he believes, a further distinction should be made between government by consent and according to law on the one side and arbitrary or lawless rule on the other. By making this distinction one arrives at a sixfold division: kingship and its counterpart, tyranny; aristocracy and its counterpart, oligarchy; democracy and its counterpart, ochlocracy or mob rule.

In fact, this sixfold division was not altogether new. All its essential features can be found in Plato's dialog *Politicus*,[23] which was written about 360 B.C., with the one exception that Plato states that arbitrary and lawless majority rule and democracy based on laws are called by the same name, while Polybius uses the term ochlocracy for the depraved form and democracy for the legal form. Since "ochlocracy" is not found in Greek literature before Polybius now extant, it is quite possible that he invented the term himself, though he may equally well have picked it up from discussions current in his time. It is of course futile to attempt to identify those "teachers of political theory" who, according to Polybius, were satisfied with the distinction between monarchy, oligarchy, and democracy, since these simple terms had been widely used in a general and vague sense ever since the fifth century B.C. at the latest, just as they continue to be used up to the present day. The point that Polybius wants to make in connection with his sixfold division is that, though kingship, aristocracy, and democracy, in contrast to tyranny, oligarchy, and ochlocracy, are all in a way good constitutions, or rather good types of government, they are all necessarily unstable, since each of them easily and even inevitably degenerates into a depraved type. Hence, the problem is to find a type of government which is free from this weakness of all simple forms of rule; the solution is a system which combines all the three fundamental types, that is, a mixed constitution.

To prove his point Polybius has first to demonstrate why the simple forms of political rule are necessarily unstable, and this leads him to the problem of the origin of the state. In order to solve this problem he imagines, as Plato for similar reasons had done in his *Laws*,[24] that a great catastrophe had destroyed all human communities and only a few scattered individuals had survived. Then he asks the question: What agent in such circumstances would make these individuals seek out one another to form a community, and what form of government would they be likely to adopt? His answer is that the agent is the weakness (ἀσθένεια) of the individual when left to his own devices, and he points out that this same agent makes many animals which are impotent and defenseless as individuals live together in herds. He uses this analogy to draw the conclusion that just as animals in a flock or a herd take the strongest and bravest animal among them as their leader, so human individuals, when they first formed a community to defend themselves against wild beasts and against aggression on the part of individuals or groups of their own kind, undoubtedly flocked around the strongest and bravest of their group, seeking protection in his leadership. The first and original form of some kind of human political community, therefore, is the rule of the strongest, or a kind of monarchy.

It is interesting to compare Polybius' theory with the theories of his most famous predecessors. Both Plato and Aristotle had asked the question: What agent makes human beings live together in political communities? Both had given an answer somewhat different from the one given by Polybius. They found the fundamental motive not in weakness (ἀσθένεια) but in a lack of self-sufficiency (αὐτάρκεια). This lack of self-sufficiency includes, of course, physical weakness as one of its aspects, but not the most important one.

Plato, in his *Republic*, when discussing the foundations and the origin of human society, begins by pointing out [25] that human beings have a very great variety of needs, but also a very great variety of abilities to satisfy these needs. No human individual, however, is able to develop fully all the manifold abilities that are potentially inherent in the human race. A man who concentrates on agriculture, or on the building of houses, or the making of shoes or clothes, will be much more efficient in his special kind of work than a man who tries to do all these different types of work himself. Hence, human beings, in order to live a life corresponding both to their needs and to their potential abilities, will have to collaborate with one another on the basis of a differentiation and division of labor. A human society, therefore, is not like a herd of animals, all of whom, apart from the difference between males and females, have essentially the same function. It is not a mere conglomeration of individuals pooling their strength to defend themselves against external dangers, but an organic whole with different parts. It follows further that not every association of a considerable number of human beings can be called in the full sense a human society or a state. It can be called so only if and when it has become sufficiently differentiated to be self-sufficient, or at least to approach self-sufficiency when taken as a whole. It is characteristic that Plato finds the first principle of the formation of a human society in a property that human beings do not share with other animals, or at least which other animals do not have to the same degree, while Polybius finds it in a quality that human beings have in common with other animals; he brings in peculiarly human qualities only when discussing the second step in the evolution of the human state.

Aristotle, in the first book of his *Politics*,[26] follows Plato in making the lack of self-sufficiency the primary factor in the formation of human society. He also agrees with him in pointing out that man is much more a "political animal" than even an ant or a bee, not to speak of other gregarious animals. But he goes much further than his predecessor. He asserts that human society is prior to the human individual because a human being cannot even become a real human being without associating with other human beings. A child born of human parents but growing up without any contact with his own kind will remain an animal in human shape; and, generally speaking, a being living outside the human community must be either less or more than a human being. This conclusion, in Aristotle's opinion, is borne out by empirical observation. An outcast, who, though he has grown up among other men, is compelled to live permanently outside human society, will, if he does not perish, gradually become a savage, fiercer and more dangerous than any beast, while the man who has developed the divine spark to the full, the wise man and true philosopher, will, to be sure, not be able to live entirely without associating with other human beings, but in so far as he has grown beyond what is purely human, he will need human society less and less.

With these observations Aristotle emphasizes the absolute necessity of human society much more than even Plato did, for, if what he says is true, it is not only man's physical life and the satisfaction of his material needs that depends on society, but his very existence as a human being. There is, however, also another, and in a way opposite, aspect of Plato's theory that has been more fully elucidated by Aristotle. In his *Politics* [27] Aristotle asserts that the human community "comes into being for the sake of bare living," that is, for the sake of the preservation of physical existence, but that once it has come into existence "it exists for the sake of the good life."

What "the good life" is, is explained in the *Nicomachean Ethics*.[28] In this work Aristotle makes a distinction between pure and impure pleasures. Impure pleasures are those that cannot be fully experienced without either preceding or succeeding pain or discomfort. Thus, the fullest pleasure of eating or drinking is not possible without preceding hunger or thirst; contrariwise, there are many pleasures, including too rich and refined a table, that in the end will produce illness and pain. Pure pleasures are those which can be experienced to the fullest extent without any preceding or succeeding pain or discomfort. Such pleasures are most often produced by a serious activity congenial to him who engages in it. There is, furthermore, a natural connection between the pleasure that a man experiences in such an activity and his native ability. A man who is extraordinarily fond of music and takes a very great pleasure in making music is likely to become a

good musician if he practices this art, and, vice versa, a man with a
great talent for music will generally find a great pleasure in it. The
good life, therefore, and true happiness do not consist in an abundance
of physical pleasures, not to speak of material possessions, nor in
continuous amusement—since amusement is truly pleasurable only
as a form of recreation, not as the main content of life—but in an
individual's freedom to engage, as far as possible, in those serious
activities that are most congenial to him. It follows that to the division
and differentiation of labor which, as Plato had pointed out, is necessary to provide for the great variety of physical and spiritual needs
there corresponds, to some extent, a differentiation in the inclinations
and abilities of human individuals for the various activities necessary
to take care of those needs and in the pleasures experienced through
the exercise of these activities.

At the end of the *Nicomachean Ethics* [29] Aristotle points forward
to his *Politics* as the natural sequence to his discussion of "the good
life." This latter work, however, was obviously never completely
elaborated. The first book of the *Politics*, which is most closely connected with the end of the *Nicomachean Ethics*, consists of three sections dealing with the foundations of human society and the state,
with slavery, and with economic theory. These sections, however,
though giving a most concentrated exposition of Aristotle's thought
on these matters, have remained mere outlines or sketches and refer
only incidentally to "the good life." They do not contain any elaborate discussion of the relation between the perfect state and "the good
life." On the other hand, the seventh and the eighth books of the
Politics, which do deal with the problem of the best state in its relation
to virtue and happiness, most likely belong for the most part to an
earlier period of the development of Aristotle's political philosophy [30]
and were probably intended to be replaced by an exposition based
on the results of the discussions of the tenth book of the *Nicomachean
Ethics*. Apparently this new exposition was never written, so that an
authoritative statement by Aristotle on his latest ideas concerning
this question is lacking. Yet, since he says expressly that human society
and the state "exist for the sake of the good life," it appears safe to
assume that Aristotle must have considered as at least one of the
criteria of a good state that its citizens, as far as circumstances permit,

are able to engage in those serious and beneficial activities that are most congenial to them, or that they are at least not prevented by the state from doing so.[31]

There can be no doubt that Polybius was familiar with Plato's *Republic*. The extent of his knowledge of Aristotle's latest and most mature political thought is less certain. It is most improbable that he knew his *Politics*, though he probably knew the works of some of Aristotle's disciples on political theory.[32] But it is sufficient to be sure that he must have been acquainted with the theory that the lack of αὐτάρκεια in the individual human being was the cause and origin of human society in order to ask why Polybius not only replaced this theory by the assertion that the origin of the state is to be found in weakness rather than in a lack of self-sufficiency, but does not even so much as mention the earlier theory.

In fact, Polybius and his predecessors differ not only in the answer which they give, but to some extent also in the question which they ask. Both, to be sure, wish to explain the "origin" of the "community" in which human beings are accustomed to live. But Plato and Aristotle wish to explain, above all, the "origin" of the differentiated society in which we, as individuals, have different functions, and which enables us through this arrangement to become and to be human beings in the fullest sense, while Polybius wishes to explain why we live in a community in which there exist certain definite power relations among the individuals.

In these different contexts the word "origin" also assumes somewhat different meanings. Plato in the first part of his discussion describes a simple and "primitive" society, so primitive indeed in its spiritual needs, or rather in its lack of spiritual needs, that Glaucon in the dialog [33] says that he finds it difficult to see in what way this society differs from "a pigs' state." Yet this society, with its weavers, tailors, shoemakers, toolmakers, metalworkers, architects, export-import traders, and shopkeepers, is much more differentiated than the most primitive societies of which we know, and in this sense "more advanced" in its material culture. Plato can hardly have been unaware of this fact. Thus, when he asks "What is the 'origin' (ἀρχή) of human society?", he obviously does not mean to ask the "historical" question, "For what reasons did human beings *first* band together?"

but rather, "What is the fundamental or primary agent that makes them live together as they now do?" In other words, he aims at an analytical rather than a historical construction. It is different with Polybius. He too, in discussing the "origin" of the human community, does not relate ascertainable facts, but his is a historical construction, an attempted answer to the question "What made human beings *first* band together?" and in this context the answer "weakness" is not inappropriate. Nor is his reconstruction of the most primitive form of "political power" inappropriate. In very primitive societies physical prowess and distinguished bravery in combat are still indispensable qualities of a chieftain or a ruler. Even in the *Iliad* or the old Slavic or Germanic epics the physical strength and the daily demonstrated bravery of all leaders and rulers played a very great role.

What Polybius tries to reconstruct is a state much more archaic and primitive than the society described in the Homeric or similar epics. In terms of Aristotle's philosophy one might say that Polybius tries to reconstruct that phase in an evolutionary process when human society "comes into existence for the sake of bare physical survival," while both Plato and Aristotle try to lay bare the foundations of a human society that "exists for the sake of the good life." [34] This difference has rather far-reaching implications.

Greek political terminology does not clearly distinguish between what we call society and what we call the state.[35] The word "polis," which Plato and Aristotle use in the context discussed, means primarily the city community, in its wider sense any political community, or to use the modern terminology, the state *together* with its social foundation or understructure, while the word "politeia," which Polybius uses, designates the political structure of such a community, or, more specifically, the distribution of competences and powers in such a community.[36] It is evident that when Plato in the *Republic* and Aristotle in his *Politics* speak of the *origin* of the polis, they are thinking primarily of human society and only at a much later point in their discussions come those problems which concern what we would call the state. But does Polybius speak of the "state," if we assume that a *state* presupposes an administrative machinery and the existence of more or less fixed institutions regulating the power relations between the different elements of the body politic? Since, in contrast to Plato

and Aristotle, he thinks from the beginning in terms of power relations, one may say that Polybius speaks of the germ from which the
state was ultimately to develop, but not of a state in the full sense of
the word.

Closely related to this is the further difference that Plato and
Aristotle, when they discuss the origin of society, begin with the question of "happiness" [37] and "the good life," and only at a much later
stage arrive at the problem of the stability, internal strength, and
external success of different types of states, while Polybius begins at
once with this latter question. In modern times Plato and Aristotle
have often been characterized as idealists, and Polybius has sometimes been contrasted with them as the first "realist" among political
philosophers. Polybius himself would certainly have agreed with this
estimate. The term "pragmatic," which he coined for his historio-
graphical method, though of a somewhat wider meaning, includes
what we mean by the term "realistic." Polybius refused to consider
Plato's ideal state on the same level with states that had had a concrete historical existence,[38] and his own concept of the best state or
the best constitution was not a construction of something that had
never existed and may never exist, but was directly derived from
actually existing states such as Sparta and Rome.

Yet this distinction between the idealists Plato and Aristotle and
the realist Polybius is rather superficial. In the last phase of the development of Aristotle's political philosophy the question of the best
state, though not completely abandoned, recedes rather into the background and is largely replaced by a more empirical study of the means
of improving existing constitutions under various historical circumstances and of making them more stable.[39] Yet it is exactly in this
same and latest phase of Aristotle's development as a political thinker
that the inquiry into the social or "societal" foundations of the state,
and with it the question of "the good life," play a fundamental role
in his whole political theory. In fact, it is not difficult to see that the
necessity of inquiring first into the general anthropological foundations of human society in order to arrive at a complete and sound
theory of the state is quite independent from the search for an "ideal"
state. One may ask, therefore, whether a political theory that concentrates exclusively on the power relations existing in a state, and

this in terms of more or less clearly defined competences, can be really quite realistic, or, more precisely, whether a theory conceived in such narrow terms can even correctly evaluate the power relations themselves and the stability of the system to which they belong. This question can be answered only in much later stages of the present inquiry and on the basis of the historical evidence provided by the history of the Roman constitution.[40]

The second step in the original development of the state, according to Polybius,[41] is the transition from the rule of the strongest and bravest to true kingship, which is based on the administration of justice. This is at the same time a transition from a condition that is common to human beings and other gregarious animals to a type of community which only human beings are capable of organizing. Such a transition becomes possible because man, unlike other animals, lives not only in the present but also in the future. His ability to reason from the present to the future is the source from which the notion of a moral good ultimately springs, and with it the possibility of a human community or state based on and devoted to the preservation of justice. The growth of this state out of the notion of justice is described in the following fashion.

When, for instance, adult human beings see that children who have been brought up with great care and pains by their parents do not show gratitude and do not take care of their parents when they have grown old, then even those who are not directly concerned will be indignant over the children's behavior. They will be indignant because they realize that if children in general behave this way, then they themselves will not be taken care of in their old age. Thus they are aware that it is in the interest of everybody that children be punished if they do not pay back the debt of gratitude they owe their parents. Similarly, if a man harms a person from whom he has formerly received help and support, there will be general indignation because everybody applies the case to himself. Thus, the notion of gratitude as a socially desirable attitude or a "moral good" is formed, and such is generally the origin of all moral concepts.

Once the moral concepts have become firmly established in a community they will have a profound influence on the form of the state and of the government. If the man who, because of his strength and his bravery in fighting the enemies of the community, has become the leader and the ruler of the human herd always supports the general sentiment in questions of "justice" and decent behavior and uses his strength to force the recalcitrant and "unjust" members of the community to live according to rules derived from these concepts or sentiments, then the majority of the people will retain him as ruler; they will even support him by their combined strength after he has grown old and has lost that physical strength and power through which, in the beginning, he had obtained the first place in the human herd. It is in this way that the primitive monarchy of the strongest is gradually replaced by the kingship of the just. This kingship tends to become hereditary, because people expect the children of a just and wise father to develop the same qualities and so be fit to become kings. So far Polybius' theory.

The notion of the just and wise judge as the natural ruler was widespread in the ancient Orient; it appears for the first time in Greek literature [42] in the guise of an Oriental story. This story, as told by Herodotus, differs in some respects from Polybius' version. When the Medes, so the story goes, had freed themselves from Assyrian domination, they lived for some time in complete liberty. But this liberty led also to much lawlessness. A man by the name of Deiokes, who was hungry for power and wished to become a tyrant, realized that he could use this situation for the attainment of his aspirations. Within a lawless world he decided to be straightforward and just and to work for justice within his village. After some time his fellow townsmen made him their judge, and as the fame of his justice spread, more and more people from distant places came to ask him to act as arbitrator in their quarrels with one another. After this had gone on for some time and he had become famous all over the country, he suddenly declared that he could not continue to neglect his own affairs in order to serve as arbitrator for others. When the lack of his former services was severely felt everywhere, the Medes came together and decided to make him king, since under his rule there would be law and order in the country. Deiokes accepted on the condition that they would build him a strongly fortified place and grant him a military force under his exclusive command. This granted, he built himself an extremely

strong fortress, introduced a very strict court ceremonial, and withdrew from all direct contact with the people. He had his supervisors
and his spies everywhere in the country and was very harsh in enforc-
ing a rule of strict justice.

There is an interesting difference between Polybius' historical construction and Herodotus' story, which is, of course, also a historical
construction, in the guise of a story. In the first case the chieftain, who
owes his chieftainship originally to his physical strength and bravery,
retains his power when his strength is gone because he has used it to
defend justice, while in the second case power not possessed previously
is *acquired* through the administration of justice. But the idea which
is common to both reconstructions, namely, that a renown for justice
may give power, is not altogether lacking in sound historical sense.[43]

Still more important, however, is Polybius' theory of the origin of
human morality and of the notion of justice. According to Polybius
the notion of justice originates from the ability of human beings to
reason and to realize in advance that the harm which is done to another
human being may also be done to themselves if such conduct is generally acknowledged as unobjectionable by everybody. It is very widely
assumed that Polybius took over this theory of the origin of morality
and of the notion of justice from the Stoic philosopher Panaetius of
Rhodes, who like Polybius himself was a friend of the younger Scipio
and with whom Polybius may have been well acquainted in his later
years, though this cannot be proved.[44] The reason for this assumption
lies in the fact that the passage in which Polybius develops his theory
about the origin of the notion of justice has a close parallel in a passage
in Cicero's treatise *De officiis*,[45] which, according to Cicero's own testimony, is based on a work of Panaetius.

It is, however, characteristic of Polybius that he derives morality
and the notion of justice, together with the emergence of a society
in which the principle of justice is enforced, *exclusively* from enlightened self-interest and the ability to reason by analogy about the future.
In consequence of this ability men are indignant when they see that
children do not pay back the debt of gratitude they owe their parents.
The question of why the parents have done so much for their children
in the first place remains undiscussed, but since Polybius does not mention any principle except enlightened self-interest, one would have to

assume that they do it in order to have someone who will take care of them in their old age. This, however, is no longer in agreement with Cicero-Panaetius, who continues in the very next sentence with the assertion that "nature" has made human beings in such a way that they love not only themselves but also their offspring, their wives, their family, and generally their fellow human beings with whom they have to live. Here, then, the egotistic principle of enlightened self-interest is clearly supplemented, though not completely replaced, by the altruistic principle of a natural love of various degrees for other human beings, without which genuine gratitude could not even come into existence. For if the parents take care of their children only in order to have someone take care of them in their old age, the children may still keep this bargain because they, in their turn, wish to be taken care of by their children. But in such a bargain there is hardly more room for a feeling of personal gratitude than in the relation of a man to his life insurance.

The one-sided application of one of Panaetius' principles to the exclusion of the other is neither Panaetian nor Stoic. In fact, if one looks for an explanation of the origin of the state as a guarantor of justice purely on the basis of enlightened self-interest, it is to be found in Epicurean rather than in Stoic philosophy; it is an Epicurean doctrine that natural justice must be derived from an agreement concerning that which is useful or advantageous for everybody, namely, agreement not to harm others on the condition of not being harmed by them.[46] Nobody, as far as I know, has yet claimed that Polybius was an Epicurean, and this for very good reasons. For much in Polybius' philosophy of life, especially his positive evaluation of the active life, the life of the practical statesman, and his notion of honor, which has found expression in many parts of his work, are absolutely irreconcilable with Epicurean philosophy.

If, then, a strong agreement with Epicurean doctrines in his theory of the origin of a society which protects justice does not make Polybius an Epicurean, it is no more permissible to regard him as a Stoic or a Panaetian because of the agreement of one of his statements made in the context of his theory of the origin of the notion of justice with a statement that in all likelihood goes back to Panaetius. The relation of Polybius to Stoic philosophy, to be sure, is somewhat stronger than

his relation to Epicureanism and deserves somewhat closer attention since it is characteristic of his relation to philosophical theories and
systems in general. Polybius uses a great many terms that play a central role in the philosophy of Panaetius and of his Stoic predecessors.
But he uses such terms with a meaning frequently quite different from
the meaning which they have in Stoic philosophy. Thus, to give only
one example, the term κατόρθωμα in Stoic philosophy, where it is
a central concept of ethical theory, means an absolutely correct action
resulting from absolute virtue and absolutely correct insight on the
part of the man who acts. In Polybius it very often means simply "success." [47] This in itself would be sufficient to prove that Polybius cannot
have been a Stoic, though he was undoubtedly influenced to some extent by Stoic philosophy, just as he was influenced by the theories of
a number of non-Stoic philosophers. The nature of this influence can
be more strictly defined by determining Polybius' relation to some
fundamental Stoic doctrines.

Two basic concepts in Stoic ethics are the notions of "the beautiful"
(τὸ καλόν) and "the useful" or "the expedient" (τὸ συμφέρον). The
concept of "the beautiful" has a wider meaning in Greek, and especially in Greek philosophy, than in most modern languages. It means
everything that calls forth spontaneous and disinterested admiration.
It can therefore also be applied to the moral field, where it designates
any action that evokes spontaneous and disinterested approval, as in
someone risking his life to save someone else's, but also outstanding
honesty in all matters. Thus, "the beautiful" in this sense can be equated
with what we would call "the moral good." Its opposite is "the ugly"
or "the shameful" (τὸ αἰσχρόν), that which calls forth spontaneous
disapproval. It is, then, one of the most fundamental tenets of Stoic
moral philosophy that what is morally bad or shameful can never be
really useful or expedient, since the harm that such action does to the
soul of its perpetrator is much greater than any profit that he can
derive from it. In fact, the older and sterner school of Stoics contended
that such external goods or profits, even if acquired honestly, are no
goods at all, but indifferent (ἀδιάφορα).

Though Panaetius deviated from old Stoic orthodoxy in several
respects, there can be no doubt whatever that he retained its doctrine
according to which there can be no real clash between the morally good

or beautiful and the useful or expedient, since nothing can be expedient that is not at the same time morally good. This is proved by the fact that Panaetius, according to Cicero,[48] intended to write a book in three parts, the first on the morally good or beautiful, the second on the useful or expedient, and the third on the apparent conflict between the morally good and the seemingly expedient. This last section (which was not completed) was to show that there could be only an apparent, not a real, conflict between what is good in itself and what is good or expedient for an individual or for a group.

The manner in which Polybius uses these Stoic terms is then most significant. When speaking of Philopoemen [49] he says that

the morally beautiful and the expedient come very rarely together, and there are few people who can bring them into harmony with one another. For we all know that most of the time the morally good is far removed from immediate expediency and vice versa. But Philopoemen made this his aim [that is, to bring them into harmony] and he actually achieved it, for to bring back [to Sparta, their home country] the exiles who had been captured by the enemy was a most beautiful deed, and to weaken or subdue that Lacedaemonian city was most expedient [for the Achaean League].

This whole paragraph, with the exception of the last sentence, might well have been written by a Stoic, though it does not follow the strictest Stoic terminology. A Stoic like Panaetius might very well have said that it is most difficult for an ordinary man to bring the morally good and the expedient into harmony because it is not easy to realize that the seemingly expedient is not expedient if it is not morally good. But when we come to the last sentence we are suddenly in an entirely different world. True, it was one and the same action of Philopoemen, which resulted in the weakening of Sparta, an event most expedient from the Achaean point of view, and which at the same time made it possible for Philopoemen to do "a fine thing" by bringing the Spartan exiles back into their home country. But these two results are merely incidental to one another; and this kind of reconciliation of the "morally good" with the politically expedient is certainly often excellent policy, but it has no more to do with Stoic than with Christian ethics.

All this is most characteristic of Polybius' relation to Stoic philosophy and to Greek philosophy in general, with which, as a further analysis will show, he was very familiar. He uses the concepts, terms, and theories of the philosophers as his intellectual tools with which to describe and, so to speak, to dissect reality as he sees it. But fundamentally his viewpoint remains that of a historian and of a practical statesman whose guiding principle is "good realistic common sense," and not absolute logical consistency. It is quite possible that he was not conscious of the fact that he used the Stoic theory concerning the relation between the morally beautiful and the expedient in such a way as to reveal himself to be miles away from true Stoic doctrine.

There is, however, another point that requires further elucidation, and this will lead back to Polybius' theory of the origin of the notion of the moral good and of the state as a guarantor of justice. The rationalism of Polybius' attempt to derive the moral notions exclusively from enlightened self-interest and the ability of calculating from the present to the future agrees perfectly with the rationalism of his theory of religion. If all human beings had enough of that calculating ability there would be no need for religion, since everybody would behave decently out of enlightened self-interest. But since this is not so, it is good that the common crowd should believe in the gods and in divine punishment, and the wise man therefore will consider religion one of the greatest supports of the state, even though he is not a believer himself. This is his opinion where he deals with the question ex officio, so to speak, and on a purely theoretical level. But reading his whole work one discovers that on some occasions he makes concessions to the belief in divine powers, though in a somewhat skeptical and tentative fashion, while on still other occasions he shows a spontaneous indignation over violations of sacred objects that does not seem to be quite in agreement with his theoretical convictions.[50]

The same inconsistency can also be seen in the moral field, where the moral *indignation*, which he ascribes to the men who first observed ingratitude in children and which in his history he himself often expresses over many things, does not seem to agree completely with his assumption that the moral concepts are derived from purely rational calculations.[51] But these are not the only cases in which a certain discrepancy between his purely rationalistic opinions and his somewhat less rationalistic convictions or sentiments can be observed. There is another instance in which Polybius uses the Stoic concepts of the "beautiful" and the "expedient" in a not quite Stoic fashion, though in this case the deviation from true Stoicism is in a different direction. When he speaks of the fate of Carthage and Greece in the fateful year 146 B.C.,[52] he says that one should consider the fate of the Greeks, who (through their own folly) came under the domination of Rome after a crushing defeat but survived, more pitiful than the fate of the Carthaginians (who were completely exterminated), unless one pays no attention to what is befitting and "beautiful" and bases his judgment merely on what is "useful." Here, once more, the Stoic terms appear, and in an entirely different context. Yet again they are not used entirely in the Stoic sense, for the "beautiful" here has rather the meaning of traditional honor; this is not quite what this concept meant to the Stoics, though they approved even of suicide if a man could no longer live in agreement with Stoic principles. But this would hardly have applied to the Greeks in general after 146 B.C.

Thus, while the use of the term "the beautiful" in this passage deviates to some extent from genuinely Stoic usage, it nevertheless, through the notion of "the beautiful" in the sense of the glorious, the noble, the honorable, also brings in an element that is foreign to the rationalistic theory of the origin of morality and justice which Polybius expounds in the sixth book. This theory is built exclusively on the notion of the "useful" or the "expedient," that is, on the same criterion which in the passage on Carthage and Greece appears as so much lower than the criterion of "the noble."

This shows again conclusively that on the purely theoretical level Polybius has a strong tendency to think exclusively in terms of power relations, of political expediency and political success, and of enlightened self-interest, but that this absolutely pure rationalism is sometimes alloyed with other elements that have their origin partly in traditional notions of honor and the like, partly in very genuine but less rationalistic feelings. The introduction to his third book [53] shows that in his later period the "beneficial" became a criterion along with success. But this is hardly sufficient reason to explain all the apparent and real discrepancies in Polybius' moral philosophy as evidence of different phases in his development; and it will be seen that in the political theory expounded in the sixth book there is but very little evidence of the viewpoint which Polybius, according to his own testimony, adopted when he set out to write the last ten books of his work.

IV

The Cycle of Constitutions and the Mixed Constitution

POLYBIUS' RECONSTRUCTION of the origin of the state is followed by his theory of the cycle of constitutions.[1] This theory is extremely simple. Hereditary monarchy has come into being because people believe that the children of a just ruler are likely to become just rulers also. As long as the first origin of monarchy and its true purpose are not forgotten, this system serves the community well. After some time, however, the descendants of the original king come to believe that the rulership is theirs by right and that their power must serve the satisfaction of their every desire. Thus they become haughty and overbearing and begin to encroach upon the private rights of their subjects. In this way kingship is turned into tyranny. When this has become unbearable, the most high-minded, noble, and courageous of their subjects will conspire to overthrow the monarchy, and when they find support among the people, the end of monarchy is not long in coming; the people choose the men who have played the foremost roles as their leaders in the liberation from oppression, and thus tyranny is replaced by aristocracy. This regime, in turn, works well at first. The new leaders are pleased with the trust they have received and rule for the benefit of the community as a whole. Again the rule becomes hereditary, and again after a time the descendants of the original leaders, having forgotten the origin and purpose of the existing political system, become haughty and overbearing and abuse their power. Thus aristocracy is gradually converted into oligarchy. Finally, when this has become intolerable, there is again a revolution, this time directly of the people. Because of their bad experiences with monarchy the people do not wish to return to that form of government. The only way left seems to be to retain the power themselves, and consequently oligarchy is replaced by democracy. This political order again works well temporarily, for everybody is jealous of the liberty and equality that the people have at last attained. After some time, however, the people get so accustomed to the enjoyment of liberty and equality that these great goods no longer mean anything to them; individuals and groups begin to struggle with one another for influence and power. Demagogues spring up who know how to win followers by "paying the people out of their own pockets" (by means of taxes and subventions paid from those taxes), until their regime ends in complete anarchy and disorder. Then there comes the last turn of the wheel; the community reverts to monarchy, since there must be someone to restore law and order.

This, according to Polybius, is the natural cycle of pure and simple constitutions. He claims that whoever has understood the law of this cycle clearly and correctly may still be mistaken in forecasting the exact time when a change in a given state will take place, but will hardly err in judging the stage in development or decline it has reached at any given moment, nor at what point in this development it will change to a different form of government. This is certainly a rather astounding claim, as made in this form and following upon the very simple exposition of the theory of the cycle of constitutions.

The observation that under certain conditions an existing political order may be destroyed by a *Putsch* or a revolution was first made, at a very early time, of course. In fact, in the very earliest documents of Greek political thought extant, this observation assumes the form of the warning that a state of lawlessness or of social injustice may easily lead to a revolution and that the outcome of such a revolution is very often the establishment of a tyrannical regime. Quite different, however, from this very common observation is the idea that certain forms of government naturally and inevitably fall into lawlessness and then are replaced by other forms. This is the idea which underlies Polybius' theory of the cycle of constitutions: and this particular idea found its first expression within extant Greek literature in one of Herodotus' famous stories.[2]

After seven Persian nobles, as Herodotus tells it, had done away with the false Smerdis, who had usurped the Persian throne, they deliberated what form of government should be adopted. The first pleaded for democracy, the second for an oligarchy. Then Darius expressed his opinion in favor of monarchy, with the following argument: If you have an oligarchy, you will have factions and strife between them. This will lead to bloodshed until one man is the victor, and then there will be monarchy. If, on the other hand, you have democracy, lawlessness and disorder will develop until the people find a leader who suppresses the evildoers. This man will earn the admiration of the people and he will become their ruler. Thus, here too the end is monarchy. Why then not begin with monarchy, since we will end with monarchy anyway? This argument of Darius is accepted by the majority of the seven nobles, and, in the further course of the story, Darius becomes king.

Problem stories in historical guise like this were a familiar expression of popular speculation on all sorts of topics in the ancient Orient, especially in those border lands where Orient and Occident met. Like most of them, Herodotus' story appears in Oriental guise and has some Oriental elements.[3] The outcome of the story and the special weight given to the arguments of Darius are, of course, determined by the fact that Persia was a monarchy. But the story also contains very pronounced Greek elements. It is most unlikely that in ancient Persia a discussion concerning the best type of government to be chosen could actually have taken place among Persian nobles, since the monarchy seems to have been generally taken for granted. Furthermore, the plea for democracy and against monarchy with which Otanes, one of the seven nobles, opens the discussion, though referring to the bad experiences of the Persians with Cambyses and the false Smerdis, describes the psychology of a Greek tyrant who has to reckon with strong antimonarchic tendencies among his subjects rather than that of a Persian king secure in the possession of his legitimate power. The "most beautiful name" which, according to Otanes, democracy has been given (namely ἰσονομία, equality before the law) is a typical expression of Greek political ideals of the fifth century. Thus it is almost certain that the political speculations underlying the story are largely Greek. It is significant then that in Otanes' attack on the monarchic system of government the point is made that even the best man will inevitably be corrupted by the possession of unrestricted power. This conviction plays a very great role in later Greek political theory and, in slightly modified form, is of course also the basis of Polybius' theories of the cycle of constitutions and of the preferability of the mixed constitution. At the same time one may say that, since this conviction implies that a king in the course of time almost inevitably becomes a tyrant, the Herodotean story anticipates not only the natural transition from democracy to monarchy in Polybius' cycle but also from kingship to tyranny; [4] with the significant difference, however, that Herodotus' version clearly implies that the monarch who has come to power through a civil war will almost inevitably become a tyrant in consequence of the difficulties that he has to face, while consistent application of Polybius' cycle theory would imply that the deterioration sets in only with the descendants of the monarch.[5]

A still more elaborate description of what at first sight may appear to be an inevitable transition from one type of government to another is found in Plato's *Republic*.[6] This description requires a somewhat more detailed analysis because of its great importance for the problem of the origin of Polybius' cycle theory and also because it is doubtful whether Plato's intentions were correctly understood by Polybius or even by Plato's immediate disciple, Aristotle.

After the discussion of the ideal or perfect state has been brought to completion, in Plato's *Republic* Glaukon proposes to examine also, though much more briefly, the different types of imperfect or faulty states. The proposal is accepted and executed in the form of a discussion of the transition from one type of government to another; each case is accompanied by an analogy of the transition from a father whose character corresponds to that of the first government to a son whose character corresponds to that of the next one. However, the types of governments considered by Plato are only partly identical with those which enter into Polybius' analysis of the natural cycle of constitutions. The constitutions discussed by Plato, apart from that of the perfect state, are (1) those similar to Crete or Sparta; (2) oligarchies, in which money plays the decisive role as the distinguishing factor between the ruling class and the rest of the people; (3) democracies; and (4) tyrannies. All other forms are considered as being somewhat in between these pure and fundamental types of constitutions.

The perfect state is an aristocracy in which the wisest men rule disinterestedly and for the benefit of the whole people. It is converted into a timocracy, or a state after the fashion of Crete or Sparta, when the rulers no longer consider the working and producing population as their friends and "bread-givers," but as their subjects and slaves. In the state that results from this change of attitude the guiding principle of the ruling class is no longer service to the community, but ambition and honor. Honor and distinction are gained especially in war, and therefore the ruling class in a timocracy will be inclined to engage in continuous warfare.[7]

A further deterioration sets in when money begins to play a dominant role in society and the state. At the end of the process, wealth rather than bravery and prowess in warfare gives influence, power, and honor.[8] In this way a timocracy is gradually converted into an oligarchy, in which the wealthy rule and the poor have no share in the government. Such a state is much worse than a timocracy. For the rulers in a timocracy, though harsh and selfish, are at least distinguished by personal ability, while the possession of money is no proof of any particular ability of the owner. On the contrary, the possession of excessive wealth tends to make a man idle and useless to the community, while at the same time the accumulation of wealth in the hands of a comparatively small group creates as its counterpart a completely impoverished proletariat which is equally useless to the community. What is still worse, as a consequence the whole community tends to split into two parts, the wealthy and the poor, who, instead of being friends since they are fellow citizens, become deeply hostile to one another.

The proletariat thus formed may again be divided into two groups: those who are resigned to their fate, and those who rebel against it.[9] Those in the latter group become dangerous to the existing order, especially when they are joined by former members of the ruling class who have been financially ruined by their more greedy fellow oligarchs and who have now become furious enemies of their former associates. In time the wealthy steadily decrease in number and those who remain lose their physical stamina, because they have been accustomed to live in luxury. When the poorer classes become aware of this, they cannot in the long run fail to realize that power based exclusively on money is actually based on a fiction, and that they can rid themselves of their masters as soon as they decide to do so. When they have reached this point the time is ripe for a revolution. Wealthy people who refuse to give in are killed or exiled; the rest have to live with the remainder of the population on an equal footing. In this way democracy supersedes oligarchy.

The principle of the perfect state was service to the community; of the timocracy, personal distinction or honor; of oligarchy, money. The principle of democracy is freedom.[10] But freedom in a democracy that originates in the manner described is above all the liberty of everyone to do as he pleases. A natural consequence of such freedom is disrespect for the law and laxity in its application. Known criminals who should have been or actually have been legally condemned to death, and therefore by right should be dead, dare to show themselves in broad daylight, and no one seems to mind or even take notice. In such a democracy teachers are afraid of their pupils, and parents of their children. But freedom and equality do not eliminate political ambition. Under the new order there will still be poor and wealthy, though the latter are no longer the rulers. In these circumstances ambitious politicians will try to win favor with the masses by taking money from the rich and distributing it among the people.[11] In the end the most radical, the one who advocates a complete redistribution of wealth, will become the leader of the masses. Since his program arouses strong antagonism and hostility among the more prosperous part of the population, he will ask for extraordinary powers to cope with this violent opposition. Once he has obtained these powers, together with the command over an armed force that obeys him blindly, he becomes a tyrant; and this is the end of democracy.

At first, as long as he is still dependent on the support of the majority, the tyrant is affable and friendly,[12] but since he cannot fail to meet with opposition and find competitors for power, he must use harsh means to secure his position. By these measures he incurs the hatred of a large part of the population, and since people are looking for a leader to free them from his tyranny, he has to start foreign wars in order to keep the people occupied and have one purge after another at home in order to eliminate those who might become dangerous to him. When this stage has been reached, the people realize too late what a monster they have nursed to political power and that too much freedom breeds the most terrible despotism and political slavery.

This is a brief summary of Plato's description of the imperfect or faulty types of government and of their transition from one to another. It is clear that this is not a cycle of constitutions. What Plato describes is, on the contrary, a continuous downward movement that begins with the ideal state and ends with the worst possible type of government, which in Plato's opinion is not even worthy of the name of "state" or government: tyranny. But it is interesting to see that Aristotle when discussing this part of Plato's *Republic* [13] blames Plato for not having made it a cycle, or for not having completed the cycle. For he says, "Plato does not say whether there is a further transition from tyranny to some other form of government or not, and if so, for what reason and to what form of government . . . But according to his scheme the transition should be to the first and best state. For in this way it would be continuous and a cycle."

It is not easy to determine whether Aristotle meant to say that Plato himself had thought of a cycle but did not complete it, or whether he blamed Plato for not having conceived of the movement as of a cycle. At any rate, it is evident that Aristotle believed Plato to have conceived of the transitions described by him as compulsory and necessary in the sense that a timocracy must always turn into an oligarchy, an oligarchy into a democracy, and a democracy into a tyranny. If this assumption is made it is quite logical to demand a cycle, for if the development down to tyranny is compulsory and universal but stops there, then all states in the course of time must have become tyrannies, which is contrary to experience. But it is not likely that Aristotle interpreted Plato correctly in this respect. The fact alone that Plato admitted that there were other "intermediate" forms of government, beside the five discussed, seems to indicate that Plato reckoned with the possibility confirmed by historical evidence that the development might also take different turns, and that he regarded the transitions which he describes merely as especially illuminating examples. In this case he could very well stop with tyranny, leaving it open as to what type of government it would turn into. Plato believed that tyranny, though in itself the worst constitution, offered a unique opportunity of creating a good state without a revolution, if a tyrant could be persuaded to become a philosopher and to give up part of his power voluntarily; [14] but in the face of overwhelming historical evidence he can hardly have believed that a tyranny would automatically turn into a philosophers' republic.

It would appear, then, that Aristotle misunderstood Plato in this respect. This misunderstanding is most significant because it shows how easily Plato's description of a transition from one type of government to another could lead to the idea of a cycle. Aristotle himself, of course, is opposed to this idea, since he points out that while many constitutions are unstable, there is no necessity for an oligarchy to be always turned into a democracy and a democracy into a tyranny, but that any kind of transition is possible, from tyranny into another tyranny, into an oligarchy or into democracy, from democracy into oligarchy, from oligarchy into tyranny, etc. In this respect Aristotle is, of course, historically right. Polybius, on the other hand, adopted the theory of the cycle in its strictest form.

It is not absolutely impossible that some unknown author had elaborated a similar theory before Polybius and after Plato, since cycle theories of all kinds abound in antiquity, especially in the period between these two authors. It is therefore natural that many attempts should have been made to show that Polybius must have taken over his theory ready-made from some earlier writer. It has also been claimed that this writer must have been a Stoic, a Pythagorean, or a Peripatetic, or even some known individual philosopher, for instance Dicaearchus. In order to support such theories some scholars have contended that Polybius himself was not capable of so profound an elaboration of Plato's ideas and that this alone proves that there must have been some intermediate author whom he copied.[15]

All these arguments are not very convincing. The cycle theory in the form in which it is presented by Polybius is anything but profound. It is a gross oversimplification, essentially of the same kind as his oversimplified analysis of the Roman Republic which he cannot possibly have borrowed from someone else. Hence it is most characteristic of Polybius' own method. If carried to their logical conclusions, the attempts to find some intermediate author between Plato and Polybius merely lead to the fiction of a Polybius before Polybius, like the famous "final solution" of the Homeric question: "It has now been proved that the *Iliad* was not written by Homer but by another poet of the same name." It is much more important to find out by what general ideas Polybius was influenced and how he adapted them to his special purpose.[16]

That Polybius was acquainted with Plato's *Republic* can be proved beyond doubt.[17] That he was acquainted with the eighth book of this work is clearly implied in his statement that Plato "and others" may have dealt more thoroughly and more adequately with the transition from one form of government to another but that he is going to present the matter in a simplified form in order to make it more easily understandable for the average reader and to adapt its description to the special requirements of "pragmatic history." [18] Whether the "others" to whom he refers were definite authors, possibly of the Hellenistic age, whom he had read, or whether they merely represent some vague memory that others might also have touched upon the problem, is difficult to tell. Polybius was, after all, deceived by his memory when he enumerated Xenophon among the authors who had likened the Cretan constitution to that of Sparta.[19] But all this is of little importance. What has been said about a Hellenistic model for Polybius' cycle theory is the merest guesswork, without a leg to stand on. How easily one could derive a cycle theory from Plato is proved by Aristotle; and that the simplification of the theory is Polybius' own work and not that of someone else is attested by his own unmistakable words, which, in this case, we have not the slightest reason to mistrust. In fact he appears to realize somewhat that he has not only simplified but oversimplified the matter. He adds, though, that whatever defects his brief presentation of the theory of the cycle of constitutions may have will be compensated for by his more detailed discussion of specific historic constitutions later on.

These later compensations, however, do not bridge the deep difference between Polybius' and Plato's treatment of the matter. This difference is essentially the same as that which was found in their theories of the origin of human society. Polybius concentrates exclusively on power relations and on the effect of the possession of power on human individuals or groups. Plato does not neglect these factors, but includes in his analysis a great many social, economic, and psychological factors which may have a profound influence on changing power constellations, but cannot be adequately described in terms of power relations only. Many of Plato's observations have an almost uncanny reality for the present day. If it were not so certain that his description of a democracy in which known criminals walk around in broad daylight without anyone taking notice of them, and in which teachers are afraid of their pupils and parents of their children was written more than two thousand years ago, one might easily believe it to be a satire on certain aspects of American democracy in the middle of the twentieth century. Similarly, his analysis of the way in which a demagogue rises to power through the promise of a new distribution of wealth, especially of the land, and after having seized absolute power in this way is driven by the inner logic of his system to establish an ever more cruel system of oppression, at the same time engaging in foreign aggression in order to keep the people occupied, might have been derived from the experiences of the last four decades.

There is nothing of this burning present-day actuality in Polybius' description of the natural cycle of constitutions. This may, of course, partly be due to chance, since some two to three hundred years ago Plato's remarks would not have been quite so directly applicable to the contemporary scene. But a comparison of the constructions of Polybius and those of his predecessors Herodotus and Plato with the historical reality of their own times and of preceding periods leads to similar conclusions, and it is significant that in this respect the philosopher Plato keeps nearer to historical experience than the historian Polybius.

In the Herodotean story the emphasis on transition from both oligarchy and democracy to monarchy is, of course, predetermined by the necessity of letting the movement end with monarchy. But the description of the transition from oligarchy to monarchy through the struggle between various aristocratic factions until the leader of one of the factions wins out and sets himself up as a tyrant is certainly true to often-repeated experiences in Greek states of the sixth century; however, the result here is, of course, not a monarchy of the Persian type but a tyranny of the type which many Greek cities, including Athens, experienced in the period of the transition from oligarchy to democracy. The description of the transition from democracy to monarchy in Herodotus is much less specific, and in this case it is somewhat difficult to find the historical model. But the fact that the explanation does not, as in Polybius, follow a set pattern that repeats itself with every transition from one type of government to another seems to indicate that it must somehow be based on historical experience. Finally, the first section of the story concerning the psychology of the tyrant who is displeased if someone admires and praises him only moderately, but also dislikes those who praise and admire him immoderately since he knows that they cannot be sincere, and who is afraid of anyone who stands out by superior qualities, is most admirably true to life. Similar experiences of the Greeks with the city tyrants of the sixth and early fifth centuries have found expression in innumerable stories. One of the most striking is the famous anecdote of how Thrasybulus, by simply walking through a grainfield and cutting off the ears that stood out above the others, silently advised Periander of Corinth how to retain his tyrannical power.[20]

The transition from the ideal state to timocracy, discussed in the eighth book of Plato's *Republic*, has, of course no equivalent in history, since the ideal state has never existed. But the parallel transition [21] from a father who is a perfect gentleman to a son who becomes a disgruntled reactionary of rude manners is obviously portrayed from life. It has even been suggested that the model of the portrait of the old gentleman may have been Plato's father, Ariston, though in this case the son would not have been portrayed after Plato himself. But there were many men among Plato's uncles and cousins who could have served as models for the description of the reactionary son.

In his description of the transition from timocracy to oligarchy, Plato doubtless follows closely the development which had actually taken place in Sparta in the second half of the fifth century and the beginning of the fourth, and which had not yet come to an end at the time when he wrote the *Republic*. Concerning the beginning and the causes of this development the ancient sources disagree to some extent. There is general agreement [22] that at some time there had been no great inequality of wealth among the Spartiates, that is, the descendants of the last wave of Doric conquerors of the southwestern Peloponnesus. It is further agreed that this equality continued for some time, because to sell one's land or to buy land from another Spartan was frowned upon socially [23] and was even either partly or altogether prohibited by law.[24] There is some disagreement concerning the causes of the later change. According to a tradition mentioned for the first time by Plutarch,[25] a certain ephor named Epitadeus caused the revocation of a law regulating the inheritance of landed property, and so broke the dam which until then had prevented any great inequality in the possession of landed estates. This innovation is not known to earlier writers such as Xenophon and Aristotle.[26] The latter ascribes the unfortunate development to a fault in the legislation of Lycurgus [27] himself, which frowned upon the sale of land belonging to citizens, but made it possible to bequeath it freely and to give large dowries in landed estate to women. In the course of time this practice, in Aristotle's opinion, caused the growth of large estates on the one hand and, on the other, the impoverishment of many people in a country in which landed property was the only source of income.

But whatever the causes of the development may have been, as early as the second half of the fifth century at the latest a great inequality of wealth had developed among the Spartan citizens, which caused the wealthy to form a new aristocracy within the aristocracy which the Spartiates constituted in regard to the rest of the population.[28] This naturally evoked great resentment among those who, because of their poverty, were excluded from the higher group. The situation became much worse after the Spartan victory in the Peloponnesian War brought great wealth to Sparta, but almost exclusively to those who belonged to the new ruling circle and who had been wealthy before, for now the greed for money was added to the greed for landed property. The new kind of wealth had to be displayed in order to be enjoyed. This led to a breakdown of the old Spartan laws of austerity among the new ruling class and greatly increased the resentment of the poor Spartan citizens who felt that they were the true representatives of old Spartan mores and customs. It is evident how closely this development resembles Plato's description of the transition from timocracy to oligarchy.

The models for Plato's construction of the transitions from oligarchy to democracy and from democracy to tyranny are much more difficult to find, and it seems likely that what he draws in both cases are really composite pictures. Some elements of these pictures he may have taken from events that had happened in Sparta in the beginning of the fourth century. One of the Spartans who did not belong to the new aristocracy of the "equals," Kinadon, had tried to stir up a revolt against them,[29] attempting to enlist also the support of Perioeci and other men who did not have full citizen rights,[30] obviously with the aim of bringing about a greater democratization of the Spartan constitution, though it is not known what his exact plans were. This conspiracy was discovered in 398 B.C. and quickly suppressed. But there were also other and similar movements. Lysander, the victorious Spartan general of the Peloponnesian War, is said to have planned to replace the hereditary Spartan kingship by an elective monarchy,[31] probably with the aim of becoming sole king, that is, in Greek terminology, a tyrant. Undoubtedly it was not only his military glory but also the internal strains and unrest in Sparta that made it possible for him to nourish such plans, and since it was the conservative party that defeated his aims, it is likely that he too tried to win support by advocating reforms. So there was for a time the possibility not only of a transition from oligarchy to democracy but also from oligarchy to tyranny.

Both these attempts, of Kinadon as well as of Lysander, had come to nothing before Plato wrote his *Republic*, and the strictly oligarchic regime had been restored. But the internal strains had not been eliminated, and about a hundred years after Plato's death the reform movement found the support of two successive kings and led to changes in the Spartan constitution, resulting first in the suppression of the ephorate and the one-man kingship of Cleomenes and later in the tyranny of Nabis. Thus those beginnings which Plato had witnessed in his lifetime did, some one hundred to one hundred and fifty years after his death, result in a development not quite unlike the one that he describes.

But Plato's analysis of the last two stages in the constitutional changes which he postulates is not altogether a prophecy based on contemporary movements in Sparta. Some features of his description of democracy—for instance, his mocking remarks about known criminals who walk around in broad daylight without anyone taking notice, though according to law they should be dead—are certainly based on conditions prevailing in Athens in his time.

It is somewhat difficult to find a clear example in pre-Platonic Greek history of the transition from democracy to tyranny as Plato describes it. Elements of what he describes may be found in Athenian history of the early sixth century, and similar occurrences may have happened in that period elsewhere. But generally speaking these occurrences belong rather to the period when tyrants came to power as leaders of the people against oligarchic regimes, so that they should be listed as transitions from oligarchy to tyranny rather than as transitions from democracy to tyranny. Aristotle, on the other hand, observes [32] that, according to historical experience available at his time, when a demagogue tried to make a revolution through the promise of a redistribution of land, the wealthy usually struck first and re-established a strictly oligarchic regime. But Plato is all the more to be admired, considering the rather insufficient historical evidence existing at his time, for having been able to give so excellent a description of a development that has occurred many times after his death, both in ancient and in modern times.

It is not necessary to show in detail how far Aristotle's analysis of natural changes of constitutions [33] agrees with historical evidence, since his whole discussion of the subject is based on the large collection of the histories of constitutions that he had made in collaboration with his disciples and since he himself illustrates everything with concrete historical examples.

The difference between Polybius' theory of the cycle of constitutions and the theories of his predecessors is striking. Polybius begins with the transition from primitive monarchy to aristocracy. Now it is true that in early Greek history a great many of the old patriarchal and democratic monarchies were gradually replaced by oligarchies, one of the outstanding examples being Athens. But there is no indication whatever that these old monarchies were overthrown because the kings, in the course of time, had become tyrannical and overbearing. The reason in most of the cases, and specifically in Athens, was just the opposite. With more settled conditions the large landowners gradually became so powerful that the power of the kings became steadily weaker, until finally monarchy was abolished altogether.[34] In later times a tyrant who had inherited his rule may occasionally have been overthrown in the way and for the reasons that Polybius describes. But this was certainly not at all characteristic of the transition from primitive patriarchic monarchy to oligarchy. Here again it is the application of a stereotyped formula concerning power relations and the corrupting influence of absolute power to the total neglect of social and economic causes which is characteristic of Polybius' construction.

This is hardly less true of the other transitions in Polybius' general scheme. Most amazing, however, is his apparent claim that the transition must always follow the cycle from monarchy to oligarchy to democracy and back to monarchy, though Aristotle had pointed out long before that history provides examples of any kind of transition: from monarchy directly to democracy, from democracy to oligarchy, from oligarchy to tyranny, and so on.[35] For even though it is most improbable that Polybius had read Aristotle's *Politics* he can, as a historian, hardly have been completely unaware of the fact that history did not always follow the cycle which he describes and on the basis of which, he claims, it is possible to predict the future.

This is of crucial importance for the evaluation of Polybius as a political thinker. As pointed out before, Polybius did admit that the cycle theory as presented by him was an oversimplification. This statement has been interpreted to mean that all Polybius wants to say is that in a state with a simple constitution the governing part has too much power and therefore tends to become insolent and overbearing, a situation which in the course of time will lead to a revolution. The description of the cycle then is merely an illustration of this fundamental fact and does not mean that the constitutions must actually follow upon one another in the sequence indicated. This interpretation of Polybius' statement, however, is demonstrably false. There remains the hard fact that, according to Polybius' own claim, predictions can be made on the basis of the cycle theory and these predictions concern not only the future deterioration of a government as such but also the form of government which will succeed it, since this can be inferred from the point in the cycle at which the present government finds itself. There can not, therefore, be the slightest doubt that Polybius took the cycle theory much more seriously than the interpretation mentioned admits.

This is further confirmed by what Polybius himself says concerning the nature of his oversimplification. For when he speaks of it he adds that the deficiency will be corrected through the more detailed analysis which he will give later. Yet the only correction that can be found in the later parts of the sixth book is the observation that some cities, like Athens and Thebes, for some time overcame the natural handicaps of their simple constitutions through the merits of outstanding political leaders like Themistocles or Epaminondas. Thus it is clear that in Polybius' opinion the oversimplification consisted merely in the omission of special circumstances which might temporarily prevent the mechanism of the cycle from having its full effect. He certainly did not mean to express any doubt of the accuracy of the cycle theory as such. It is equally clear that his reference to Plato implies that he considered Plato's description of the transition from timocracy to oligarchy to democracy to tyranny [36] as a somewhat more elaborate way of describing essentially the same cycle that he was going to describe, but with less emphasis on what appeared to Polybius the essential point. Obviously he believed that Plato also had meant to speak of a development that always follows the same pattern, and not merely to give examples of typical transitions from one type of government to another out of a much greater number of other possibilities.

Thus it is impossible to eliminate the fundamental deficiency of Polybius' cycle theory by arguing that he did not really mean what he appears to say. Nor can the deficiency be explained as the result of a change in Polybius' views and of his failure to revise his work thoroughly enough to remove the discrepancies caused by the clash between his earlier and his later views. The deficiency is right in the cycle theory itself. For anyone who would make historical predictions on the basis of the theory, even if only to the extent to which Polybius declares this to be entirely feasible, would be very much mistaken indeed. Similar but much more intricate difficulties and deficiencies can be found in Polybius' general theory of the mixed constitution. It is entirely wrong to explain them away, either by specious interpretation or by the assumption that they are due to a change in his views, as the majority of recent commentators have done. One must try to find out their cause and origin and use the results of this inquiry to attain a better understanding of Polybius' way of thinking. Only in this way will it be possible to distinguish what is valuable in his theory from the deficiencies which it has in the special form in which it is presented by him.

The only possible way out of the vicious cycle of constitutions, according to Polybius,[37] is to be found in the mixed constitution which is a well-balanced combination of all the simple constitutions. This theory also has long antecedents and, as with the other theories discussed so far, the social and the political aspects of the underlying problem are in the beginning closely related to one another. The problem with which Solon had to deal in Athens at the beginning of the sixth century B.C. had been above all a social and economic one, concerning the indebtedness of the Athenian farmers to the big landowners, the bondage in which the debtors were kept, and the provision that they could be sold into slavery abroad if they could not pay the interest, a provision of which very extensive use seems to have been made in the period preceding the Solonian reforms.[38] Solon solved the social and economic problem by a cancellation of the debts of the farmers, the abolition of debt slavery and bondage, and a provision that made the land, which until then had been the unalienable property of the family, freely salable, so that mortgages could be taken on the land rather than on the body of the owner. At the same time this new regulation had the advantage of appeasing the desire of the landowners for the outright acquisition of more land, which made the new order at least a little more acceptable to them. But a political question was also involved.

Solon had been called upon to act as mediator between the two conflicting groups when a revolution of the distressed peasants against the oppression by their creditors was brewing.[39] At the same time he seems to have enjoyed the special support of a third group, the new merchant class, who needed free labor for their ships and shipyards but could not obtain it as long as the majority of the poor population was kept in bondage on the land by the big landowners. Nevertheless, both of the conflicting parties appear to have nourished the hope that Solon's decision would be essentially in their favor. The poorer classes especially appear to have believed that Solon might be induced to set himself up as a tyrant, as other popular leaders elsewhere had done in the same period, and drive the leading aristocrats into exile with their support and introduce much more radical reforms than he actually did. Solon, however, refused to follow such a course and become the instrument of one party. In his poems he says that he wished to give both parties neither more nor less than what was due them, that he held out his strong shield over both of them, not allowing either to triumph over the other in violation of justice, that he found no pleasure in achieving anything by the forceful methods of tyranny, and that he did not wish to see the noble and the common people have an equal share of the rich soil of the fatherland.[40] In other words, while he relieved the poor of bondage and of the intolerable burden of their debts and made it possible for them to earn a living as free men, he did not promote equality of property. The same idea of justice found expression in the political order which he established. For the highest administrative offices, the archons and the treasurer, were to be held by men exclusively from the highest property class,[41] but appointed by lot from candidates previously elected in the tribes through an election in which all citizens participated. The lesser administrative offices and membership in the council were, in a similar way, reserved for people belonging to the three higher property classes. But all citizens of voting age of all four property classes participated in the elections and had the right to vote in the ecclesia or the assembly of the people, which had the final decision in all the most important issues.

Thus the Solonian constitution in a way clearly represented a mixture of oligarchic and democratic elements, and therefore may be called a mixed constitution of a sort. But the slogan of Solon's time and of the following century was not "the mixed constitution" but "the middle of the road" ($\tau\grave{o}$ $\mu\acute{e}\sigma o\nu$, $\dot{\eta}$ $\mu\epsilon\sigma\acute{o}\tau\eta s$) and "the middle-of-the-road party" ($o\acute{\iota}$ $\mu\acute{e}\sigma o\iota$).[42] These slogans played a very great role, especially in the last decades of the fifth century when a reaction had set in against what many considered the excessive democracy which had gradually developed in Athens after the Persian Wars. In this period the middle-of-the-road men advocated a return to the "ancestral constitution" ($\pi\acute{a}\tau\rho\iota os$ $\pi o\lambda\iota\tau\epsilon\acute{\iota}a$), which some identified with the constitution of Solon, others with the constitution of Cleisthenes adopted after the overthrow of the tyrants at the end of the sixth century, because they believed that these constitutions avoided the faults both of excessive oligarchy and of excessive democracy. However, the question most frequently discussed in that time was not how democratic and oligarchic features could best be mixed in such a middle-of-the-road constitution, but rather how large a part of the population should share in the fundamental political responsibility and power.[43]

Since in the earliest discussions of mixed or middle-of-the-road constitutions the problem of the relative political power to be given to the wealthy and the poor plays a predominant role, it should perhaps also be mentioned that towards the end of the fifth century a number of rather fantastic proposals were made for the solution of the problems resulting from the unequal distribution of wealth. Thus, a certain Phaleas of Chalcedon advocated [44] a law by which the wealthy were to be compelled to give their daughters large dowries while the girls themselves were obviously supposed to marry poor men, and the sons of the wealthy were supposed to marry girls without dowries. In this way a continuous redistribution of wealth was to be guaranteed. The architect and city planner, Hippodamus of Miletus, had a somewhat more elaborate plan [45]—to divide all the land into three parts. One part was to be distributed in equal shares among the farming population as outright property, one part was to be assigned to the priests and temples, and one part to the standing army. According to Aristotle, Hippodamus did not make it quite clear who was to work these two latter parts, but the produce from them at any rate was to be used for the sustenance of the groups to which they were assigned. The craftsmen and merchants were to have no land since they could buy what they needed with the money earned through their professions.

The theory of the mixed constitution, in the narrower sense in which "mixed constitution" means above all a system of checks and balances, appears for the first time [46] in Plato's political writings. Here, however, it is presented not so much in connection with social and economic problems but with the problem of absolute power and the desirability of preventing a concentration of power within the political community. In his *Republic* Plato had placed hardly any restrictions on the power of his philosopher kings or rulers to decide and regulate everything according to their superior insight without being bound by any hard and fast laws or regulations. In his *Statesman* he begins [47] by emphasizing again the absolute superiority of the insight of a wise man over any possible legal regulation, because any law must necessarily be couched in general terms and human life is too manifold and varied in its incidents for any possible general regulations to do justice to it. He even compares the law to a stubborn old man who will not listen to reason and refuses to understand that this or that individual case is an exception to the rule and requires an individual solution. But after having made this point Plato observes that only the perfectly wise and incorruptible statesman can be intrusted with the power to decide everything according to his superior insight and that human beings are apt to be corrupted by the possession of power.[48] The second best course, then, is to establish a strict rule of law. For such a rule, however imperfect it may be because of the inevitable rigidity of any set of general rules, is infinitely better than unchecked power of unwise or corrupt politicians.

In Plato's last work, the *Laws,* the notion that men are inevitably corrupted by the possession of unchecked power recurs several times [49] and is now expressed in the most forceful terms. The conclusion is then drawn that power can be checked only by preventing its concentration, which is achieved by its distribution among various agencies and by special devices designed to preserve the existing distribution of power. The first scheme of this kind discussed in the *Laws* [50] is incorporated in the historical legend of the settlement of the Peloponnesus by the Dorians and the establishment of the three kingdoms of Argos, Messene, and Lacedaemon. According to Plato, the Dorians at that time decided to have the same fundamental laws in all three kingdoms and provided that if in any one of them, either the king or kings—there were two kings in Lacedaemon—would encroach upon the rights of the people, or if the people would deny the king what was due him by law, the other two nations and their kings were bound by oath to come to the support of the part that had been wronged. This is especially interesting because we have here the scheme of a federation or a federate state with a mutual guaranty of the constitutions of the member states, each of these states being a mixture of democracy and monarchy, a democratic monarchy or a democracy with a monarch as its head.

The second example discussed in the same work [51] is that of the Spartan constitution as it is supposed to have developed after the mixed constitutions of Argos and Messene had been destroyed in spite of the mutual guaranty. This is a much more elaborate scheme, but restricted to one state. The first check on the absolute power of the monarch is the fact that there are two kings of equal power in Sparta. But since royal power was still "seething" or "boiling over," there was a second check through the power of the gerousia, the council of elders, which at the same time represented the moderating influence of the wisdom of old age. Finally, since this still was not enough, a further curb was added through the institution of the ephors. No mention is made of the power of the people, but since it is said that in Sparta alone was the old middle-of-the-road structure preserved in this way, the idea is obviously that through this system of checks and balances an encroachment on the rights of the people was prevented. Finally, the importance of the *distribution* of power is emphasized by the remark that the oath by which the three kings and nations promised one another help against any violation of constitutional rights proved to be an insufficient check against the lust for power.

The third example of a mixed constitution in Plato's *Laws* is the state whose laws and institutions are described in detail in books six and following. Of this state Plato says [52] that, like all good states, it must hold the middle ground between monarchy and democracy, a statement which Aristotle criticized with the remark [53] that what Plato actually describes is rather a mixture of democracy and oligarchy.

It is not without profit to analyze the reasons for this disagreement. On the face of it Aristotle is of course right. For there is no monarch in the ideal state which Plato describes in his *Laws*. But what Plato means is obviously that there must be someone who leads and controls the state through his wisdom and insight and is at the same time, so to speak, the living representative of the legal order. It does not matter very much then whether this highest authority is represented by the nocturnal council. Since this council has more than one member one may call it oligarchic. Yet there can be no doubt that it represents the monarchic element which Plato has in mind; and in this respect Plato is essentially quite right. For the nocturnal council has exactly the functions of a king,[54] and is not an oligarchy in the traditional sense of the word, that is, the political representative of a socially prominent ruling class. In spite of the great powers given to this nocturnal council, Plato, however, in the *Laws* also makes provision for a certain control by the people over the government, since he clearly sees the danger that otherwise even the best government might be corrupted by the possession of absolute power. This is why he says that in a good state there must be a mixture of monarchy and democracy. What he has in mind here, then, is clearly a system of checks and balances.

But Plato, in the construction of the ideal state of the *Laws*, pays attention not only to this side of the question. He is also interested in the social side of the problem. He no longer believes in communism as he did when he wrote the *Republic*. He permits the development of a difference of wealth and is even willing to grant the wealthy a larger share in the administration of the country. Yet he is still anxious absolutely to prevent the emergence of a class of the very rich and a class of the very poor in his ideal state. It is the combination of these various provisions that makes Aristotle say that the ideal state of Plato's *Laws* is really a mixture of democracy and oligarchy. But here we are no longer dealing with systems of checks and balances but with the middle-of-the-road theory.

Aristotle's *Politics*, which, as observed before, may not have been read by Polybius, are so full of observations concerning all sorts of mixed and middle-of-the-road constitutions that it is impossible to discuss or even mention all of them in the present context. It must therefore suffice to speak of some of the most important ones. It appears to be a general principle with Aristotle that the more mixed and middle-of-the-road a constitution is the better and more stable it will ordinarily be. Thus, he says,[55] one should not call those measures truly oligarchic that make a state more oligarchic, but those which make it more stable, and one should not call truly democratic what makes a democracy more democratic, but what makes it more stable. But what makes a democracy more stable is exactly what makes it less democratic, and what makes an oligarchy more stable is what makes it less oligarchic. He says [56] that the best mixture between oligarchy and democracy is that which makes it impossible to say whether the result is a democracy or an oligarchy because the mixture of the two elements is so even. A mixture of more than two constitutional forms or types is better than a mixture of only two, according to him.[57] He points out [58] that a middle-of-the-road constitution can be best achieved by a mixture of the elements of two or more constitutions. Finally, he pays a great deal of attention to the social and economic foundation of various constitutions and points out [59] that a sound middle-of-the-road constitution can hardly exist for any length of time where there is an excessive difference of wealth between the rich and the poor and that such social conditions will either result in excessive oligarchy or in excessive democracy, both of which will turn into tyranny in the end.

This selection of quotations from Aristotle's *Politics*, though incomplete, shows clearly that Aristotle posed four closely related problems: (1) How is it possible to prevent a class war resulting from a split of the population into a group of excessively rich and a large mass of excessively poor? (2) How can the government be given a sufficiently broad basis without making it dependent on every whim of the ignorant and unreasonable masses? (3) How can one prevent the concentration of too much power in the hands of any governmental agency or ruling class? (4) By what principles or criteria should the distribution of power in a state—which must necessarily be unequal—be regulated? [60]

The solution of the third problem is a system of checks and balances. But in Aristotle's opinion a system of checks and balances is not enough, since it cannot work properly if the social order is unstable or out of balance with the political order. The establishment of a really sound mixed or middle-of-the-road constitution requires that all four problems be solved to a reasonable degree. Aristotle's discussion of the problem, though sketchy in regard to some details, is much more comprehensive than that of any of his known ancient successors, and it is a pity that Polybius obviously never became acquainted with it.

One of Aristotle's most famous disciples, Dicaearchus of Messene, who lived about a century and a half before Polybius, is credited with a work entitled *Tripoliticus*, in which he tried to show that the best constitution was a mixture of monarchy, aristocracy, and democracy; he seems to have discussed the Spartan constitution as an example.[61] The same theory is attributed to "the Stoics" by Diogenes Laertius [62] in his life of Zeno. In the *Florilegia* of Stobaeus [63] one finds a frag-

ment or an epitome of a treatise ascribed to Archytas which says that
the best constitution must be a mixture of democracy, oligarchy,
monarchy, and aristocracy, and exemplifies this theory with the Spartan constitution. It is generally agreed that this cannot be a fragment
from a genuine work of the Pythagorean Archytas, who, in 367 B.C.,
was head of the government of Tarentum and was acquainted with
Plato, but belongs to the pseudo-Pythagorean literature which developed after the first century B.C.[64] But Rudolf von Scala has tried to
prove [65] that this fragment, as well as a number of fragments attributed to the "Pythagorean" Hippodamus, who is obviously meant
to be identical with the architect and city planner mentioned above,[66]
are ultimately derived from and reflect the contents of Stoic treatises
contemporary with or earlier than Polybius. The arguments set forth
in support of this theory, though they have been widely accepted, are
really not very strong. But the whole question is not of major importance in the present context, since there can be no doubt whatever
that the theory of the mixed constitution had a long history before
Polybius. Furthermore, it has been shown [67] that Polybius is certainly
not an orthodox Stoic but uses Stoic philosophy and Stoic theories
just as freely and without any scrupulous attention to their original
meaning as he uses the theories of other philosophers. It is much
more important to analyze further the use which Polybius made of
the abundant theories existing at his time.

The only way out of the vicious cycle of constitutions, according to
Polybius, as mentioned before, is the mixed constitution. This, he
says,[68] was clearly realized by Lycurgus, the great Spartan lawgiver.
For Lycurgus saw that just as iron is destroyed from within by rust,
and wood by grubs and worms (if they are not destroyed by some
external cause), so the simple constitutions have congenital diseases
that destroy them from within. Therefore he adopted a system that
was not simple and one-sided, but united all the advantages and
characteristic features of the best governments so that none of the
elements could grow unduly powerful, since the power of each one
of them would be counteracted by that of the others. In this way, he
believed, the political system would remain for a long time in a state
of equilibrium. And in fact, Polybius points out, as a result of the

adoption of this system the Lacedaemonians retained their liberty for a much longer time than any other people we know of.

Since the chapter on the cycle of constitutions had stressed the instability of simple constitutions, the chapter on the mixed constitution created by Lycurgus very appropriately stresses the stability of this constitution. Between the two chapters, however, there is a short section on the Roman constitution.[69] The Roman constitution is, of course, the most outstanding example of a mixed constitution, and, as has been seen before, it is because of the fundamental importance of this constitution to the success of the Romans in the late third and in the second century B.C. that Polybius has inserted his excursion into political theory in the sixth book. Yet the section mentioned, which—apart from a few words in the introduction to the sixth book—is the first passage in which the Roman constitution appears, does not characterize it as a mixed constitution, much less speak of its stability. On the contrary the section emphasizes that if any constitution has come into being in a perfectly natural way, it is the Roman constitution, and that therefore it will follow the general laws of nature, which will make it possible to predict its rise and also its future decline. In other words, while we expect the stable Roman constitution to be contrasted with the unstable constitutions of the cycle, we learn to our amazement that the Roman constitution follows essentially the same laws, so that not only its rise but also its decline can be predicted.

This real or apparent contradiction has always appeared puzzling; and it is quite natural that it should have been taken as an indication that here, as in other places, we have a later insertion, written from a changed point of view. When Polybius first started on the elaboration of his political theory, so the argument goes, he was convinced that the Roman constitution was the most stable of all constitutions; to show this is obviously the purpose of the detailed analysis of this constitution which occupies a large part of what is extant of the sixth book. But when, in his old age, he lived through the first stages of the so-called Gracchan revolution, he became doubtful whether the Roman constitution was really so stable as he had believed it to be. He finally came to the conclusion that the Roman constitution as a natural constitution must follow the same laws as other constitutions and that therefore its future decline and the course of this decline can be predicted. Thus he inserted the puzzling passage, which somewhat contradicts what he had written before. But he never revised the book as a whole, and so the two contradictory versions are now found side by side.

On the other hand, it has been argued that there is no fundamental contradiction, but that the two versions are perfectly reconcilable if they are understood correctly. For, it is held, what Polybius says in this intermediate passage by no means implies that the Roman constitution is as unstable as the simple constitutions. It merely implies that, like all things human, it is not eternal. But this is also true of the Lacedaemonian constitution of Lycurgus, through which, Polybius claims, the Spartans preserved their liberty much *longer* than any other people. Yet in this case surely there can be no doubt that he wishes to contrast the Lacedaemonian constitution with the constitutions of the cycle because of its stability. In fact, it may be said, a later passage,[70] in which Polybius compares the Roman and the Carthaginian constitutions and says the Romans were stronger because their constitution was still in the oligarchic stage while the Carthaginians had already passed to the democratic one, shows clearly what was in Polybius' mind. The simple constitutions, it would then seem, follow a development in which a comparatively good and healthy state follows each time upon a revolution, but is soon in its turn followed by a decline that becomes ever more rapid until the next revolution brings in a different type of government. With a naturally developing mixed constitution it is different. The revolutionary reversal from monarchy to oligarchy is here replaced by the development of a mixture of monarchic and oligarchic elements, in the course of which the oligarchic element gradually gains in strength. But while the oligarchic element is still developing, democratic elements also gradually come in, so that a three-fold mixture is produced. In this way the rapid decline characteristic of simple constitutions is avoided, and with it the revolutions that intervene each time the lowest point of the decline has been reached.

Nevertheless a mixed constitution that has grown naturally is no more absolutely stationary than anything else that has a natural growth. The curve of its rise and decline is merely much longer and more even, since it has no steep downward movements between monarchy and oligarchy, oligarchy and democracy, but rises steadily, as one element after the other is added to the mixture until the most perfect mixture is reached. Only then may it again decline slowly as the element last added, the democratic element, gradually becomes prevalent. This would also agree with Polybius' apparent assumption that a mixed constitution is strongest when the aristocratic element is at the height of its strength. For since the oligarchic element is the second of the three to grow in strength, its summit would coincide with the time of the most perfect mixture reached. On the basis of some remarks which Polybius makes at the end of the sixth book,[71] one might even say that his conclusion was that the Roman state, after a long development of the type described, would also end with complete democracy, which in its turn, according to the cycle theory, must turn into monarchy. In this way he would have predicted what actually was to happen in the middle of the first century.

Such arguments certainly carry considerable weight and contain important elements of truth. Yet they no more provide a completely satisfactory explanation of what we find in Polybius than does the assumption that the apparent discrepancies in his theory are the result of later additions to an earlier text and his failure to revise the whole book from the new viewpoint. True, it would have been absurd to assume that the Roman state and the Roman constitution, however good, would last forever; and the idea that a mixed constitution is much more stable and will last much longer than any simple constitution is not irreconcilable with the assumption that a mixed constitution, especially if it has come into being through some kind of natural growth, will also have its natural decline, though this decline will be much slower in coming than in a simple constitution. Yet it is not without cause that so many intelligent readers have been puzzled by what Polybius says. Everyone who has read through Polybius' exposition of the cycle of constitutions, with its strong emphasis on the instability of simple constitutions, must expect that when the mixed constitution is introduced, its stability will be stressed; he is naturally somewhat stunned when he learns instead that the decline of a mixed constitution like that of Rome can also be predicted. If such a statement had to be made, then it should at least have been coupled with a remark to the effect that such a constitution is not ever lasting either, but that, because of the different character of its development, it will last much longer and, while at its peak, will give a state greater strength than a simple constitution ever will. The complete absence of any such statement at this juncture and the fact that the stability of the mixed constitution is mentioned only in the next chapter, which deals with the "artificial" constitution of Lycurgus, makes the passage very confusing to the reader. It may of course be argued that the difficulty is due merely to a certain awkwardness of Polybius as a writer which can also be observed elsewhere in his work. But one may ask whether the special awkwardness of this passage has not special implications.

After having described the cycle of constitutions Polybius claims that, by observing the point of the cycle at which a (simple) constitution stands, it is possible to predict, within certain limits, its future development. Then he adds that by the same method of observation one can also understand the first formation, the growth, the summit and maturity, and the subsequent decay of a naturally growing mixed constitution such as that of Rome and hence make predictions concerning its future.

It is evident from the context that Polybius here means to compare the natural development of the Roman constitution with the equally natural course of the cycle of constitutions. But with what aspect of the cycle? With the whole cycle? There is the difference that the whole cycle has three high points and three low points in which the changes occur, while in the development of the Roman constitution there are only one high point and two low points, at the beginning and at the (anticipated) end. The comparison then might be with the development of each of the simple constitutions within the cycle. But here there is the difference that each constitution within the cycle reaches its high point almost immediately after the revolution producing it and then enters into a period of decay that is slow in the beginning and becomes ever more rapid towards the end. In regard to a naturally growing mixed constitution such as the Roman, Polybius emphasizes, on the other hand, the *slow* growth to maturity which, after a long period of strength and stability, will be followed by a similar period of decay.

Now it can of course be said that the development of a mixed constitution must not necessarily correspond to that of the cycle of simple constitutions or of its several parts in every respect. For Polybius it is quite sufficient that both developments are natural and therefore to some extent predictable. But it is easy to show that here is a more deep-seated difficulty, which has caused endless controversies among modern commentators on Polybius political theory.

Polybius' description of the natural development of the Roman Republic suggests the comparison with the growth, maturing, and aging of a living being; and this is the way in which it has been understood by many readers and commentators, though Polybius does not make the comparison in so many words.[72] But when Polybius speaks of the decay of simple constitutions, he does not compare it to the aging of living beings but to the decay of iron or wood through rust or worms. This comparison is quite appropriate where it stands. For the simple constitutions do not grow but are made by revolutions. In the same way iron and wooden things do not grow—wood may grow, but that is not the point here—but may decay from within, as the ancients believed, just as the simple constitutions decay through some inherent weakness. Thus it is quite clear that the case of the cycle of simple constitutions or of the development of an individual constitution within the cycle is not as analogous to the case of the mixed constitution as it may appear at first sight.

Still another simile is used by Polybius in his description of the constitution of Lycurgus. This constitution-maker, who, according to Polybius, saw the deficiencies of the simple constitutions and found a remedy against them, does not act like a doctor who cures a human being of an illness that might have caused his premature—but not his natural—death, nor like a man—in our times we would say a chemist—who finds some solution or process by which a piece of dead matter can be preserved from decay, but like a construction engineer. This makes it perfectly clear that Polybius mixes his similes. It is therefore not permissible to say that Polybius cannot have thought of the growth and aging of living beings in describing the Roman constitution because that does not fit the cycle of simple constitutions or that he did not intend to apply the cycle theory in a modified form to the growth of the Roman constitution because then the analogy of

the growth of a living being would not fit. For he is demonstrably
not so logical and consistent in his comparisons and similes.[73]

At the same time it is perfectly clear that the awkwardness of Polybius' analysis in these two chapters cannot possibly be explained by
the assumption of later revisions and additions. For the different parts
of his analysis hang so closely together that they cannot be separated
from one another.[74] Obviously it is necessary to find a different explanation; and it would hardly have been worth while to discuss
Polybius' use of similes so much in detail if this inquiry did not lead
to a better understanding of the way in which Polybius arrived at his
political theory.

No one who has read the first chapters of the first book of the work
of Polybius can doubt that what set Polybius' political thinking in
motion was his observation of the enormous staying power of the
Roman Republic after the disaster of Cannae and the inner strength
which enabled it subsequently to conquer, within an amazingly short
time, the greater part of the world then known. He looked for an
explanation of this phenomenon. He found it in the excellence of the
Roman constitution. This constitution appeared to correspond to an
ideal that had been elaborated before by various Greek political theorists. Thus it seemed obvious that in this case political philosophy
could be used as an instrument of historical analysis.

Greek political theory had stressed the stability of the mixed or
middle-of-the-road constitution. This was just what Polybius needed,
since it was the stability of the Roman Republic that needed explanation. There was some slight inherent difficulty since the stability
which Polybius had to explain was the stability against attacks from
without while Greek theory had stressed the stability against disturbances and revolutions from within. But these two types of stability
could be considered as merely two aspects of essentially the same
thing, though it will be seen that certain difficulties in Polybius'
analysis of the Roman Republic arise from his failure to make the
distinction. These difficulties, however, are not of essential importance
at the present moment.

In emphasizing the stability of the mixed constitution Polybius
had to contrast it with the instability of simple constitutions. He found

examples of unstable simple constitutions discussed in Herodotus and in the eighth book of Plato's *Republic,* probably also in the works of some Hellenistic authors, though this is not absolutely certain. On the basis of what he found in the works of his predecessors he developed the simplified theory of the cycle of (simple) constitutions. He claimed that this simplified theory enabled the historical and political observer to make predictions concerning the future development of the cities or countries observed. This was very important for him since he considered it the very essence of "pragmatic" history that it enables the historian to make historical predictions.

In elaborating the theory of the mixed constitution as a means of making the political order more stable, Polybius' predecessors had availed themselves of the example of Sparta. Common opinion had been that this state owed the excellence of its constitution to the wisdom of one man: Lycurgus. In this case then the mixed constitution was considered the result of a rational construction. This explanation was accepted by Polybius. But in trying to apply the same explanation to Rome, Polybius could not fail to observe that the Romans did not know of any single man who was responsible for their apparently excellent constitution. On the contrary, this constitution appeared to be the result of a long process. On the basis of what he was able to find out about Roman history, Polybius had to accept this explanation: in contrast to the Spartan constitution, which was supposed to have been created by one rational act, the Roman Republic appeared to present an example of a mixed constitution which had grown and developed in a natural way. The analogy of biological growth then suggested itself easily, especially since in Polybius' time this analogy was used very widely in a great many different fields. It was then only one step further to the realization that, if this analogy were taken seriously, the future of Rome could also be predicted within certain limits, since natural growth, after a period of maturity, is inevitably followed by natural decay. What greater discovery could a "pragmatic" historian make? On the basis of Polybius' convictions as to what "pragmatic" history should be, his course of thought is perfectly natural. It does not matter very much whether the process of thought by which he arrived at his conclusions required a few hours or a few months. It certainly need not have extended over many decades and it must have come to its conclusion before Polybius started to write the chapters under discussion.

The incontestable awkwardness of Polybius' presentation of his theory in these chapters is not, then, the result of later revisions, but of his whole method of dealing with his subject. He has to explain a historical phenomenon. In order to do this he brings in a number of theories, analogies, similes, which he has borrowed elsewhere: the theory of the natural instability of simple constitutions which he transforms into the theory of the cycle of constitutions, the analogy of biological growth and of decay through aging, the analogy of the decay of various sorts of matter through internal weaknesses, etc. These theories and analogies may quite properly be used in order to illustrate certain aspects of the historical phenomena that Polybius wishes to explain. But each time the internal logic of the theory or analogy used carries Polybius somewhat beyond the point up to which it really applies, especially whenever the theory or analogy appears to favor Polybius' desire to make historical predictions possible. This is profoundly characteristic of Polybius' way of combining historical analysis with general theory and also the cause of some of the weaknesses of his analysis of the Roman constitution. It is therefore fundamentally important not to obscure this fact by the assumption that every difficulty in his work is due to later revisions.

This does not mean that there are no discrepancies in Polybius' work that can only be explained as due to a later change in his outlook. In his introduction to the sixth book,[75] Polybius says that it is not in quiet and ordinary times that the mettle of individuals and states and their constitutions are tested, but in periods of extraordinary misfortune or extraordinary good luck and prosperity. This, he says, is the reason why he inserted the discussion of the Roman constitution after the narrative of the battle of Cannae. In one of the later chapters of the sixth book,[76] Polybius tells why he does not consider the constitutions of Athens and Thebes worthy of special discussion, in spite of the fact that these cities had had periods of extraordinary success, which, according to Polybius' general principles, might be attributed to special merits of their respective constitutions. In this context Polybius says that Athens always resembled a ship whose master has no authority.[77] In such a vessel, he says, the crew will readily cooperate and obey the captain as long as they fear the disturbed sea or a threatened storm. But as soon as the danger has passed they begin to show contempt for their officers and to quarrel with one another, so that the ship which has successfully weathered the storm may be wrecked while the sky is perfectly clear.

Now the most convincing proof of the excellence of the Roman constitution was the ability of the Romans not only to emerge from the catastrophe of Cannae unscathed, but to conquer nearly the whole known world immediately afterwards. But the Athenians with their democracy had also been able to weather the greatest storms, because danger and distress make people in a democracy collaborate with one another. Thus, the difference in this respect does not appear to be so fundamental. At the end of his analysis of the Roman constitution Polybius points out [78] that such a constitution will prove its worth in times of emergency, because then all the different elements of the state will vie with one another in working for the common good, *and* in times of great success, because it prevents any of the elements of the state from exceeding its bounds. Yet at the end of the whole book [79] he speaks of the destruction of a state through too great prosperity in terms so general that he seems to include Rome.

Discussions of this question may have been more or less current in Rome in Polybius' time, especially in his later years. Plutarch in his biography of the elder Cato mentions a dispute between Cato and Scipio Nasica in the Senate,[80] one pleading for the destruction of Carthage, the other for its preservation, and both of them on essentially the same grounds. For Cato argued that the Roman state had degenerated so much through success and prosperity that, if the Carthaginians were allowed to exist and grow again in power, the Romans at some later date might no longer be able to cope with them as they had done in the past. Nasica, on the other hand, argued that just for that very reason Carthage, as the only potential enemy left, must be preserved, because this danger was the only thing that could prevent further degeneration of the Romans. Many scholars assume—and it is indeed not improbable—that the discussion in this definite form is an invention of Posidonius who, in the earlier decades of the first century B.C. wrote a universal history in continuation of the work of Polybius. But even if the story is not strictly historical, it indicates clearly that discussions of this sort were in the air during the last decades of Polybius' life.[81]

It may then of course still be argued that there is no absolute contradiction between the different parts of Polybius' analysis. For if one accepts his view that the naturally grown mixed constitution was subject to gradual decline as part of his original theory, one may argue that the Roman constitution would have overcome even the dangers of prosperity at the peak of its development, but was no longer able to do so after it had passed this peak. In regard to Athens, on the other hand, one may point out that Polybius himself attributes part of the success of Athens to the good luck of having had most outstanding statesmen just at the time when they were most needed, and that the stability of Rome, as Polybius himself mentions, was more lasting than that of Athens. But it is not difficult to see that these arguments are rather forced. No interpretation can get around the fact that, as the position of the theoretical discussion in the whole work indicates, the proof of the excellence of the Roman constitution is originally and essentially based on the endurance and stability of Rome in distress, and that the strength of this argument is undermined if the despised democracy of Athens has shown the same durability under similar circumstances. It is also self-evident that doubts as to the stability of the Roman constitution must have been much more pressing in Polybius' later years than at the time when he began his work under the overwhelming impression of the success of the Romans in the years from the beginning of the second century to the final defeat of Macedon in the battle of Pydna. Since direct proof of a change in Polybius' views is also provided by the introduction to his third book, there is no reason to doubt that some of the discrepancies in the sixth book are due to later insertions. These insertions, however, concern a special point which originally had not appeared significant, and the way in which this point is now introduced is also characteristic of Polybius' process of thinking.

There are three entirely different grounds on which the future downfall of the Roman Republic could be predicted. In the first place it is an axiom with all Greek philosophers that nothing is everlasting in this world. Hence even the most perfectly organized and most stable political body will sometime be destroyed either from the outside or through internal decay. This is what Plato says of his ideal state in the *Republic*,[82] though he believes that so perfect an organization would be more resistant to decay than any state that has yet actually existed. The same general conviction or feeling is expressed by Scipio when, looking down on the ruins of Carthage, he weeps at the thought that the same fate will some day befall Rome. But the awareness of this general fate of all things human permits only the prediction that a state will sometime decay and fall, not the time when such an event is likely to occur.

The application of the general theory of biological growth and decay together with a somewhat modified application of the cycle theory to a naturally grown mixed constitution permits a closer prediction of the future. The historical observer has to determine the point in the natural development which the constitution has reached. On the basis of this observation he will then be able to predict within certain limits what further course the development will take and approximately how much time it may require.

Even on the basis of the application of this theory, however, Polybius originally appears to have believed that a well-constructed mixed constitution or a naturally grown mixed constitution in the period of its maturity could withstand the strain of exceptional prosperity no less well than the strain of distress and misfortune. In his later years, on the contrary, he appears to have inclined to the belief that too great external power and prosperity might be a much more dangerous test for any constitution than even the greatest dangers from without or a crushing defeat by a foreign enemy, the like of which even a democracy such as Athens had been able to survive.

This new belief was in no way in contradiction to the earlier one that a naturally grown constitution will undergo an aging process and finally die a natural death. A man, after all, may also die of a disease in the flower of youth or in his best years. But it is a new consideration that is brought in, and it is clearly in disagreement with Polybius' earlier opinion that a mixed constitution was equally resistant to the ills resulting from excessive prosperity as to those caused by external attacks. On the basis of this new consideration the historical observer may then make a still closer diagnosis of the future prospects of a constitution or of a political community. This diagnosis in turn may then enable him either to predict what is likely to happen or to find a remedy for the ills of the state.

This latest element in the political theory of Polybius is directly derived from historical observation, while some of the other elements, as has been demonstrated above, are the result of the simplification of theories taken over from others, or of the application to politics of more or less inadequate analogies. It is essential for a correct evaluation of Polybius' political philosophy to distinguish these elements from one another. For his historical observations are nearly always excellent. This is also true of his initial discovery that the internal and external strength of Rome had something to do with its constitution or political order and that this political order had some affinity to what the Greeks had called a mixed or middle-of-the-road constitution. Polybius was much less fortunate in applying to his historical object the intellectual tools which he borrowed from others. Instead of transforming and refining these tools until they were perfectly adapted to the work that was to be performed, he merely simplified them. As a result he did not succeed in bringing all his observations together in one consistent theory, nor are the theories in the form in which he presents them quite sufficient to explain the phenomena that he tries to analyze. It is most unlikely that had Polybius had the time to revise his whole work on the basis of his latest opinions the discrepancies that we find in his theory would have disappeared completely. For this reason the historical analysis which he has undertaken must be resumed and enlarged.

V

Polybius' Analysis of Constitutions
Other Than the Roman

In connection with the exposition of his political theory, Polybius discusses at some length three "constitutions" beside that of Rome, namely, those of Sparta, of Crete, and of Carthage. In addition he mentions briefly the constitutions of Athens and Thebes, but merely in order to show that the temporary prominence of these cities was due not to the excellence of their constitutions, but to especially fortunate circumstances. The most important of these circumstances was that they happened to have outstanding political leaders at a time when they were most needed. But since no state will at all times have leaders of such extraordinary qualities of intellect and character as Themistocles or Epaminondas, the prominence of Athens and Thebes was short-lived as compared with that of Rome, Sparta, and Carthage. The Cretan constitution is also not considered a model constitution by Polybius. He discusses it at somewhat greater length merely in order to refute what he considers an egregious historical error shared by a great many political philosophers of earlier times. This critical discussion is of great significance both for an analysis of Polybius' political thought and for the history of the theory of the mixed constitution before him. In earlier times the Cretan and the Spartan constitution were considered very much alike. While Polybius, however, accepts the traditional view of Sparta, he rejects the traditional view of Crete, and therefore both constitutions must be discussed together.

Crete and Sparta

Polybius begins his discussion of the constitution of Crete, or rather the constitutions of the Cretan cities,[1] by expressing his amazement that so many of the most famous authors—Ephorus, Xenophon, Callisthenes, and Plato—should have considered the Cretan constitution both similar to that of Sparta and praiseworthy. For, he says, the very opposite is true. One of the most remarkable features of the Spartan constitution is the provision that all citizens have an equal share of the land. In Crete the law permits the acquisition of as much land as the buyer can pay for, without any limits whatsoever. In Sparta, wealth in money is despised, so there is no competition among the Spartans in this respect. Among the Cretans the greed for money is so great and so universal that they alone among all nations do not regard as dishonorable any kind of gain, however sordid. The Spartans have hereditary kings, and the members of their council of elders or senate are elected for life. In Crete all magistrates are elected by a democratic procedure and on an annual basis. By eliminating all major differences of wealth among the citizens of his country Lycurgus created that internal harmony and unity which, together with the bravery for which the Spartans were educated from their early youth, made Sparta so strong and for many centuries invincible. The history of Crete, on the other hand, is full of internal discord, revolutions, and civil wars caused by the enormous inequalities in wealth and by the universal greed for money.

Having thus pointed out what he considers the fundamental differences between the Cretan and the Spartan constitutions, Polybius goes on to show that the Cretan laws and institutions are by no means praiseworthy. He does this in a somewhat indirect fashion. Good laws, he argues, are apt to make people act decently in private and public affairs. By the same token, where people in general live decently and public life is free from corruption, one may draw the conclusion that the institutions are good; where the opposite is the case, they are bad. Now the Cretans are known as liars and cheats in private life, and they are renowned for their immoral political scheming. Hence, their laws and institutions cannot be praiseworthy.

What strikes the reader most in this violent attack on the admirers of Cretan political institutions is Polybius' complete disregard of any chronological considerations. He considers the Spartan constitution of Lycurgus one of the most outstanding models of a mixed constitution. But, according to his own testimony, this constitution had been destroyed long ago, partly in consequence of an inherent fault in its construction, partly through external circumstances. In asserting that the Cretan political order was in no way comparable to that of Sparta and certainly not praiseworthy, he argues, on the other hand, from contemporary conditions in Crete, or at least makes no attempt whatever to show that the conditions which he condemns had also existed in the past. It does not seem to occur to him that possibly the praise of Cretan institutions which he found, or believed that he found, in authors most of whom had lived some two hundred years before his time might have been justified in regard to an earlier period.

In actual fact, the historical evidence that we have about the earlier history of the island of Crete, though scanty, seems to indicate that there was a period in which there existed a great similarity, if not in all, still in a great many respects, between the social and political institutions of the Dorians in Crete and those of the Dorian Spartans.[2] But because of a difference in external circumstances the development in each country took a different turn. In both countries a gradual loosening of the old customs and institutions appears to have set in at an early period. But while this development continued to take its natural course in Crete, the Spartans, towards the end of the seventh century B.C., returned to the old customs and even strengthened them through certain new political devices. In consequence the Spartan state and society, for a considerable period of time, retained a certain archaic rigidity which distinguished it from all other political regimes in Greece, until, after the Spartan victory in the Peloponnesian War, the process of disintegration set in anew and, within a surprisingly short time, caused the breakdown of Spartan predominance.

To analyze the reasons both of the parallelism and the difference in the development of Crete and Sparta, or at least to point out similarities and differences on a synchronistic basis, would certainly have been a task worthy of a historian interested in the causes of the stability and instability of social and political institutions. Aristotle, in his *Politics*, which Polybius did not know,[3] has to some extent attended to this task. It is most significant for Polybius as a historian and political thinker that he does not appear to have been aware of it.

Perhaps it is possible to find out some of the reasons for his failure.

In the first place it is clear from many passages in his work that Polybius greatly disliked the Cretans because of the role they had played in wars in which the Achaean League had been involved.[4] His feelings in this respect obviously were only slightly less violent than his feelings towards the Aetolians, the traditional enemies of the Achaeans. But the Spartans had also often been enemies of the Achaean League. Thus there must have been a difference. This difference is not difficult to find. It is obviously twofold. First, the relations between the Achaeans and Spartans were somewhat more ambivalent. For some time Sparta was a member of the Achaean League and at the time when Polybius and his father Lycortas had been politically active, there had always been an Achaean party in Sparta. What seems to have aroused Polybius' ire most appears to be the fact that Cretan mercenaries served as bodyguards under the Spartan tyrant Nabis and helped him kill the supporters of the Achaean cause at Sparta.[5] More important, however, is another factor. Ever since Plato's *Laws* the Spartan state had been considered a model of a mixed constitution; and in fact the distribution of power between the hereditary kings, the gerousia, the popular assembly, and the ephors lent itself easily to an analysis from this point of view. The conditions in Crete were much more complicated. A hereditary kingship appears never to have existed there from the beginning, that is, from the time of the Dorian conquest, and other political and social institutions which the Cretans originally shared with the Lacedaemonians developed differently in the different parts and cities of Crete.[6] For this very reason a synchronistic comparison of the development of original institutions in the two countries would have been most instructive.

At this point, however, the limitations of Polybius as a historian and political thinker again become apparent. He makes certain pertinent historical observations. He is, for instance, quite right in rejecting both the idealization of early Cretan institutions that had become current in Greek political literature and the identification or near-identification of these institutions with those attributed to Lycurgus, which, for the most part, actually belonged to a time when Sparta had long been out of contact with Crete. Polybius is also right in his opinion that the theory of the mixed constitution as he conceives it is hardly applicable to Crete. But neither the historical nor the political analysis is carried through to the end, and what he has to say about Crete remains purely negative. His examination of the Spartan constitution is more important and must therefore be discussed in somewhat greater detail.

Polybius' idea of this constitution is in the briefest terms, the following: Lycurgus, realizing the instability of all simple constitutions, created a mixed constitution in which the power of the kings was counterbalanced by the power of the people, and in which the council of the elders, or gerousia, represented the wisdom of old age and had the function of preventing either of the two other elements from acquiring too much power, since it would always throw its own weight on the side of the weaker party.[7] By establishing an equal distribution of wealth and making a hard and simple life obligatory for everybody, Lycurgus at the same time eliminated the main cause of discord which proved so dangerous in other cities; and by the introduction of a kind of money that could not be used outside of Lacedaemon, he prevented the import of luxury goods from abroad and the corruption that might have resulted from it. These measures would have been wise ones if at the same time he had educated his fellow citizens to avoid any aggressive or ambitious foreign policy. That he did not follow such a course, but made them the most warlike and aggressive tribe in Greece, led finally to the destruction of his whole system. For a simple economy of self-sufficiency, eliminating as far as possible all foreign trade, might not affect the strength of a country in dealing with its immediate neighbors, but was certainly not fit to support an expansionist policy necessitating the conduct of wars far away from home. Once such a policy was adopted it must therefore inevitably destroy either the country or the established system.

This is very briefly Polybius' view of the nature of the Spartan constitution and of the reason for its later destruction. It is perhaps not beside the point to observe that the artificially constructed constitution of Lycurgus, according to Polybius, comes to fall through a fault in its rational construction, while the Roman constitution, which has grown by a natural process, will finally decline in the further course of this natural process. The question of whether the decline of the latter might be prevented by some rational device or devices, just as

Lycurgus stopped the cycle of constitutions by the introduction of his rational system, remains unanswered.

It is, of course, impossible within the present context to discuss in detail the ancient tradition concerning the elusive figure of Lycurgus. But there can be no doubt that what was later known as the constitution of Lycurgus was in many respects the result of a long development and not of a single act. Even Polybius, though he does not mention it, cannot have been completely unaware of this fact. For ancient tradition is unanimous in dating the introduction of the double monarchy which is so characteristic of Sparta, and which, as Plato pointed out, established a check to the power of one king through the power of the other, much earlier than Lycurgus. What Polybius obviously meant was that Lycurgus through his legislation tried to create a perfect balance between the three main elements represented by the kings, the gerousia, and the people. He may have believed that the gerousia, which, in his analysis, is the main balancing factor, was first introduced by Lycurgus, though even this is not certain.

Much of the early history of the Spartan community is uncertain and obscure, but some of the most important factors can be established with a reasonable approximation to certainty. There can be hardly any doubt that the monarchy and perhaps even the double monarchy goes back to the time of the conquest of the Eurotas valley, the site of Sparta, by the Dorian invaders. The andreia or syssitia and the organization and training of the boys in agelae, as the Cretan analogy shows,[8] obviously go back to the same early period. In primitive tribal monarchies of this kind the power of the king or kings is almost always controlled and restricted by the assembly of the warriors, which in the case of Sparta is customarily designated by the name apella.[9] There is no reason to believe that it was any different with the early Spartans.

Some time after the conquerors had become firmly settled, and especially after Messenia had been added to the conquered territory through the so-called First Messenian War, a landed aristocracy seems to have come into being. As in other countries, especially in Athens, this landed aristocracy gradually gained in political power. It is possible that the power of the aristocracy expressed itself politically mainly through a council which was the precursor of the later gerousia, but in which, in those older times, only the leading members of the aristocratic families were represented.[10] But while in Athens, for instance, this development finally led to the abolishment of the monarchy and while a Doric monarchy seems never to have existed in Crete, the monarchy in Sparta continued, though it was reduced in power. There is no reason to assume that those Spartan citizens in that early period who did not belong to the new aristocracy were ever reduced to a state of economic distress and political nullity comparable to that of the poor Athenian farmers before the Solonian reforms. Thus some kind of mixed constitution or balance of power between the kings, the aristocracy represented by a council, and the people represented by the assembly of the warriors seems to have developed in Sparta naturally and at an early time.

The reason why the development in Sparta was different from that in other countries, including Athens and even Crete, where an aristocracy of wealthy landowners came to wield all the power for some time until the poor began to revolt against their regime, is not difficult to find. The Spartans ruled as conquerors over a subject population. All Spartans, of all classes, in a way constituted an aristocracy or an oligarchy in respect to the rest of the population; a split among themselves would therefore have endangered their position. Yet this alone, as the example of Crete shows, might not have sufficed permanently to prevent the aristocracy of the wealthy which had gradually been forming within the larger aristocracy from grasping all political power if it had not been for a special event of very great importance.

In recent times various attempts have been made to show that there was no break in the internal development of Sparta and that the Spartan constitution, which is described by Xenophon, Plato, Aristotle, Polybius, and others, was the result of a natural evolution, in the course of which the *damos* or people, as in other countries, gradually acquired more power. If this opinion is accepted it would follow that the development in Sparta differed from the development in other Greek cities only in so far as in Sparta the people exercised this power through new agencies which were incorporated in the framework of the old institutions, while elsewhere the old institutions were completely abolished and replaced by new ones.[11] Yet the special character of this evolution in Sparta was hardly due exclusively to the innate conservatism of the Spartans, and it cannot be considered a mere coincidence that the new forms seem to have been developed shortly after the so-called Second Messenian War.[12] This war had been the result of a rebellion of the Messenians against their Spartan overlords. It had dragged on for a period of about thirty years and had brought the Spartan community to the brink of destruction. Even after the Messenians had been finally subdued before the end of the seventh century, it took a long time for the Spartans to recover their former strength and their position as the leading power in the Peloponnesus. The war had required a concentration of all the forces of the community, and it was indubitably due to this necessity that, contrary to the development in Crete, the old Dorian institutions were not only retained and restored in Sparta, but, as Ephorus pointed out,[13] "improved upon" and made more rigid.

The most important political feature of the new order was the rise of the ephors to a position of power in the community. Doubtless there had been ephors before. Whether their function in earlier times had been exclusively or mainly a priestly one, as many modern scholars assume,[14] is not so certain. If Ephorus' observation that they had functions analogous to that of the kosmoi in Crete is correct, they probably had something to do with the supervision of the training of the youth; this is not unlikely in view of the role they played in tightening the control of the state on its citizens. At any rate it is certain that the five ephors of old had been closely connected with the five *komai* (settlements or quarters) into which Sparta was divided. They appear in some way to have been the chiefs of the groups of citizens corresponding to these komai.[15]

In recent times the position of the ephors has often been likened to that of the tribunes of the plebs in Rome.[16] If the tribuneship of the plebs, as many scholars assume, developed from the chieftainships of the Roman tribes, the analogy is apt in regard to this particular factor. It is also true that the rise of both the ephors and the tribunes of the plebs was connected with the rise of the "people" to greater political power. But beyond these two factors, the first of which is rather uncertain, the analogy is utterly misleading, for the tribuneship of the plebs in Rome continued for a long time to be a countermagistracy, a piece of institutionalized revolution.[17] The power of the tribunes, mainly negative, was positive only in so far as they could force the government, through their ability to make trouble, to introduce legislative proposals which it would never have initiated of its own accord.[18] Only in a rather late phase did the power of the tribunes become more positive, and even then it was in no way comparable to that of the ephors in Sparta.

The ephors, on the other hand, had from the end of the seventh century the greater part of the civil executive power and, in addition, a far-reaching judicial power. Above all, however, they were the main agents by whom the state exercised a strict and narrow control over all citizens, including even the kings. Their power, therefore, was much more direct and positive than that of the tribunes of the plebs. Or, to express it more concisely, the rise of both the ephors and the tribunes of the plebs to greater political power was connected with and was the consequence of an upsurge of "democratic" forces against an aristocracy. But the tribunes of the plebs remained for a long time the official agents of the resistance of the "people" to the arbitrary rule of an aristocracy that continued to control the state, while the ephors became the agents of the state in its control over the individual citizens, including the aristocracy and even the kings. It is likely that this tightening of the control of the state through the agency of the ephors was not the result of a long development, but of a decisive act, and it is not improbable that this act was the work of an individual "lawgiver," whether this lawgiver was Lycurgus, whom ancient tradition, however, places in an earlier period, or Chilon, as some modern scholars have assumed.[19] In any case it is the result of this act that Plato and others describe as "the Lycurgan constitution."

If one wished to apply Polybius' theoretical concepts to the results of modern inquiries into the history of the Spartan constitution, he might say that the mixed constitution of Sparta came into being through a "natural" and gradual development, which, however, was brought to its conclusion by a conscious and rational act, the like of which Polybius makes responsible for the constitution as a whole. All through this process the successive forms of government would not have been destroyed, as they were in other communities with similar developments, but would have remained as elements in the resulting mixture. Considering finally the fact that the ephors, a fourth element in addition to the kings, the gerousia, and the apella, acquired a nearly unchecked and arbitrary power over the individual citizen, though not over the community as a whole, one is tempted to say that with the rise of the ephors the cycle had come around full swing. An element of tyranny was thus added to the elements of primitive kingship, aristocracy, and democracy, all of which were also preserved.[20]

Such an interpretation of the historical evidence in Polybian terms, however, would of course have to be taken with more than the proverbial grain of salt, and I have introduced it here mainly in order to show how easily these Polybian concepts lend themselves to all sorts of more or less forced constructions. In fact, the analysis undertaken so far should have made it amply clear that Polybius' distinctions between good and bad, mixed and simple, naturally developed and artificially created constitutions are not sufficient for an understanding of the Spartan state of the sixth and fifth centuries. The problem of the nature or the essential character of the Spartan constitution has at least three, possibly four, main aspects, all of which have to be carefully considered.

If one concentrates exclusively on the full Spartan citizens, who constituted an ever smaller minority of the whole population of the Spartan territory, and within this group again on the different political agencies and their competences, then there can be no doubt that Sparta had not only a "mixed constitution" but a most complicated and elaborate system of checks and balances. It is not possible within the present study to discuss in detail all the very complicated questions arising from the imperfections and the occasional ambiguity of the ancient tradition concerning the distribution of power between the various elements of the Spartan state.[21] But it will be quite sufficient for the present purpose to mention some of the best established facts. The kingship was hereditary in the two Heraclid families, but whenever for any reason the succession was in doubt, the people decided by vote who should succeed to the crown. Ordinarily the kings ruled for life, but each individual king, though not both kings at the same time, could be put on trial and punished by a fine, by exile, or even by death. The ephors could coerce, arrest, and even punish a simple citizen and could give orders to the kings and suspend a king from office and put him on trial, though they could not punish him without the approval of the assembly of the people. But they were annual magistrates who had to give account of their conduct when their year of office was over and could be tried and punished for malfeasance in office. The assembly of the people had no legislative initiative but had the decision over peace and war,[22] the decision in all changes of the existing law, and also the final decision as to guilt or acquittal; it probably also had the final say in approving or rejecting a proposed punishment in trials of kings and magistrates. The gerousia deliberated the proposals to be brought before the assembly of the people and decided whether they were to be put to the vote; it had also very important judicial functions. These few examples show sufficiently that there were no executive, legislative, or judicial branches of the government, but that the executive power was shared by the kings and the ephors, the legislative power by the people and the gerousia, and theoretically also by the kings, and the judicial power by the ephors, the gerousia, and the assembly of the people. Thus, there can be no doubt that there existed a very complicated system of checks and balances, though not of the kind advocated by Montesquieu.

We are accustomed to connect a system of checks and balances with what we call liberalism, but the Spartan state was anything but liberal in the modern sense of the word. If by totalitarianism we mean a strict control by the state over the life of the individual, then the "Spartan state of Lycurgus," in which a citizen was not allowed to go abroad except in military service or on an official mission before he had reached an age of forty years "beyond the year in which he had become an adult," in which the education of the boys from the sixth year onward was entirely directed by the state, and in which the adults were also under constant control through the obligation of participation in the syssitia and the incessant military training, was certainly one of the most totalitarian that have ever existed. In this sense the Oriental despotism of the Persian kingdom was much more liberal than Sparta.[23]

It is also noteworthy that within the Spartan state the life of the Spartan citizens was much more strictly controlled than that of the Perioeci, who were the subjects of the Spartans and did not have the rights of full citizens. Nevertheless, the Spartans considered themselves, and were considered by many other Greeks, as the freest of the free. In order to understand this it is necessary to distinguish between different concepts of freedom. The subjects of a Persian king were at the mercy of the arbitrary will of their master. He could have the ears, the nose, or the head of a subject cut off without having to account to anybody for the justice or injustice of his action. It is this dependence on the arbitrary whim or will of a person that the Greeks, especially the Spartans, considered the most abject slavery. In this respect the Spartans were actually free. For though the ephors had a very large discretion in punishing anyone for violating the law, they were accountable for any misuse of their power after their year of office was over. In a way then the Spartans were actually freer than the citizens of Athens, where a chance majority in the sovereign assembly of the people could condemn the commanders of the battle of the Arginusae to death unjustly and not be accountable to anyone for this miscarriage of justice. It is clear that this freedom from the arbitrary exercise of power was a result of the system of checks and balances existing in Sparta, but that this system was perfectly reconcilable with a totalitarian control of the state over the lives of its citizens.

It is likely that the tightening of the control of the state over the lives of the individual citizens after the Second Messenian War was connected with an attempt to bring about a greater equality of property among the Spartan citizens and to preserve this comparative equality in the future. Aristotle [24] considers this one of the outstanding features of the "Lycurgan constitution." There are also other reasons for attributing such an attempt to this period. The new order of the sixth century was obviously connected with a strong "anti-luxury" movement and an attempt to control the life of the citizens in this respect. This movement is connected with the introduction of the famous iron money, and this money cannot possibly be older than the beginning of the sixth century.[25] There was a tradition that the Spartans had very bad institutions [26] "before Lycurgus" and that there had been a period of constant internal strife,[27] probably because of the unequal distribution of wealth and its political consequences, if one may judge from analogy with other Greek cities. That there was a period of luxury and good living in Sparta down to the Second Messenian War, and possibly even on a slightly reduced basis for a short time afterwards, is proved by archeological evidence. On the other hand, there

was also a tradition affirming that after the first settlement of the later
Spartans in the Eurotas valley each family was assigned a piece of
land of approximately equal size or value and that even later each
Spartiate received a lot of land which remained his inalienable property during his lifetime.[28] This tradition is very likely correct, and the
reform of the sixth century may then have taken the form of a
reaffirmation and stricter application of old Dorian principles and
institutions that in the meantime had more or less fallen into desuetude, just as was obviously the case with other features of the reform.

If this assumption is correct, one may regard this attempt to control
the distribution of property among the Spartan citizens as one of the
totalitarian features of the Spartan constitution. Yet if one considers
the fact that the early history of the theory and practice of mixed constitutions is closely associated with attempts to combat and remedy
the economic, social, and political evils concomitant with an excessive
inequality in the distribution of wealth, he has to admit that the attempted control is not quite unrelated to this aspect of the Spartan
state either. Therefore, though the different aspects of the Spartan
constitution must first be viewed separately if it is to be fully understood, they must then also be considered in their relation to one another. But first it is necessary to turn to the fourth aspect of this constitution.

All three aspects mentioned so far are those of the political community of the full-scale Spartan citizens, the Spartiates. But these
citizens, as mentioned earlier, only constituted an ever smaller proportionate part of the population of the Spartan territory. The remainder
consisted partly of the "free" Perioeci, who were the subjects of the
Spartans and served in the army, but had no active political rights,
partly of the unfree Helots who, though they were assigned to the
estates of individual Spartans, were considered the property of the
community.[29] This is why Sparta in the fifth century is usually considered an oligarchy rather than a mixture of monarchy, oligarchy,
and democracy, since the Spartiates together undoubtedly ruled as an
oligarchy over the rest of the population. Both descriptions of Sparta
are perfectly correct. If one looks merely on the Spartan citizens, they
have a most elaborate system of checks and balances. If one looks at

the relation of the Spartiates to the rest of the population, it is a pure oligarchy. But how does this affect the advantages ascribed to a mixed constitution?

The main advantage ascribed to a mixed constitution in earlier literature is the strict preservation of the Spartan kind of freedom. It is interesting to observe that Polybius, when speaking of the Spartan constitution, twice points out [30] that this constitution enabled the Spartans to preserve their freedom longer than any other nation, while, when speaking of the Roman or Carthaginian constitution or of the mixed constitution in the abstract, he speaks of stability and success. Obviously this advantage of a mixed constitution does not apply to the subjects of the Spartans. The Helots are slaves and have no protection whatever against the arbitrary whims of any one among their masters.[31] The Perioeci are not free in this respect either, for though they are under less strict control than the Spartan citizens, they have no equally effective redress against arbitrary treatment by a Spartan magistrate or other official since they are not members of the apella. But in regard to the Spartiates themselves, this advantage of the mixed constitution is effective without restriction and in no way affected by the fact that the Spartans as a whole constitute an oligarchy over their subjects.

The question of the stability of a political arrangement of this kind is obviously much more complex. Polybius believed that the only fault of "Lycurgus" was that he made the Spartans aggressive while giving them an economic system that was most unsuitable for a policy of expansion.[32] But it is now no longer difficult to see that this explanation is not sufficient. It is true that it was the expansion of Spartan power overseas in the last phase of and after the Peloponnesian War that brought about the disintegration of the Spartan state. But the policy of the Spartans in the fifth century was anything but aggressive or expansionist, at least not of their own free will. Whether they were driven into the war against Athens by their Peloponnesian allies or whether they themselves decided to fight against the Athenians,[33] there can be not the slightest doubt that they were moved by their own and their allies' fear of the growing power of Athens and not by any desire for expansion on their own part.

What is really interesting is not the presumed discrepancy between an expansionist spirit of Spartan policy and an economy not suited for political expansion, but the reason why the Spartans who spent their whole lives in excessive military training were not at all expansionist or aggressive. As pointed out before, the totalitarian control of the Spartan state over its citizens was the price which the Spartans paid for their domination over their subjects, the Perioeci and Helots. They knew very well that, considering the extreme disproportion between the numbers of the rulers and the ruled, any attempt to expand beyond the limits of the Peloponnesus would be dangerous to the internal stability of the established system. Their entrance into the Peloponnesian War, therefore, was not an expression of exuberant aggressive strength but of the consciousness of their weakness. Yet at the same time one may say that, apart from this danger arising from without, the pressure from below in a way made the Spartan constitution even more stable, since it made the Spartans realize that only by the strictest self-discipline and by the most meticulous adherence to their established laws and customs could they uphold their domination. Polybius might then still have been right in his assumption that this system could be destroyed only through a collision with the outside world, though one would have to add that the reason why it could not survive a major collision of this kind was not only its insufficient economy, but also that the system was so delicately balanced that it was apt to be destroyed by any major concussion.

But this is not yet the whole story. Aristotle in his *Politics* has tried to show that, though the weakness of the Spartan state came into the open through the Peloponnesian War, disintegrating forces had been at work from within for a long time before that event. He pointed out that the provisions made by "the Lacedaemonian lawgiver" to prevent the development of a great inequality of wealth among the Spartan citizens proved insufficient. For, though the Spartan law "frowned upon" [34] the sale of land by Spartan citizens, it did not prevent them from giving large dowries to their daughters and placed no difficulty in the way of the accumulation of wealth through inheritance. Whether or not Aristotle is quite correct in his evaluation of the causes of the development is disputed. But there can be no doubt as to the accuracy of his description of the conditions that had developed at the beginning of the fourth century, nor as to the fact that the development that led to this result must have started long before the Peloponnesian War.

However defective, therefore, our knowledge of the earlier history of Sparta may be, and however controversial much of this history may have remained to the present day, what can be established with a reasonable approximation to certainty is quite sufficient to make it possible for us to analyze Polybius' method in dealing with historical phenomena like the Cretan and Spartan constitutions.

Apart from the predilection of Athenian oligarchs and reactionaries of the fifth century for oligarchic Sparta, which does not interest us in the present context, there had been two reasons why the Spartan constitution had found many admirers in the fifth and fourth centuries B.C. One of these had been the strict organization and education of the youth, the austerity of the life of the adults, the strict control of the state over the lives of the individuals by which this austerity was enforced, and the military prowess of the Spartans that resulted from it. This is the aspect of the Spartan "constitution" which is stressed by Xenophon in his *Constitution of the Lacedaemonians*, and by Plato in the eighth book of his *Republic*, where he describes Sparta as a timocracy.[35] For in a state like this, as Plato points out, distinction can be won only by military exploits and this kind of honor is therefore the reward for which most citizens compete. It is also in this respect that Plato and others in earlier Greek literature find Crete similar to Sparta. The other reason for admiring Sparta was its mixed constitution and the special kind of freedom resulting from it.[36] This is the aspect of the Spartan constitution which is stressed by Plato in his *Laws*.[37]

There is, finally, one feature in the Spartan constitution which belongs essentially to the first of these two aspects, but is not quite unrelated to the second one. This is the attempt to prevent by legal measures the development of considerable inequality of wealth. For though this comes essentially under the head of state control and an enforced simplicity of living and though a system of checks and balances on the purely political level in itself has nothing to do with the regulation of the distribution of property within a community, the middle-of-the-road men as early as the fifth century had begun to realize that an excessive inequality in the distribution of wealth might make it difficult if not impossible to establish or to preserve a well-balanced political system.

Polybius is, of course, primarily interested in Sparta as an example of a mixed constitution, and where he first speaks of Sparta,[38] he takes into consideration only this aspect of its constitution. But later, when he compares the Cretan and the Spartan constitutions with one another, and the Spartan constitution with that of Rome,[39] it is no longer this aspect on which he focuses his interest. He makes only one point that has to do directly with the problem of the mixed constitution, when he points out [40] that in Sparta the kingship was hereditary and the kings ruled for life, the gerontes or senators being likewise elected for life, while in Crete all offices were annual. He calls this restriction of office to one year a democratic institution. This point would be well taken if it were not for the fact that in Polybius' analysis of the Roman constitution the consuls, who are also elected annually, represent the monarchic element.

Apart from this, Polybius in this whole section deals only with the control or the lack of control of the state over the individuals, the influence of the laws on the private habits of the citizens, the distribution of wealth and use made of it, and so on. This is quite understandable in view of the fact that it had been with respect to these elements that the Cretan and the Spartan constitutions were likened to one another and that both of them were praised.[41] But it is clear that "constitution" in this latter connection is not the same thing that Polybius means when he speaks of the mixed constitution as a mixture of monarchy, oligarchy, and democracy or as a system of checks and balances. It would certainly have been worthy of consideration to determine whether or not the two aspects of the Spartan social and political order, which Polybius considers in the context last mentioned, are necessarily related to one another. But, in contrast to Aristotle, Polybius does not discuss this problem. So here again there is no integrated analysis of the various aspects of the historical phenomena under consideration.

Even more serious is Polybius' failure to see that the disintegration of Sparta was not due exclusively to its inability to expand without destroying itself, though the forced expansion after the Peloponnesian War undoubtedly accelerated the process and brought it into the open but that the process of disintegration itself, as Aristotle pointed out had begun long before. It had begun with the development—against the intentions of the "Lycurgan" laws—of a large inequality of wealth among the Spartan citizens. A very considerable inequality of wealth need not become dangerous to a political order as long as both the rich and the poor feel that they are not impaired in their status as citizens. In the Athens of the period before Solon one of the main factors in stirring up a revolutionary spirit among the indebted peasants had been their consciousness that they were by right and descent Athenian citizens, but in consequence of the laws about debts were deprived of all qualities of citizens. In Sparta active citizen rights were dependent on participation in the common meals or syssitia. When, therefore, a considerable number of Spartans became so impoverished that they were unable to pay the contributions for these meals, they were *de facto* deprived of their most important, active citizen rights [42] and became hypomeiones, that is, neither Perioeci nor, of course, Helots, but a group somewhere between Spartiates and Perioeci with apparently no very clearly defined status at all.[43] At the same time the numbers of the ruling class and the full-scale citizens thus became ever smaller and the discrepancy between the numbers of the rulers and the ruled ever more excessive. In times of emergency the attempt was then made to remedy this situation by giving Helots who had distinguished themselves as faithful servants of their masters, probably in higher functions as overseers and administrators on the Spartan estates or in other capacities, some kind of citizen rights, if they were willing to serve, or after they had served for some time, in the Spartan army. These newly created citizens of a sort [44] were called *neodamodeis* and appear to have received some land of their own so that they owned something comparable to the κλῆρος of the full-scale Spartans. As long as these conditions lasted—and in a way they lasted for a considerable time—the mixed constitution with all its benefits continued, of course, to be valid for those Spartan citizens who enjoyed their social and political status unimpaired, though the number of such citizens became exceedingly small. But it is clear that under such conditions a mixed constitution cannot make a community strong in its dealings with other nations, as in Polybius' opinion a mixed constitution is bound to do, and this quite regardless of the economic and financial resources of the community as a whole. It is no less obvious that the internal stability of the constitution in such a case will not be too great; and this is also borne out by the historical evidence.

If Polybius had carried his analysis to this point and then made a comparison between Sparta and Rome, he would have found, to be sure, that there were very essential differences between the two communities which accounted for the difference in their success in expansionist enterprises. But he could also hardly have failed to notice that, as early as the first decades of the second century and even earlier, certain analogies began to develop that might have made it possible to predict quite some time before the Gracchi that Rome in a not too distant future might become threatened by serious dangers from within, and not merely because of a natural development towards greater democracy. Above all, however, he could not have based his theory exclusively on an analysis of power relations seemingly expressable in well-defined competences. Thus here again the result is the same. There can be no doubt that Polybius is dealing with historical phenomena of the first rank. He tries to analyze them by means of theories which are certainly relevant. But when it comes to the details of his analysis the result is somewhat disappointing, and a large part of the work that he undertook has still to be done.

CARTHAGE

The section on Carthage in the sixth book of Polybius' work [45] falls into two parts, both of which are rather short. In the first part Polybius tries to show that Carthage, like Sparta and Rome, had a mixed constitution, but explains the inferiority of Carthage in its struggle with Rome by the supposed fact that Carthage, as the older of the two states, at the time of the Second Punic War had already reached a stage in which the perfect balance between the three elements of which a perfect constitution must be composed had been destroyed, since the democratic element had become stronger than the two others.

In the second and longer part Polybius adds further reasons why the Romans proved superior to the Carthaginians in these wars. First of all there is the difference in their whole military system. In the beginning, Polybius points out, the Carthaginians enjoyed a great advantage at sea because of their long experience and consequent skill in maneuvering ships. The Romans, on the other hand, had a great advantage on land because they had always relied on citizen armies and had themselves fought along with their allies, while the Carthaginians had always been accustomed to using mercenary armies, which are never quite reliable, and had failed to develop a warlike spirit and military discipline among the majority of their own citizens. He also argues that the advantage of the Romans was greater, because a tradition of military discipline and daring can, to some extent, make up for a certain lack of skill and because skill in a special field can be acquired more quickly than a military tradition. This advantage of the Romans, Polybius points out, was all the greater since the Italian race was by nature both physically stronger and bolder than the Phoenician and the Libyan races, of which the population of the Carthaginian territory was made up, and because the Romans had managed to increase these natural qualities by customs and traditions of which Polybius adduces a number of examples. Polybius observes finally that the attitudes of the Romans and the Carthaginians in regard to monetary gain or profit were entirely different. In Carthage the profit motive ruled supreme and nothing that led to monetary gain was considered shameful. In Rome, on the other hand, it was considered most disgraceful to accept bribes and to acquire riches in an improper fashion. As a consequence bribery in the elections for public office was an accepted practice in Carthage, while in Rome it was punishable by the death penalty.

In this second part, then, Polybius mentions a number of reasons for the inferiority of Carthage as compared to Rome which are not, or at least not directly, connected with the character of the constitutions of these cities or the stage which these constitutions had reached in their development. As to the last point mentioned by Polybius, everyone knows that not so very long after Polybius' death bribery in elections became as universal in Rome as it had been in Carthage in Polybius' own time. In addition Polybius doubtless exaggerated the difference which may have existed in the middle of the second century between Rome and Carthage as to bribery. The very fact that twice within Polybius' own lifetime, in 181 and 159 B.C., new and severe laws against corruption in public elections had to be introduced, though there had been an earlier law against the same offense, shows clearly that the standard of public morality in Rome was no longer so high as Polybius would have us believe.

Polybius' remarks on the difference between the Roman and the Carthaginian military systems, on the other hand, are undoubtedly pertinent. In fact, these differences alone might suffice to explain the final victory of Rome, in spite of the initial superiority of the Carthaginians. There appear to have been two decisive factors: first, rather early in the First Punic War the Romans had learned how to defeat the Carthaginians at sea by inventing the corvus (a gangway for boarding an enemy ship), a device which permitted them to turn a sea battle into something very closely resembling a land battle; second, the large land empire which Hamilcar tried to create after the First Punic War, the resources of which were to enable the Carthaginians to conquer the Romans on land, remained too loosely knit, partly because the Carthaginians were unable to match the military tradition which the Romans had created in the course of several centuries. If this is accepted, one might argue that Carthage would have been defeated by the Romans, regardless of any deficiencies in its constitution, for no other reason than that its military system was inferior to that of the Romans. Similarly, Sparta, in Polybius' opinion,[46] had come to grief because her economic and social system did not permit her to engage over a long period of time in large wars far from the home base.

In Polybius' opinion, however, this analogy to Sparta is only part of the truth, and not the most important part. There is the fundamental difference that the Spartan mixed constitution was the conscious and artificial creation of a genius, while the Carthaginian constitution, like that of Rome, was the result of a natural process of growth and therefore also subject to natural decay, with the one decisive difference that Carthage had progressed farther on the road to decay after having reached the summit of its development. Obviously there is no contradiction in the assumption that the defeat of Carthage was partly due to this latter factor, partly to the deficiencies of its military system. Yet, as will be seen later, there is a certain significance in the fact that one part of Polybius' explanation of the downfall of Carthage runs parallel to his explanation of the final disintegration of the artificially and rationally created constitution of Sparta, while another part is based on the idea that a naturally grown mixed constitution, such as that of Rome, must at a predeterminable point of its development inevitably begin to decay.

What Polybius says [47] about the constitution of Carthage as a mixed constitution is very little indeed. There were kings in Carthage, he says, there was something of the nature of a gerousia, which represented the aristocratic power, and the people were master of those things "which pertain to them." [48] But at the time of the Punic Wars the constitution had passed the high point of its development so that the people had the greatest influence in public decisions, while in Rome the Senate was the most influential factor. [49] The first part of this description appears to characterize the Carthaginian constitution as a well-balanced mixed constitution, which it is supposed to have been at the height of its development. [50] The terms used in this description characteristically emphasize again the similarity with Sparta. The second part, which deals with the state of Carthaginian constitutional development reached at the time of the Punic Wars, emphasizes again the comparison with Rome.

Unfortunately, our independent knowledge of the Carthaginian constitution is rather scanty, so that it is impossible to check the accuracy of Polybius' remarks in detail. Yet what can be gleaned from Aristotle and other ancient sources is sufficient to throw more light on the character of Polybius' analysis.

The comparison between the Carthaginian and Spartan constitutions is made for the first time in extant Greek literature by Isocrates in his *Nicocles*. [51] He says that both constitutions are excellent, adding that they were oligarchic "at home" and monarchic in war. Aristotle, to whom we owe the only other detailed description of the Carthaginian constitution that has come down to us, [52] starts with the same comparison, [53] but he is mainly interested in the question of how far these two constitutions can be considered as truly aristocratic, that is, as constitutions favoring the rule of "the best men." He emphasizes from the beginning the stability of the two constitutions as compared with those of most Greek cities, pointing out that neither Sparta nor Carthage had experienced a violent overthrow of the government within time immemorial. There is, he says, the further similarity that in both cities one finds the institution of common meals, or syssitia, and both have kings and a gerousia, or council of elders. Likewise the magistracy of the so-called One Hundred and Four corresponds to that of the Spartan ephors. There are, however, he seems to say, the following important differences: first, the Carthaginian kings are not always taken from the same family nor, on the other hand, are they chosen without regard to their familial descent,[54] and second, if kings and gerousia agree with one another they can, but need not, submit their decrees to the popular assembly for ratification. If, on the other hand, they disagree, then the people decide, and if anything is submitted to the decision of the people, anyone can get up and express his opinion about it, which is not the case in Sparta and Rome, where the people can vote only aye or nay. The most influential body, Aristotle continues, is elected by the pentarchies and the pentarchies elect themselves (to wit, by co-optation) and rule for a longer time than all the other magistracies; for they rule both before and after their term of office.[55] As special peculiarities of the Carthaginian political system Aristotle points out finally that the magistrates and public officers receive no pay for their services and are not chosen by lot as in Athens, that the same man can hold more than one office at the same time, and that the highest offices can be bought.[56]

A large part of this report is rather puzzling and in need of interpretation. What Aristotle says about the kings seems to mean that the "kingship" was not strictly hereditary as in Sparta, where the kings were always taken from the two branches of the gens of the Heracleidai, but that the "kings" were always chosen from a certain number of noble families. This is confirmed by the fact that of the "kings," or suffetes, whose names we know, an even greater proportionate number belong to a few selected families than is the case with the Roman consuls of the same period.[57] The same evidence appears to indicate that the office of "king" was annual, but there appear to have been no restrictions on re-election. The suffetes, therefore, seem to have been functionaries of the state and at the same time representatives of the ruling aristocracy rather than hereditary kings, so that the designation "king" can be applied to them only if this term is used in a very wide sense.

What Aristotle says about the other Carthaginian institutions is even more puzzling. The functions of a body of one hundred and four can hardly have been similar in every respect to those of the five Spartan ephors. What Aristotle probably means is that this body, like the ephors in Sparta, exercised a control over the other magistrates, including the kings. But the Council of One Hundred and Four appears to have been a kind of high court, whose functions were mainly, if not exclusively, judicial,[58] while the ephors had not only judicial but even more important executive functions. Aristotle speaks also of a Council of One Hundred, which, he says, was the "greatest" or highest magistracy in Carthage.[59] It is very probable but not absolutely certain that this Council of One Hundred is identical with the Council of One Hundred and Four.[60]

Polybius, on two occasions,[61] distinguishes between the Carthaginian gerousia and a Carthaginian senate (σύγκλητος), of which the gerousia appears to have been a part, either a permanent steering committee or a narrower and higher council within the larger council. If the members of the Council of One Hundred and Four were chosen from among the senators, as Justin says,[62] and if the "senators" in this context mean actual members of the Senate, it would seem to follow that the Senate must have been considerably more numerous than the Council of One Hundred and Four. There are other indications that point in the same direction. On the basis of certain passages in ancient authors, it has been argued that the Senate had probably three hundred members and the gerousia thirty. But these conclusions are quite uncertain.[63] About the pentarchies nothing is known beyond what we learn from the passage in Aristotle's *Politics* mentioned above.

It is clearly not possible within the framework of the present study to deal with all the puzzling problems presented by ancient tradition on the Carthaginian constitution; and the evidence is in any case too scanty to make a definite solution possible. But what we do know shows clearly that the Carthaginian political system was essentially aristocratic or oligarchic and certainly did not represent at any time a perfect balance of monarchy, oligarchy, and democracy. As in many purely oligarchic systems there seems to have arisen, from time to time, a certain danger that one of the leading families might rise above the others and establish a monarchy. This does not prove, however, that there was a balance between a monarchic and an oligarchic element in the political system. On the contrary, this is one of the dangers which threatens any "simple" oligarchy at any time. The provisions, on the other hand, that certain questions *could* be referred to the people, that if the suffetes and the Council disagreed, appeal *had* to be made to the people, and that in such cases anyone could get up and speak to the point may be considered as democratic elements in the constitution. Yet it is obvious that in a system in which the people had no legal way of influencing public decisions except when the chief executives and the oligarchic council either disagreed with one another or, out of their own free will, decided to refer a question to the people, there can be no question of anything like an equal balance between the oligarchic and democratic factors.

There remains the question of the weakening of the Carthaginian system through democratization. Unfortunately we do not know too much about the details of possible constitutional changes in Carthage within the last century of its existence. The most important change of which we know is the law introduced by Hannibal in 197 B.C., which provided that the members of the High Court were no longer to be selected for a lifetime but had to be newly elected every year, with the provision that a member could not be elected more than twice in succession.[64] Even though we do not know who was to elect the High Court, which is, of course, a very crucial point, it is clear that by this measure Hannibal tried to diminish the power of the leading families represented in the High Court in its earlier form. It has been questioned whether the new law remained in force after Hannibal had gone into exile a year later.[65] Yet in spite of all these uncertainties, one thing is certain. The law by which Hannibal tried to break the resistance of the traditional High Court to his reforms was made by the people. It was probably a case of disagreement between the suffetes or between a suffete and the Senate in which the suffete, as authorized by the existing constitution, appealed to the people. But in this case the decision of the people meant a very incisive constitutional innovation directed against the majority of the ruling oligarchy. There is no evidence whatever indicating that there were other very incisive changes in the Carthaginian constitution in the same period. But there is plenty of evidence to show that there was a long and sometimes violent struggle between the family and supporters of Hamilcar and

Hannibal on the one hand and the majority of the Carthaginian aristocracy on the other, a struggle in which appeal not infrequently was made to the people. Naturally such a dissension within the ruling aristocracy, with the people called in as arbitrators, increased the power of the people in that period and, in addition, must have tended to make them more conscious of their political power.

This, then, in all likelihood is the nature of the "democratization" of the Carthaginian constitution to which Polybius refers. In other words, it is not certain whether there was a lasting change in the governmental structure, the mode of election to the ruling bodies, etc. But if there was a lasting change of this kind, it was undoubtedly preceded by a period in which such changes had not yet occurred, and in which, nevertheless, the power of the people and their consciousness of this power had already increased in consequence of the dissensions within the ruling oligarchy and the inherited provision of the constitution according to which such dissensions were to be decided by the people. Likewise, if there was no lasting change in the legal foundations of the constitution, assuming that after Hannibal had gone into exile the old High Court was restored and its members became again life members, this can still not have led to a complete restoration of the distribution of power as it existed before the dissensions started. For the evidence shows that the dissension continued in different forms and that the people retained the new sense of their potential influence and power which they had acquired.

There can be no doubt, then, that Polybius was right in speaking of a democratization of Carthage within the period in question, if democratization means a shift towards greater power and influence of the people. But this was not the democratization of a political order which, as the result of a long evolution, had become an almost perfect mixture of monarchy, oligarchy, and democracy. It meant, on the contrary, the strengthening of the power of the popular assembly in a system which, as Aristotle rightly pointed out, had been preponderantly aristocratic, with some slightly democratic institutions as safety valves.

Still more important for a critical evaluation of Polybius' general political analysis is the fact that the democratization which did take place did not, or certainly not completely or even preponderantly, find expression in new laws or in a change of institutions, as was the case in Athens when democracy was restored after the rule of the so-called Thirty Tyrants, or, on a minor scale, in Rome through the so-called *lex Hortensia* of 287 B.C., by which plebiscites acquired the force of laws. On the contrary, everything indicates that the actual shift in the balance of power at Carthage was much greater than the changes in legal and constitutional institutions would indicate and that the shift in actual power preceded whatever institutional changes did occur.

If, therefore, as Polybius believes, the superiority of a mixed constitution over all other constitutions lies in the fact that it creates a balance of power between the different elements in the state, then it is obviously not sufficient to consider the legal foundations and the institutional structure of a state, but also necessary to find out what shifts of power are possible within a given political system without a corresponding change in the legal or institutional structure. Furthermore, it will be one of the most important tasks of adequate analyses of political systems to distinguish those power shifts which find expression in changes of constitutional law and institutional devices from those which do not, and to study the complicated interrelation between both types of changes in the distribution of power within a political community. That Polybius fails to make clear and explicit this fundamental distinction, without which no adequate analysis can be undertaken, is another serious deficiency in his political theory, which will become very noticeable in his analysis of the Roman constitution.

There is just one more point which must be mentioned. Concerning the Spartan constitution, it was observed that the constitution described by Polybius applied only to Spartan citizens, but that the question of the causes of the stability or instability of the Spartan constitution cannot be discussed in a satisfactory manner without taking into consideration the fact that the Spartans ruled over a much greater number of Perioeci and Helots who had no share in the constitution described by Polybius. The cases of Carthage and Rome are, of course, similar, since both of them ruled over large populations with no, or no full, citizen rights. But it will be expedient to reserve a further discussion of this aspect for the analysis of the Roman constitution, since we know so much more about Rome and its empire than we know about Carthage.

VI

TRACES OF POLYBIUS' ACCOUNT OF THE

DEVELOPMENT OF THE ROMAN CONSTITUTION

POLYBIUS' ANALYSIS of the Roman constitution consisted of four sections.[1] The first contained a description of the development of the Roman constitution or governmental system, in the course of which, in Polybius' opinion, it finally became a perfect example of a well-balanced mixed constitution. The second section consisted of a systematic analysis of the Roman constitution at the time when it had reached its highest degree of perfection, i.e., towards the end of the third century and the beginning of the second century B.C. This section had the purpose of showing how at that time political power was evenly distributed among the consuls, who represented the monarchic element, the Senate, which represented the aristocratic or oligarchic element, and the people, who represented the democratic element in the state. The third section gave a more detailed account of certain special aspects of the Roman political order. The fourth section, finally, presented a comparison between the Roman constitution and the constitutions of some other cities or nations for which especial excellence had been claimed.

Of these four sections the second and the fourth appear to have been nearly completely preserved in the *excerpta antiqua* contained in the Codex Urbinas.[2] Of the third section a detailed description of the military institutions of the Romans has been preserved in its entirety. But this part is not of major interest for our present inquiry except in so far as it constitutes a parallel to the discussions of the defects of the military institutions of the Spartans and the Carthaginians,[3] and has, of course, the purpose of showing that the Romans were superior to other nations, not only through the excellence of their constitution but also through their military system. It is possible that the same

section dealt also with other more special matters and that it was here
that Polybius gave the more detailed description of the Roman institution of the dictatorship which he promises in a passage of the third
book,[4] though it is also possible that this description formed part of
the first section mentioned above, which dealt with the development
of the Roman constitution.[5]

Of the first section, which is, of course, of the greatest interest in
connection with our attempt to evaluate the historical foundations
of Polybius' political theory, only very small and, from the point of
view of political theory, very insignificant direct excerpts have been
preserved, partly through quotations by later authors, partly through
the Constantine excerpts *De virtutibus et vitiis*,[6] and partly through
marginal notes in the Codex Urbinas. But when in 1821 Angelo Mai
discovered large parts of the first books of Cicero's treatise *De re
publica* in a Vatican palimpsest, Berthold Niebuhr, who helped to
decipher the text, recognized at once that the summary of the history
of the Roman constitution which Cicero inserted in chapters 1–37 of
the second book of this work must be largely dependent on Polybius.
In recent years a number of attempts have been made [7] to distinguish
in Cicero's work those parts or ideas which he has taken over from
Polybius from his own additions, which in part, of course, may also
have been influenced by other authors, and to reconstruct, as far as
possible, Polybius' analysis of the history of the Roman constitution
on this basis. Naturally the results obtained in these difficult investigations differ a good deal from one another. Yet there is also a large
area of agreement.

Obviously it is not feasible within the framework of the present
study to discuss, in regard to every single passage in Cicero's second
book, all the arguments that have been set forth to prove that it was
copied from, or influenced by, Polybius, or that, on the contrary, it was
added by Cicero as a result of his own thinking or under the influence
of some other author. There are, furthermore, quite a number of
passages that are really not very relevant to our problem.[8] Therefore
it appears permissible to follow a somewhat different method.

A critical survey of Cicero's philosophical and theoretical writings
(in contrast to his orations) clearly shows that in the vast majority of
cases the logical and systematic skeleton of these works is taken over

from a Greek writer, while the illustrative details, the anecdotes, observations, historical illustrations, and sometimes also argumentative discussions of points of details, are very often added by Cicero himself. It has, furthermore, been observed [9] that Polybius' idea of the growth of the Roman constitution does not altogether coincide with that of Cicero. Polybius emphasizes [10] that the Roman constitution grew to perfection through many struggles and troubles, and that the cause of its becoming increasingly more perfect was that in the moments of crisis which occurred again and again in this process, the responsible men saw and chose "the better course." Cicero, on the other hand, using a quotation from Cato, i.e. not from Polybius, emphasizes [11] that no *one* man could have created so excellent a constitution, since no one can oversee everything, and that the Roman constitution was the product of many excellent men in many generations, each one of whom made his own contribution. These two explanations are not in contradiction to one another. But there is clearly a certain difference of outlook. It is also obvious that the Ciceronian idea leaves the author a good deal of freedom. Every great man—in the early period every king—makes his contribution to the organization of the state according to his personal genius, but there need be no systematic sequence of these contributions. This is in harmony with Cicero's inclinations as an author who likes to pick up his problems at random. On the other hand, it has been seen, and will be shown again in the discussion of Polybius' analysis of the Roman constitution at the height of its development, that Polybius has a certain tendency to do violence to historical reality when he makes an attempt to show agreement with his conceptual schemes. This is especially clear if one compares with the historical facts his theory of the cycle of constitutions and his claim that one can, to some extent, predict the future on the basis of this theory.[12] Since Polybius obviously believed [13] that a naturally growing mixed constitution nevertheless follows, though in a different fashion, the cycle of constitutions, it is to be expected that something of this forced systematization was also inherent in his account of the development of the Roman constitution.

A survey of the first chapters of Cicero's *De re publica* shows that actually each political leader—especially in the history of the monarchic period (in this case each king with the exception of the last, who

turns kingship into tyranny)—is credited with a positive contribution
to the Roman political order not directly connected with the principle
of the mixed constitution. This idea of the fundamental character of
the history of the Roman monarchy was later more fully elaborated
by Livy in the first book of his historical work. But at each turning
point—in the history of the monarchy, at each accession of a new
king—there is also a step, mostly forward but also sometimes backward, in the development of a mixed constitution. These points are
sometimes hardly elaborated but they are always there, and their
arrangement is very systematic. In fact, the sequence of these steps
is so regular that it is safe to say that actual history never takes such
a logical course. Considering then what has been observed concerning
the general inclinations of Cicero and of Polybius in dealing with such
matters, it appears safe to assume that those observations in Cicero's
work which belong to this scheme are generally derived from Polybius. On the other hand, what is said about the positive contributions
of each king to the political order may largely belong to Cicero,
though some of it may also be taken over from Polybius. The origin
of any additional material that belongs neither to the first category
nor the second is much more difficult to determine, and may in some
cases be unidentifiable. But perhaps one negative conclusion may also
be drawn. The preceding chapter has shown—and the following chapters on Polybius' analysis of the Roman constitution at the point of
greatest perfection will show again—that Polybius, when dealing with
the Spartan, the Carthaginian, the Cretan, and the Roman constitutions, failed to consider certain factors that are of fundamental importance for the evaluation of their stability and of their character
as mixed constitutions. If in the extant parts of Cicero's second book
no trace of any consideration of these same factors can be discovered,
it appears more than probable that Polybius did not discuss them in his
account of the development of the Roman constitution either.

It is then necessary to begin with a summary of those sections of
Cicero's work which are relevant to the history of the Roman constitution, and to interpret and discuss those passages the meaning of
which is not clear at first sight.

Through the union of the Latin settlers of Rome with the Sabines,

Rome in the beginning had two kings, Romulus, its founder, and Titus Tatius, the Sabine king, who had become Romulus' co-ruler. Together with Titus Tatius, Romulus selected a council consisting of the most outstanding citizens to serve as the kings' advisers. This is the origin of the Roman Senate, whose members were called *patres* (fathers). The kings furthermore divided the people into three tribes and thirty curiae.[14] After the death of Titus Tatius all the power resorted to Romulus alone; he nevertheless made even greater use of the counsel and the authority [15] of the Senate than before. In this respect Romulus showed equal insight with Lycurgus, who had been the first to see that a monarchy will function much better if the authority of the most outstanding citizens is joined with the domination of the king. Moreover, Romulus distributed the people of the lower classes among the outstanding citizens as their clients, a measure that proved extremely beneficial. He kept the people in bounds, not by cruel punishment, but as far as possible by the imposition of fines.[16]

After the death of Romulus the royal council—i.e. the Senate—attempted for some time to rule without a monarch, but the people did not cease to demand the restoration of the monarchy. When finally their demand had to be met, the Romans, though a young and inexperienced people, showed an insight which had been lacking in Lycurgus. They realized that the choice of a king ought not to be determined by heredity, but by the worthiness of the person to be selected for that exalted office. They therefore established an elective rather than a hereditary monarchy.[17]

The first successor of Romulus, then, was elected on the proposal of the Senate by the people in Comitia Curiata, i.e., in an assembly in which the vote was taken by curiae. It was not a Roman citizen but a Sabine from Cures, Numa Pompilius, who was elected in this fashion. Immediately after his election Numa asked the people to confirm by law his imperium, i.e. his command over the Roman army. The people acceded to his wishes and a lex curiata was passed accordingly.[18] After his accession Numa divided man by man among the citizens the land that had been conquered under his warlike predecessor. He created many religious institutions and accustomed the minds of the Romans, who had become savage through continuous warfare, to the arts of peace.[19]

After the death of Numa, Tullus Hostilius was elected king of Rome. As in the case of his predecessor, his imperium was confirmed by a lex curiata. He was the first to make an attempt to establish something like principles of international law by his creation of the *ius fetiale*. Most important was the introduction of the rule that no war was to be considered just that had not been duly announced and declared. Thus the important distinction between just and unjust wars was introduced for the first time.[20]

One more important innovation is attributed to Tullus Hostilius by Cicero, but since there is a lacuna in the text at the end of the section dealing with this king, the meaning of this innovation is not quite clear. The extant part of the text says that Tullus "did not dare to make use of his royal 'insignia' [or rather, of the external tokens of his royal power] without a special law passed by the people." In this way he showed "how much the Roman kings at that time were aware that some power must be given to the people." The last sentence of this section, of which only nine words have been preserved, seems to indicate that "the tokens of royal power" are the twelve lictors who preceded the king when he appeared in public. Since the lictors are not mentioned in the sections dealing with earlier kings, it has been conjectured [21] that, according to Cicero, the institution of the lictors was first created by Tullus Hostilius, and that its introduction marked an increase in, and emphasis upon, the coercive powers of the king. This may very well have been the sense of the original tradition. But the introductory sentences in Cicero do *not* emphasize a possible increase in the power of the king but, on the contrary, the increased respect of the king for the right of the people to give or withhold privileges and power. The intention, therefore, seems rather to draw an analogy between Tullus and Numa: the latter had been the first to consider it necessary to ask the people specifically to confirm his military command; his successor, Tullus, goes a step farther and begs for a specific confirmation of his coercive powers in peace.[22]

Very little is said about the fourth king, Ancus Marcius. Cicero mentions [23] that he was a grandson of Numa. This is probably meant to indicate that by now the principle of heredity had begun to play a certain role, though Cicero hastens to add that the king was duly elected by the people and that his imperium was confirmed by a lex curiata. No constitutional innovations are attributed to this king, but he is credited with the establishment of a settlement or colony of Roman citizens at the mouth of the Tiber, the first *colonia civium Romanorum*.[24]

L. Tarquinius, who was to become the fifth king of Rome, came first into prominence through his close association with Ancus Marcius, whose advisor he had been for a long time. His affability and benevolence as first counselor of the king had made him so popular that after the death of Ancus Marcius he was unanimously elected his successor. After having had his imperium confirmed by a lex curiata he doubled the number of the members of the Senate, but with the provision that those who had been Senators before his accession—and, one must assume, those descendants of old senatorial families who would replace them after their deaths—were to be called [*patres*] *maiorum gentium*, the newly appointed senators, and, one has probably to understand, their successors chosen from other than senatorial families, [*patres*] *minorum gentium*. He made it a custom always to ask the Senators of the former group first for their opinion when he consulted the Senate. He also doubled the number of the *equites* (knights) in each of the three centuriae of the Tities, Rhamnes, and Luceres, the intercession of a famous augur having prevented him from adding three new centuriae to the three original ones as he had intended to do.[25]

The sixth king, Servius Tullius, ruled, or rather administered, the state first without having been elected by the people, but with their tacit consent. He had been chief counselor of L. Tarquinius, and when the king had died, he concealed the fact for some time, appearing in royal attire and acting as supreme judge, claiming that he did so on order of the king, who was ill. In this role he managed to win the favor of the populace by his great affability and by freeing, at his own expense, a great many citizens from the burden of their debts. Then, when the death of Tarquinius had finally been announced and the burial had taken place, Servius approached the people directly, offering himself as a candidate for the kingship, and was duly elected. Following this a lex curiata confirming his imperium was passed.[26]

There follows in the extant text of Cicero's treatise, after a major lacuna, a report on the most important constitutional innovation attributed to Servius Tullius. He is said to have divided the whole citizenry into centuriae, which from then on became the voting units both in elections and in the legislative process, with the exception that the *lex de imperio* had still to be passed by the Comitia Curiata. According to the new order the number of centuriae of equites was increased to eighteen. The rest of the citizenry was divided into five classes according to property qualifications, and this in such a way that the first class, i.e., the most wealthy class apart from the knights, consisted of 70 centuriae, while all the other four classes together comprised only 105 centuriae.[27] Cicero points out [28] that it was the fortunate result of this new division that the poorer people, or the masses, did not have the majority of votes, the wealthy people having a greater voting power than the poor, but that nevertheless nobody could complain that he was excluded from the vote.

Servius Tullius was the last of the series of real kings, for with his successor, Tarquinius Superbus, the monarchy deteriorated into tyranny. On the occasion of this important turning point Cicero inserts some general reflections and again draws a comparison between Sparta and Rome. Sparta, like Rome, Cicero says,[29] had a constitution mixed of three elements, to be sure, but the mixture was more of the kind that existed in Rome at the time of the monarchy rather than later when the Republic had reached its highest perfection. For though the constitutions of Lycurgan Sparta, of Carthage, and of Rome at the time of the monarchy were all mixed—there being a Senate in early Rome, and the people also having certain definite political rights— these mixtures were not well tempered. They could not be well tempered because wherever there is a monarch with the title of king, who rules for a lifetime, the royal power will always stand out above all else, and such a state must, therefore, be called a monarchy. Monarchy, however, he considers, is the most unstable of all forms of government because, through the vice of one man, the monarch, it can be converted with the greatest facility into the worst type of government (that is, tyranny). Apart from this, monarchy or kingship is not bad in itself; in fact, it may be preferable to any other simple constitution as long as it remains what it should be, namely, a system under which the welfare of the citizens, the rule of law, and internal peace are guaranteed through the power, the justice, and the wisdom of one man. Yet it must also be observed that even under the best monarch a people lacks many things; the most important lack is liberty, which does not consist in having a just master but in having no master at all.

This last statement is again followed by a lacuna in the text so that we do not know whether the discussion of monarchy and the comparison of Rome with Sparta and Carthage was carried any further, nor is it absolutely certain whether these remarks were in the dialog attributed to Scipio, who is the main speaker, or whether they were remarks made by one of the other interlocutors. The story of the accession of the seventh and last king of Rome, Tarquinius Superbus, is also lost in the lacuna, except that we learn he came to power through the assassination of his predecessor.[30] From the context, however, as well as from the parallel account in Livy,[31] it can be inferred with certainty that, according to Cicero's account also, Tarquinius was not recommended by the Senate nor elected by the people, and that his imperium was not confirmed by a lex curiata. In other words, he was a usurper according to Roman laws, though he was a legitimate descendant of L. Tarquinius. We learn from the extant parts of Cicero's treatise [32] that Tarquinius Superbus was at first successful in foreign wars, but when he had reached the summit of his insolence he was deprived of his rulership by the people, who rose against him on the instigation of L. Brutus. By becoming the author and leader of this revolt, Cicero adds, Brutus showed that in Rome nobody could consider himself a private citizen (i.e., remain unconcerned and inactive) where the liberty of the people was at stake. As a result of the revolt Tarquinius and his whole family were exiled from Rome.

This section on the rule and the overthrow of Tarquinius is followed by another discussion of a general nature, this time on the difference between a king and a tyrant.[33] The tyrant is defined as a *rex iniustus* (an unjust king), and tyranny as an abuse of royal power. These observations are followed by another lacuna of two pages in the manuscript. In the short section following this lacuna [34] Cicero observes that the names of the gerousia in Sparta and of the senatus in Rome have the same meaning, but that the number of the members of the gerousia was too small. He adds that it is not enough to give the people a little power, as Lycurgus and Romulus had done, for this will not quench the people's thirst for liberty but make it stronger, since they get just a taste of it but not more, and that under such a regime there will always be fear that it may degenerate into tyranny. The example of Tarquinius Superbus shows that even where there has been a long succession of good monarchs such fears are always justified.

Following these observations there is again a lacuna of very considerable length. But where the text begins again we find the interlocutors of the dialog [35] still talking about kingship and tyranny, and the observation is made that after the expulsion of Tarquinius Superbus the Romans hated the very name of king as much as they had longed for a monarch after the death of their first king, Romulus. The whole section on the advantages and dangers of monarchy, both limited and unlimited, must therefore have been of great length.

Cicero's account of the establishment of the Roman Republic and of its first institution is again lost in a very extensive lacuna in the manuscript, and when the text begins again [36] we are in the midst of a discussion of the safeguards of the rights of the people against the arbitrary powers of its magistrates. But there is a reference in St. Augustine [37] which obviously belongs to the lost beginning of this section of Cicero's treatise. It says that the Romans, since they could not tolerate any kind of regal power any longer, from then on elected annually two supreme commanders (and, one has obviously to understand, heads of the state) [38] who were called *consuls* from the Latin word *consulere* (obviously here in the sense of "taking care of something") rather than *reges* or *domini,* two designations which are derived from the verbs *regere* (to rule) and *dominari* (to dominate or to be master).

The text after the lacuna concerns itself with further restrictions of the power of the consuls beyond those which followed from their collegiality and from the limitation of their term of office to one year. The most important measure mentioned in this context is a law which, according to Cicero, was the first law passed by the Comitia Centuriata.[39] This law, which was introduced by P. Valerius Publicola, established the right of the so-called *provocatio ad populum,* making it unlawful for a magistrate to have a Roman citizen executed or flogged without permitting him first to appeal against such punishment to the assembly of the people. Cicero adds that, after a provision had been accepted (in 450 B.C.) to the effect that the *decemviri legibus scribundis*,[40] who had been appointed for that year, be exempted from the *provocatio ad populum*, the Valerio-Horatian Laws (which were passed two years later) provided that in the future no magistracy not subject to the *provocatio* should ever be created.[41] We learn further that Publicola introduced another law according to which the twelve lictors were to follow either of the consuls in alternate months so that there should not be more "tokens" of the coercive power of the supreme magistrates in the Republic than there had been under the monarchy.

Cicero's account of the early republican constitution, then, clearly began with a discussion of the restriction of the powers of those magistrates who, in the Republic, were entrusted with the functions formerly exercised by the kings, though it may of course have contained considerably more than we have now. It is followed by a section which discusses the power and position of the Senate in proportion to those of the two other elements of the body politic. Cicero points out that the power of the consuls was limited in the various ways described in the previous section but was otherwise royal in nature and scope. The people, though protected by law against unlimited use of the coercive power of the magistrates, had but little positive influence on the conduct of affairs. But it was the Senate that wielded the greatest power in the earliest period of the Roman Republic. What contributed most to making the Senate more powerful than the people was the provision that bills passed by the assemblies of the people acquired legal validity only after they were ratified by the auctoritas [42] of the Senate.

In this connection Cicero discusses also briefly the institution of the dictatorship which was introduced for the first time in this period.[43] Of this institution he says only that the power of the dictator came very close to that of a king, but adds that nevertheless (i.e., even when a dictator had been appointed) everything remained in the hands of the principes, i.e. the first citizens, the members of the Senate, who had the highest authority; it was the people who had to give way (that is, to the power of the dictator).[44] In other words, Cicero emphasizes again that in this early period of the Republic there was no real balance between the power of the three elements of the body politic. By far the greatest power was in the hands of the Senate, who

represented the oligarchic element. There were also considerable re-
mainders of the monarchic powers now wielded by the consuls and,
in times of emergency, in even greater measure by the dictator. But
the democratic element was still very little developed.

It is, however, in Cicero's next chapter [45] that we learn of an event
which marks the first step towards an increase of the power of the
people. The plebeians, Cicero tells us, being hard pressed by debts,
seceded to the Mons Sacer or, according to another tradition, the
Aventine, refusing to serve in the army under the leadership of the
patricians. This led to the creation of the institution of the *tribuni
plebis*, which the patricians were forced to acknowledge, and by which
the power of the Senate was for the first time checked to some extent
and actually decreased.[46] However, Cicero continues, in spite of this
new institution the authority and power of the Senate continued to be
very great. This was due mainly to the egregious qualities of the
majority of the Senators, who were not only very wise and brave men
who supported the state by their excellent counsel in peace and their
brilliant leadership in war, but who also led exemplary lives, being
more restrained in indulging in sensual pleasures than the rest of the
people. In fact, they did not even raise themselves very much above
the common people through the use which they made of their
wealth.[47]

There follows a short chapter [48] which tells of the attempt of a
certain Sp. Cassius to use the popularity he had acquired with the
people to restore the monarchy, with himself as monarch. He is accused by his quaestor, however, and when his own father confirms
his guilt he is executed after an unsuccessful appeal to the people.[49]

The last surviving section of Cicero's work that deals with the
history of the Roman constitution [50] tells the story of the *decemviri
legibus scribundis*. Within the period in which the authority of the
Senate was still supreme it was decided, with the passive agreement
of the people,[51] that the consuls and the tribunes of the plebs should
abdicate to make room for a commission of ten men who were to create
a code of laws and at the same time to act as rulers of the country.
These men were to be exempt from the *provocatio ad populum* and,
since during their rule there were no tribunes of the plebs, also from

tribunician intercession. During the year for which they had been elected this commission actually composed an excellent law code which was written down on ten tables. But since the commission was of the opinion that these ten tables were not sufficient and that therefore their business was not completed, they were at the end of the year replaced by another commission of ten that was to complete their work. This second commission of ten men, however, did not show the same high notions of their duties as the first. Only one of them distinguished himself by permitting a man whom he believed to be a murderer to appeal to the people, though as a member of the commission he was exempt from the *provocatio ad populum*. At the end of their term of office the new commission refused to abdicate or to appoint successors. They tried to continue their rule, acting in a very oppressive manner, and at the same time introducing new laws that were greatly prejudicial to the plebeians, as, for instance, a law forbidding intermarriage between plebeians and patricians. As a reaction to this unlawful or obnoxious behavior of the Ten-Man Commission there was a second secession of the plebeians to the Mons Sacer and later to the Aventine.

At this point there is another lacuna in the manuscript, and when the discussion starts again it has turned to other matters. Yet there can, of course, be no doubt that the outcome of the rebellion of the plebeians against the *decemviri* was described in the chapters that have perished in the lacuna. According to the Livian tradition the outcome was that the *decemviri* had to abdicate, the consulship and the tribunes of the plebs were restored, the powers of the tribunes were increased and confirmed by new laws, and other important concessions were made to the people through the so-called Valerio-Horatian laws.[52]

Since the lacuna following this section comprises only eight pages, since Cicero, as has been shown above, usually concludes every section of his history of the Roman constitution with a somewhat more general discussion of certain points of political analysis suggested by the constitutional development just recounted, and since after the lacuna he deals with other matters, it seems clear that Cicero did not pursue the history of the Roman constitution any farther. At any rate, it is absolutely certain that he cannot have discussed its later phases in detail, as there is not room for such a discussion in the missing parts of his work. The reason then, for Cicero's choice of a stopping point, must be that he believed that with the overthrow of the second commission of *decemviri*, and the acknowledgment of the new powers of the people through the Valerio-Horatian laws, the most important phase of the development of the Roman constitution had ended. And, in fact, if one considers the way in which the development of this constitution to this point is described by Cicero, such an assumption is quite understandable. In the first phase it was the monarchy that predominated, though certain democratic and aristocratic elements were brought in from the beginning. In the second phase, which lasted from the establishment of the Republic to the rule of the second committee of *decemviri*, the Senate, i.e., the patrician aristocracy, predominated. Yet a rather strong monarchic element remained in the office of the consuls, who had very far-reaching powers. Only the democratic element, as we are told again and again, remained politically weak. After the overthrow of the *decemviri* and the second secession of the plebeians, the power of the democratic element was greatly increased while the power of the aristocracy was weakened. Hence, the element that had been weakest in the preceding period having been strengthened, and the previously predominant element having been reduced in power, while the third element, which had been neither too strong nor too weak, remained the same, a nearly perfect balance of the three elements was established, and the ideal of the well-balanced mixed constitution was realized. If then it can be shown that Cicero stopped with the Valerio-Horatian laws, because he believed that through them a perfect balance of monarchy, oligarchy, and democracy had been achieved, it can hardly be considered a coincidence that Polybius says [53] that the Roman constitution had continued to be excellent ever since the year 449 B.C., i.e., since the time of the overthrow of the second Commission of Ten Men. In other words Cicero clearly accepted Polybius' contention that it was at that point that the Roman constitution came, so to speak, to maturity, and that it continued in this state of maturity for a long period of time. One can then hardly avoid the further conclusion that Polybius also carried his analysis of the development only to this point.

Even the most superficial survey of the preceding summary of Cicero's account of the history of the Roman constitution shows that each of those parts of his work in which he deals successively with the six first kings of Rome contains a section that corresponds to the notion of the development of the Roman constitution that Cicero attributes to Cato and another section that corresponds to Polybius' notion of its development. The sections of the first type are in most cases somewhat longer and more elaborate; the sections of the second type are in most cases shorter but obviously, if taken by themselves, much more closely related to one another, and in fact are clearly part of a tightly knit account. In the account of the last king, Tarquinius Superbus, a section of the first type is missing, quite naturally so, since as a tyrant he did not make a positive contribution to the Roman political system. But in that part of Cicero's work which deals with the early history of the Republic, the two types can again be distinguished, though less clearly than in the part that deals with the history of the monarchy. It is the sections of the second type which make it possible to gain some insight into the way in which Polybius dealt with the history of the Roman constitution.

The first relevant point in the extant parts of Cicero's work is the observation that Romulus and Titus Tatius, the early kings of Rome, created a council of advisers consisting of the most outstanding citizens (the later Senate), and that after the death of Titus Tatius, when all the power had reverted to Romulus alone, the king paid even greater attention to the advice of the Senate than before. But perhaps it is possible to reconstruct to some extent a still earlier part of Polybius' account of the Roman constitution. At the very beginning of the second book [54] Cicero tells the story of how Romulus and his brother Remus had been brought up by a she-wolf and how, when they had grown up in this way, they distinguished themselves so much through their physical strength and the fierceness of their character that all the inhabitants of the region "obeyed them willingly." In this form the story appears to be nothing but the traditional fairy tale and of no importance for the political theory that is later to be developed on the basis of the constitutional history of Rome. But, as Taeger [55] has pointed out, there is an account of Romulus and Remus in the work of Diodorus [56] which fits in very well with Cicero's story, but gives considerably more. This is all the more important since there can be no doubt that Diodorus has made extensive use of Polybius in other parts of his work.

Diodorus in the passage quoted tells the same story as Cicero and in almost the same words, but adds that Remus and Romulus established security for the herdsmen of the region in which they lived by combating and killing robbers, and at the same time remained friendly and considerate towards all peaceful people. By their moderation and by the help which they gave the weak they won such general acclaim that everybody acknowledged them as guarantors of peace and security and obeyed them willingly. It is not difficult to see that this agrees perfectly with Polybius' theory [57] that primitive monarchy develops when those who distinguish themselves through their physical strength and bravery also show a strong sense of justice, and become the protectors of the herd of peaceful human beings against its enemies.

So far, then, the rise of Romulus and Remus to the Roman kingship provides simply an example of the natural origin of primitive kingship according to Polybius' general theory. The later double kingship of Romulus and Titus Tatius was of course a part of Roman tradition, and could not be passed over even if it could not be related to any specific point in the general theory. It has been pointed out that this double kingship in a way anticipates the institution of the two consuls in the later Republic, and that it can also be considered as a temporary analogy to the double kingship existing in Sparta. But since Cicero is completely silent on these two points it is doubtful whether Polybius had reflected on them.

The next steps in the development are perfectly clear. The first deviation from the development of the simple cycle as described by Polybius is the introduction, under Titus Tatius and Romulus, of an aristocratic council. Cicero's text does not suggest that this council represented an aristocratic element that could in any way have counterbalanced the power of the king, but its importance becomes at once clear when the king has died. Since the king left no heir it looks for some time as if the Senate, as the only surviving part of the government, would take over, so that there would be a transition directly from early kingship to aristocracy without the intermediate stages of the development of a tyranny and its overthrow by revolution. However, just because the people so far have had only good experiences with their monarchs, they demand the restoration of the monarchy, and the Senate finally must give in.

Yet the restoration of the monarchy is accompanied by more and more important deviations from the development within the cycle of simple constitutions. In the first place, the principle of heredity which, according to Polybius, plays such a harmful role in the natural cycle, is not applied. The method by which the king is elected asserts the political influence of the Senate, which acquires the right to propose and recommend candidates for the kingship when a king has died. Still more important is the fact that the assembly of the people not only acquires the right to accept or reject the candidates so proposed, but is also allowed to assert its temporary sovereignty by ratifying the military command of the king by a special law.[58] Again this does not mean that the Senate or the people could in any way counterbalance the power of the ruler once he has become king. On the contrary, Cicero (or Polybius) emphasizes repeatedly that the king, once he has become king and imperator, rules supreme. Yet, in contrast to the purely hereditary monarchy of the simple cycle, since the death of Romulus the aristocratic and the democratic elements in Rome do have well-defined and important active rights in the interval between two kings and in regard to the choice of their ruler.

The relevant factor in the history of the following kings is obviously the mode of succession. The accession of Numa Pompilius appears to have established the principle of the elective monarchy. Yet since this principle has been established only by precedent and not by law, and is not yet confirmed by a long tradition, there is still the danger that it may be superseded by other principles. Most obnoxious, in Polybius' opinion, at least in the long run, is the principle of heredity. Yet he himself has tried to show how easily it can creep in: it seems so plausible that the children of a wise and good monarch, who have a good *Erbmasse*, who have been brought up and educated by an excellent father, and who, through living with the king, have become acquainted with the problems of government from their early youth, should make very good rulers, and in fact for some time it may work out extremely well. Nevertheless, when this belief is constantly applied, it will, so Polybius believes, inevitably result in a degeneration of monarchy to tyranny.

In exact correspondence with this Polybian scheme, with Ancus Marcius the principle of heredity comes in for the first time, but in scarcely a noticeable way, and in a perfectly innocuous fashion. He is the grandson of Numa Pompilius, but he has all the good qualities that the grandson of so good and great a monarch ought to have, and he is elected because of them and not because of any hereditary claim as such. Yet later, with Tarquinius Superbus, the principle of heredity is applied in its undiluted form, and at once the monarchy is converted into a tyranny.

The second principle that may enter into competition with that of a purely elective monarchy is the principle that the first adviser, the right-hand man of the king, should be chosen as his successor. It is perhaps not beside the point to observe that this principle has a certain affinity to the principle of adoption as it was practiced in certain periods of the Roman empire. Obviously, if one accepts Polybius' conviction that the best man should have the monarchic functions in the state, whether the state be a monarchy or a mixed constitution, this principle is better than that of pure heredity. Such a right-hand man of the king will ordinarily have proven his wisdom and capability by the time he is called upon to rule, while in the case of the son of a king this may not always be true. In fact, both of the men who become kings in this fashion later turn out to be excellent rulers.

Yet the danger inherent even in this principle becomes apparent through a comparison between the accessions of L. Tarquinius and Servius Tullius. Though Tarquinius appears to be predestined to become the successor of Ancus Marcius because he has all the qualities and the experience required of a king, his elevation to the throne follows in every detail the established custom. He does not begin to rule in his own name until he has been duly recommended as a candidate by the Senate and then elected by the people. Servius, on the other hand, rules first through deception, seemingly under the authority of his predecessor but actually on his own responsibility, and it is mainly in this period that he manages to win the favor of the populace so that, when the death of Tarquinius is finally revealed, he has no difficulty obtaining popular confirmation of his rule. However, the other traditional step in the selection of a new king, recommendation by the Senate, is completely omitted. This difference in the modes of accession of L. Tarquinius and Servius Tullius is emphasized by a parallel difference in the accession of the hereditary kings Ancus Marcius and Tarquinius Superbus. Ancus Marcius corresponds to L. Tarquinius inasmuch as his accession, in spite of the fact that he is the grandson of a former king, does not violate the established procedure in any way. Servius Tullius and Tarquinius Superbus both break with the established custom, though there is the important difference that Servius, who has no claims on the basis of heredity, knows that he must save appearances, while Tarquinius Superbus pays no attention to tradition but boldly claims the superiority of his birthright over any traditional rights of the Senate and the people. Cicero does not stress these points as has been done here, but the analogy can hardly be fortuitous. The very fact, therefore, that Cicero does not emphasize them appears to prove that they must have been taken over from elsewhere. They obviously belong to a definite conceptual scheme, the like of which cannot have been originally inherent in the legends which the Romans told about their early kings, but they fit in very well with Polybius' general theories. For all these reasons there can hardly be any doubt that this scheme formed part of Polybius' analysis of the history of the Roman constitution.

It is not difficult to discover the continuation of essentially the same pattern in Cicero's account of the constitutional development in the early Republic. In spite of the fact that some first elements of a mixed constitution had developed in the monarchic period, this period ended with a tyranny because the balance between the three elements had been too uneven. But the overthrow of the tyranny follows much more quickly than history had shown to be usual in the cycle of simple constitutions, and though the second phase brings the oligarchic element to the fore, a strong monarchic element is retained in the form of the consulate. In fact, the consuls retain practically all the powers that the kings had possessed. The difference is merely that there are two consuls who keep check on one another instead of one king who rules unchecked, and that the consuls are elected for one year only while the kings, when once elected, rule for life.

Cicero does not indicate, at least in the extant parts of his work, the reason why the development in this respect took so different a turn from the ordinary cycle of constitutions, but one may guess that in Polybius' opinion it was not unrelated to the fact that the monarchy had been moderate for such a long time and that the tyranny had lasted for such a short period that the benefits of a good and restricted monarchy were still vividly remembered. At any rate, it is absolutely essential for Polybius' theory that a strong monarchic element be carried over into the oligarchic phase from the preceding period, since otherwise a well-balanced mixed constitution could not result.

The general theory requires also that in the second phase the democratic element be at first still very weak, and this is exactly what Cicero emphasizes again and again. But it must not be completely absent either, so that a comparatively easy and nonviolent transition to the third phase can take place. Thus the election of the chiefs of the Republic by the people is carried over from the period of the monarchy. There is the introduction of the *provocatio ad populum* as an innovation in favor of the common people in the very first years of the Republic. But since no perfect balance is yet achieved, the political order, as Cicero points out,[59] remains unstable, and there follow upon one another three events that illustrate the continuing struggle until finally the perfect state of mixture is attained. First there is the secession of the plebs which, through the establishment of the plebeian tribuneship with its great privileges and powers, results in a considerable strengthening of the democratic element. Then there is an attempt to restore the monarchy; this, however, is easily defeated. But since the system is really out of balance through the greater weight on the oligarchic side, it is from this side that the greatest danger threatens. Thus, just as the monarchy—in spite of its having been tempered almost from the beginning by certain oligarchic and democratic elements—had finally followed the pattern of the cycle of constitutions and ended in a tyranny, so now the second phase ends with the establishment of an undiluted and oppressive oligarchy through the refusal of the second Commission of Ten Men to comply with the provisions of the constitution. It must be pointed out that this usurpation of power meant a discontinuation of the consulate, i.e., of the monarchic factor which had been retained after the overthrow of the monarchy, as well as an abolishment of the rights of the people, which had been partly inherited from the early monarchy, and partly acquired in the first years of the Republic. But just as in the time of Tarquinius Superbus the inevitable revolution had come quickly and in a comparatively mild form—the tyrant merely being driven into exile instead of being killed—so now the overthrow of this oligarchic regime is even quicker. And as in the first case the result of the overthrow of the tyrant was not a purely oligarchic regime but one in which a strong monarchic factor remained, so now the result of the revolution is not a radical democracy, but the Senate remains as the representative of the aristocratic element in the state and retains a great part of its power. There seems to be even the further analogy—though this is not pointed out by Cicero in the extant parts of his work—that the revolution could hardly have been so easy and mild, and yet at the same time so successful, if the people had not during the preceding secession acquired an organization under their tribunes which had been acknowledged as legitimate, just as the form of the antimonarchic revolution had been conditioned by the fact that the Senate had already had a legal position under the regime of the kings.

As soon as these points, which are directly relevant to the development of a mixed constitution, are placed side by side, disregarding all other elements of Cicero's story, one cannot fail to see a very rigid systematic pattern closely related to Polybius' political theory. This relation will become still more apparent when we check Cicero's story against what we know of the historical reality.

How much of the remainder of Cicero's account is derived from Polybius is more difficult to determine. There can be no doubt that some of the "positive" contributions to the development of the political order ascribed to individual kings must have been mentioned by Polybius also, as, for instance, the distribution of the people into curiae and later into centuriae, since the vote in elections, which play such an important part in Polybius' scheme, was taken according to these divisions. Considering Polybius' interest in religion, or rather in the function of religion in a well-ordered political society, it is not unlikely that he said something about Numa Pompilius and his role in the creation of a system of religious institutions, though this is by no means certain. Whether Polybius spoke of the contributions to the creation of a code of international law which Cicero attributes to Tullus Hostilius is still more uncertain, especially in view of Cicero's own very pronounced interest in all questions of law. Within the framework of the present study it would hardly be rewarding to discuss the probable derivation of all the passages of this kind in Cicero's work. It must be sufficient to say that most of this material may, but not necessarily must, come from Polybius.

There are, however, a few special points that require further discussion. Since Polybius, in the extant parts of his sixth book, makes an elaborate comparison between the constitutions of Rome, Sparta, and Carthage, it seems natural to assume that the repeated comparisons between certain phases in the development of the Roman constitution with certain aspects of the constitutions of Carthage and Sparta are also taken over from Polybius. Yet a closer inspection of the relevant passages shows that the problem is not quite so simple. There are three references to Lycurgus in the extant parts of Cicero's second book. On the first occasion Cicero says [60] that Romulus showed the same insight as Lycurgus in realizing that a monarchic government will function better if the authority of the most outstanding citizens is joined to the royal power of the king. The second passage [61] asserts that the Spartans and the Carthaginians had mixed constitutions, to be sure, but mixed constitutions that were not well tempered or well balanced, for as long as there is the continued power of one man, especially under the name of king, the monarchic element will always predominate and the danger of its being converted into a tyranny will never be absent. In the third passage [62] Lycurgus is criticized for having made the gerousia—i.e., the Spartan Senate—too small, giving it only twenty-eight members. At the same time another parallel between Romulus and Lycurgus is drawn: both of them, it is said, gave the people only enough power to wet their thirst for liberty without satisfying it, which of necessity was bound to cause unrest and instability in the state.

The most interesting passage is obviously the second one. It has been pointed out [63] that Polybius in the extant parts of the second book obviously means to characterize the Lycurgan constitution not only as a mixed constitution of some kind but also as a well-balanced one. It is inferior to that of the Romans not so much because of any weaknesses in its governmental structure or in the way in which political power is distributed, but rather because its economic structure is not calculated to support an expansionist policy, which the Spartans nevertheless attempted. Hence, it is argued, what Cicero says about the imperfection of the Lycurgan system in this respect cannot have been taken over from Polybius.

There is, perhaps, still stronger evidence to prove that what Cicero says about Carthage cannot have come from Polybius. For according to Polybius, Carthage proved weaker than Rome because it had reached a later stage in constitutional development, and therefore had shifted from a predominance of the aristocratic to that of the democratic factor. This view is clearly irreconcilable with what Cicero says about the Carthaginian constitution. True, if the Carthaginian constitution was not invented like that of Sparta, but had grown in a natural process like that of Rome, there must have been a stage in its development in which the monarchic factor predominated. But it is clearly not an early stage of this constitution that Cicero has in mind, but either the Carthaginian constitution as such, without regard to its different phases, or the Carthaginian constitution at the time of the contact of Carthage with Rome—i.e., the time when, according to Polybius, the Carthaginian constitution had progressed considerably on the road to democracy. How then could Cicero be induced to see the fundamental weakness of the Carthaginian constitution in the prevalence of the monarchic rather than the democratic factor?

There are two factors which Cicero designates as dangerous: that a man should rule perpetually, and "the royal name." We have seen that the title of the suffetes was translated by the Greeks with the word βασιλεύς or "king." Whether there was a period in which the suffetes were elected for life is contested,[64] but it certainly was no longer the case in the third century B.C. and later, and, as pointed out before, Cicero cannot have meant to refer to some early period of Carthaginian history. It appears, therefore, that the only possible historical basis for his observation concerning the perpetual power of a man in regard to Carthage is the free re-eligibility of the suffetes [65] and the fact that frequently in the course of Carthaginian history outstanding men, or even a series of outstanding men from the same family, continued to wield great power and to hold the highest positions in the state through their influence either with the aristocracy or, especially in the latest phase in the history of Carthage, with the people. Cicero's addition is, then, in all likelihood, due to the traditional aversion of the Romans to the title of king or *rex*, and, as far as Carthage is concerned, perhaps also to the fact that in Roman tradition the great enemies of Rome, Hamilcar and Hannibal, were considered to be the men who brought about the downfall of Carthage through the perpetual ascendancy which they achieved in their country by appealing to the passions of the people. What Cicero considered the prevalence of the monarchic element in the Carthaginian republic would then at least partly coincide with Polybius' "democratization." But it is certainly noteworthy that neither Cicero nor Polybius pointed out the preponderantly oligarchic character of the Carthaginian state which stands out so clearly in the remaining ancient tradition.

The two other references to Sparta in Cicero's second book are less significant, but the first one seems to indicate that Cicero slightly altered a remark that he probably found in Polybius. It is very likely that Polybius compared the introduction of a council by Romulus with the function of the gerousia in the constitution of Lycurgus. The fragments of the sixth book show that the analogy with Sparta was constantly in his mind, and since the creation of the Senate in his opinion was not the result of a compromise, but of the free will and insight of the king, he can hardly have failed to make the comparison with the same feature in Lycurgus' rationally contrived constitution. On the other hand he can hardly have formulated the comparison in the same way as Cicero did since Lycurgus, in Polybius' opinion, did not try to create "a better-functioning monarchy" but a mixed constitution. In view of this it is not improbable that Polybius referred to Sparta and possibly to Carthage also on the same occasion on which Cicero describes the constitutions of both these cities as not really well tempered. Here again, then, Cicero would have somewhat changed what Polybius had said. But what this was can no longer be reconstructed.

There are two more points that must be briefly mentioned. What Cicero says about the merits of the distribution of the common people among the aristocracy as their clients is not likely to come from Polybius since this was a characteristically Roman institution for which a

Greek hardly had much understanding.[66] Somewhat more difficult to
determine is the relation between Cicero and Polybius in the former's
account of the first secession of the plebs and of its aftermath. The
assumption that one of the main causes of the first secession was the
intolerable burden of debts which the majority of the plebeians owed
to the patricians seems so firmly established in the later Roman tradition that one can hardly assume that it originated later than Polybius.
But one may very well doubt whether it is much older. Though it
is probably a historical fact that a first secession of the plebs did take
place in the early half of the fifth century B.C. the details of the event
as told by Livy and other ancient writers are certainly a later invention.[67] What is said about the indebtedness of the peasants as the cause
of the revolt has a striking similarity to the conditions which prevailed
in Athens before the Solonian reforms. Yet it is not at all likely that
the economic and social conditions of Rome in the early fifth century
should have been analogous to those prevailing in Attica in the late
seventh and early sixth centuries. The Attic soil was notoriously
poor. The country began to become overcrowded at an early period,
and soon after Solon it became completely impossible to feed the
population except by very large imports of grain from overseas. Such
conditions developed in Italy only centuries later. There is absolutely
no reason to believe that the Roman peasants of the fifth century were
not able to produce enough food on their farms to support themselves
and their families. Why then should they have become burdened with
debts, especially since a money economy had not yet developed at
that time in Rome? Apart from this the outcome of the struggle of
the patricians and plebeians shows clearly that it was the wealthy
plebeians who were leading in this struggle and that the grievances
of the plebeians were of a totally different nature from those of the
Attic *pelatae* of the early sixth century.[68] It is therefore not unlikely
that the picture of this struggle which we find in Cicero, Livy, and
other Roman authors was colored by the mistaken attempt to explain
them on the analogy of the social conflicts preceding the Solonian reforms in Athens. But it is impossible to tell whether this explanation
stems from Polybius or from some other early author.

What Cicero says about the simple life of the senators of that
period, on the other hand, is hardly Polybian, but is an addition ac-

counted for by the romantic notions of the early Roman Republic which had developed since the time of the Gracchi.[69]

The comparison between Polybius' account of the history of the Roman constitution and what we know of the actual facts can be kept rather brief. Nobody doubts any longer that the history of the Roman kings as it appears in the Roman tradition, including Cicero, is very largely legendary. Since, according to this very tradition, the last two kings did not rule very long, the number of seven kings is too small to cover the period between the founding of the city and the establishment of the Republic. The positive contributions to Roman life and Roman institutions which are attributed to the individual kings are distributed differently among them in different branches of the tradition, which shows that there were names and institutions which were brought together in a more or less arbitrary fashion. For example, it has been shown that the story of the Tarquin kings veils, though rather thinly, the fact that towards the end of the monarchic period Rome was under some kind of Etruscan overlordship.

At the same time it is clear that at the time of Polybius the legend, though it undoubtedly existed, cannot yet have been definitely fixed. There must have existed a great variety of alternative versions among which an author could make his choice. This explains why it was so easy to make the history of this epoch fit into a rather abstract scheme. On the basis of institutions and formulae which survived from the monarchic period in later times, partly in Rome itself, partly in other Italian communities, and also on the basis of certain indications in the legend, one can conclude that the kingship in Rome was not hereditary but elective. It is also very likely that in the earliest period the monarchy was more "democratic" than later, the kings having to invoke the decision of "the people," i.e., the assembly of warriors, in regard to the most important questions concerning the whole community, especially decisions involving peace and war. But under Etruscan influence the monarchy appears to have become more absolutistic, a development which, in the tradition and also in Polybius' account, is reflected by the story of the Tarquins, especially of Tarquinius Superbus. The historical foundations of all the rest of Polybius' account, or rather Polybius' reconstruction, of the monarchic period appear to be rather slight.

There has been much argument in recent times concerning the degree of reliability or unreliability of the ancient tradition concerning the earliest period of the Republic from its establishment to the *decemviri legibus scribundis*. There can be little doubt that the patrician aristocracy was the decisive factor in the state and that it exercised its power chiefly through the Senate, though by no means exclusively. Furthermore, everything indicates that the consuls were provided with far-reaching power. It is extremely probable that there were two consuls from the beginning of the Republic, though recently an attempt has been made to show [70] that there was a one-man consulship in the period before the *decemviri legibus scribundis*. That the institution of the *provocatio ad populum* goes back to the earliest time of the Republic is also very likely; in fact, it may even date back to the time of the monarchy. The historicity of the first and even of the second secession of the plebs has been contested in modern times, and there can be no doubt whatever that the detailed account that Livy later gave of these events [71] is largely an invention or construction, probably not of Livy himself, but of Roman annalists of the first century B.C. But a number of Roman institutions which certainly existed in the later fifth century and the fourth century B.C. can hardly be explained except on the assumption that some events of the general nature of these secessions actually did occur in the period indicated by the Roman tradition.[72] To this extent, then, Polybius' account is probably correct. While there is very little historical foundation for Polybius' belief that an aristocratic and a democratic element were introduced into the Roman political system through the sheer wisdom of her earliest kings, there cannot be much doubt that the development, in the early history of the Republic, of something which, in a way, may be called a mixed constitution was actually due to the fact that the long struggles between the patrician aristocracy and the plebeians did not, as happened so often in the Greek cities of the classical period, result in alternate, but for the time complete, victories of one party over the other, but were resolved in ever-new compromises.

This brief survey is perhaps sufficient to show that Polybius' account

of the early phases of the development of the Roman political order is
a historical construction and that it is not likely that the actual course
of events followed the systematic pattern which Polybius thought he
could discover in it. Nevertheless the same survey has also shown that
Polybius' analysis, in spite of its obvious deficiencies, is not altogether
unrelated to historical reality. It is not entirely wrong to say that the
early monarchy probably combined monarchic with democratic features, and that gradually a strong aristocratic element developed
which became dominant in the early Republic. It is also true that
against this latter factor democratic elements began to assert themselves in the struggle of the plebeians against the patricians, though
this movement is far too complicated a historical phenomenon to be
adequately expressed in the terms just used. Finally there is even
some justification for the claim that the very far-reaching powers
of the consuls constituted something comparable to a monarchic factor,
though it will be shown later that the essential function of monarchy
in the true sense is different.

Still more important, however, is the question of what elements of
general political theory Polybius introduced into his analysis, or rather
reconstruction, of the early development of the Roman constitution,
and how far these elements are reconcilable with one another and with
historical reality.

Polybius started with the theory of the cycle of constitutions. In
the first two phases of this cycle the principle of heredity plays a decisive role in causing the later deterioration of constitutions which had
worked well when they were first established. Thus it is quite natural
that the dangers inherent in this principle are brought out in Polybius'
reconstruction of the different phases of the history of the early kings
of Rome. His main point, however, seems to have been that where
there is a monarchy the principle of heredity will always creep in
finally, even if an attempt has been made to eliminate it. If this was
Polybius' opinion it appears to be confirmed by the history of the
Roman emperors long after Polybius had written his work.

The problem then remains: How to stop the cycle, or at least make
it slow down? Polybius offers two solutions, the rational one, of which
Lycurgus is the main example, and the natural one, exemplified by
the naturally growing mixed constitutions of Carthage and Rome

In the latter case the constitutions of the cycle do not follow upon one another but are added to one another and grow together until a well-balanced mixture is achieved which for some time becomes ever more perfect until it finally begins again to dissolve. This process, as we have seen, is likened to the biological process of growth and aging, and on the basis of this analogy its stages appear to become to some extent predictable. In the analysis of the growth of the Roman mixed constitution, however, an element of rational choice is also introduced when it is said that the deviation from the cycle of simple constitutions was made possible because, in times of crisis, the representatives of the different classes in the state "showed insight and took the better course."

At this point it becomes again apparent that the different elements of general theory which Polybius uses in his analysis are not completely integrated with one another and that therefore the analysis itself remains somewhat inadequate. Where there is a rational choice there is also an element of freedom. Once a rationally constructed mixed constitution has been introduced it may be predictable that under normal circumstances it will be more stable than a simple constitution. But it is certainly not predictable that a man or men with the insight to create such a constitution will at a given time or place be in the position and have the power to create it. This applies to an even greater degree to the periods of crisis in a naturally growing constitution. If what Polybius says is correct, then the continuation of such growth and the preservation of the constitutional order will depend on the insight and the decisions of those in power, though Polybius would be right in pointing out that once the development has been started in the right way it will be easier to make the right choice and to arrive at reasonable compromises than it would be under simple constitutions, where one individual or class or group has all the power and hence, when corrupt, cannot be deprived of this power or restricted in its use except through a revolution. Yet as soon as an element of freedom of choice is introduced into the process the analogy of the biological process of maturing and aging can no longer be rigidly applied.

All this may appear extremely elementary; and it has often been said that the biological analogy in Polybius' theory must not be taken too seriously. The fact, however, is that Polybius did not make it quite clear how far the different principles of explanation that he uses apply actually to the historic phenomenon which he wishes to explain. This has induced many of his modern commentators to emphasize one of these principles to the exclusion of the others. This will again become clear when we turn to Polybius' analysis of the Roman constitution at the height of its perfection. For the present it will be sufficient to consider some of the more general implications of Polybius' method.

Though the so-called Lycurgan constitution was not a written constitution in the literal sense, the so-called rhetra notwithstanding, it may, as a presumedly rational construction, be compared with modern written constitutions, while the Roman political order, though a considerable part of it consisted of published laws, may be likened to what we are used to calling unwritten constitutions, of which the British constitution is at the present the most outstanding example.

The opinion has often been expressed, and not without justification, that a naturally grown constitution is preferable, because no legislator or body of legislators, however enlightened they may be, can foresee and make provision for all possible future contingencies, and because a written constitution, even allowing for amendments, is inevitably somewhat rigid. A naturally growing constitution, it is then said, is by its very nature flexible and adaptable, and moreover the product not of the genius of one man or group of men but of the combined wisdom of centuries. Against this view it can be said that a naturally grown constitution is not the result of wisdom but of compromises between conflicting parties which were effected under very special historical circumstances and in a fortuitous fashion, and that it may remain burdened with the results of such compromises long after they have lost their meaning. The history of the Roman constitution, as will be seen in the following chapters, provides a great deal of evidence in favor of this latter view.

If this is acknowledged it becomes evident that one may distinguish "naturally growing" constitutions in the sense just outlined from constitutions created by one deliberate rational act, but that the concept of natural growth, if applied to constitutions, cannot mean what Polybius makes it mean, i.e., something analogous to the growth of living beings with its natural division into periods of childhood, adolescence, maturity, and old age. There is no natural lifespan of a mixed constitution, no natural limit of years, decades, or centuries, beyond which a naturally grown constitution cannot last. Much less, of course, is there any necessity for such a constitution to follow in a slightly modified form Polybius' scheme of the natural cycle of constitutions. If a mixed constitution grows slowly out of a simple constitution, as may very well happen, there will, of course, be a period in which it is formed, and since all things in this world are bound to perish some time, there will be a period of decay and dissolution if it is not destroyed by some external event. But how long it will last and what turns it will take in its development is not determined by some inevitable pattern, nor by a process of aging, but only by the nature of the conflicts, stresses, and difficulties which arise in its history, and by the wisdom or lack of wisdom of the political leaders and groups who must find the resolutions of those conflicts.

All this may seem to be an obvious truth which hardly deserves such a detailed discussion, but there can be no doubt that Polybius did not recognize this truth, or at least not clearly. Any survey of the history of political theory down to the present day will show that in this respect he has had a great many successors. The consequences of this failure, both of Polybius' general theory and his historical analysis, are great. He seems to think that a rationally constructed constitution, if faultless, would be virtually everlasting. It can perish only through a fault in its construction as, in his opinion, was the case with Sparta, or through an overwhelming catastrophe that destroys it from the outside. A naturally growing constitution, on the other hand, he believes, will follow a predestined pattern and, like any naturally growing living thing, has a limited lifespan. However, the opposite is true. Even the most perfect, rationally constructed constitution, if absolutely rigid, would perish within a period of time not altogether unpredictable because it cannot adapt itself to changing conditions. In fact, all rationally constructed constitutions, including the written constitutions, change constantly through varying interpretation and application far more than through formulated amendments. Only in this way are they able to survive. But in so far as this is so, they are subject to the same general laws as the naturally growing constitutions.

If Polybius had seen this he would not have concentrated in his historical survey on the formative period of the Roman constitution from legendary Romulus to the overthrow of the decemvirate and to the Valerio-Horatian laws. He would, on the contrary, have seen that the period from these latter events to Polybius' own time (i.e., the period when in his opinion the Roman constitution continued to be particularly well arranged) was by far more important for a theory of the mixed constitution. He would also have been aware that it was not sufficient to give a static picture of the power relations between the three determining factors in the Roman Republic, but that it was necessary to pay at least some attention to the constant shifts of power which occurred within the very period in which the Roman constitution was "at the height of its perfection." In this respect also Polybius' analysis of the Roman constitution will therefore have to be enlarged and supplemented if we wish to test his belief in the superiority of the mixed constitution by checking it against historical reality.

VII

POLYBIUS' ANALYSIS OF THE ROMAN
CONSTITUTION AT THE TIME OF ITS
GREATEST PERFECTION; LEGAL, TRADITIONAL,
AND FACTUAL FOUNDATIONS OF THE
DISTRIBUTION OF POWER IN THE
ROMAN REPUBLIC

SINCE A TRANSLATION of the extant parts of Polybius' sixth book is given in Appendix I, his analysis of the Roman constitution can be summarized very briefly. It is divided into two main parts. In the first part Polybius enumerates first the powers of the consuls, then of the Senate, then of the people. In the second part he tries to show how each of these different elements is kept in check by the others.

The powers of the consuls, he says,[1] are the following. All other magistrates, with the exception of the tribunes of the plebs, are subject to their orders. They bring all urgent matters, including foreign embassies, before the Senate and execute the decrees of that body. They convoke the assemblies of the people, introduce the bills on which the people have to vote, and direct the execution of the assemblies' decisions. They have complete authority over everything that belongs to the preparation for war and unrestricted power to inflict punishment on those who serve under their command in the army. They are not dependent on anyone's authorization in spending money from the public treasury. Considering all this, Polybius adds, one might easily conclude that Rome is essentially a kind of monarchy.

The Senate, Polybius continues,[2] has control over the treasury, with the exception of the money that is expended by order of the consuls, but all expenditures made by other magistrates require authorization by the Senate. Crimes committed in Italy and requiring public investigation *are the concern* of the Senate. The Senate *makes provision* for the settlement of disputes between communities and private persons in Italy that are of public interest, and likewise, through embassies, for the settlement of similar problems arising outside Italy. The Senate decides how embassies arriving in Rome should be received and what answers they should be given. Polybius adds that the people have nothing to do with these matters, and that, considering all these important functions and powers of the Senate, a person coming to Rome while the consuls happen to be absent might easily come to the conclusion that the political order of Rome is completely aristocratic.

Yet, he continues,[3] the most important part of the government is really reserved for the people. Since all public offices are elective it is the people alone who bestow public honors, and since the people alone have the power to impose the death penalty on Roman citizens [4] (Polybius should have added "except while the latter are serving as soldiers in the field"), and have also the final decision in certain cases in which fines are to be imposed, they have a very important share in the administration of justice. It is the popular assemblies that have the power to approve or reject laws (but, Polybius might have added, they have no legislative initiative [5]). They have the decision over war and peace and over the ratification or nonratification of all kinds of treaties with foreign nations. Thus, considering the great share which the people have in political power, one might say that the Roman system is essentially democratic.

The second part then begins with an analysis [6] of the ways in which the power of the consuls is counterbalanced by the Senate and the people. The consuls, as has been pointed out before, seem to have the most unrestricted power in all military matters. Yet if the Senate *prevaricates and is deliberately obstructive*, the soldiers will get no food, no pay, and no clothing, so that the war which a consul may be conducting cannot be brought to a successful end. The Senate also decides whether the consul, when his term of office is over, can retain command over his army until his military enterprise is completed, or whether he has to make room for a successor. Finally, a victorious general cannot celebrate his victory by a triumph, or at least not with proper magnificence, unless the Senate grants the necessary money. The consuls are no less dependent on the people, for the people, by refusing ratification, can annul all treaties or other agreements that a consul may have concluded with an enemy or a foreign nation, and, in addition, on laying down his office a consul has to give account of all his actions to the people.

Likewise, the Senate is kept in check by the people.[7] For the final decision in regard to crimes that the Senate may investigate lies with the people, especially where the death penalty is concerned; this penalty, as pointed out before, can be imposed upon Roman citizens not actually in military service only by the people. Furthermore, the people can reduce the privileges, public honors, and powers of the Senate, or even the private possessions of the senators, if someone can be found who will introduce such a bill in a popular assembly. (This condition has of course to be stated, because, as mentioned before, the people had no legislative initiative. But what Polybius does not say is that since the tribunes of the plebs had the right to introduce legislation, the legislative initiative was not restricted to the two other branches of the government.) Finally, if one of the tribunes of the plebs intercedes, the decrees of the Senate cannot be executed, and the Senate cannot even assemble. The tribunes, however, must act in agreement with the wishes of the people.[8]

Finally, the people are dependent on the Senate,[9] for, since all public contracts are made under the authority of the Senate, businessmen, contractors, and workers who gain a living by working for the state are dependent on the good will of the Senate and will therefore be anxious not to offend this body. In addition, the judges in the most important actions at law are taken from the Senate so that here again the people are dependent on the good will of the senatorial aristocracy. The people are also dependent on the consuls, since they are under their absolute authority while doing military service.

A reader of Polybius' analysis of the Roman constitution at the time of its greatest perfection will almost inevitably be impressed by its apparent lucidity and precision; and in fact a great many famous political philosophers have expressed their admiration for it either directly, or indirectly by borrowing from it or imitating it. Yet on closer inspection one can hardly fail to discover some irregularities in the seemingly harmonious proportions of Polybius' edifice. While we are told how the consuls are kept in check by the Senate and by the people, and the people by the Senate and the consuls, we learn only how the power of the Senate is counterbalanced by that of the people, but not that it is also kept in check by the consuls. Yet this is the least important point. For though Polybius does not mention the consuls in his chapter on the restrictions of the powers of the Senate, he has pointed out earlier that it is the consuls who introduce all important business in the Senate. From this function of the consuls, who (though Polybius does not mention this directly) presided over the sessions of the Senate when they were present at Rome, one may infer that there was some checking power of the consuls on the Senate, though this aspect of the Roman constitution is not discussed in detail.

However, there is another aspect of the relations between the consuls and the Senate which is somewhat puzzling. When the consuls are present in Rome, Polybius says, Rome appears to be a monarchy, but when they are absent from Rome it appears to have a purely aristocratic regime. It is certainly somewhat surprising to learn that whether a country is to be considered as having a monarchic or an oligarchic government depends on the presence of the chief executive or chief executives in the capital.

Still more puzzling is what Polybius says about the control of the treasury. First we hear that the consuls can make any expenditures from the public treasury at their own discretion and without authorization by anyone else. Then we learn that the public finances are under the control of the Senate, with the exception of the outlays made by the consuls. At this point a logical contradiction of the first statement is avoided by putting forth the exception. But from a practical point of view the two statements are not much less puzzling, since one naturally asks what happened if the consuls and the Senate wished to spend the available money for different purposes. This difficulty comes clearly into the open when, in a still later chapter, we learn that the consuls cannot even bring to a successful conclusion a war in which they are engaged for their country if the Senate makes difficulties by withholding food, clothing, and money for their soldiers. If the consuls could take whatever sums they wished from the public treasury, why could they not do so in order to get supplies for the army, instead of being dependent on the good will of the Senate?

The powers attributed to the Senate in the first part of Polybius' analysis are fewer than those attributed to the two other branches of the government, and what is more, the terms in which these powers are described are much weaker than those by which he describes the powers of the consuls or of the people: the consuls "are in control," "have almost absolute authority," "have the right," "have unrestricted power," and so on; the people "have alone the power," "decide," "are the only court that can impose," "have the final decision," etc. Where the powers of the Senate are enumerated a similar expression is used only once, namely in reference to their control over expenditures from the treasury; but in regard to this power we learn that the Senate had to share it with the consuls. For the rest we are informed simply that something "is the concern of the Senate," that "the Senate takes up certain matters," or that "the Senate makes provision for" something. Is it merely for the sake of stylistic variation that Polybius uses different and weaker terms when speaking of the powers of the Senate, or were the powers of the Senate actually less well-defined or less well-founded than those of the consuls and of the assemblies of the people? In the latter case one might be tempted to draw the conclusion that the balance between the three branches was not quite even and that the Senate was the weakest of the three. Yet most modern historians are agreed that at the time of the Second Punic War and in the time of Polybius it was really the Senate that had the greatest political power, and Polybius appears to agree with them when he says [10] that Carthage was defeated because she already had reached a stage in which the people had the decisive power, while in Rome the Senate was in the period of its greatest strength.

Finally, in the last section of the second part, Polybius tries to show how the power of the people is checked by the consuls and the Senate. Yet he does not mention any check on the power of the people in their official assemblies, but speaks only of the dependence of a large section of the people individually on the good will of the Senate and the consuls, while when speaking of the restriction of the power of the Senate, he says that the Senate as a political body can be deprived of

its powers by the assembly of the people "if someone can be found who
will propose a law to that effect." In other words, the power of the
people against the Senate is a clear political right; the power of the
Senate to check the people is exercised through indirect political and
economic pressure. Such pressures undoubtedly have always played a
very great part in the distribution of power within a state, and Polybius is therefore quite right in mentioning them. But it is somewhat
misleading and does not make for clarity to place legal competences
and power that may be exercised through indirect pressures on the
same plane in the analysis of a constitution. This is especially true of
the Roman constitution, for it will be seen [11] that the people actually
deprived the Senate of one of its most important legal political rights
at a time when their own legal competences were not sufficient to
achieve this aim, and when they had to use indirect political pressure
to attain it. Thus Polybius' analysis in this respect reveals itself as
incomplete since it gives the impression that political pressure could
have been exercised only by the Senate.

There was, on the other hand, even in Polybius' time a deficiency
in the legal competence of the popular assembly, namely the lack of
legislative initiative. He hints at this in the words, "if someone can
be found who will introduce a bill to that effect," but he does not
clearly explain it. In fact, the preceding quotation from Polybius'
analysis does not reveal, but rather conceals, a most important problem. In Polybius' time the tribunes of the plebs had the right to introduce bills which, if accepted by a majority of votes, became law. Of
these tribunes of the plebs Polybius says a little later that "they are
obliged always to do what appears good to the people and must always
aim at the satisfaction of the desire of the people." [12] If this is literally
true, then the words "if someone can be found who will introduce a
bill to that effect" are almost superfluous. For if the people are clamor-
ing for a law the tribunes will be obliged to introduce a bill in com-
pliance with their wishes. That Polybius nevertheless inserted the
sentence, "if someone can be found etc.," appears to indicate that he
was not quite certain that the tribunes would always act in accordance
with the will of the people; and in fact less than twenty years after
Polybius had written the sixth book of his work, during the tribuneship of Ti. Gracchus a plebeian tribune, M. Octavius, not only did not

support but actually vetoed the introduction of a bill which the overwhelming majority of the popular assembly wanted to become law. This shows that it is necessary to make a more detailed analysis than that of Polybius if the complicated interplay between legal competences and extralegal political pressures which developed under the Roman constitution is to be fully understood.

This brief survey will have been sufficient to show that Polybius' seemingly lucid account of the distribution of power in the Roman Republic presents a great many difficulties, several of which can be discovered (though not completely understood in their import) without any knowledge of the history of the Roman constitution not derived from Polybius' own report. In attempting to find a solution of these difficulties it will perhaps be instructive to remain as long as possible within the boundaries of the knowledge provided by Polybius himself, and to bring in extraneous information only as it becomes strictly necessary.

The most puzzling point in Polybius' report is in his remarks about the control over the finances in the Roman Republic. Who had the first right to make disbursements from the public treasury, according to his account? Obviously the consuls; for, while in the beginning of the second chapter Polybius says that the Senate had "complete control over the finances," he hastens to add "with the exception of the expenditures made at the order of the consuls." Likewise, when he later points out that a consul cannot even bring a war to successful conclusion without the good will of the Senate, he does not say "if the Senate refuses to grant the necessary money," but "if the Senate prevaricates," or more literally, "if the Senate uses deliberate chicanery." Clearly, then, the legal right in such cases was on the side of the consul. But it is equally clear that in Polybius' opinion the consul could not effectively make use of his right if the Senate chose to be obstructive. Therefore we have here a clear case of a discrepancy between legal and actual powers, though Polybius does not say so expressly.

How could this discrepancy arise? A large part of the answer can still be given on the basis of Polybius' own report. The conduct of a war is obviously the occasion on which a consul—or if there were two wars at the same time, both consuls—had to be away from Rome.

When the consuls are away from home, Polybius says, the Roman state appears to be an aristocratic republic. The Senate's actual, though not in all respects legal, control over the treasury during the absence of the consuls can now serve as a concrete illustration of this general statement. Obviously when both consuls were acting as supreme commanders in different wars—fought simultaneously in different parts of the world at a considerable distance from the capital—neither of them was able to make unrestricted use of his right to withdraw any amount of money he wished from the public treasury as long as the available funds were not absolutely unlimited. What was taken by one consul could not be taken by the other; and it is equally clear that enough money had to remain in the treasury to care for the most urgent needs of the civil administration. Considering the comparative slowness of communication in antiquity, and the fact that the consuls, when engaged in a war, had to devote most of their time and attention to the military—and sometimes political—problems before them, it was quite impossible for them to keep sufficiently informed of the state of public finances to know exactly what amount they could spend without exhausting the treasury or making it impossible to take care of other essential matters. There had to be, therefore, some agency which decided how much money should go to one consul, how much to the other, and how much should be spent for other purposes. This agency, then, was the Senate. So much can be seen purely on the basis of what we learn from Polybius himself, and this is sufficient to make it clear that the discrepancy between legal rights and actual power was at least partly the product of a conflict between inherited legal provisions and practical necessities that had developed under changing circumstances; for in the old times when Rome was still small and its wars were fought not far from the capital, this particular problem did not arise.

In actual fact the history of the control of the finances in the Roman Republic is a good deal more complicated, and in order to understand it completely it is now necessary to bring in extraneous knowledge. Polybius himself says [13] that the most comprehensive item of expenditure, that for the construction and repair of public works (provision for which was made every five years by the censors), was under the control of the Senate. The censorship had first been introduced in the year 443 or 436 B.C., and there can hardly be any doubt that before that date the control of the finances had been entirely in the hands of the consuls, though, as in all important matters, the consuls would have consulted the Senate on this subject whenever decisions of higher importance had to be made.[14] It was the purpose of the introduction of this new magistracy to relieve the consuls of part of the administrative burden which, with the growth of Rome, had become too great for two men.

From the beginning the censors were entrusted with keeping the citizen lists, which included the voting lists, the army list, and the tax lists. Their other tasks and related powers appear to have developed gradually from this original function. Thus, when with the expansion of Roman domination in Italy there developed the necessity for large public works—buildings, roads, aqueducts, harbors, and so forth—which the consuls because of their other tasks were totally unable to supervise, it was natural that this function should be taken over by the censors who, through their concern with taxation, were already engaged in the supervision of public finances. It then became customary for the Senate to deliberate every five years on how much money should be assigned to the censors for works to be undertaken at public expense, while the distribution of this money and the conclusion of individual contracts with builders were left to the discretion of the censors. Since censors, however, were elected only every five years, and their term of office was only one year (later one year and a half), there arose, not infrequently, the necessity of providing for additional public works while there were no censors. In this case it was again the Senate which "advised" what works were to be undertaken, how much money should be assigned for them, and which of the existing officials was to be entrusted with their supervision. Still later, when Rome had extended its domination beyond the boundaries of Italy, when more armies than the consuls could effectively command had to be kept in the field or as garrisons, and when allocations had to be made for these purposes and for the administration of the provinces, it was again the Senate that actually controlled these matters.

Thus, in the course of time, the control of public finances slipped completely from the hands of the consuls. But, as Polybius indicates, it was still the official theory that the consuls did not require the authorization of the Senate when they wished to make disbursements from the public treasury; they still were officially the holders of its keys.[15] But it is equally clear that in actual fact they now always abided by the decisions of the Senate, even where it was most inconvenient for them, and where they may have felt that the Senate engaged in chicanery.[16] What is interesting in this development is the fact that this transfer of one of the most important functions and powers in the state, the control of finances, from the consuls to the Senate does not appear to have been effected by any laws, but came about through practical necessity and custom. When it had become perfectly clear for some time that the consuls were practically unable to control the public finances and that the Senate was the only agency which possessed both the necessary knowledge and authority to control the state funds, it became the custom for the consuls to abide by the decisions of the Senate even when they believed them to be wrong,[17] and even though they were still aware that they had a legal right to disregard them.

Public finances, however, are not the only field in which the power of the Senate, in the course of time, increased enormously through practical necessity. Polybius mentions it as one of the functions of the Senate to determine how foreign embassies coming to Rome should be received and what answer was to be given to them. As in other connections, the expression used by Polybius to designate this power of the Senate is rather vague. But it is clear that the Senate had something to do with the conduct of foreign policy. We know from Polybius and other sources that the declaration of war, as well as the conclusion of peace and any other treaties with foreign nations, was subject to the final decision of the assembly of the people. The proposal for any such measure had to be introduced in the assembly by a magistrate, and usually, though not necessarily, on the advice of the Senate. The assembly was then free to accept or reject the proposal. But since the people could not conduct the negotiations, it was not too difficult, at a time when foreign affairs had become rather complicated, to force the hand of the assembly. A famous case of this kind happened in the aftermath of the Second Punic War, when, immediately following this war which had been so costly to the Romans, the Senate wished to declare war against Philip of Macedon, and the assembly of the people voted almost unanimously against the proposal.[18] Yet the

Senate succeeded in conducting the negotiations and in presenting the situation in such a way that not very long afterwards the people reversed their decision. Where foreign affairs have become too complicated for the people to form a well-founded opinion about them, the actual power in this field will naturally fall to him who controls the negotiations with foreign powers.

Again it appears beyond doubt that originally, and in fact throughout the first centuries of the Republic, the conduct of such negotiations had been the domain of the consuls, though they acted of course after consultation with the Senate. Since the consuls' term of office was restricted to one year, and foreign policy, even in the early period of the Republic, must have required some long-range planning, the influence of the Senate in foreign affairs must have been rather strong at all times, and this inference is confirmed by the ancient tradition. Yet in this respect also there is a marked change in the period of Polybius. The reasons for it are quite analogous to those in the field of finance. As in the course of the third century the political horizon of the Romans widened and they came in contact with greater powers, long-range foreign policy became still more important, and this in itself was bound to increase the influence of the permanent body which advised the changing consuls, since it would have been disastrous if each new pair of consuls had entered upon a new foreign policy. Still more important is the fact that in the beginning of the second century b.c. foreign affairs became so complicated that the consuls, who at the same time were overburdened with military tasks, became totally unable to handle them. Thus the Senate took over and not only received foreign embassies in the absence of the consuls, but sent out commissions and individuals with the order to conduct negotiations on prescribed lines, to make demands, to threaten war, or to make offers. In this period the consuls, when present in Rome and presiding over the Senate, may still have had considerable influence on the latter's decisions, but when they were absent from Rome and concerned with problems of foreign policy they became essentially agents of the Senate, not very different from the commissioners who were sent out directly by that body. Or, to describe the facts still more accurately: there are some instances in which a consul tried to follow a somewhat more independent course in negotiating with emissaries of foreign powers. But since what he did had to fit somehow into the over-all picture of Roman foreign policy and since this picture was for the most part determined by what had been decided before the consul's term of office and by what was done by agents of the Senate, his freedom of choice was very greatly limited. For the same reason the consuls, even when present in Rome, were no longer able to conduct Roman foreign policy with the mere advice and help of the Senate because this policy involved too many things which were completely beyond their reach.

Foreign policy, then, is another field in which the functions and concomitant powers of the Senate increased enormously through sheer practical necessity and without any corresponding change in the laws of the country. This change was all the more important because the apparent success of the Senate in this field greatly increased its prestige with the people.

Another privilege of the Senate mentioned by Polybius was its power to prolong the military command of a magistrate. This power, again, had been only recently acquired. The term for this prolongation of command was *prorogatio imperii*. Such extension of a military command beyond a magistrate's term of office became necessary as the number of wars which the Romans had to conduct simultaneously increased, and as wars, which in former times had been conducted only in summer time, extended through the winter; i.e., the time when the new magistrates and commanders entered their office. The term *prorogatio* (derived from *rogatio*, which means a bill introduced in an assembly of the people) indicates that such extension of office originally had to be voted on by the people, and since the commanders were elected by the people for one year, it is logical that an extension of their command beyond this term should also have had to be granted by the people. In fact, tradition tells us [19] that this was the case when such a step was taken for the first time in 327 B.C. and for some time afterwards. But as early as the last decades of the third century B.C. we find that such extensions of military command took place on a simple senatus consultum, and this is obviously the custom that Polybius describes. It is generally assumed that the change was made by a law, probably of 227 B.C. (the year in which the third and fourth praetorships were introduced), though we have no tradition whatever about such a law. But assuming that there was a law by which the people granted the Senate the right to extend the military command of magistrates without confirmation by an assembly of the people, it is still clear that the change was brought about by practical necessity. As the military tasks of this kind increased it must often have become necessary to make the decision quickly whereby a commander was entitled to retain his command, and in such cases the Senate probably expressed the opinion [20] that it was in the interest of the state that he retain it provisionally until confirmation by an assembly of the people could be obtained. Perhaps it is then not completely impossible that, after this had happened many times, confirmation was more and more delayed, and finally forgotten, until in the end it became the custom for the Senate to act on its own. But if a law was passed giving the Senate this power officially, as is more probable, it was passed because of the same practical necessity.

Another important power of the Senate was its share in the distribution and assignment of provinces. "Province" did not originally mean a territory, but a field of activity, and came to mean a territory only when later it happened more and more often that the field of activity of a magistrate was identified with a territory. Since the two consuls had equal power but their tasks were manifold, it was not practicable that they should always attend to everything together. Therefore, especially if a war was to be waged, a decision had to be made as to which of the two should take command in the war and which should stay in Rome as head of the civil administration. According to custom this was left to the discretion of the consuls. They could decide the question by mutual consent or they could draw lots, as very often was done. But they could also invoke the decision of the Senate. It is probably on this basis that the Senate occasionally made an attempt to take the decision into its own hands.

There is an interesting case in the beginning of the third century. Livy reports [21] that in 295 B.C. the Senate assigned the command in Etruria to the consul Q. Fabius. But the other consul, P. Decius, protested against this interference, which shows that in this case the consuls had not agreed to submit the question to the arbitration of the Senate. The question was then brought before an assembly of the people, which confirmed the decision of the Senate. But this, as later developments show, did not mean that from then on the power of assigning provinces to each of the consuls was in the hands of the Senate. On the contrary, it meant that in case of a difference of opinion in this respect between the Senate and one of the consuls—if the consuls agreed with one another the Senate had no power anyway—the Senate and the consul were two parties between whom the people had to decide.

The influence of the Senate in the assignment and distribution of provinces increased nevertheless in the course of time, though not without occasional resistance of the magistrates to the Senate's arrogation of new powers to itself. In 210 B.C., for instance,[22] the Senate had "decreed" that one of the consuls should conduct the war against Hannibal while the other should go to Sicily and at the same time take over the command of the navy. No objection was raised to this decree, since it was natural that the consuls should take over the two main commands in the war against Carthage. However, the Senate did not say which consul should take over which command; therefore, the consuls drew lots. The result of this lottery was that the command in Italy fell to Valerius Laevinus, the command over the navy and in Sicily to M. Marcellus. When this became known in Sicily the Sicilians complained bitterly because they had experienced the harshness of Marcellus on an earlier occasion. Then the Senate requested the consuls "to consult the Senate concerning an exchange of their provinces." Upon this Marcellus declared that he was willing to exchange his province for that of his colleague if the latter were agreeable, but that *he did not recognize any right of the Senate to request him to do so.*

Five years later a quarrel arose because Scipio, as consul-elect, was said to have stated that if he was not going to be assigned the task of carrying the war into Africa he would appeal to an assembly of the people.[23] The case is quite different from the case of Valerius Laevinus and Claudius Marcellus. The quarrel did not concern the distribution of tasks between the two consuls, but the task or province itself. Since the other consul-elect, P. Licinius Crassus, happened to be Pontifex Maximus and was not allowed to leave Italy because of his priesthood, it was clear that any task outside of Italy to be taken over by a consul would have to be assigned to the other consul, i.e., to Scipio. The question therefore was whether the war was to be carried into Africa at all.

It was customary for the consuls to consult the Senate at the beginning of their terms of office concerning the most important tasks to
which they would have to attend. In accordance with this custom Scipio
consulted the Senate as to whether he should carry the war into Africa,
i.e., whether carrying the war into Africa should be one of the provinces of the consuls. Yet he had let it be known, even before he had
entered upon his office, that if the Senate should decide that the war
should not be carried into Africa he would not abide by the decision
of the Senate but would appeal to the people. This attitude, according
to Livy,[24] naturally caused great resentment in the Senate. For it was
said that it was making a farce of the consultation of the Senate if the
consul let it be known beforehand that he would listen to the advice
of the Senate only if it agreed with his own previously expressed
wish. After Fabius Maximus had pointed this out and had strongly
advised against Scipio's plan another leading senator, Q. Fulvius, who
had been consul four times and once censor, refused, when called upon
to speak, to give his opinion unless Scipio promised to abide by the
decision of the Senate.[25] At the same time he called upon the plebeian
tribunes for support.[26] After some discussion the latter decided: (1)
to support the refusal of Fulvius and other senators to discuss the
matter unless Scipio promised to abide by the decision of the Senate,
and (2) in case Scipio did make this promise, to see to it that he could
not go back on it. Upon this Scipio asked permission to consult with his
colleague, and following this consultation agreed to abide by the decision of the Senate. Now the Senate resolved that Sicily and a fleet
of thirty warships should be entrusted to one of the consuls (i.e., to
Scipio, since the other consul could not leave Italy), who would be
given permission to carry the war into Africa "if this should be in the
interest of the Roman Republic." When Scipio consequently went to
Sicily the Senate "prevaricated" so that Scipio could not go to Africa
during his consulate.

This story is most instructive as an illustration of the complicated
interrelations between the different governmental agencies in that
period. The decision over war and peace had always been the preroga-
tive of the assemblies of the people; but no such decision needed to be
made since the war with Carthage had been in progress for a long
time and was not yet at an end. When there was a war it was clearly

part of the competence of the commanding general to decide how and in what place the army should attack the enemy. Yet since it was the task of the Senate to advise the consuls, it had always been customary to consult the Senate on major decisions and in more recent times this custom had come to imply the assignment of major fields of activity to the consuls at the beginning of their year of office. There can be no doubt (and it is additionally confirmed by the story as told by Livy) that the consuls were not obliged to abide by the decision of the Senate. Yet the authority and prestige of the Senate at that time were so great that it was not easy to act against it. Scipio obviously neither dared to break with the custom of consulting the Senate on the major decisions of the year nor did he dare to act contrary to the wishes of the Senate without appealing to the decision of the people. He appears to have tried to make the Senate vote in agreement with his wishes by declaring beforehand that otherwise he would not obey. But in this way he only increased the difficulty. For now the senators could declare, not without justification, that this was an insult, and could refuse to enter upon the customary debate.

The role played by the tribunes of the plebs in this impasse is also very interesting. The tribunes were in no way obliged to obey the Senate. But at that time their solidarity with the Senate was already so great that they supported the Senate leader Fulvius against the independent-minded consul. They said that they would use their power of intercession if the consul should try to appeal to the people against the decision of the Senate. They also supported the refusal of the leading senators to debate the question unless the consul promised to heed the advice of the Senate. But this clearly left it open to the consul to act without consulting the Senate at all. In this situation Scipio consulted with his colleague and came to the conclusion that it would be better not to violate the established custom in so flagrant a fashion. But the Senate also realized that it would be better to compromise on an issue in which it had the established custom, but not a law, on its side. Thus the Senate approved of Scipio's carrying the war into Africa, "if this should be in the interest of the Republic," but then maneuvered so that Scipio was unable to carry out his intentions anyway. The Senate's weakness on the legal side and its actual strength, both through established custom and through the force of circumstances, could not be better illustrated than by this example. It is also interesting to see that in the end it was the Senate that prevailed in this conflict with a consul who even at that time enjoyed an enormous prestige and obviously could reckon with the support of the popular assembly if it was consulted.

The cases discussed so far concern the assignment and distribution of special tasks or "provinces" to the regular consuls who officially had the over-all direction of the affairs of the state. But now there were also "provinces" in the geographical sense. Since the year 366 B.C. an increasing number of praetorships had been created to relieve the consuls of part of their burden and to attend to special tasks. By the beginning of the second century B.C.—the exact date is 197 B.C.—the number of praetors had been increased to six, the first praetor (since 366) having the jurisdiction in Rome, the second (since 242) the jurisdiction in causes between citizens and noncitizens, the third and fourth (since 227) in Sicily and Sardinia respectively, and the fifth and sixth in the two Spanish provinces. This increase in the praetorships is a development which also shows the transition from nonterritorial provinces to fields of activity that are circumscribed by limits of a territory rather than function. These praetors were elected by the people, so that the Senate was not directly concerned. Yet, since it was an acknowledged principle that the Senate should use its authority to make provisions for emergencies, it happened even in this period that two provinces, in this case the *jurisdictio urbana* and the *jurisdictio peregrina*, were assigned to the same man in order to make the praetor who normally would have acted as judge *inter cives et peregrinos* available for a military command.[27]

Much more important is the development in regard to the assignment of provinces in the second century. The rapid expansion of Roman domination in the eastern Mediterranean and then in Africa in that period required the creation of an increasing number of special military commands, which, after the victory, gradually turned into administrative-diplomatic assignments until they finally became governorships. Yet until the Sullan reforms no new praetorships were created and the new posts were filled by the device of the *prorogatio imperii*. While in the beginning the *prorogatio imperii* had been an emergency measure and the command accordingly had been prolonged only for a short time or "until the completion of the task on hand," it now became customary to assign a command or governorship for a regular year by *prorogatio*. Thus the comparatively recently acquired control over the *prorogatio imperii* and the newly increased influence in the assignment and distribution of provinces combined to enlarge the power of the Senate over the magistrates and thus over the Republic. Naturally this power was greatest in the period of transition when ever-new decisions had to be made. In the second half of the second century, when conditions had become more settled, when a number of definitely circumscribed territorial provinces had been created and certain customary rules concerning their assignment and distribution had developed, the discretionary power of the Senate in this field became somewhat less great. Yet it remained very considerable.

The different and to some extent contradictory aspects of this process are well illustrated by a plebiscite introduced and carried by C. Gracchus during his tribuneship in 123 B.C.[28] By this plebiscite the Senate was ordered to designate before the elections the "consular provinces." This meant now the territorial provinces which the consuls of the following year were to take over after the end of their consulate. The purpose of the law was to prevent the Senate from knowing to whom the provinces would actually fall. The plebiscite therefore was obviously meant to restrict the powers of the Senate and to prevent political intrigues. Yet at the same time it indirectly confirmed—even though on a very restricted scale—the role which a long time before the Senate had arrogated to itself in the distribution of provinces.[29]

With these examples the analysis of those powers of the Senate which developed through a change in circumstances and the practical necessities arising from them could be concluded; for the evidence is clear enough. But since Polybius mentions among the functions of the Senate its role in the administration of justice and in the control over the noncitizen communities of Italy, a few words about these two subjects may be added.

As almost everywhere in the chapter on the powers of the Senate, the expression used by Polybius to characterize this competence of the Senate is extremely weak: "All those crimes committed in Italy which require a public investigation, for instance conspiracy, poison-

ings, and assassination, *are the concern of the Senate.*" In actual fact
the Senate in the time of the Republic never acted as a law court or
possessed any private or criminal jurisdiction,[30] but there were several
ways in which either the Senate as a body or individual senators concerned themselves, or were concerned, with the investigation or punishment of crimes. In the course of time, as the advice given by the
Senate assumed more and more the form of directives given to the
magistrates, the Senate not infrequently requested a consul or a praetor to make an investigation when crimes had been committed or were
suspected of having been committed, and to see to it that the culprits
were found and punished. It could instruct the magistrates under
what law or laws the members of certain organizations which appeared
obnoxious to the Senate could and should be prosecuted. It could,
and often did, promise rewards to informers, and sometimes requested
magistrates to grant impunity to participants in illegal activities or
associations if they were willing to turn state's evidence. It could also
ask the assembly of the people to order the creation of a special law
court to deal with a crime or a set of crimes which appeared dangerous
to the community. Furthermore, it became customary to select the
jurors for these law courts from among the senators, especially in the
trials of provincial governors accused of extortion, until, in 123 or 122
B.C., C. Gracchus, or perhaps his fellow-tribune M'.Acilius Glabrio
on his instigation, introduced and carried a bill according to which
the jurors in these trials were to be selected from equites who were
not senators.[31] Indirectly, therefore, the Senate had a very considerable influence in the field of jurisdiction, even though it never acted
as a law court in the republican period.

The position of the Senate in regard to the noncitizen communities
in Italy, which Polybius also mentions, is extremely complicated. Since
the Romans claimed a kind of sovereignty over communities and
nations with which they had treaties and which they also called their
allies, the boundaries between foreign policy and jurisdiction are here
fluid and not always easy to define. It is not possible, therefore, to
deal with this matter adequately in the present context, and it must
suffice to state that in this field, as in the field of jurisdiction over
individuals, the influence of the Senate undoubtedly increased within
the period preceding the Second Punic War. But the implication of

this development within these fields is not so easy to see as in the fields of finances, of foreign policy, and of the distribution of provinces.

The increase of the power of the Senate in the absence of any proportionate corresponding legislation is all the more remarkable because in the very same period in which this happened the Senate was, in two steps, deprived of one of its most essential legal powers. First, through the Publilian law of 339 B.C., the Senate was deprived of its right to invalidate a law accepted by the assembly of the people by withholding its *auctoritas* or ratification,[32] though the same law ordered the Senate to give its authorization *before* the law was put to the vote in the assembly of the people. Much more important was the second step, the Hortensian law of 287 B.C., which was passed after the third and last secession of the plebs, and which ordered that henceforth plebiscites, i.e., bills that could be introduced by the tribunes of the plebs, which were voted on by the plebeians to the exclusion of the patricians, and which required no authorization by the Senate if accepted by the plebeian assembly,[33] were to have the force of laws.

Thus it is obvious that the powers of the Senate not only increased without the increase finding expression in corresponding legislation, but this happened at a time when the people made strenuous and, on the purely legal side, successful attempts to decrease these powers. In order to understand this paradoxical phenomenon it is necessary to distinguish clearly between the legal and extralegal foundations of the Roman constitution.

Though the Roman constitution was of course not a written constitution, there existed at the time of Polybius a great many laws which we would consider constitutional laws and which were preserved in their original wording. This was most probably the case with the Publilian and Hortensian laws mentioned above, with the law by which the second praetorship was introduced in the year 243 B.C., and with many other laws which, by their content, can be characterized as constitutional in the sense in which we use this word, though they had been passed, like all other laws, by a simple majority of an assembly of the people. Whether the law by which the first praetorship and the two curule aedileships were introduced in 367 B.C. was still extant in its original wording at the time of Polybius is doubtful—it was not in the time of Livy—but when the law was passed it certainly must have contained specifically worded regulations concerning the powers and functions of these new magistrates. The laws of the Twelve Tables which had been composed by the two Commissions of Ten Men of 450 and 449 B.C., and which were not constitutional laws, were still recited in the schools at the time of Cicero though the original tables themselves appear no longer to have been in existence at that time. Authors of as late a period as the Augustan age even believed that they knew the original wording of the Valerio-Horatian law by which, in 449 or 448, the inviolability of the tribunes of the plebs was legally confirmed, though they do not quote it in the original fifth-century Latin.[34]

All these laws, however, are in a way amendments of an existing constitution. If one asks on what basis the remainder of the constitution rested, the usual answer is, on custom or on the *mos maiorum*, the ancestral tradition. This answer is not wrong, but it requires considerable clarification.[35] We know hardly anything about the way in which the republican "constitution" was created and formulated towards the end of the sixth century B.C., after the overthrow of the monarchy. The art of writing was doubtless known at that time in Rome, though it was not yet used very much. At any rate, the most fundamental principles of the new political order must in some way have been formulated at that time. One formula, for instance, still used in later times—the formula *in re pari maior causa prohibentis*, which meant essentially that in case of a definite conflict of opinion between the two consuls, who have equal power, the opinion of him who negatives a proposed action shall prevail—seems to go back to the very earliest Republic, though its earliest extant quotation is late and again not worded in the Latin of the sixth century B.C. Yet if one may judge on general grounds and on the analogy of what happened in sixth-century Athens, it does not appear likely that the constitutional competences of the consuls, for instance, were described and formulated in detail, much less that such formulations were recorded in writing. It is much more probable that the consuls took over all the functions of the former kings, subject to the new restrictions imposed on them with the abolishment of the monarchy, and that it was these restrictions, if anything, that found expression in definite formulae, whether the latter were written down in the form of constitutional documents or not.

Thus we find that even in the very beginning of the Roman Republic it was the *changes* in the constitution which were definitely formulated, and not the body of the constitution. If, then, one goes back to still earlier times in order to find out where these remaining parts of the constitution came from he loses himself in the darkness of a period about the legislative processes of which not only we, but also the Romans of the time of Polybius, had no definite knowledge. Therefore, since nobody knows or knew of a formulated law by which the various functions and powers of the consuls were defined, it is perhaps legitimate to say that the consuls held these powers, in so far as they had not been abolished by a later law, by ancestral custom. Yet it is essential to understand that these powers, which were inherited from the beginning of the Republic, were considered to belong to the consuls *by right* no less than if a law conferring them had been known, since all those provisions which were taken over into the new order at the time of the establishment of the Republic, even if not expressly defined and formulated, were considered as constitutional law. In fact, what Polybius says about the right of the consuls to make any expenditures they wish from the public treasury without authorization of the Senate shows that this right was still considered constitutional law when it was no longer effective in practice.

From this *mos maiorum*, which was intended as constitutional law though not formulated in a dated legal document,[36] one must distinguish that kind of *mos maiorum* which developed without such legal intent out of practical expediency and necessity. This latter kind might become very strong. The acceptance even by the enemy of the Senate C. Gracchus, of the (purely customary) right of the Senate to determine which provinces should be consular and which praetorian is proof of this. Yet such a right could always be challenged as long as someone happened to remember that it had only sprung from custom and had never been confirmed by law. Above all, however, such practices were not from the beginning *mos maiorum*. There is by necessity a first time for any such practice to be introduced, in a situation that cannot be handled effectively in any other way. It would be rather ridiculous to call "ancestral custom" a practice that had been introduced for the first time only some twenty or thirty years before, nor is there any evidence that the expression was used in such cases in antiquity, though this has been done occasionally in recent articles on problems of Roman history of the Republic.

It is then this time of transition that was decisive for the final acceptance of the practice. If the practical necessity was very strong the new custom prevailed: if not, it could not only be challenged but the challenge might be successful. Again the distribution of provinces can be used as an example, since the Senate did not succeed in obtaining complete control over it. This example is rather interesting, since it is doubtful whether it was really in the interest of good administration to let the drawing of lots decide which of the consular tasks an individual consul or praetor would undertake. But the fear that, in consequence of the factional struggles constantly taking place in the Senate, the decision would be more through favor than according to the appropriateness of the assignments was too strong, and so the practice of senatorial decision in this area had to be abandoned. This happened because in the period of transition the practice was challenged again and again. But if a new practice went unchallenged for a very considerable period of time it appears gradually to have been accepted as binding and nobody asked any longer whether it had a foundation in law or not.

The evidence presented so far tends to show that within the two hundred years from the middle of the fourth century to the middle of the second, the power of the Senate increased enormously, although in the beginning of that period the Senate had been deprived of most of its legal powers by law, and although it seems that hardly any laws increasing the power of the Senate were passed throughout the whole period. The reason for this growth of the Senate's power seems to have been practical necessity: the consuls could no longer attend adequately to the tasks which were theirs according to the old constitutional regulations. Thus the Senate had to take over a large part of the consuls' functions, and naturally acquired all the powers connected with them.

This, however, is still a very imperfect answer to the question of why the powers of the Senate grew so rapidly in this period. The consuls were no longer able to attend to all the tasks with which they had been entrusted because of the growing needs of an expanding empire. Thus the increase of the powers of the Senate seems to be due to the expansion of Roman domination first over the Italian peninsula, then over the whole Mediterranean world. But most modern students of Roman history agree that the expansion of Roman domination brought about the downfall of the Roman Republic and of the oligarchic senatorial regime, and made its replacement by a monarchy inevitable. If this view is accepted one would then have to arrive at the somewhat strange conclusion that the direction of the expanding Roman empire had to pass from the hands of the monarchic element in Rome—the consuls—into those of the oligarchic element—the Senate —because the administration became more complex, and that it had to pass from this oligarchic regime to a monarchic one when the administrative tasks became still more complex. This seems to show that the course of history cannot be adequately explained in quite such simple terms, and that possibly the apparently inexorable historical necessity may to some extent depend on the kind of institutions that human beings create and on the decisions that they make.

The question that must be asked at this point is obviously twofold. Why were the consuls no longer able to handle the administrative tasks? And why was it the Senate to which most of the functions that they could no longer exercise accrued? The greater part of the answer to the second question must be reserved for later chapters, where there will also be discussion of the questions of why the Senate later lost the same functions and powers and why the development ultimately resulted in the establishment of a monarchy.

A first but somewhat superficial answer to the first question has been given by Polybius, and a somewhat more explicit answer is implied in the analysis attempted above. The consuls were no longer able to attend efficiently to all their traditional tasks because they had to act not only as heads of state but at the same time as supreme commanders in the field, and because the military and administrative tasks had multiplied in the century from 250 to 150 B.C. But the Hellenistic kings also frequently commanded their own armies and yet did not lose control over foreign policy or finances in their kingdoms; the administrative problems of the Seleucid empire, for example, cannot have been much less great than those of Rome at the end of the third or at the beginning of the second century B.C.

The real answer is that the consuls had no cabinet. In the very earliest period of the Roman Republic, when Rome was still small, there appear to have been only two magistrates, the quaestors, besides the consuls. Their duties and functions in that early period were not yet restricted to the financial field, but they were subordinate to the consuls on the governmental level in general.[37] Furthermore, in this earliest period the quaestors were not elected by the assembly of the people, but were selected by the consuls themselves. Thus there existed no official distinction of provinces or fields of activity except in so far as the consuls might agree to distribute their tasks among themselves, and as they delegated certain of these tasks to their general assistants, the quaestors. The introduction of the censorship in 443 B.C. was therefore a great innovation in two respects; for the censors not only relieved the consuls of part of the administrative burden, which had become too heavy, but they were the first magistrates in Rome to whom a restricted field of activity was assigned ex officio (i.e., by virtue of their office). Unlike the quaestors, furthermore, they were directly elected by the people, and since they were elected only every fifth year and for a term of only one year, so that their orders remained valid[38] through the following four consulates, they were largely independent of the consuls. The censorship, however, was always officially considered inferior to the consulship and in the early period was not yet (as it was in later times) the most honored office in the Republic.

If the ancient tradition is correct,[39] one year before the introduction of the censorship an attempt had been made to solve the problem of the overburdening of the consuls in a different fashion. Instead of two consuls, three generals or "military tribunes" with consular power had been elected. But after three months they had been replaced by two consuls. The expedient found in the following year through the introduction of the censorship may at first have appeared more satisfactory, but it soon proved insufficient. Therefore the Romans a few years later (in 438 B.C.) returned to the solution which had been attempted, but quickly abandoned, in 444: the election of three military tribunes with consular power. At first this expedient was used only rarely, when the military tasks were especially heavy—i.e., when several wars were being fought simultaneously in different places. But with the rapid expansion of Rome towards the end of the fifth century and the beginning of the fourth, the election of more than two military tribunes instead of two consuls became for a considerable time almost the rule, and the number of consular tribunes was often increased so that in some years there were four or even six consular tribunes, all with equal competence and power.

This was an arrangement which could function only so long as many of these tribunes were engaged as commanders of armies in different locations. It could no longer function when, some time after the conquest of Rome by the Gauls in 388 B.C., the Romans had reconquered most of the territory lost in consequence of this temporary catastrophe, and were compelled for some time to turn to other urgent tasks. The most important problems with which they were faced at that time were the rebuilding of what had been destroyed by the Gauls, and the litigation developing from the fact that many property rights had become uncertain when so much territory had been conquered and in turn reconquered by the warring parties. Obviously two consuls, with not only the functions of heads of state and of supreme commanders, but also of heads of the city administration and of supreme judges, were no longer sufficient to attend to all these tasks. It was equally clear that the election of three, four, or six supreme magistrates with equal competence and power was no solution either, since they would be in each other's way. There was an urgent need for another differentiation of functions.

The decisive step was taken in 367 through the creation for the following year of three new magistrates—the praetor, who took over the judicial functions of the consuls, and the two *aediles curules* who were entrusted with the most important tasks of the city administration— city police, market police, sanitation, supervision of building, and so on. These new magistrates, like the censors, were elected by the people, and they were elected for specialized duties. They were considered inferior and in a way subordinate to the consuls. The praetor received, in addition to his judicial function, an *imperium minus*, which meant that in case of an emergency he could act as supreme commander of an army, but in a case of conflict with a consul would have to obey the latter's orders. Yet since these magistrates were elected directly by the people, and since the consuls, who were elected at the same time, had no influence on their selection, they attended to their tasks quite independently of the consuls. Above all they did not form a cabinet. There were no regular meetings of the consuls with the other higher magistrates, except inasmuch as all of them, when present in Rome, would attend the meetings of the Senate, all being senators ex officio.

It is very likely that when in 242 another praetor was added to relieve the original one of the jurisdiction between citizens and noncitizens, and in 227 two more praetors for the first territorial provinces of Sicily and Sardinia respectively, each praetor was at first still elected for his specific task. But some time earlier it had become necessary to create, so to speak, temporary additional magistrates by the device of the *prorogatio imperii*, which, as shown above, by an inevitable process became one of the most important privileges of the Senate. In the course of this process it became necessary with increasing frequency for a praetor elected for a judicial function to take over a military command, and again it fell to the Senate to advise when this was necessary and who should take over the command. Finally when the number of praetors was further increased at a time when the numerous tasks for which they were now needed were still in flux, it became entirely impossible for each praetor to be elected for a specific task. Regularly the "provinces" were distributed by lot. But this is also the period in which the Senate attempted to usurp the distribution of provinces; in this attempt, however, it was only partly successful.

All this makes it abundantly clear that the historical necessity by which the Senate acquired all the functions described above and the political power inevitably connected with those functions, was a necessity only because and as long as the consuls had no cabinet but were surrounded by magistrates directly elected by the people and, if not in theory, at least in practice, very largely independent of the consuls.

But why, then, was this strange arrangement made? The answer is suggested by the fact that within the same period in which the new magistracies were created, the quaestorships, which originally had been filled by men selected by the consuls, were also made elective,[40] and it was also in the same period that the people struggled violently, and successfully, to deprive the Senate of its most important legal powers. There can then be little doubt that the main reason was the fear that the consuls might become too powerful if they were allowed to choose their own cabinet ministers.

This makes the problem of historical and practical necessity appear again in a somewhat different light. It was not necessary for the powers of the Senate to grow as they did, nor would this have happened if essentially the same powers had been given to the consuls or to some third agency. But when the attempt was made to restrict the powers of the consuls and of the Senate at the same time, and this while the tasks of the government were increasing, the powers which the consuls were prevented from acquiring simply accrued to the Senate. In other words, there was a time in which there existed the possibility of a free choice by the people to allow either the consuls or the Senate, or possibly some third agency, to acquire these powers, but it was not possible to prevent these powers from developing altogether. Wherever there are urgent tasks which must be done, the agency which attends to them will always acquire the powers which are inevitably connected with this function, and when the attempt is made to prevent this by purely negative laws, the result will merely be that these powers will arise in some unexpected place. What is more, where there is an urgent need for a central direction of many functions it will not even be possible to distribute these powers in such a way that no single agency will become very powerful, but there will also of necessity develop a certain concentration of power if the state is not to perish.

It is at least partly, though not exclusively, such observations which have given rise to the theory that so-called systems of checks and balances are nothing but pleasant illusions, and that in fact there will always be some group or agency which has the decisive power, though this power may in the course of history go from the hands of one group or agency into the hands of another, and though there may therefore be times of transition in which it is not clear in whose hands the decisive power is. But, it is often believed, these will always be times of trouble and disorder.

The adherents of this theory will, as a rule, readily admit that in some countries the unpleasant fact that there is always some supreme power may be hidden from the eyes of the common man by all sorts of constitutional trappings, but in actual fact they believe the difference is not very great. In regard to Roman history the members of this school will say that in the republican period Rome had simply an oligarchic regime and under the empire a monarchic one, whatever the official theory in either period may have been.

There is another school of thought which admits that where the tasks of government are comparatively simple, a genuine distribution and consequent dilution of power is possible, but that in times of stress and emergency in large states such a system must inevitably break down. This school will concede that within certain periods of the earlier history of the Roman Republic there may have existed something approaching a system of checks and balances, or at least a certain actual balance of power between the different parts of the community. But, in their opinion, when Rome expanded beyond a certain area its government became gradually more and more oligarchic. Finally, when the tasks of the government had become more complicated and a still greater centralization became necessary, the oligarchy, in their opinion, inevitably broke down and was replaced by a monarchy. Especially in regard to the last phase of the development this theory has been dominant in the nineteenth century and is still very widely accepted.

Thus the history of Rome and of the Roman constitution appears to provide an excellent testing ground for these various theories, including the theory of Polybius. But in order to apply the test adequately it will be necessary to look at the Roman constitution from many more angles. What has been discussed so far is only a beginning and not yet sufficient as a basis for an adequate solution of the fundamental problem.

VIII

MIXED CONSTITUTION, SEPARATION OF POWERS, AND SYSTEM OF CHECKS AND BALANCES; CHECKS BEYOND BALANCES AND EMERGENCY PROVISIONS

THE CENTRAL THEME of Polybius' political theory is what he calls the "mixed constitution." But his analysis of the Spartan and Roman constitutions shows that a mixed constitution to him is essentially a system of checks and balances. In recent times it has often been said [1] that one must distinguish between a mixed constitution and a system of balances. But no attempt appears to have been made to describe exactly what a mixed constitution and a system of checks and balances have in common and in what respect they differ from one another, much less to apply this distinction systematically in an analysis of the constitution of the Roman Republic.

In order to determine what "mixed constitution" means, or what it meant originally, one must first describe the simple constitutions of which it is supposed to be a mixture. A monarchy is a governmental system in which the supreme power is in the hands of one man, an oligarchy is a system in which the supreme power is in the hands of a definitely circumscribed minority group, and a democracy is a system in which it is in the hands of the people, or one may say, of changing majorities. A mixed constitution, then, by definition is a system in which the supreme power is shared by, and more or less equally distributed among, these three elements. In such a system the powers of the three elements will be balanced against one another, and since by being balanced they inevitably constitute a check upon one another, a mixed constitution will always be a system of checks and balances. This is the way in which Polybius appears to have looked at the matter; and taken in the abstract and without relation to historical reality this seems very simple and plausible.

In terms of historical and political reality the problem is not quite so simple. Even Athenian democracy of the late fifth century, which is perhaps the most extreme democracy that has ever existed in a political community on a higher level of civilization, could not entirely dispense with a government in which there was at least something like a highest magistracy and also a council with important political functions—in Polybius' terms, a monarchic and an oligarchic element. But since all the more important decisions were made directly by the assembly of the people, in which every male citizen could not only vote but speak on the issues at hand, since the magistrates were not selected from a privileged group,[2] and since every provision was made to assure that the archons and the members of the council would not become the rulers or masters of the people but remain its agents and servants, the Athenian constitution has never been considered a mixed constitution nor a system of checks and balances, but simply as "democratic." In the United States none of the members of the government or of the legislature are chosen from a privileged family or privileged group. The President and the members of the legislature are elected by the people, and the government and the legislators are at least theoretically considered agents and servants, not masters and rulers of the people. It has become customary in recent times to call the United States a democracy, and in fact the similarity of its governmental system to that of a democracy is very great. But it is also generally known that, in contrast to the Athenian constitution of the second half of the fifth century B.C. the American constitution was meant to represent, and to some extent actually still represents, a system of checks and balances. This system of checks and balances, however, is not usually called a mixed constitution.

In republican Rome the consuls were elected by the people and were considered the agents of the community rather than its masters or rulers.[3] But throughout the greater part of the history of the Roman Republic they were selected from a privileged class. Polybius calls this system a mixed constitution and describes it as a system of checks and balances. Yet it is not difficult to see that Sparta, where the kings were hereditary and not, like the consuls, elected by the people as temporary agents of the community, comes nearer to the original meaning of the term "mixed constitution" than Rome. Thus in historical reality the distinctions are not so clear, and there are many transitions from one form to the other, though it remains true that a mixed constitution is always a system of checks and balances of some sort, while a system of checks and balances is not necessarily a mixed constitution.

However, the survey which has led to this first conclusion is still very imperfect. It has been based on a tentative distinction between political systems in which the government or the head of the government are rulers and masters, and systems in which they are servants of the people. Most of these concepts are in need of further clarification. "The people" in modern times, but also according to some ancient authors, is often identified with the majority. But Aristotle pointed out long ago that a majority can be just as tyrannical as an individual tyrant or a privileged minority—as a racial or religious majority may, for instance, tyrannize over racial or religious minorities, or a chance majority over individuals and groups. The stock example in antiquity of the latter possibility is the infliction of the death penalty on the generals of the battle of the Arginusae by the majority of the Athenian ekklesia.[4] It is the purpose of systems of checks and balances, if such a thing exists, to curb this many-headed tyrant, the majority, no less than individuals or minorities aspiring to arbitrary power, under the rule of laws which are, or ought to be, for the benefit of the community as a whole and not only for the benefit of the majority.

If, then, we speak of agents or servants of "the people," this should mean agents of the community as a whole, and not merely of the majority or a large minority that may pretend to be the majority, or even to be the whole. But the concept of "agent or servant of the people" is also in need of further clarification. Just as a person or a political body which takes over important political functions will inevitably acquire the power that is necessary for the execution of this task, thus it is impossible to acquire or to retain political power without fulfilling, however imperfectly, certain fundamental functions of an agent or servant of the people. Even the most oppressive tyrant, if he is to retain his power, will have to serve the community by protecting the public order against ordinary criminals and by making provision for defense against a foreign enemy. Likewise, a minority that has acquired political power by the accumulation of wealth could not have accumulated that wealth and could not have continued to hold its power if it had not in some ways served certain interests of the community, though these interests might possibly have been better served in a different way. On the other hand, even the most devoted and unselfish servant on a high level in the community will sometimes, on his own authority and responsibility, have to take energetic coercive action against individuals or groups. Thus, a ruler is inevitably to some extent a servant of the people, and the high-level servant of the people is to some extent a ruler. Nevertheless, it is not only possible but necessary to make the distinction, though it is not quite so simple as it may appear at first sight.

Polybius rightly begins his political analysis with a discussion of the way in which political power is acquired. But he fails to make another most fundamental distinction. According to his theory the cycle of constitutions begins with kingship, which becomes hereditary, the descendants of kings ultimately tend to become tyrants, and are finally overthrown to make room for an aristocratic regime, and so on. The logic of his theory of the cycle, then—though he does not make this quite clear—demands that the overthrow of democracy result in the establishment of kingship, with which the cycle began. Historically, however, democracies have hardly ever been directly replaced by that type of monarchy which in antiquity as well as in modern times has been designated by the name of kingship. In the overwhelming majority of cases they were overthrown by popular or oligarchic leaders, who then set themselves up as sole rulers. Such monarchs, who came to power as leaders and through the support of political parties, were not called kings by the Greeks of the 6th, 5th, and 4th centuries, but tyrants. In the beginning of this period of three hundred years the word had no derogatory meaning. It was, on the contrary, a highly honorific title, derived from the title of certain Oriental rulers, who, in the 7th and 6th centuries had been greatly admired by the Greeks. It is only in the course of the period from the sixth to the fourth century, though comparatively early, that tyrant became a word of opprobrium, and by the beginning of the fourth century this development had progressed so far that any bad or unjust monarch could be called a tyrant, though the original meaning of the word was not yet quite forgotten.

In Polybius' time, unfortunately, this original meaning had been largely obscured, and this prevented him from making a distinction which early Greek history could have taught him to make, and which, as will be seen, would have been of fundamental importance for his political theory. The rulers whom the early Greeks called tyrants came to power as leaders of a party and were supported in power by that party, though once they had established their rule they might also support it by a military force, which was at their service first, and only secondarily at the service of the people. Though, therefore, as rulers they inevitably had to serve the community as a whole to some extent, most of them ruled essentially *for* one part *against* another part of the population.

Some of the Greek tyrants, especially of the sixth century, undoubtedly fulfilled important historical missions—those of that early period, for instance, performed the mission of freeing the impoverished majority from the unbearable economic and political oppression to which they were subjected by aristocracies of wealthy landowners. Yet few escaped the natural consequences of the manner in which they had come to power. Pisistratus, who enjoyed the great advantage that Solon had already carried through the most necessary reforms before him, tried to take a position above the parties after having achieved his main aims. But he was twice driven into exile, and when his son and successor, Hippias, made an attempt to retain his power by force, he became so much hated that the assassins of his brother received semidivine honors as tyrannicides in spite of the fact that they had killed him for private and not for political reasons. Pittacus of Mytilene abdicated voluntarily after having carried through and consolidated the reforms that he considered necessary, and earned the honor of being counted among the Seven Wise Men. But this required extraordinary skill and self-abnegation, and he had to go through desperate struggles before he was able to abdicate. These were the two great exceptions.

Most of the tyrants took what appeared the easier course of ruling with and for their party, and with the support of their military guards against the rest of the population. In this case the fact that reforms were carried through, not by compromise and persuasion but one-sidedly and by force, and that there was no hope of a change of regime except by violence and revolution, naturally created bitter resentment on the part of a large section of the population. In order to overcome the opposition resulting from this resentment, harsh and oppressive measures had to be used, which in turn caused new resentment and potential opposition. Thus, tyranny entered upon a vicious circle from which there was rarely an escape until the system broke down or the tyrant was assassinated, and it is no wonder that the term "tyrant," which once had been a title of honor, within a short time became one of the most hateful words.

This distinction between tyranny and kingship in the original and technical sense is much more important for political theory than the traditional distinction between good and bad, just and unjust mon-archs, which has been adopted by Polybius: for the lusts and desires of an individual as an individual are necessarily of limited scope. This fact can also be illustrated by an interesting example from ancient history. In recent times there has been a tendency to contend that Nero, for instance, cannot have been the kind of man described by Tacitus, because it has been found that the provinces flourished under his rule. But there are numerous uncontestable historical facts which prove that Nero was everything Tacitus says he was, though Tacitus' portrait of Tiberius, for instance, may be distorted. The condition of the provinces has nothing to do with this question. For, since Nero's perversions were only those of an individual, they were not felt beyond his immediate entourage, except perhaps for a lesser influence in the capital; in no way did they affect the empire as a whole. The ruler, on the other hand, who rules essentially as the leader of a party and without a fixed limit of time, is *ipso facto* a tyrant in the technical sense of the word, and if he starts on the vicious circle of oppression of the opposite parties and ever-stricter suppression of any kind of active or passive resistance, the resulting oppression, regardless of the char-acter of the ruler as an individual, will be infinitely more extensive and effective than that which may be found under the rule of a perverted king.

Polybius' discussion of the origin and nature of kingship is much more adequate than his explanation of tyranny as a mere degeneration

of kingship. Kingship, in Polybius' opinion, is based largely on heredity, though there may also be an elective kingship which he appears to
prefer. But even those monarchies which later became hereditary must
at some time have come into being without the benefit of heredity, and
these, Polybius believes, were for the most part established when a
man was made king because of signal services rendered to the community as a whole, most frequently in the field of military leadership
or the administration of justice. This is an oversimplification. Yet it is
not quite wrong.[5] It implies that whatever the king's relation to the
people, it is a direct relation to the community, without the inter-
mediation of a party. This is the fundamental distinction between
tyranny and kingship. As always with historical phenomena, there are
of course certain intermediate or transitional forms.[6] Tyrants have
tried to free themselves from the consequences of the mode in which
they gained their power, and kings have sometimes had to use the
support of a party. Yet, generally speaking, the difference between
the two forms of government in history is unusually clear-cut, for the
transition from tyranny to kingship, where attempted, has mostly
proved extremely difficult; kings on the other hand, who had to rule
with the support of a party, have always by instinct made the most
strenuous efforts not to become the mere exponents of this party.

   In an analysis of the theory of the mixed constitution it is of fundamental importance to make this distinction between tyranny in the
technical sense and kingship as clear as possible, because tyranny cannot
enter into or form an element of a mixed constitution, while kingship
can.[7] In the course of history there have been many different concepts
of the relation of a king to his people, ranging from the concept of
Oriental despotism, which in its most extreme form implies that the
country and its inhabitants are the property of the king or despot, to
the idea that the king is the first servant of his people. There have also
been a great many different forms of royal succession, the most important of which are: heredity by natural descendance and blood relationship; heredity through adoption; and elective kingship. Yet all
these different concepts and forms have something in common by
which kings—and this includes Oriental despots—are fundamentally
distinguished from tyrants as well as from any other kind of head of
state or government. Kings differ from archons, consuls, presidents,

or prime ministers not merely by the fact that their term of office
usually ends only with their death. The Athenians are said to have
had for some time archons who were elected to govern for a lifetime,[8]
but these archons were not considered to be kings. On the other hand,
the Greeks occasionally speak of kings whose term of office was restricted to a number of years.

Wherever kingship, in the full sense of the word, has existed in
history, the king has never been a mere agent of the people, nor has
the king's importance for the community been restricted to his direction or participation in the direction of public affairs. Beyond anything
that a king may do or have the power to do, it is his main function to
be a symbol of the public order as a whole. Hence the special sacredness that surrounds the person of a king and which, where kingship
has survived, is still to some extent acknowledged even in our practical
and disillusioned age. In periods in which kingship was most fully
alive this sacredness of the king was so strong that it was acknowledged
even by those who felt compelled to revolt against the king.[9] Tyrants
have often aspired to this sacredness as symbols and leaders of their
country, but this is the one thing in which a tyrant, because of the
very nature of tyranny, cannot succeed, while the sacredness of even
a "bad king" in a monarchic period is not seriously affected by his
personal shortcomings.

This peculiar character of kingship is of fundamental importance
for the position of kingship within a mixed constitution. The position
of a Roman consul, a president, or a prime minister is fully determined by the functions that are entrusted to him, by the power that
goes with these functions, and by what he can make of both of them
through his personal capacities. Kingship may first have come into
being through merit—i.e., through functions well performed—but
once it is firmly established, the position of the king is prior both to
whatever concrete functions he may perform and to his personal capacities. This is especially clear in hereditary kingship, where the selection
of the individual who is to become king is completely independent of
his personal capabilities. This was also the case with the Spartan kings
under what Polybius called the mixed constitution of Sparta. But this
was not true with the Roman consuls. The full importance of this
difference in the position of kings and consuls within a mixed constitu-

tion or within a system of checks and balances will become apparent in the continuation of the historical analysis of the Roman constitution. For the present one illustration may be sufficient.

The active functions and powers of the Spartan kings under the so-called Lycurgan constitution were restricted much more than the powers of the consuls under the Roman Republic. Yet the kingship in Sparta did not lose its political importance, while the consulship under the later principate ceased to be an office giving political power when its most important functions had been taken over by the princeps. Clearly, the reason is that the authority of a king was not restricted to his active functions, while that of a consul was. For the same reason Cleomenes, for instance, could use his authority as a king to overthrow the constitution and do away with the ephors, while nobody was ever able to use the consulship to overthrow the Roman constitution, though a man like Octavian, who had succeeded by other means in making himself master of the state, might use the consulship for some time as part of the system of devices by which he tried to legitimize his position.

What has been said concerning the priority of the position and authority of the king over his actual functions within the governmental machinery is of course also true of an aristocracy. But here some additional factors have to be considered. Plato and Aristotle make a fundamental distinction between an aristocracy that has come to power through political merits and an aristocracy whose power is derived essentially from wealth. They call the first type aristocracy or timocracy and the second one oligarchy, a terminology that differs somewhat from that of Polybius. This distinction is not quite unjustified, though historically it is not always easy to draw the line between the two types. But it is common to both types that, just as in the case of tyrants and kings, the power of the aristocracy is prior to its active political functions. (However, in the case of the tyrant this power rests on the support of his party, in the case of the king on respect for the king as the symbol of the community, in the case of a hereditary nobility on respect for nobility of birth, and in the case of oligarchy on the influence derived from wealth and money.) The ways in which an aristocracy can make political use of its power are manifold. It may openly monopolize all higher political offices and functions, as was the case in the early Roman Republic, or it may merely make it more difficult for men who do not belong to the aristocracy to attain the highest positions; the attainment of such a position in spite of these difficulties may then automatically give permanent status as a noble. This was the case in the later Roman Republic. Political influence may also be exercised in a more indirect fashion. Always, however, where there is a true aristocracy the number of those who belong to the aristocracy will be greater than the number of aristocrats who at any time actually perform or participate in the highest political functions. This is the fundamental difference between an aristocracy and a hierarchy of officials.

A clarification is also necessary in regard to the term "people." In the political sense this word as used by Polybius in regard to Rome designates only the totality of Roman citizens, which means that it excludes not only foreigners but slaves and all those numerous inhabitants of territory under Roman domination which at the various periods of Roman history did not have full citizen rights. Furthermore, it must be taken into consideration that Polybius uses the term "the people" very often to designate the assemblies in which the Romans voted on laws or in elections, but that in these assemblies the voting power of different groups of Roman citizens was by no means the same. This factor therefore must also be considered in any evaluation of the Roman constitution as a mixed constitution or as an effective system of checks and balances.

On the basis of these general considerations some defects of Polybius' analysis of the Roman constitution stand out very clearly. Polybius identifies the Senate with the aristocratic element in the political order of the Roman Republic. But probably at no time, and certainly not throughout the major part of the history of the Roman Republic, was the Senate identical with the aristocracy. No analysis that neglects this fundamental fact can give a correct picture of the distribution of power in the Roman Republic. Likewise, Polybius designates the consuls as the monarchic element in the Republic. But though the consuls in the beginning of the Republic probably inherited most, if not all, of the functions and concomitant powers of the kings, they lacked from the beginning the fundamental characteristic of true monarchs: their powers as consuls were not prior to, but entirely the result of, the functions for which they were elected, except in so far as the consuls were at the same time members of the aristocracy. But this is a different matter.

In order to determine how far the early Roman Republic corresponded to the concept of a mixed constitution or of a system and checks and balances, it is, then, of paramount importance to clarify as far as possible the interrelations of the consuls, the Senate, and the popular assemblies, and also the relation of the consuls and the Senate to the patrician aristocracy and of the assemblies of "the people" to the total population and to the aristocracy. This task is by no means easy, because the ancient tradition on the early Roman Republic is very unreliable, and there is hardly anything in this tradition that has not been contested by some scholars, not to speak of the innumerable theories and historical constructions by which some scholars have tried to replace the ancient tradition. It is therefore necessary to say as briefly as possible which part or parts of the ancient tradition appear sufficiently supported by intrinsic and extrinsic evidence to be accepted as truly historical.

The origin of the aristocracy of the early Roman Republic, the so-called patriciate, is contested. Polybius seems to have believed that it originated from the counselors selected by the kings according to their wisdom. In recent times the theory has been defended that the patricians, like the higher castes in India, were the descendants of a conquering group or race, while the plebeians were the descendants of the conquered native population. Certainly this latter theory is almost completely wrong.[10] Most probable and also most widely accepted is the theory that the patriciate ultimately originated from military distinction and leadership. Since it was always a custom of the Romans to distribute conquered territory as a reward for military merits, the leaders who had distinguished themselves acquired wealth which continued in their families. Thus military leadership and economic superiority were combined in the same families and the power of these families was likely to increase all the more rapidly, as in a primitive and early period sudden inroads of hostile bands often must have called for quick action under the leadership of a local chieftain rather than for a military effort of the community as a whole. The earliest division of the Roman army into curiae or co-viriae, i.e. (local) bands of men, indicates clearly that at that time the Romans, even if their entire military power was called into the field, fought under their local leaders, who were in turn under the supreme command of the king. It is then only natural that these local chieftains should have formed the council of the king, so that Polybius' theory of the origin of the patriciate is perhaps not completely wrong, though insufficient.

But whatever the origin of the patriciate may have been, at the beginning of the Republic we find the patricians to be a closely knit group which combined wealth (consisting entirely or nearly entirely of landed property) with a virtual monopoly of military and political leadership. Its exclusiveness had become such that it did not admit any newcomers, at least not from among their own fellow citizens; exceptions were made only for a very few of the most outstanding families of some conquered towns incorporated in the Roman state, and this also only in the earliest period. All the rest of the citizens, whatever their economic status or their military or political merits, were counted as plebeians and were, together with their families and descendants, definitely excluded from the patrician aristocracy for all time.

Though several ancient authors, including Livy,[11] assert that from the beginning of the Republic plebeians were admitted to the Senate, a careful analysis of the evidence leads to the conclusion that this was not the case, and that the Senate became accessible to plebeians not earlier than the last decades of the fifth century B.C.[12] Undoubtedly, therefore, the Senate was one of the agencies by which the patrician aristocracy exercised its political power. Yet the Senate was not identical with this aristocracy, for it is extremely improbable that at any time within the period of the Republic the Senate comprised all the adult male members of the patrician families, and such certainly was not the case in the second half of the fifth century B.C. and later.

Of the definitely formulated foundations of the political power of the Senate, the most important was the rule that bills accepted by a majority vote in the popular assembly did not acquire the force of law until they had been approved by the Senate and the latter had officially given its auctoritas.[13] Whether such a rule had existed under the kings and before the establishment of the Republic is extremely doubtful. It is likely that it came into existence with the beginning of the Republic, though as long as bills could be brought before the assembly of the people only by the consuls, and as long as there was no conflict between the consuls, or between one of the consuls and the Senate, regarding desirable legislation, there may have been little need for such a rule. At any rate there can be no doubt that the rule was acknowledged as valid from the later part of the fifth century B.C. to the year 339 B.C., when it was modified by the Publilian laws.[14]

In the monarchic period the Senate had acted as an advisory body to the king. It is very likely that there were periods during the early Roman monarchy in which the local chieftains who were members of this body had considerable power and were able to exert very strong pressure upon the king. Yet there is no indication that they ever had the power to give orders to the king nor, what is more important, is there any indication that at any time of the Republic was it considered a legal or constitutional obligation of the consuls to obey a senatus consultum in the same way in which they were obliged to obey a law that had been accepted by the people and approved by the Senate.[15] Nevertheless, there is little doubt that in the earliest period of the Republic the Senate was at least as powerful as in the time of Polybius, but for different reasons.

The consuls, as the supreme magistrates of the Republic, were elected by an assembly of the people, the Comitia Centuriata, and had their mandate and their powers as agents of the people, i.e., the community as a whole. But though the tradition is not absolutely clear, there can be little doubt that from the beginning of the Republic only patricians could become consuls. This was certainly the case from the middle of the fifth century to the year 367 B.C., when the plebeians finally compelled the patricians to present a plebeian candidate for one of the consulships for the following year. The consuls in turn chose their quaestors also from among the patricians, and even after the quaestorship had become elective, the quaestors continued to be patricians for rather a long time. It is only in 409 B.C. that we find the first plebeian quaestor. Thus during the first hundred years of the Roman Republic the government consisted exclusively of patricians.

As supreme executives, and at the same time supreme judges, the consuls of the early Republic had an enormous discretionary power. But since there were two consuls with absolutely equal power, and the provision that in case of conflict the consul opposing an action should always prevail over the consul proposing it, they kept one another in check. Their term of office was only one year, but they remained senators for life. What is perhaps still more important, the patricians as a whole formed a very closely knit social unit, all of them having essentially the same background. They were not like the aristocracies of many Greek cities (including Athens, but not Sparta) of the seventh and sixth centuries, which were divided into two groups with somewhat divergent interests: namely, those whose wealth consisted mainly in landed property, and those whose chief economic interest was in overseas trade. This is probably at least one of the reasons why the rivalries between individual noble families and individuals which existed of course in Rome, as in any other aristocracy, did not in that early period become disruptive, and why the aristocracy as a whole remained in complete control of its members, while in many Greek cities individual aristocrats made successful attempts to rise over their fellow nobles by espousing the cause of the common people and established themselves, with the people's support, as tyrants.

Thus the position of the consuls in the early Roman Republic was a double one. They were elected as agents of the community as a whole, and there can be no doubt that they received all their legal powers from the people by whom they were elected, and not from the Senate or the patricians. Yet at the same time they *were* patricians, and naturally considered themselves representatives of the patrician aristocracy. Ancient tradition is full of stories of how many of them dealt harshly with the people and looked down on them as a lower class. No doubt most of these stories are legends, yet their persistence shows that the general conditions they describe must be to some extent historical. This is also confirmed by the fact that the devices by which in the course of time the plebeians tried to break the arbitrary power of the patriciate were mostly directed against the highest magistrates, which shows clearly that in internal policy the people considered the consuls largely as instruments of the patrician aristocracy.

According to the ancient tradition the resistance of the plebeians against the patricians started within the first decades of the Republic. The necessary condition for the effectiveness of this resistance must then have been created still earlier; i.e., in the last phase of the monarchy. In this respect again the ancient tradition, however unreliable in its details, is in all likelihood correct. In the earliest period, as pointed out before, the Roman army was divided into curiae or coviriae, local units under local leaders, which in a major engagement served under the command of the king. But everything indicates that in the last phase of the monarchy the Greek phalanx was introduced, and with it new weapons, new tactics, and a new organization of the army. In purely local engagements the Romans may still for some time, then, have fought under local leaders. But the core of the army with which the community waged its wars was now the heavy-armed infantry fighting in closed ranks and supported by a cavalry also fighting in closed formations. This army was divided into centuriae, and these centuriae now also replaced the curiae as the voting units in the assemblies of the people.

The details of the development of this new system are uncertain and controversial. Livy and Dionysius of Halicarnassus attribute to the king Servius Tullius a complicated organization of eighteen centuriae of cavalry and five classes of eighty, twenty, twenty, twenty, and thirty centuriae of infantry, respectively, the first class being the most heavily armed, and each of the following classes somewhat lighter armed than the preceding one, plus five centuriae of craftsmen, musicians, and of the propertyless, or proletarians. According to the same tradition the distribution of the citizens into these classes was made according to property qualifications.

It is generally agreed that it is quite impossible that this system existed in the early period to which it is ascribed by Livy and Dionysius of Halicarnassus. Apart from this, the same authors in other passages indicate clearly that there was a time in the early Republic when there was only one class besides the centuriae of the equites or cavalry, namely, the class of the heavily armed infantry fighting in the phalanx, and that all the others were considered *infra classem* (below the class), though men of this group may have been used to support the phalanx in battle in the same way in which a Greek phalanx would be supported by lightly armed groups. On the other hand, there can be no doubt that the system of 193 centuriae, erroneously attributed to Servius Tullius, did exist in later times, at least for voting purposes.[16]

But whatever the details of the development may have been, the transition to the new military system shows that there must have been a substantial number of citizens who did not belong to the patrician aristocracy, but had enough wealth to provide themselves with the expensive armor of the heavily armed soldiers. For down to the last decades of the second century B.C. it was always the rule that the soldiers had to buy and take care of their weapons themselves. The units of this army, then, were not local groups of retainers and dependent peasants serving under a local lord or chieftain, and were therefore not bound by loyalties naturally arising from such an arrangement. But since it had always been the people in arms who elected the supreme commander of the army, and with it the head of the state, this function quite appropriately was taken over by the new army, which also then had the final decision in regard to peace and war and in regard to foreign treaties, and which, when lawmaking became one of the functions of the popular assembly, accepted or rejected the proposals for laws.

The importance of this new military system for the political order in Rome can hardly be overestimated. Since the heavy armed infantry now formed the core of the military strength of the Roman state, and since its units were no longer under the direct influence of local lords, they could not fail to develop a certain feeling of their worth and a certain resistance to the overlordship of the great. It is then not at all unlikely that the formation of the closely knit and exclusive aristocracy of the patricians was nothing but the reverse side of the same development, i.e., the means by which the leading families tried to retain their supremacy in a totally changed situation.

It seems that the consequences of this change were not restricted to the purely political sphere. The relations between the local lords and their retainers or *clientes* and other dependent peasants appear to have been close and by no means one-sided. How seriously the obligations of the lord or *patronus* to his clients were taken can be inferred from one of the laws of the Twelve Tables which ordered that a lord who had betrayed his client shall be cursed and excluded from the company of his fellow citizens.[17] This law shows also that by the middle of the fifth century this relation between the lord and his retainers was not yet a thing of the past. The antagonism between patricians and plebeians therefore must have been of a different nature; it is likely that it was connected with the process by which the patricians tried to establish an absolute barrier between themselves and the rest of the population. The law of the Twelve Tables forbidding intermarriage between patricians and plebeians that had to be revoked a few years later is perhaps the strongest expression of this process.[18]

Unfortunately the ancient tradition concerning the struggles between patricians and plebeians in the fifth and fourth centuries is obscured by the tendency of the Roman historians to interpret the history of this early period by analogy with the internal conflicts of the time from the Gracchi to Sulla. According to the tradition the conflict arose from a demand of the plebeians for a more just distribution of land, and from the harshness with which the patricians exacted the payment of debts. That the demand for a more just distribution of conquered land played a role in the struggles of the fifth century is indeed quite likely. But the agrarian laws or bills which Livy constantly mentions in his history of the fifth century and the first half of the fourth century are so clearly modeled after the laws of the late second and the first centuries that there can be no reliance on the details of the tradition. The story of the indebtedness of the plebeians and of the harshness of the patricians in dealing with their debtors may be earlier and may go back to Polybius. But if it does, it is quite possible that the analogy of the Athenian peasants of the sixth century may have played a role, especially since there is some evidence to show that resistance to the patricians originated with the more wealthy plebeians rather than with those who were economically distressed.

Where the tradition concerning the causes of the struggle is so obviously unreliable, the only evidence we have of its true nature comes from its lasting results. This evidence fortunately is very clear. According to the ancient tradition there were within the fifth century B.C. two major secessions of the plebs, each accompanied by a threat to establish a separate community and an absolute refusal to do military service under patrician command, and in addition a great number of minor military strikes. According to the same tradition, during the first secession the plebeians established the *sacrosanctitas* or inviolability of their elected leaders, the tribunes of the plebs, by an oath— obviously to defend this sacrosanctitas against anyone trying to encroach upon it [19]—and demanded for them the *ius auxilii*, i.e., the right to come to the aid of any plebeian against the legitimate coercive powers of a consul or other magistrate, by stepping with their inviolable body between the plebeian and the magistrate trying to arrest or punish him. As a result of the second secession the sacrosanctitas of the plebeian tribunes and their ius auxilii was confirmed by one of the Valerio-Horatian laws of 449 or 448 B.C. which threatened violators with a curse and exclusion from all intercourse with Roman citizens.

Again the details of the story of these secessions as told by Livy are full of forced and improbable analogies with later events, and the accounts are therefore almost certainly unhistorical. Yet it is quite unjustified to reject for this reason the core of the story itself. There can be not the slightest doubt that the sacrosanctitas and the ius auxilii of the tribunes of the plebs existed throughout the later history of the Roman Republic, and the archaic form of the Valerio-Horatian law which made them legal shows that this law must have belonged to a very early period. Such a strange institution does not come into being without a struggle nor without a corresponding cause. This struggle can hardly have been a violent and bloody revolution, which would have ended in the victory of one party and the suppression of the other, but must have been rather a rebellion without bloodshed and ending in a compromise—something in the nature of a secession or a strike, which is exactly what the tradition, if one eliminates all details and embellishments, essentially affirms.

Much more important within the present context, however, is what one can learn concerning the causes of the struggle from its results. The creation of inviolable tribunes fitted out with a ius auxilii is hardly the most direct way to bring about a juster distribution of land. It may be used as a means of protecting debtors from their creditors, but if that had been the only reason, the effect would go far beyond its cause. Actually the institution clearly reveals its purpose: the general protection of private citizens against arbitrary and oppressive actions of the elected magistrates; and since the protection worked only for plebeians, it is clear that the magistrates whose actions had given rise to the rebellion and the resulting new institution had felt and acted essentially as members of the patrician aristocracy.

That this was in fact the main issue in the struggle is confirmed by

its other lasting results. By far the most important of these is the
publication of the Twelve Tables, which brought, at least to some
extent, an end to patrician monopoly of the knowledge of the law,
and in this way caused the administration of justice by the consuls to
become somewhat less arbitrary.[20] The ius auxilii of the tribunes and
the publication of the Twelve Tables then obviously supplemented
one another in providing a measure of protection for the plebeians
against the arbitrary rule of the patrician magistrates, and it is clear
that they were for the benefit of all plebeians, the wealthy as well
as the poor.

The two other major successes which the plebeians attained in the
further course of the fifth century—the revocation of the law forbidding intermarriage between patricians and plebeians five years after it
had been included in the Twelve Tables [21] and the admission of
plebeians to the consular tribuneship towards the end of the century—
were clearly for the benefit of the most outstanding men among the
plebeians, and not for those on the lowest social level. It is then still
quite possible that the two factors discussed above—demands for a
juster distribution of land, and the indebtedness of a large section
of the plebeians—may have had something to do with the struggle
between plebeians and patricians in the fifth century. Undoubtedly
the plebeians who were leading in the struggle must have had a large
following to be successful, and it is therefore not unlikely that economic questions were involved. But the demonstrable results of the
struggle prove that the main issue was a different one.

The question may of course be asked why there had to be two
secessions and a series of minor military strikes if the leaders in the
struggle were the more wealthy and independent plebeians, since
they must have had the majority in the centuriate assemblies which
made the laws. The answer, however, is not difficult to give. Livy
mentions a great many laws of the first half of the fifth century as
having been passed by the Comitia Centuriata. The historicity of
many of these laws is doubtful for internal reasons. The laws of the
Twelve Tables are the first Roman laws of which the wording has
been partly preserved, and the Valerio-Horatian laws which followed
immediately upon the publication of the Twelve Tables are the
earliest laws passed by the Comitia of which a summary has come

down to us. It is therefore not absolutely certain whether there existed laws in the full sense (i.e., definitely formulated laws laid down in writing) before the Twelve Tables, though it appears that in the period from the establishment of the Republic to the middle of the fifth century the first definitely formulated and written international treaties were made. But even assuming that there were such laws, it certainly was a fundamental principle with the Romans to the end of the Republic that the popular assemblies had no legislative initiative; proposals for laws could be made only by the magistrates presiding over the assemblies. These presiding magistrates in the Comitia Centuriata were the consuls, who would naturally not introduce legislation restricting their own powers or prejudicial to the interests of the patricians unless they were under strong pressure.

Such pressure was brought to bear on the patricians in the strongest form by the two secessions and in a somewhat milder form by the military strikes which, according to tradition, occurred between the two secessions. At first, of course, these strikes and secessions must have had the nature of rebellion. But as a result of the second secession the pressure of the plebeians for legislation seems to have been given a legal or semilegal expression. The patricians acknowledged the right of the plebeian tribunes to convoke the plebeians alone (i.e., to the exclusion of the patricians), and to make them vote on proposals for laws which they desired to have enacted. This right of the tribunes was called the *ius cum plebe agendi*, and the proposals approved by a majority of the plebs in a regular assembly (concilium plebis) were called *plebei scita* (plebiscites). Until the year 287 B.C. such plebiscites did not have the force of law, but they constituted a formal demand of the plebeians on the patricians and the curule magistrates either to make certain concessions which could be made without legislation, or to introduce the proposal which had been accepted by the Concilium Plebis as a formal bill in the Comitia Centuriata.[22] If the patricians and the curule magistrates did not accede to such demands, the tribunes could negotiate with the Senate and the consuls and then make the plebeians vote again, either on the same proposal or a modified one, and if repeated negotiations and repeated demands were not successful, the pressure might still be increased by military strikes or civic strikes (for instance, refusal to participate in elections). This seems, in fact, to have happened not infrequently in the further history of the Roman Republic down to the year 287; after that year such pressure was of course no longer necessary, since from then on plebiscites accepted by the plebeians *ipso facto* had the force of laws. It does not seem that a right to go on military or civic strikes was ever acknowledged. But the right to make formal demands for legislation in the way described was acknowledged. In this way the plebeians did acquire some kind of legislative initiative, though at best only at second hand. For proposals for plebiscites could not be introduced in the plebeian assemblies except by the elected plebeian tribunes who, however, at least in the earlier period, would naturally be inclined to listen to the wishes of their fellow plebeians. But even if such proposals had been introduced in the Concilium Plebis and passed by it, they could not be brought before the legislative assembly unless a curule magistrate could be induced to do so.

The results of the struggle between patricians and plebeians in the fifth century B.C. as described so far are essentially what Polybius calls the perfect mixed constitution of the Romans which continued to be excellent down to the time of the Second Punic War, and even to Polybius' own time. It is not difficult to show that this presumedly perfect mixed constitution is very different indeed both from the original concept of a mixed constitution and from the modern concept of a system of checks and balances based on a separation of powers, or rather of what Montesquieu's theory describes as a distribution of functions together with the powers inherent in the performance of these functions.

Whatever Polybius may say about the consuls as the monarchic factor in the state, nothing is clearer than that the consuls did not have or take a position above the aristocracy, and did not counterbalance the power of the patricians in the way in which medieval and modern kings may have counterbalanced the power of the aristocracy. On the contrary, everything indicates that though the consuls were elected by the people, or rather by the assembly of the warriors, they were actually instruments of the patrician aristocracy, so that their functional powers augmented the political strength of the aristocracy instead of counterbalancing it. The case of the people is different. They actually did gain considerable potential power probably even before the overthrow of the monarchy, and certainly in the course of the fifth century. But even after the battle of the two secessions had been won these powers remained but imperfectly legalized.

The resemblance of the Roman constitution of the late fifth century to a system of checks and balances based on a separation of powers is still less great than its resemblance to a mixed constitution in the original sense of the word. There was no separation of the executive, the legislative, and the judicial powers. The consuls united the executive and judicial powers in their hands, and in addition held the legislative initiative. The Senate and the assembly of the people shared the legislative power, the first through the requirement of the *patrum auctoritas*. The tribunes of the plebs and the plebeian assemblies under their presidency also had in a way a share in the legislative initiative, but only indirectly. Apart from this the Senate had the function chiefly of advising the consuls, but because of the Senate's essential character as the representative body of the patrician aristocracy, its advice carried very great weight with the consuls, who felt above all as members of their class.

Obviously, then, there was no balance of power between a monarchic, an aristocratic or oligarchic, and a democratic element in the Roman Republic of the late fifth century. There may be said to have been a certain balance of power between the patricians and the plebeians, but this was anything but a balance of positive functional powers, the latter remaining almost completely in the hands of the patrician Senate and the patrician magistrates. The powers of the people, on the other hand, were mostly negative, consisting of the power of rejecting proposals for laws made by the consuls in the Comitia Centuriata, the power of the tribunes to protect individual plebeians from the coercive power of the curule magistrates, and the semipositive power of making official demands for legislation and of making trouble if such demands were not met.

It is not certain whether (and perhaps not likely that) the tribunes of the plebs in that early period possessed the very far-reaching power of intercession which appears to have developed in the course of time from their ius auxilii, and by virtue of which the tribunes, by their simple veto, could not only forbid any individual intended action of a magistrate within Rome, but in addition could forbid generally, and in advance, any action which any magistrate might undertake in execution of a senatus consultum.[23]

All this is certainly very different from the beautifully balanced system that Polybius describes. Yet with this crude system—if these more or less fortuitous results of a struggle can properly be called a system—the Roman Republic actually showed an internal stability, and at the same time adaptability to changing circumstances, which hardly any other ancient community possessed. This is the phenomenon that has to be explained.

The development did not stop with the gains made by the plebeians in the course of the fifth century. Toward the very end of that century the plebeians finally attained access to the highest magistracy in the form of the consular tribuneship, but not to the consulship itself. As long as the elections of consular tribunes instead of consuls continued to be the rule rather than the exception this did not matter very much. But when in the beginning of the third decade of the fourth century it became apparent that the annual election of from three to six magistrates of the highest rank no longer served the needs of the community, and therefore that the consulship would have to be restored, the question became acute.[24] The majority of the patricians contended that plebeians, though they had become eligible to the consular tribuneship, could not become consuls. This, if the consular tribuneship was to be abolished, would have meant that from then on the plebeians were to be permanently excluded from the highest office, although they had already attained access to its counterpart in the preceding period. No wonder that a violent struggle arose over this question. The plebeians passed one plebiscite after another demanding that a plebeian candidate be admitted for one of the two highest positions if the consulship was to be restored. After the struggle had lasted for ten years with intermittent military and civic strikes, the patricians gave in. One of the plebeians who had led the struggle as a tribune of the plebs was admitted as the first plebeian candidate for the consulship, and was promptly elected. At first the patricians tried to reserve the newly created minor curule offices of the praetorship and the curule aedileships, and also the censorship, for members of their class, but once the dam was broken the flood could not be stopped, and the plebeians gained access to curule aedileship nearly at once and to the praetorship and the censorship some decades later.

As a result, then, of this struggle, which lasted for more than a century, the political monopoly of the patricians was finally broken, and the plebeians attained access not only to all the highest political offices, but, since the curule magistrates became members of the Senate, also to the Senate. It is conceivable that if the process by which the plebeians gradually conquered the highest offices and the Senate had been rapid in the following decades, these governmental agencies would as a consequence have ceased to be (and therefore to feel as) representatives of a privileged class, and would have been reduced to their functions as instruments of the community as a whole. But the process was very slow and the development took a different turn.

Once a man had become a senator he remained a member of the Senate until his death unless he was removed from the Senate by the censors because of misconduct. Until the year 172 B.C. the principle prevailed that one of the consuls must be a patrician. Until 343 B.C. the patricians sometimes even used an interregnum, when the candidates for office had to be presented by the patrician interrex, to present only patrician candidates, and so forced the people to elect two patrician consuls. The first plebeian censor was elected for 351 B.C., the first plebeian praetor for 337 B.C. Though individual plebeians therefore appear to have attained access to the Senate as early as the end of the fifth century B.C., it was a long time before they formed a considerable portion of this body, and even longer before they were in the majority. Likewise, the majority of the highest positions in the state continued to be held by patricians for quite some time after the plebeians had attained access to these offices.

There can hardly be any doubt that these facts had a decisive effect on the attitude of the plebeians toward the magistrates and the Senate, and that the further development of the whole political order was largely determined by this attitude. As pointed out before,[25] the people's distrust of their magistrates and their desire not to let them become too powerful is virtually the only explanation for the strange custom of electing all incumbents of the highest offices in the state directly instead of permitting the consul to select (subject to the approval of the people if necessary) the members of the cabinet, as in the early Republic the consuls had actually selected their quaestors. A similar attitude of the plebeians toward the Senate is illustrated by the successive attempts of the plebeians to deprive the Senate of its right to withhold its ratification of laws which had been passed by the popular assemblies, attempts which in the end were successful. But the most striking illustration of the attitude of the Roman people towards its government is the excessive veto power which the tribunes of the plebs acquired in the further course of the struggle. In the beginning the tribunes' right of intercession had probably been largely identical with their ius auxilii, i.e., it had meant that a tribune could step with his sacrosanct body between a consul and a plebeian and so prevent the former from punishing or arresting the latter. But some two centuries later, and from then until the end of the Republic, it was acknowledged as constitutional law that the simple veto of any tribune of the plebs could not only prevent or stop, within the city of Rome, any action that any magistrate, including even his fellow tribunes, intended to take in pursuance of what he considered the duties of his office, but could even by a simple announcement prevent and make illegal in advance any actions that a magistrate might take, or intend to take, in execution of a senatus consultum to which the tribune of the plebs objected.

All this clearly shows that, even after plebeians had attained access to the Senate and to the highest offices of the state, the plebeians long continued to consider the government not as an agency of the community, over which they must try to gain a positive influence or control, but as something alien to their interests and against which they must defend themselves by depriving its different parts of as much power as possible, and by establishing special but purely negative safeguards against its encroachments. The result in the first respect was probably not quite what the plebeians intended it to be. For, as we have seen, the power which the people tried to keep from the consuls largely accrued to the Senate through practical necessity, and it was the Senate in which, for obvious reasons, the patrician predominance continued for the longest time. Further, when this predominance was finally broken, the Senate became the center and the instrument of a new patrician-plebeian aristocracy. In the second respect the plebeians were eminently successful, as the increase in the veto powers of the tribunes show; but this left the community with an excess of negative powers the like of which can hardly be found in any other state in history. Before discussing the causes and the effects of the rise of a new aristocracy after the patrician predominance had finally been overcome, it will be necessary to discuss briefly some of the technical devices by which the excess of purely negative powers was prevented from becoming destructive to the state.

According to Polybius, the greatest advantage of a mixed constitution in which the powers of a monarchic, an oligarchic, and a democratic element are equally balanced is that in times of prosperity none of these elements can degenerate through too great a security in the possession of power, since all of them keep one another mutually in check, while in times of adversity they can all work together and support one another for the common good. If this is correct, it would seem to apply naturally either to a mixed constitution, in which monarchic, oligarchic, and democratic elements are in balance, or to a system of checks and balances, in which the various main governmental agencies have a more or less equal share in the supreme power, and so keep one another in check because none of them can function properly without the collaboration of the others. This appears also to have been Polybius' opinion. But it has now been shown that, at least during the earlier part of the period during which, according to Polybius, the Roman constitution continued to be excellent, there was no equal distribution of the power to act, but such a superabundance of negative powers to prevent action that, on the face of it, it is difficult to understand how the government could function at all. Yet this is the period in which the Romans not only survived the conquest of the city of Rome (with the exception of the fortress of the capitol) by the Gauls, and the consequent desertion of all their subjects and allies, but conquered, and after the conquest continued to hold, the greater part of the Italian peninsula.

The factors which made this paradoxical phenomenon possible are manifold. But one of these factors is undoubtedly the fact that the Romans apparently developed an elaborate system of provisions for emergencies almost from the beginning of the Republic. These provisions made it possible to keep the most dangerous negative powers in abeyance when and where this was necessary for the safety of the state, and permitted these powers to remain in force or be revived automatically when and where there was no such necessity.

The purely negative principles which had become incorporated in the Roman constitution were the power of each of the two consuls to veto an action or intended action of the other consul; the *provocatio ad populum*, or the right of any Roman citizen to invoke the decision of the assembly of the people against the imposition of the death penalty, a right which was so liberally interpreted as to allow a citizen to avoid execution by going into voluntary exile during the voting process until the vote had decided against him; and finally, and by far the most important, the tribunician power of intercession.

The most common form of public emergency is war, and since the Romans were almost constantly involved in wars this kind of emergency was more or less permanent. Since it was customary in time of war for one consul to take over the command of the army while the other either remained in Rome to direct the civil administration, or, if there was another war at the same time, commanded another army in a different place, the veto power of consul against consul under ordinary circumstances did not constitute a major danger, since the separation of functions made direct interference difficult though not impossible. But the *provocatio ad populum*, and even more the tribunician intercession, would have been a very serious hindrance in the conduct of military operations if they had not been limited.

This difficulty was met by the distinction of two fields, *domi* and *militiae* (at home and in the field), a distinction which corresponds to some extent to the modern distinction between ordinary and military law, but with the important difference that in Rome the distinction was partly geographical, inasmuch as in ordinary times military law was excluded from what the Romans called the *pomerium* of Rome, while the tribunician power of intercession was restricted to the capital. The *provocatio ad populum*, on the other hand, did not apply to soldiers in actual service in the army. This had the advantage that the consuls had sufficient coercive and discretionary powers where these were necessary to secure the external safety of the state, but were automatically de-

prived of unchecked power when they approached the heart of the
state, the seat and ultimate source of all political power, where too
great an authority invested in an individual might have become dangerous to the liberties of the people.

In times of ordinary wars this distinction of the two spheres was
usually sufficient, but when the capital itself was threatened, either from
without or from within, or when there was a serious dissension between
the consuls, an additional safeguard was needed. This was provided by
the institution of the so-called dictatorship which appears to have been
introduced in the very early time of the Republic.[26] There was no
geographical restriction on the powers of the dictator. The dictator had
no colleague with equal powers and so could not be hampered in his
freedom of action by the principle *in re pari maior causa prohibentis*. He
was, at least in the earlier period of the Republic, not subject to the *provocatio ad populum*, or to tribunician intercession, but while his extraordinary or emergency powers had no limit in space, they were subject to
a strict limitation in time. A dictator could not be appointed for a longer
period than six months. He could abdicate and lay down his powers as
soon as he believed that he had fulfilled the task for which he had been
appointed, even on the very next day after his appointment, but he
could not retain his power beyond the limit of six months. After that his
power ceased automatically and nobody had to obey his orders any
longer.

It is also noteworthy that until the last decades of the third century
B.C. dictators were not elected by the people but were appointed by one
of the consuls, though the Senate could of course ask a consul to appoint
a dictator. But in this case the consul, as generally in regard to senatus
consulta, was not strictly obliged by law to comply with the Senate's request, and he could also appoint a dictator on his own responsibility.
These provisions were probably more favorable to liberty than is apparent at first sight, for in this way the dictator could not claim to owe his
power to popular support, and could not try to retain it after his term
was over with the help of the group or party that had elected him.

From the purely technical and legal point of view, then, the distinction between the two fields of *domi* and *militiae*, together with the dictatorship as an emergency institution strictly limited in time, appear to
present a very neat solution of the problems presented by the super-

abundance of negative powers which had developed in the Roman Republic in the course of its internal constitutional struggles. Historically, however, and in terms of actual powers to act and to prevent action, the question is somewhat more complicated.

Unfortunately, the ancient tradition concerning the history of the Roman Republic up to the beginning of the third century B.C., and to some extent even to the second half of that century, is very unreliable in regard to details. Consequently we do not know exactly in what way the ius auxilii of the tribunes of the plebs developed into the far-reaching power of intercession which the tribunes possessed in later times. But it is very likely that this development was closely connected with the ability of the tribunes to cause trouble by making the people vote to support their wishes by military or civic strikes, and that such strikes played a very great role in the struggle of the plebeians, first against the exclusive political privileges of the patricians, and later for greater positive powers, can hardly be doubted.

If this is so, it is obviously not sufficient to say that the tribunician power of intercession did not apply outside the pomerium of Rome, and that the dictator was not subject to it, for a military strike certainly affected the sphere *militiae* even if it happened *domi*. If, then, in such a case a dictator was appointed, the question arises as to how the mere appointment of a dictator could make the plebeians obey the draft which they had not obeyed under a consul. In fact, Livy tells of numerous instances in which a dictator was appointed in order to break the resistance of the plebeians. But he also mentions several cases in which the dictator had to argue with the people or ended by introducing legislation according to the wishes of the plebeians, the most famous case being the laws introduced by the dictator Publilius Philo in 339 B.C., by which the power of the Senate to withhold its auctoritas of bills passed by the Comitia Centuriata was restricted.[27] At this point, therefore, the problem of obedience to legally constituted authority comes in. But this most important general problem cannot be discussed adequately before some additional aspects of the relation of the Roman people to its government have been studied.

The situation which has been described so far changed in one very fundamental respect with the last secession of the plebs in the year 287 B.C. and the Hortensian law, which was the most important consequence of this secession. By giving legal force to proposals accepted by a majority vote in the Concilium Plebis (i.e., the official voting assembly of the plebeians alone), the law provided the people for the first time with some kind of legislative initiative—not, it is true, in the sense that any member of a popular assembly would thenceforth have the power to make proposals for new legislation, as was the case in the Athenian democracy—but through the ten tribunes, who, as Polybius says, were considered the servants of the wishes of the people. It is not always realized, and Polybius, it would seem, did not realize, that through this law for the first time in Roman history a popular assembly attained a truly active share in the government. As long as legislation could be introduced only by curule magistrates, and these magistrates were representatives of a ruling aristocracy, the provision that laws could be made only by the people in its legally constituted assembly in actual fact left to the people only the negative power of rejecting new legislative proposals. Since through most of the third century there was also an increasingly rapid influx of plebeians into the Senate, one may perhaps say that in this period for the second time an opportunity offered itself for the development of a system of checks and balances in the modern sense, i.e., a system in which the governmental functions and concomitant powers are distributed between different high agencies and bodies, all of which, however, have no political powers or privileges beyond those inherent in the functions with which they are temporarily entrusted by the people. Again, however, the actual development did not take such a new turn, but continued largely in the old direction.

One of the most important factors in this development was the fact that the Senate, in spite of the influx of plebeians, who even finally constituted a majority, continued to be an aristocratic body, and that in the course of time there came into being a new plebeian-patrician senatorial aristocracy larger than the Senate. The Senate then became the representative and the instrument of this new aristocracy, though perhaps not quite to the same degree as it had been the instrument of the patrician aristocracy in the earliest period of the Republic. In addition, the conquest of new territories of enormous wealth led to the rise of a new privileged group, the financial aristocracy of the equites, who also gained considerable political influence. These phenomena will later have to be discussed more fully in a different context.

On the part of the people, on the other hand, there still continued the emphasis on the restriction of the power of government. There were, it is true, no more civic or military strikes after the secession of 287 B.C. The following hundred and fifty years were singularly free from internal disturbances. But this was no more than natural, for the strikes had been the instrument by which the plebeians had forced the curule magistrates to introduce legislation which the people desired, as long as they had no legislative initiative. When, therefore, through the Hortensian law of 287 plebiscites, which were initiated by the plebeian tribunes, acquired the force of laws, there was no longer any need for the pressure exercised by civic and military strikes. Hence these strikes naturally ceased until new reasons for internal disorders of a different kind arose a century and a half later.[28]

The tribunician power of intercession, however, retained its full range, though in actual practice it was used more sparingly during the same period of a hundred and fifty years, and for reasons that will be discussed later, it was used increasingly often in support of decisions of the Senate rather than against them. Yet it was also in the course of the third century B.C. that the dictatorship gradually came under all the limitations to which the consuls had been subject ever since the tribunician power of intercession had attained its full range. At an unknown date in the very early part of the third century, or possibly a few years before its beginning, the dictatorship became subject to the *provocatio ad populum*. Not very much later it became subject also to tribunician intercession. Finally, the last steps were taken during the Second Punic War, when the danger to the state from Hannibal's invasion of Italy called for extreme measures and made a succession of dictatorships necessary. It is all the more significant that it was exactly in this time that the dictatorship was deprived of its last distinctive characteristics. In 217 B.C. a dictator was for the first time elected by the comitia.[29] In the same year the people decreed that the magister equitum should have equal powers with the dictator.[30] These strange acts find their explanation in the fact that both consuls had to be absent from Rome in order to lead the armies in the field, and that therefore there was urgent need for a central authority in Rome to direct the civil administration, and above all the military supply system for the armies on the front. Since both consuls were absent, it would have been too cumbersome to ask one of the consuls to appoint a suitable dictator, and so the process of popular election was substituted for the usual procedure. But the decree giving the magister equitum equal powers with the dictator shows that the people were no longer inclined to give supreme power to one man, even temporarily and in an emergency.

The new procedure chosen in regard to the dictatorship in the year 217 B.C. was perhaps not absolutely absurd in the very special circumstances existing at that time. But it is obvious that, generally speaking, the dictatorship now had lost its meaning as an emergency institution, for a dictator and a magister equitum with equal powers and subject both to the *provocatio ad populum* and to tribunician intercession were in fact nothing but two new consuls placed above the two consuls who had originally been elected for the year. It is therefore hardly a mere coincidence that after a few more dictatorships in the Second Punic War there were no more dictatorships for more than a century.

In this way, however, the Roman state was deprived of one of its most important emergency institutions, or rather of the only well-defined emergency institution for extraordinary emergencies.

From the end of the Second Punic War to the end of the Republic Rome continued free from external dangers great enough to make the appointment of a dictator necessary. But from the time of the Gracchi onward, when grave internal difficulties arose, the lack of an agency which could have overcome by legal means the excessive negative powers incorporated in the Roman constitution was severely felt. There was one more emergency principle that had always been acknowledged as valid by the Romans but had not found expression in definite institutions—the principle *salus rei publicae suprema lex*, which meant that when the state was in immediate danger any citizen had the right to commit any action, however criminal under ordinary circumstances (as, for example, the killing of magistrate), and would go unpunished if he could prove his action had been necessary to save the state. This was a dangerous principle because of its indefiniteness. In the troubles of the last century of the Republic the Senate made an attempt to give this principle a somewhat more definite and circumscribed application by various devices, as the so-called *senatus con-*

sultum ultimum or *senatus consultum de re publica defendenda,* the *hostis* declaration, and the *contra rem publicam* declaration. The first of these devices was an expression of the opinion of the Senate that there existed a state of immediate danger to the Republic, and that therefore extraconstitutional and extralegal measures to cope with this danger would be justified and should be taken by the magistrates if and when necessary. The second device expressed the opinion that a certain person designated had become or might become a danger to the Republic, and could or should be treated as a public enemy. The third device was an expression of the opinion of the Senate that a certain action, if perpetrated, would constitute a danger to the state, and that the perpetrator would have to be considered an enemy of the state. If, then, after the Senate had made such a declaration, someone killed a person whose activities the Senate considered dangerous to the state, the slayer could still be tried but the burden of proof that his action was not justified and should be punished was then on the accuser, instead of the burden of proof that he was legally not guilty being on the perpetrator of the deed. The Senate, however, especially in the beginning, did not make the best and wisest use of these new devices of its own invention, and when in 49 B.C. it tried to use the *senatus consultum de re publica defendenda* against Caesar at a moment in which the state was really in the most immediate danger, the device proved ineffective.

Though the downfall of the Republic in the first century B.C. had of course much deeper causes, a not unimportant role in the process was played by the continuance of excessive negative powers in the hands of every single one of the ten tribunes of the plebs, and the lack of any well-defined emergency institution or any agency that could have overcome the difficulty created by this situation with the help of legally well-defined powers and methods. Thirty years before the end of the Republic the dictatorship was revived for the first time, but now in a much more dangerous form, by a dictator who was "elected" by the people under military pressure and without definite time limit. This dictator, L. Cornelius Sulla, abdicated voluntarily after having created a new constitution which was meant to give the rule of the Senate and the senatorial aristocracy a more solid foundation. But this constitution did not last very long, and when the dictatorship was revived for the second time by Caesar, he used it as an instrument to establish a semimonarchic power for himself.

The process which ended in this way, and the role in this process of the play and counterplay of negative powers against emergency institutions and emergency principles, can be understood fully only against the background of the social and economic conditions of the time, and of the changing position of the noncitizen population both of Italy and of the Roman empire at large. Before attacking these problems, however, it will be convenient to give a brief summary of the results of the analysis so far.

Throughout the period during which, according to Polybius, the Roman constitution continued to be excellent, it was not a mixed constitution in the original sense of the word—a constitution in which a monarch, whose position and authority are prior to his active functions; an aristocracy, whose power and influence are prior to its official political functions; and the people, who of course are always prior to whatever share they may have in the control of public affairs, have (or are supposed to have) definite and more or less well-defined shares in political power, and so mutually keep one another under control. Nor was it a system of checks and balances in the modern sense, according to which all political power is assumed to emanate from the people, but the governmental functions and concomitant powers are distributed among various supreme agencies, each of which, through this separation of functions and powers and the mutual checks resulting from this separation, is assumed to be prevented from becoming too powerful and from constituting a danger to public liberties.

There were, it is true, elements both of a mixed constitution and of a system of checks and balances in the Roman political order of the time to which Polybius refers; but neither of them was fully developed. If the term mixed constitution is taken in the sense which Polybius himself gives it in his introductory chapters, namely as a mixture of monarchy (in the sense of kingship), oligarchy, and democracy, then it is certainly misleading to designate the consuls as the monarchic element in the Roman constitution. For their office was in part purely functional, like that of any president of a republic, partly one of the instruments by which the aristocracy exercised its control over the people. There was no truly monarchic element in the Roman Republic. Yet Polybius was not quite

wrong in attributing to Rome a mixed constitution or rather a mixed
political order, if this term can be used of a mixture of oligarchy and
democracy only. For though from the earliest time of the Republic
theoretically all political power emanated from the people, all active
political power, including the legislative initiative and the right to put
up candidates for election to all curule offices, was for a long time
monopolized by the aristocracy. Yet it would be wrong to say—though
it has often been said—that the Roman Republic at any time between
the first secession and Sulla was in practice, if not in theory, purely oligarchic. For ever since the tribunes of the plebs were acknowledged as
sacrosanct and had acquired the *ius auxilii* and the *ius cum plebe agendi*,
the power of the aristocracy was counterbalanced by powers of "the
people" which were for the most part negative, but nevertheless were
to a certain extent institutionalized and regulated, though they retained
also a certain revolutionary and tumultuous character.

If, on the other hand, one looks at the political order of the early
Roman Republic from the functional point of view, most of the political
powers that result from political and administrative functions of any
kind were originally concentrated in the hands of the consuls. There
was no system of checks and balances based on the distribution of power
between various political agencies, the executive, the judicial power, and
the legislative initiative (though not the power of making laws) all
being originally concentrated in the hands of the consuls. Yet the power
of the consuls that might have resulted from all these various functions
was effectively kept in check by the principle of the collegiality of the
two consuls, by the restriction of their term of office, by the negative
powers of the tribunes of the plebs, and above all by the fact that the
consuls felt and acted as members of the aristocracy. In the course of
time the functions and resulting powers of the consuls were greatly
weakened by the creation of new magistracies like the censorship, the
praetorships, and the curule aedileships, and at the end of this development by the fact that the Senate took over more and more of the functions that the consuls could no longer exercise effectively. But it is significant that the suspicion against consular powers which induced the
people to make all later magistrates independently elective and so to
prevent the formation of a cabinet headed by the consuls does not appear
to have arisen from a fear that the consuls or a consul might set himself

up as a monarch, but much more from the fear that a unified government would mean more power for the ruling aristocracy.

Thus the political order of the Roman Republic can neither be called a mixed constitution nor a system of checks of balances in the sense in which these words are most frequently used, though it contains features of both. Its most distinctive characteristic is the superabundance of negative powers to prevent action which it developed in the course of the struggle of the plebeians against the patrician aristocracy; in this it has few parallels in history, though these negative powers were at least partly checked and prevented from becoming destructive by an elaborate system of emergency institutions and emergency principles.

But however the details of the Roman system may be analyzed, the essential fact is that in spite of the predominance of the aristocracy, there did not exist unchecked and unlimited political power in Rome from the middle of the fifth century to the conquest of Rome by Sulla. In spite of the great shifts of political power that took place within that period of three hundred and seventy years, and however unequal the distribution of positive power in some phases of that period may have been, there was no authority above the law. This fact, together with the enormous staying power and success of Rome, is a historical phenomenon of the first magnitude. Though Polybius' analysis of the Roman constitution has a great many defects, he has grasped the full importance of that fact. For this reason alone his political theory is worthy of the closest study.

IX

The Social, Economic, and National

Background of the Distribution

of Power in the Roman Republic

AT THE BEGINNING and at the end of the period during which, according to Polybius, the Roman constitution continued to be excellent there existed in Rome a politically powerful and influential aristocracy, and at both times the Senate was the main, though by no means the only, political agency through which the aristocracy exercised its political power. But the Roman aristocracy at the end of the period was of a different character from that which had existed at its beginning, and there was an intermediate time in which the development might conceivably have taken a different turn. To understand the difference between the two and the process of transition from one to the other is of fundamental importance for any relevant criticism of Polybius' analysis of the Roman constitution.

The origin of the distinction between patricians and plebeians is uncertain and disputed, but there are a number of points that stand out very clearly and which, in spite of the utter unreliability of the ancient historical tradition in regard to details, cannot be doubted. In the earlier years of the Republic, if not before, the patriciate became absolutely exclusive, so that until the end of the Republic no plebeians were ever admitted to it. It is possible, though it can hardly be proved, that, as Mommsen believed, at some time all plebeians in some sense had been clients. But there can be no doubt that by the middle of the fifth century and, generally speaking, when the struggle of the plebeians against the arbitrary power of the patrician magistrates began, this was no longer the case. The fact that the law of the Twelve Tables which forbade intermarriage between patricians and plebeians, and by

which the patricians had tried to make the exclusiveness of their caste
not only politically but also socially perfect, had to be revoked after a
very short time, is conclusive proof that there were at that time plebeian families which, in social and economic status, were not very much
inferior to the patricians. The fact that the core of the Roman army in
that period was formed of plebeians who were wealthy enough to
provide themselves with the expensive heavy armor required of a
soldier fighting in the phalanx proves that there must have been a
very substantial number of people whose property gave them a certain economic and social independence. The results of the struggle
between patricians and plebeians show that it was this prosperous
plebeian group, and not the poor, who led in the struggle, whatever
the ancient tradition may say about the indebtedness of the Roman
peasants; that tradition may or may not be an invention according to
the analogy of the internal history of Athens before Solon.[1] On the
other hand, there is no reason to question the tradition that Licinius
Stolo, one of the leaders in the struggle for the admission of the plebeians to the consulship, was the son-in-law of Fabius Ambustus, a member of one of the most influential patrician families, and himself a
wealthy man, for this is the kind of fact knowledge of which would
be preserved by family tradition.[2]

One may then perhaps conclude that while the opposition to the
exclusive political rule of the patricians came mainly, if not exclusively, from the socially and economically independent among the
plebeians, and not from the poor and the dependent, these wealthy
plebeians in their turn were led in their struggle by those most socially
and economically prominent in their group. This is confirmed by a
survey of the plebeian consuls elected after the admission of the
plebeians to the consulship in 366 B.C. The first plebeian consul was
L. Sextius, the faithful associate of Licinius in the ten-year-long fight
for a plebeian consulship. About his social and economic status nothing
is known, except what might possibly be inferred from his association
with Licinius, but any such inference is necessarily very uncertain. Perhaps he is an exception, since his family does not play any role in
Roman politics after 366 B.C. But the second plebeian consul was
L. Genucius, who was again consul in 362 B.C., and a second member
of the same gens, Gn. Genucius, was consul in 363 B.C. The social and

economic prominence of this family is proved by the fact that a Genucius had been among the first plebeians to be elected to the consular tribuneship (in 399 B.C.) at a time when the patrician rule was still unimpaired. An M. Genucius even appears among the patrician consuls of 445 B.C. This is obviously an interpolation. But just as an interpolation it shows that the Genucii were so noble that they tried to claim patrician descent. In 364 B.C. either Licinius Stolo, the son-in-law of Fabius Ambustus, or Licinius Calvus, another member of the same gens, was consul, and again in 361 B.C. one of these two representatives of the gens Licinia [3] was consul.

All the thirteen plebeian consulships of the next twenty years,[4] from 360 to 341 B.C., plus the one plebeian dictatorship of that period, were held by only five men from only four families; namely, the Poetelii, the Plautii, the Popillii, and the Marcii. Of these families the gens Marcia later claimed descent from the Roman king Ancus Marcius. It was also connected in some way with the legendary figure of Cn. Marcius Coriolanus, the prototype of an uncompromising champion of the rights of the patrician aristocracy in its struggle against the early opposition of the plebeians. But whatever the origin of these legendary antecedents of the gens Marcia may be, they show that though officially plebeian, it was "almost" patrician. A member of the gens Poetelia appears among the *decemviri legibus scribundis* of the year 450 B.C.

In 342 B.C. a law appears to have been passed to the effect that from then on one of the consuls always had to be a plebeian,[5] and, according to Livy, a plebiscite initiated by the plebeian tribune, L. Genucius, demanded that the consulship, or in fact any other magistracy, could not be held more than once by the same man within a period of ten years.[6] At any rate, the first of these rules was observed from then until the end of the Republic, and the second one until at least the year 331 B.C. The quicker turnover of plebeian consuls caused by the observation of these two rules [7] brought members of a considerable number of new plebeian families to the consulate.[8] There followed upon one another within the decade from 340 to 331 B.C. P. Decius Mus, Q. Publilius Philo (the initiator of the law concerning the patrum auctoritas), C. Maenius, P. Aelius, K. Duillius, M. Atilius, T. Veturius, M. Antonius,[9] Cn. Domitius, and M. Claudius Marcellus, each one of them from a different gens, in striking contrast to the preceding two decades and a half. But the list of plebeian consular tribunes from 400 B.C. to 396 B.C. contains two Publilii Philones, two Atilii, and one Duillius. A Q. Antonius Merenda appears in Livy as one of the consular tribunes of the year 422 B.C., and a T. Antonius Merenda figures in the list of the *decemviri legibus scribundis* of the year 450 B.C. The plebeian Claudii Marcelli were probably related to the patrician Claudii, and there was also a patrician branch of the gens Veturia.[10] The fasti of the fifth century B.C. are not very reliable in details, and K. J. Beloch, for instance,[11] believes that all the names of plebeian consular tribunes are interpolations. This assumption is not very likely to be correct. But even if it were, the conclusions to be drawn would not be very different. For, since the interpolations, if they are interpolations, cannot be very late,[12] they would still prove that the plebeian families whose members were elected to the consulship in the fourth century very soon developed a taste for noble ancestry, if they did not actually have politically and socially prominent ancestors, as the listings of the fasti, if they are genuine, would indicate. After 331 there are again repeated consulates of the same men, and the accession of new families to the consulate becomes rather slow again.

It is not necessary for our purpose to go further into details in this matter. The material that has been presented does not prove that all the plebeian consuls of the first few decades after the consulate had become accessible to plebeians were automatically selected from the most wealthy and socially prominent plebeian families. Specifically, the first plebeian consul, L. Sextius, and later the Decii Mures and C. Maenius,[13] may be exceptions to the rule that this was generally the case. But there can be little doubt as to the general trend; and if a man like Sextius may have become consul because of the leading role which he played in the struggle for the plebeian consulship, and C. Maenius and the Decii Mures because of extraordinary personal merits rather than because of their family connections,[14] even they must have been wealthy enough to assume the burdens of their office in a state in which magistrates received no financial compensation or support from the community, and at a time when it had not yet become customary to contract enormous debts when embarking upon a political career and to pay them back later from gains made in war or in the administration of subjected countries.

Right from the beginning, therefore, there were two divergent tendencies. For quite some time, as has been pointed out before, the Senate did not cease to be preponderantly patrician, and what is even more important, the plebeians did not cease to consider the Senate an instrument of the patricians and to fight for a reduction of its power. The plebeians, then, who became not only senators but consuls, did not at once cease to feel as plebeians; and one of them, for example, Q. Publilius Philo, the consul and later dictator "popularis" of 339 B.C., was the initiator of the law by which participation of the Senate in the making of legislation was reduced, though his family appears to have been represented in the Senate from the beginning of the fourth century at the latest. Yet, at the same time, the fact that the great majority of the plebeian consuls in the first decades after 366 B.C. came from the socially and economically most prominent plebeian families, which in a way had been almost patrician, from the beginning created conditions favorable to the formation of a new patrician-plebeian aristocracy within which the distinction between patricians and plebeians was gradually to lose most of its political and social importance.

In spite of this it would be wrong to say that the later development was predetermined from the start. The accession of new plebeian families to the consulship took place in waves. It slackened for some time after the decade from 340 to 331 B.C., which had brought the greatest influx of new families, but was accelerated again toward the end of the fourth century. The third century down to the first years of the Second Punic War shows similar fluctuations. Most important, however, is the fact that while all the earlier plebeian consuls from lesser families (with the exception of the first plebeian consul, L. Sextius) seem to have risen to their high position through the most egregious military merits, we find toward the end of that period some consuls from new families who clearly were not elected because they had distinguished themselves in war, but because they had made themselves champions of the interests and demands of the poorer classes. The most important was C. Flaminius, tribune of the plebs in 232, and consul in 223 and 217 B.C. The ancient tradition about him is largely determined by the work of his contemporary, Fabius Pictor, the earliest Roman annalist and a member of the old patrician gens Fabia, whose leading members at that time were violently opposed to everything Flaminius stood for; thus he is described as a vicious and irresponsible demagogue. But later Roman history shows clearly that his agrarian program and legislation were certainly most beneficial, or would have been if the latter had been continued after him; [15] and if another law, which he supported strongly though he was not its initiator, the Lex Claudia, which forbade Senators to engage or participate in overseas trade, may be said to have had some less fortunate consequences, these consequences could hardly have been foreseen at his time and the intention of the law was certainly good.[16]

C. Flaminius, though the first of his gens to reach the consulate, appears to have belonged to a family that had been represented in the Senate before. His plebeian successor in his second consulate, C. Terentius Varro, was the first Roman consul of whom the tradition says expressly that he came from a socially inferior family.[17] Not very much is known about his political antecedents except that he too rose to his high position not through military merits but as a champion of the poorer classes.[18] A third man, belonging to the same group and obviously politically associated with both C. Flaminius and Terentius Varro, was M. Minucius Rufus, who in 217, through a bill strongly supported by Varro, praetor in that year, was given equal powers with the dictator Q. Fabius Maximus, whose magister equitum he had been before.[19] In contrast to Flaminius and Varro he had won some military distinction before being elevated to the highest position. But his political associations are no less clear. We also learn from ancient tradition that this political group accused the patrician faction in the Senate of having provoked the invasion of Italy by Hannibal and of then showing little energy in defeating the enemy.[20]

The movement which is characterized by the three men mentioned and which, if one may judge from its initial success, must have had considerable strength, belongs to a period in which the formation of a new patrician-plebeian aristocracy had already made a good deal of progress, and in which the Senate had already acquired some of the new powers described earlier—powers, however, which at that time were actualized mainly in times of emergency and during wars.[21] It appears at least not impossible that, if peace had prevailed over a long period of time, the new movement might have gained momentum, in consequence the consuls might have become somewhat more independent of the Senate, and in the Senate itself the influence of heredity might have been somewhat weakened. One can therefore easily understand why the group of C. Flaminius was most unhappy over the outbreak of a new war with Carthage and wanted to get it over with as quickly as possible.

This impatience, however, was their undoing. Even before the outbreak of the Second Punic War, in the course of an expedition against the Celts, Flaminius, when consul for the first time, had led a Roman army into a most difficult position from which it was saved only through the skill of his officers and the bravery of his soldiers. In his second consulate he attacked Hannibal without waiting for the army of his colleague and suffered the crushing defeat of the *Lacus Trasumennus*, in which he was killed. In the very same year M. Minucius, who had been successful in some minor battles while he was still under the command of the dictator Fabius Maximus, led his army into a trap after he had become the latter's equal in command, and was saved by his former superior. Finally, in the year 216 B.C., C. Terentius Varro, who was elected against the strongest opposition on the part of the Fabian faction and the conservative majority of the Senate, lost the battle of Cannae through his temerity. Some modern scholars have expressed serious doubt as to whether the three popular leaders were really the only ones who were to blame in all these cases. Yet there can hardly be any doubt that it was the strategy of their great opponent, Q. Fabius Maximus Cunctator, that saved Rome in the time of its greatest danger, and that it was the famous members of the old patrician family of the Cornelii Scipiones, Cn. Scipio, P. Scipio, and the latter's son, P. Cornelius Scipio Africanus, who first, through their victories in Spain, prevented Carthaginian reinforcements from reaching Hannibal at a time when they might have enabled him to conquer Rome,[22] and later won the final victory over the Carthaginians.

After the battle of Cannae the same majority of the Senate which had been so violently opposed to his election to the consulship voted to thank Varro officially for "having saved his life and for not having despaired of the Republic." They probably were aware that this gracious attitude towards him was much more deadly for him, as far as public opinion was concerned, than any vote of censure could have been. At any rate, the repeated military failures of its leaders marked the end of the new popular movement. The later years of the Second Punic War are the period of the final consolidation of the new patrician-plebeian aristocracy. This does not mean, of course, that the new aristocracy, like the patriciate of the early Republic, was absolutely hereditary and excluded all newcomers. Within the seven decades from 210 to 140 B.C. there were even five consuls who had no senatorial ancestors. But it is significant that the first and most important of them, the elder Cato, who became consul in 195 B.C., was not a progressive but a dyed-in-the-wool conservative and a champion of the rule of the Senate, and this not out of submissiveness nor any sense of inferiority, but from conviction.

There had, of course, always been factions within the Senate, and it is likely that even while Licinius and Sextius fought for admission of the plebeians to the consulate they had the support of some patrician senators.[23] Likewise, while the majority of the Senate under the leadership of the Fabii was violently opposed to Flaminius and Varro, there appear to have been some members of older senatorial families who lent them their support.[24] Such factions and divisions within the Senate naturally existed also during the late phase of and after the end of the Second Punic War. Yet the position of the *homo novus* Cato shows that something very essential had changed. One aspect of the factional struggle within the Senate naturally had always been the striving of individuals and families for political leadership. But this contest of personal ambitions for more than a hundred and fifty years had been inextricably connected with the struggle of the plebeians for more popular control of the government through a restriction of the legal powers of the Senate, an increase of the power of the popular assemblies, and a reduction of the hereditary element in the distribution of the highest positions in the state and in the Senate. This was no longer the case after the battle of Cannae. The military failures of the popular leaders, the success of the representatives of the hereditary aristocracy, and more than anything else, the steadfastness and skill with which the Senate as a body had acted in a desperate situation, gave the Senate and the old families such prestige that for a long time they were no longer threatened by attacks from below. Resistance to senatorial rule in the beginning of that period did not, as before, come from political progressives, but from the Scipios, who tried to use the popularity which they had gained through their military accomplishments in order to gain a position above the rest of the Senate with the support of the people but not for the people. In the course of the quarrels resulting from these attempts, the new man Cato became the champion of the "old traditions" and of the senatorial control over the magistrates of the Republic.

Still more significant is the fact that in the same period the tribunes of the plebs, who in the old times had been by virtue of their office the leaders of the people in their struggle against an overbearing aristocracy, began to feel more and more as members of the new aristocracy and to give increasing support to the policy of the Senate. When in 205 B.C. Scipio, as mentioned earlier, threatened to appeal to the people against an expected assignment of consular provinces by the Senate, that body invoked the help of the tribunes, and it was the latter who made Scipio submit to the wishes of the Senate.[25] In the course of the following decades the Senate not infrequently asked tribunes of the plebs to introduce in the popular assembly bills which the Senate wished to have enacted.[26] Perhaps nothing can illustrate the enormous change that had taken place towards the end of the third century better than this fact, especially if one takes into consideration that down to the year 287 B.C. the legislative initiative of the plebeian tribunes was almost by definition antisenatorial, and in a great many, if not in the majority, of cases had to be supported by strikes and other semiviolent means.

Another aspect of the new development was the formation or consolidation of an aristocracy within the new patrician-plebeian aristocracy, the so-called nobility, consisting of the families of consuls and former consuls.[27] Like the patrician-plebeian senatorial aristocracy itself, this new aristocracy within the aristocracy was not closed, nor did it of course come into being at one stroke. But in the course of time it became customary to call *nobiles* those whose ancestors had been consuls. If a man who had no such ancestors became consul, he became *nobilis* himself, yet his nobility was not quite of the same quality as the nobility of those who had many consular ancestors. It is especially significant that only a very few men who had no senatorial ancestors succeeded in reaching the consulate, probably not more than five from Cato, the first *homo novus* in the consulship twenty years after the consulate of Terentius Varro, to Q. Pompeius in 141 b.c., and after a second interval of thirty-four years, another five from Marius, who was consul for the first time in 107, down to Cicero, the last *homo novus* among the consuls of the Republic.[28] Or, to put it more precisely, there were in the last century and a half of the Republic not a few persons from nonsenatorial families who rose as far as the praetorship, and of course even more who rose to senatorial rank,[29] but very few who rose directly to the consulship, and the number of consuls who within the same period came from families with consular ancestry is extremely great.

On the face of it the existence of this aristocracy within the aristocracy may appear to be at variance with the statement made earlier [30] that a true aristocracy is always larger than the number of its members holding political office or serving in a governmental capacity. But this is not the case. Though most or, at certain times, nearly all the older members of the noble families were actually senators, it was largely because of their inherited nobility that they became senators at a comparatively early age. The political influence of the noble families was not exercised exclusively through the medium of the Senate, but in various other ways also.[31] Finally, corresponding to the distinction of the nobility as an aristocracy within the aristocracy of the senatorial families there were similar, though not absolutely analogous, distinctions within the Senate itself. The former consuls held a special position in the Senate. They were, apart from the consuls-elect after the elections, the first to be asked to speak on any proposal laid before the Senate, the remainder of the Senate listened to them with special attention, and they sometimes were called together in the house of the consul to give him the benefit of their advice.[32] In a way, therefore, one may say that they fulfilled some of the functions of a cabinet, but characteristically not as heads of the different branches of the administration, but as the most outstanding representatives of the Senate and the nobility. There also appears to have been a distinction between those senators who were asked to express their opinions (*sententiam dicere*) and those who were asked merely to vote on definite proposals (*pedibus ire in sententiam*); but it is not clear where the line between the two groups was drawn, except that former curule magistrates must always have belonged to the group of those *qui sententiam dicunt;* nor is it clear when the distinction became obsolete. It does not seem to have existed as a formal distinction after Sulla.[33]

What has been discussed so far shows clearly that at the time of Polybius, and later, there existed within the senatorial aristocracy a certain hierarchy the distinctions of which were no longer identical with those between patricians and plebeians. But the nature of this new aristocracy cannot be fully understood without discussing at least very briefly the social group from which the *homines novi,* the newcomers to the senatorial aristocracy, were recruited. These were the Roman knights or *equites Romani.* It is not necessary within the present context to discuss the origin of the *ordo equester* or the difficult question of the difference in functions and position of the *equites equo publico* and the *equites equo privato.*[34] There can hardly be any doubt that at the time of Polybius, and later, the equites were essentially identical with the highest property class, though freedmen, however wealthy, were strictly excluded, and though the censors of course had the right always to refuse to insert in the list of equites or to remove from it the name of anyone, for whatever seemed to both of them to be a sufficient reason, just as they had the right to remove anyone from the Senate.

Through the expansion of Roman domination after the Second Punic War the equites acquired important new economic and political functions. Above all, however, the newcomers to the Senate all came from this group, though in entering the Senate they had to submit to certain laws restricting their economic and financial activities.[35] It is then clear that the senatorial aristocracy was essentially constituted according to three concurrent basic principles, all of which are not infrequently discussed in Greek political theory, but most explicitly by Aristotle. In a famous passage of his *Politics* [36] Aristotle says that almost all people agree that social or political justice consists in some kind of proportionate equality; i.e., they all agree that the share which different groups or individuals should have in the government must be in proportion to some quality which they have and which can be used as a measuring stick. They disagree, however, in their choice of the quality or measuring stick to be chosen. The oligarchically minded believe that the measuring stick should be wealth, so that the wealthiest may rightly claim the greatest power in a state; the truly aristocratically minded believe that the measuring stick should be personal merit and capability; while there are others who consider noble birth, i.e., descent from men of merit, as the guiding principle.

It is interesting to see that the senatorial aristocracy of Rome at the time of Polybius was actually constituted by a concurrence of all these three principles, certainly not as an application of any abstract theory, but as the result of a historical development. Enrollment in the equestrian census (which meant the possession of considerable property) [37] was the actual, even if not the legal, precondition for admission to the Senate as well as for election to a higher office. In addition such elevation required personal merit or distinction. Such distinction could be won above all by military exploits, and this kind of distinction played a very great role in elections all through the history of the Republic. In some periods it appears to have been almost the only kind of personal distinction that counted. At other times other merits or distinctive qualities were equally, or sometimes perhaps even more, important for success in elections to curule office: championship of the cause of the people, as in the period before and in the beginning of the Second Punic War, oratorical success in trials before law courts as in the time of Cicero's rise to political prominence, and so forth. But all through the history of the Republic noble birth was also a very important factor, at least to the extent that it was much easier for a man of noble ancestry, or even merely senatorial ancestry, to get into the Senate or to be elected to higher office than it was for a homo novus. Since all this was so not by law but by custom, it must be asked why it was so, and since it was the people who elected the magistrates, this question cannot be answered without a more detailed discussion of the people as a political agent and in its relation to the senatorial aristocracy.

Before entering upon this subject it will be expedient, however, to return once more for a moment to the Senate in its dual quality of a governmental agency and a representative of a new, not strictly but largely, hereditary aristocracy. It has been shown on an earlier occasion [38] how the Senate, in the very same period in which it was deprived of its most important legal power, acquired new and far-reaching political powers through practical necessity because it was the only existing agency in the state which could effectively take over those functions which originally had belonged to the consuls, but which the latter were increasingly unable to exercise. Nevertheless there can be no doubt that the Senate would either have lost this power in the course of time—as it actually did with the downfall of the Republic—or would have been transformed from within so as to lose its character as the representative of a semihereditary aristocracy, if it had not been for the enormous prestige which both this aristocracy and the Senate as a political body acquired during the Second Punic War, and in the period of the rapid expansion of the power of Rome all over the Mediterranean world during the six decades following the war's end.

It is interesting to see how this position of the Senate, and of the aristocracy represented by it, expressed itself in, and is illustrated by, a new meaning of the term *senatus auctoritas* which developed in that time. Originally this meant the right of the Senate or later of its patrician part to grant or withhold its approval of a law passed by an assembly of the people, and in the latter case to make it invalid. In this sense the senatus auctoritas or patrum auctoritas had lost most of its practical importance through the Publilian laws of 339 B.C. and the Hortensian laws of 287 B.C.[39] But in the later Republic the term is used with a different meaning. This meaning is usually explained by the statement that when a tribune of the plebs intercedes against a senatus consultum the latter "becomes" or "is recorded as" a senatus auctoritas. This is quite correct, but is obviously in need of some further elucidation which is not given by ancient nor, as far as I can see, by modern authors. Yet the origin and meaning of the new terminology is not too difficult to discover if one considers it in the light of the general development.

A senatus consultum, as its name indicates, is an advice of the Senate, or more accurately, the answer of the Senate to a consultation of this body by a magistrate. There are numerous instances all through the history of the Republic to show that legally a senatus consultum did not have to be obeyed by a consul. Yet throughout a large part of the history of the Republic, and especially in the period of Polybius, the authority of the Senate was so great that its consulta were almost laws, and very seldom did it happen that a consul or one of the minor magistrates ventured to disagree with a senatus consultum. We have also seen [40] that when this happened, the prestige of the Senate with the people in that period was so great, and its relations with the plebeian tribunes so good, that it could use the latter to introduce legislation with the people which would compel by law a recalcitrant consul to comply with the wishes of the Senate. On the other hand it could still happen—and in the last phase of the Republic, in fact, again happened very often—that a tribune of the plebs interceded against a senatus consultum. As pointed out earlier,[41] this meant in fact not so much an intercession against the senatus consultum as such, which after all had already been passed, as an intercession in advance against any action which a magistrate might take in execution of the advice of the Senate. After such an intercession the senatus consultum could of course not legally be executed. But it is now not difficult to understand that the consultum *remained* (not *became,* as most modern historians express it) a senatus auctoritas, i.e., an expression of the authoritative opinion of the Senate that to act according to this advice would have been in the interest of the state, thus throwing all the responsibility for the consequences of preventing its execution on the interceding tribune. In other words, all the prestige of the Senate remains behind the content of the consultum, though it can no longer be a consultum in the strictest sense of the word, since it cannot be legally executed. This is also the reason why it is carefully recorded.

Only in this way, furthermore, is it possible to explain the paradoxical fact that a senatus consultum in the form of a *senatus consultum de re publica defendenda* could in a way break tribunician intercession. Yet it is incorrect to say, as most modern authors do, that an emergency decree of this kind made tribunician intercession generally invalid. This is by no means the case.[42] A *senatus consultum de re publica defendenda* was the expression of the considered opinion of the Senate that there was a state of emergency of such imminence as to justify, in order to save the state, actions which under normal circumstances would be illegal. Such an action may be in defiance of tribunician intercession, but the defiance will have to be proved to be necessary for the safety of the state. The emergency resolution does not mean or imply that *any* tribunician intercession can be disregarded while the emergency lasts.

In other words, it would be quite wrong to say that the prestige of the Senate, even when it was at its highest, placed this body above the law. On the contrary, the Senate could use its prestige to promote legislation according to its wishes, but it remained subject to existing constitutional law and to whatever laws the people passed on the initiative of either curule magistrates or plebeian tribunes. Yet in times of emergencies beyond the scope of ordinary law the Senate, by its prestige or authority, could back and in a way legalize violations of existing law, including constitutional law, if they were deemed necessary to cope with the emergency. This is a most interesting phenomenon. Plato and other ancient political philosophers had distinguished between government by force and government by law and also between government by force and government by persuasion.[43] Plato had also struggled with the problem that government without law tends to become despotic and irresponsible, while government by law tends to become formalistic and unable to deal adequately with the unlimited variety of the incidents of human life.[44] In the position of the Senate in the time of Polybius we find what may be called government by prestige, yet not by prestige alone, but rather government by law supplemented by government by prestige wherever the law proved insufficient. It will be seen later that this factor must not be neglected in a discussion of the nature and value of what is called a mixed constitution or a system of checks and balances.

Just as Polybius identifies the monarchic element in the Roman Republic with the consuls and the oligarchic or aristocratic element with the Senate, so he identifies "the people" with the official assemblies of the people, and to some extent with the tribunes of the plebs as the instruments who must always act according to the people's wishes. The assumption that they always would so act has been shown to be not quite correct, but the identification of "the people" with the popular assemblies is also open to some doubt, or must at least be considerably qualified.

It is not necessary to discuss the oldest form of popular assembly, the Comitia Curiata, since this had lost all practical importance in the period in which, according to Polybius, the Roman constitution continued to be excellent. The electoral and legislative assembly in this period, or at least in its earlier part, was the Comitia Centuriata. It is likely that in the early Republic only those citizens who were wealthy enough to serve as heavy-armed soldiers providing their own equipment voted in these assemblies. But even if one assumes that the so-called Servian order was as old as ancient tradition says it was, which is most unlikely, the voting power was still most unequally divided. According to this order the citizens were distributed in centuries belonging to different classes according to property qualifications. This distribution, acording to Livy,[45] was as follows: eighteen centuriae of knights or *equites equo publico*; eighty centuriae of the first class, originally the fully armed foot soldiers, later the highest property class after the equites; twenty of the second class; twenty of the third; twenty of the fourth; thirty of the fifth; and in addition two centuriae of craftsmen, two of musicians, and one of the propertyless or proletarians.

It is not impossible that there was a time in the early Republic when a very substantial part of the citizens served as heavy-armed soldiers in the phalanx, so that the discrepancy between the number of centuriae in each class and the number of men voting in them was not so great as later. But there can be no doubt that when the property qualification for the first class had become 100,000 or 120,000 *asses* (one $as = \frac{1}{6}$ of a pound of copper),[46] the number of people voting in the first class was much smaller than that in any of the lower classes, especially the lowest, so that the wealthy had a much greater voting power than the poor. In fact, it is easy to see that if all the centuriae of the knights and of the first class agreed, they had a majority and it was no longer necessary even to take the vote of the lower classes. It is equally clear that the one vote of all the proletarians together was of purely fictitious value. "The people," therefore, if identified with the voting assembly of the Comitia Centuriata, were really the substantial citizens. Since the Comitia Centuriata continued to be the electoral assemblies to the end of the Republic, it is not too surprising that only substantial citizens were ever elected, even apart from the fact that a magistrate without sufficient property would not have been able to sustain himself in his position.

At the same time it is clear that the relation of this assembly to the patrician aristocracy must naturally have been quite different from its relation to the later patrician-plebeian senatorial aristocracy. There can be no doubt that the majority of the people voting in the first class, and possibly even among the equites, were plebeians, and it was exactly the wealthy plebeians who were most fervently opposed to the exclusive rule of the patricians. It is quite in agreement with this general observation that according to the Livian tradition there was generally no great difficulty in getting proplebeian and antipatrician legislation passed by the Comitia Centuriata. The only difficulty was to induce the Senate or a curule magistrate to introduce such a bill, since the Comitia had no legislative initiative.[47] It is no less natural that after the full victory of the plebs, and after the formation of the new plebeian-patrician aristocracy, the Comitia Centuriata ceased to be an instrument that could be used for antisenatorial legislation. For the men of the first class had naturally a greater community of interest with the equites and the senators than with the poor, and in addition they now could hope to rise to the next higher class. It was only in the last century of the Republic that, for reasons which will be discussed later, a certain antagonism arose temporarily between the knights and the senatorial aristocracy.

The assemblies of the plebs, the concilia plebis, also voted by groups, i.e., first each individual voted in his group, then the vote of the majority within the group was counted as one vote in the final count of the group votes. The distribution within these groups in the plebeian assemblies, however, was not by property qualifications but by local districts, the so-called *tribus*. There is probably significance in the names of these tribus and in what ancient tradition tells about their origin. In the beginning there were three tribus, which had their names from Etruscan gentes; each was subdivided into ten curiae. Thus it is clear that the oldest division was closely connected with the old gentilician order.[48] Then, according to ancient tradition, this order was changed, and instead of the three original tribus, four urban tribus were created, to which, in the course of time, an increasing number of rural tribus was added, until in the year 241 B.C. the number of thirty-one rural tribus, or thirty-five tribus altogether, was reached. After this no addition to the number was made. In the tradition the replacement of the original three by the four urban tribus, and possibly the first rural tribus also, is ascribed to the king Servius Tullius and is connected closely with the establishment of the new centuriate order.[49] In fact, though the date may be contested, and the details reported by ancient writers are unreliable and contradictory, there can hardly be any doubt that the two measures belong together, since both of them are an expression of the first break of the gentilician order of the community and in the army.

The names of the four urban tribus were derived from localities. The names of the first sixteen rural tribus were derived from the names of noble gentes, while the names of the rural tribus created in and after the last quarter of the fifth century are again derived from localities. This is probably significant. It is likely that the earliest plebeians who were more or less independent of the patrician families were concentrated in the city while the majority, though probably never the whole, of the plebeian rural population were clients of the patrician families. Hence the derivation from the names of gentes of the names of the rural tribus, but not of the urban ones. The addition of the later tribus, beginning with the creation of the tribus Clustumina, which was the first of the rural tribus to have a name derived from a locality rather than from a gens, was always connected with an extension of Roman territory into former enemy country. Though large parts of the conquered land used to become state domain, and though large parts of this public land in its turn used to be "lent" to noble families, neither the plebeian settlers on such territory nor the native inhabitants who might be given Roman citizenship became clients of the noble families, and when the last rural tribus were added in the third century, the institution of clientship in its original sense had become obsolete anyway. Thus the changing of names of the Roman tribus clearly reflects changing social and political conditions.

As mentioned earlier, before 287 B.C. the concilia plebis could not make laws, but through their resolutions, which were supported if necessary by military strikes, could exercise pressure on the Senate and the curule magistrates to introduce desired legislation in the legislative assembly or assemblies. According to many passages in Livy and other ancient authors it would appear that from the middle of the fifth century B.C. there was another type of legislative assembly besides the Comitia Centuriata, namely the Comitia Tributa, which, like the Concilium Plebis, voted by tribus. The frequent and obvious confusion which can be observed in Livy between the Concilium Plebis and these presumed Comitia Tributa makes it extremely doubtful, however, whether such an assembly, which, if it had the right to make laws must have been a patrician-plebeian assembly, ever existed in that period.[50] It is likely—though with the available evidence it cannot be proved with certainty—that some time after the resolutions of the Concilium Plebis had acquired force equal to that of laws passed by the Comitia Centuriata the patricians were admitted to the former Concilium Plebis, and this body then received the name of Comitia Tributa.[51] It would then be quite easy to understand how some ancient authors could mistakenly apply the latter term also to the Concilium Plebis of the period before 287 B.C., and how this in turn could lead to the assumption that there had been in the early Republic a special assembly of that name which was different from the Concilium Plebis.

At any rate, shortly before the outbreak of the Second Punic War, some sixty years after the Hortensian law of 287, there appears to have been a reorganization of the legislative and electoral assemblies. Unfortunately, the details of this reorganization are by no means clear. There can be no doubt that the division by centuriae was connected and combined with the division by tribus. As to the way in which this combination was effected, the most plausible explanation on the basis of the available evidence appears to be the following: There were now seventy centuriae in each of the five classes (two from each of the thirty-five tribus), and in addition the eighteen centuriae of equites, plus the five traditional tribus of craftsmen, musicians, and proletarians, or three hundred and seventy-three centuriae altogether. But the references to the new order in surviving ancient literature are too brief and obscure to make it quite sure that this or any other modern explanation is correct.[52]

Much more important for an analysis of the Roman constitution as a mixed constitution, however, is the question of how far and in what way these various assemblies actually represented "the people."

Obviously a purely plebeian assembly voting by tribus, i.e. by local districts, did not give the wealthy the same absolute advantage as did an assembly voting by property classes, in which the two highest property classes had the absolute majority of votes. Thus the wealthy plebeians of the early Republic must have needed the support of the poorer or middle classes in their struggle to break, with the help of the Concilium Plebis, the dominance of the patrician aristocracy. This is also what the ancient tradition indicates.

We do not know whether the first rural tribus were created at the same time as the four urban tribus, as most modern scholars assume, or whether there was a time in which the urban tribus were the only ones that existed, as Livy and Dionysius of Halicarnassus clearly imply.[53] If the latter was the case, this was at a time when in all likelihood the majority of the independent plebeians lived in the city. But our knowledge of those early times is too scanty to permit us to draw any definite conclusions. It appears certain, however, that, after the rural tribus had been added, until the censorship of Appius Claudius Caecus in 312 B.C. only (male) landowners, and the latter to the exclusion of the freedmen, were enrolled in the tribus.[54] Appius Claudius admitted both freedmen and those citizens who had no landed property to the tribus, but in 304 B.C. in the censorship of Q. Fabius and P. Decius they were restricted to the four urban tribus. By that time the number of rural tribus had grown to twenty-seven, in 300 B.C. it was increased to twenty-nine, and in 241 to thirty-one, so that the groups mentioned had influence only on four out of thirty-one, thirty-three, or thirty-five votes. In other words, the urban tribus, which originally had probably contained most of the independent plebeians, became after 304 B.C. the tribus of the proletarians. But at that time they formed a small minority of the voting assembly.

Furthermore, as the territory inhabited by Roman citizens increased, and especially after the creation of the last two tribus in 241 B.C., when large sections of the population of Picenum and the Sabine country received full Roman citizenship and were incorporated in these new tribus, a situation developed which was very similar to that prevailing in the Achaean confederacy.[55] Since everybody had to come to the assembly at Rome in order to make use of his right to vote, and since it was much easier for wealthy people to undertake this travel from distant localities than for the poor, the number of people who came from a distance to vote was much smaller than the number of those entitled to vote, and the wealthy were favored. The effect was, of course, not quite the same in the centuriate assemblies subdivided by tribus which were introduced about 220 B.C., and which have been mentioned before.[56] For here the lower property classes had their fixed number of votes regardless of the number of individuals attending. On the other hand, the division by classes in the new order still favored to some extent the wealthier people, and the proletarians in all likelihood still had only one vote in this assembly, though this is not quite certain. At the same time, since there were many more rural tribus than urban, in spite of the fact that the urban population increased much more in proportion than the rural population, the latter continued to have a considerable advantage in voting power.

This situation continued down to about the beginning of the last century of the Republic. It began to change around this time, or a little earlier, but characteristically not through a change in the organization of the popular assemblies or in the voting order. Through the destructions of the Second Punic War, but even more through the continuous wars fought by the Romans far away from home all through the first half of the second century down to the destruction of Carthage and Corinth, many Roman peasants, who had continued to serve in the army over a long period of time, lost their farms and came to live at Rome. It had by then become customary that Roman citizens retained their tribus even if they no longer lived in the region belonging to it. Thus these new city proletarians did not, like those without property of the century after the censorship of Q. Fabius, vote in the urban tribus only, but in increasing numbers in the rural tribus, and they could always vote since they were present in Rome. If and when, therefore, only a comparative few of the voters from the country came to Rome to vote, the representatives of the corresponding tribes who stayed in Rome because they had lost their land might and often did have the majority within the tribus, and so determined its vote. If, on the other hand, many did take the trouble to come to Rome, they could out-vote the city crowd. Cicero was proud that when his recall from exile in 57 B.C. came up for the vote in the Comitia, people from all over Italy came to Rome to vote for him.[57] But with the many votes that had to be taken within a year this was but seldom the case. As a consequence we find that since the time of the Gracchi it is increasingly the city population which has the decisive vote in the popular assemblies. Towards the end of the Republic there even were clubs that would sell votes in sufficient numbers to swing an election or to carry through a law. But bribery in elections had been a matter of common concern as early as the middle of the second century B.C. It is hardly necessary to say that these popular assemblies of the late Republic were even less truly representative of "the people" than the various assemblies of the earlier period in which the wealthy had always had an advantage in voting power over the poor. But the observation may be emphasized again that in all the various assemblies of the early Republic and throughout all the changes in their form, divisions, and voting procedures, the wealthy continued to have, though in varying degree, a considerable advantage in regard to the weight of their vote, and that this changed completely in a period in which there was no essential change in the form of the popular assemblies at all. This shift of power, on the other hand, which was an important factor in bringing about the downfall of the Roman constitutional order, might have been prevented by an appropriate institutional change. Thus, in certain circumstances, a change in institutions may preserve more of their essential purpose than may a preservation of their outward form.

Up to this point "the people" has been identified with the sum total of all Roman citizens, and it has been shown that though all Roman citizens had what is now called the franchise, they never had a really equal vote. But as the Romans extended their domination first over Italy, then outside Italy over the Mediterranean world, an increasingly smaller proportion of the population of this vast empire consisted of Roman citizens with the right to vote in the popular assemblies of Rome. The political devices by which the Romans incorporated the subjected nations in their empire are extremely varied and complicated so that they cannot be discussed here in detail.[58] But, very roughly speaking, one may say that the main over-all device was the conclusion of alliances, which can be divided into two groups: *foedera aequa,* i.e., alliances in which the two contracting parties were considered as equals if not in power, at least by treaty rights, and *foedera iniqua*, in which the one contracting party acknowledged the leadership of the other party and had only unequal rights. But as the power of Rome increased the foedera aequa became very soon in fact nothing but foedera iniqua of a somewhat different kind, as the Achaeans, and before them many Italians, experienced to their distress.

From the second half of the fourth century, furthermore, the Romans in Italy largely used the device of giving Roman citizenship without voting rights (*civitas sine suffragio*) to the inhabitants of subject communities. This laid upon those presented with this citizenship the burden of serving in the regular Roman army, but also gave them the benefit of protection against foreign enemies, and to individuals there was allowed the possibility of settling in Rome and acquiring the full rights of a Roman citizen. What is more, these "half-citizen" communities retained their local self-government, having their own assemblies, councils, and supreme local magistrates, who were locally elected. Yet with all this, even after the conquest of Italy had long been completed, the major part of the Italian population remained excluded from full Roman citizenship in spite of the fact that its young men conquered the whole Mediterranean world for Rome, and the provincial population outside Italy remained excluded even from citizenship without voting rights until the last years of the Republic. Thus the mixed constitution of Rome described by Polybius applied in his own time—even in so far as he describes it correctly—only to a comparatively very small part of the population of the territory under Roman domination. Yet, paradoxically, one can hardly say that the Romans as a whole represented an aristocracy ruling over the rest of the population like the Spartans of the sixth and following centuries, for even the poorest Spartiate of the fourth century still felt as an aristocrat while this can hardly be said of the poor citizen population of Rome in the first century B.C.

The author of a recently published book [59] has contended that the failure of the Romans to extend their citizenship at the right time, first to all Italians, and then to the provincials as well, and, above all, the failure of ancient political theorists to invent the representative system and so create a means by which the citizenship of such a large population could have been made politically effective, were two of the main reasons for the downfall of the Roman Republic, and later of some of the fundamental political weaknesses of Rome under the emperors. If this theory is carried to its logical conclusion it leads to the assumption that the blame for the downfall of the Roman Republic must ultimately be laid at Polybius' doorstep.[60] Instead of admiring the Roman political system in all respects, he should have pointed out that the Roman popular assemblies had (whether adequately or inadequately) actually represented "the people" in the old city-state and even to some extent in the enlarged city-state of the earlier part of the fourth century, but that a new device had to be found to achieve the same end in the vast empire to which Rome had grown in his time, and that this new device was the representative system. Since he could have found the first beginnings of a representative system close to home, in the Achaean League and in the Macedonian republics,[61] which were created by the Romans in 167 B.C., he would merely have had to develop a more perfect system of representation applicable to the vast population of the Roman empire, and since he was a close friend of the Scipios, he could have persuaded these influential men and their circle to promote this scheme. If, then, they had succeeded in this attempt, history might have taken an entirely different turn.

In actual fact the author of the book mentioned does not go quite so far in his conclusions. He concedes that even if Polybius or some other political theorist had invented and advocated the representative system, vested interests in all likelihood would have prevented its practical application to the population of the Roman empire before it was too late for the Republic to be saved. If this restriction is made, the author's opinion is not so paradoxical as it may at first seem to be, especially if one considers the enormous role that political theory has played in shaping modern constitutions, and the fact that what we are used to call democracy in modern times is largely made possible by the representative system. Apart from this, even conceding that Polybius could not have prevented the downfall of the Roman Republic by inventing the representative system and by persuading his Roman friends to promote this scheme, it is always instructive to ask what would or might have happened if at some decisive point in history a different decision had been made, or some new idea had been brought in and had been allowed to shape the course of events.

Yet if this experiment is made, the result, I believe, will still be that, however important the failure of the ancients to invent the representative system in its modern form may be from a long-range point of view, the more immediate causes of the downfall of the Roman Republic and the decay of ancient civilization under the emperors were of a different nature. It is true that the continued exclusion of a very large section of the population of Italy from Roman citizenship caused ever-increasing resentment and, in the beginning of the first century B.C., finally led to a rebellion, the so-called Social War, which shook the Roman Republic to its foundations and which had very far-reaching consequences even after the rebellion had been subdued and the original issue had been settled by admission of all Italians south of the Rubicon to full Roman citizenship. Characteristically, however, the main reason why the Italians demanded full Roman citizenship was not their desire to have the right to vote in the popular assemblies, but the desire of the wealthy and locally prominent to be able to enter upon political careers in Rome without having to give up their local connections, the desire of the poor to be allowed to settle in Rome and participate in distribution of cheap grains, and finally the desire of all of them to have the right to appeal from the decision of a Roman magistrate to an assembly of the people. It will be seen later that this is most significant in several respects.

The civil war in Italy was just drawing to its end when the eastern provinces rebelled against the Romans, and in many towns in Asia Minor and the Aegean islands the Roman and Italian inhabitants were massacred. The reason for this outbreak, however, again was not that a demand for Roman citizenship had been refused, but the general hatred of the foreign master, and especially resentment over the exploitation by Roman governors, tax-farmers, and business people. Of course it may be argued that all or most of these evils would or might have been prevented if the population of the provinces had been represented in the central government in the same way in which all the states of the Union are represented in the United States Senate and in the House of Representatives. This argument is certainly not without weight. Yet one may ask whether, quite aside from the possibility that "vested interests" at Rome might have prevented the application of such a scheme, the representative system in its modern form could have worked at all in so vast an empire and with so unhomogeneous a population. Obviously, then, the problem cannot be stated in such simple terms, but is in need of further clarification.

According to Polybius' theory, the mixed constitution is a mixture of a monarchic, an oligarchic, and a democratic element, and the democratic element is identified with "the people." Hence, if the sum total of the inhabitants of a country are "the people," Polybius' analysis of the Roman constitution is clearly defective, since "the people" of whom he is talking in this analysis were only a very small part of the inhabitants of the Roman empire of his time. The same, however, is true of Sparta, and in this case Polybius was certainly aware of the fact. He believed that a mixed constitution, even of this imperfect kind, still had most of the qualities which made it preferable to any other, especially in that it would be more stable and would make a community strong in its relations with other countries. He conceded that the Spartan constitution was undermined by an expansion of Spartan rule for which it was not made. He believed that the Roman constitution was better constructed in this respect. In this opinion he may of course have been mistaken, and it is certainly a serious deficiency of his analysis that in comparing Sparta and Rome he mainly compares their respective abilities to wage wars far from the home base, but does not discuss in any detail the problems arising when an attempt is made to keep not only a subject population within a comparatively small territory, but the population of a large empire, under control in peacetime.

At this point the problem of the nature and value of the mixed constitution indeed becomes closely connected with the problem of the causes of the downfall of the Roman Republic. Was the destruction of the republican form of government simply the inevitable result of rapid overexpansion? If so, in what specific way or ways did overexpansion destroy the system of checks and balances on which the Republic, according to Polybius, had rested? Or could this result have been avoided, and was the invention and application of the representative system the only possible, or at least the best, way of avoiding it? Certainly the rule and the administration of so vast an empire could not remain indefinitely restricted to so small a minority as the Roman citizens at the time of Polybius were of the population of the empire as a whole, and all the less so since these Roman citizens were anything but a socially homogeneous group. A gradual extension of the rights and duties of citizenship was certainly necessary and actually took place within the next few centuries. But this required a long process of assimilation, at the end of which the introduction of such a device as the representative system might have been beneficial. It is hardly imaginable that this system would have worked if it had been artificially introduced in the first century after the conquest of the Mediterranean world had been completed. But by the end of this century the Roman Republic had already given way to the rule of Caesar.

Still more important is another factor. The resentment of the Italians who had not been admitted to full Roman citizenship was partly caused by the interference of the Roman government with the local administration of the half-citizen communities, an interference which was not compensated for by full citizen rights. But ironically the admission to full citizenship brought with it a further reduction in local self-determination. This is characteristic of the general development of the pattern of government in the following centuries, far beyond the end of the Republic. Though many of the earlier emperors, beginning with Caesar, favored and tried to promote local self-government and self-administration, the general trend was toward ever-greater centralization of military, administrative, and economic controls all over the empire, a centralization which made much faster progress under the "good" than under the "bad" emperors, which proceeded parallel with the process of assimilation and the extension of citizenship to an ever-increasing part of the population of the Roman empire, and which, in the course of time, became absolutely suffocating.[62] It is very doubtful whether a central congress in which all the provinces would have been represented, could or would have counteracted this development. Therefore, though there can hardly be any doubt that the rapid expansion of Roman domination in the early half of the second century B.C., and the impossibility of extending Roman citizenship effectively and quickly over the whole empire, were among the main causes of the downfall of the Roman Republic, the failure of the ancient political theorists to invent and advocate the representative system cannot be considered the decisive factor, and the more immediate and specific causes must be found elsewhere. But before the attempt can be made to find and analyze these causes it will be necessary to consider one more aspect of the social and economic background of the distribution of power in the Roman Republic.

In criticizing Polybius' analysis of the Roman constitution we have found that there is nothing monarchic about the consuls except what is inherent in their official functions, but that there was an aristocracy, or rather that there were at different times different types of aristocracies more comprehensive than the Senate, which was the body by which they were to some extent represented, and that "the people" likewise comprised more than the various functional popular assemblies. Since Polybius has analyzed only the interrelations between the Senate and the people, his analysis must be supplemented by an attempt to show in what way the various aristocracies and "the people" acted upon one another, and in this connection it will also be possible to show in what way, toward the end of the Republic, certain individuals could attain semimonarchic positions.

No aristocracy can come to power or stay in power without the support of a sizable section of the population not belonging to the aristocracy but especially dependent on it. In the early Republic this factor was provided by the clients in the original and technical sense of the word, the dependent peasants and retainers of the patrician gentes; there can be no doubt that the patricians would not have been able to resist the rise of the plebeians for such a long time, and that the struggle between patricians and plebeians would not have ended in a compromise, if it had not been for the clients.

Clientship in its original form and meaning had probably become a thing of the past at the time when the plebeians attained access to the consulship. Yet in ever-changing forms it continued to be a very essential factor in Roman political life to the end of the Republic. The first plebeian consul, Sextius, was probably elected to this high position because of his leadership in the struggle of the plebeians for greater political influence, and not through the help of any special clientele of his family or of his own. But the very fact that for many decades afterwards only members of the socially and economically most prominent families were elected to the consulship indicates that these families also had their clients, not in the original sense of the word but in the sense of a large group of people who were either economically dependent on them, or otherwise expected help and support from them in their economic, social, and political ambitions. The same must, of course, have continued to be true to an even larger extent of the powerful patrician families. In later times, when the wealthy nobles owned large numbers of slaves, the fact that, according to Roman practice, slaves who were set free immediately acquired Roman citizenship but remained bound to their former masters by strong ties of obligation, must also have contributed to the increase of the political influence of the nobles, and all the more so since the vote in the popular assemblies, until 139 B.C. in elections, and until 131 B.C. in legislative assemblies, was not secret.[63]

These various forms of clientship in the nontechnical sense of the word, then, played a very great role in the maintenance of the essentially aristocratic character of the Roman government in spite of the fundamental change from the patrician aristocracy of the early Republic to the patrician-plebeian senatorial aristocracy of the later Republic. They constituted at the same time a very important factor in the struggle of individuals and individual families or gentes for leadership within the aristocracy and in the state.

Strong loyalties and allegiances of this kind, competing with the loyalty and allegiance of the individual to the community as a whole and to the state, have often proved very dangerous and disruptive. Yet this appears not to have been the case in Rome before the end of the second century or the beginning of the first century B.C., in spite of the fact that the earlier history of the Roman Republic is full of struggles for power between various factions within the aristocracy.[64] The reasons, however, why this was so are not too difficult to find. If one disregards the early struggles between patricians and plebeians, which are of a different nature, Roman history down to the last century of the Republic is remarkably free from ideological parties. The reason for this was at least partly that the natural tendency of dissension over questions of internal and foreign policy to crystallize in the formation of more or less permanent political parties was to some extent counteracted and deflected by the crosscurrents of family policies, i.e. the struggle of individual families for political leadership. None of these families ever became wealthy enough to dominate the state by means of its dependents or clients. One of the most characteristic features of Roman internal politics in the middle period of the Republic, and, though in a somewhat different way, still later, is the constant formation of political alliances between aristocratic families or individuals for mutual support in the struggle for leadership and power. At the same time the mutual jealousies were naturally very strong, and the history of the Scipios shows that, as soon as there was a danger of an individual or a family rising above all others, the majority of the aristocracy formed a coalition to prevent this. No less important, however, was the fact that there was a considerable body of citizens who were not closely or permanently tied to any of the noble families, and while these men might not participate very much in the everyday struggle for political power, they could always make their influence felt when an important issue was at stake.

This situation did not change visibly before the last century of the Republic. But the origins of the development which ultimately led to a fundamental change are to be found far back in the second half of the third century B.C. The conquest of Sicily by the Romans in the First Punic War and the subsequent collection of taxes from that fertile country in the form of grain brought a great amount of grain to Italy which could be sold cheaper than was possible for the Italian farmer. This had no very dangerous consequences as long as the Italian farmers could produce most of their needs on their own farms. But when, in the course of the Second Punic War, Italy had been thoroughly devastated by the armies of Hannibal, and the houses and implements on many farms had been destroyed, many farmers had to go into debt in order to replace what they had lost. At this moment the low price of grain became of crucial importance. The situation was still further aggravated by the Roman conquests of the first half of the second century B.C. On the one hand the import of cheap grain increased still further, so that even the dyed-in-the-wool conservative Cato, who was, however, also a shrewd economist, had to turn to cattle raising, and had to admit that to grow grain was no longer profitable in Italy on any scale.[65] But in order to make cattle raising profitable one had to have more land than the smaller farmers in Italy possessed. On the other hand, the long absences of a great part of the Italian peasants in military service all over the Mediterranean world made it still more difficult for them to keep their farms going. Thus an increasing number of them sold their farms either from necessity or because it was the easiest way out of the difficulty. This process was greatly facilitated by the fact that other factors developing at the same time made it easy for them to find buyers.

By the Lex Claudia, which had been passed with the support of C. Flaminius in the first years of the Second Punic War,[66] senators were prohibited from engaging in overseas trade, and probably also in banking and high finance. At any rate, they did not engage in tax farming or similar enterprises. Their high station in life required a high permanent income. Being debarred from other profitable enterprises, they had to derive this income from landed property. The booty from the great wars in the East during the first half of the second century B.C. provided a great many members of senatorial families who served in high military positions with the necessary funds with which to buy additional land. The enormous influx of slaves from the newly conquered provinces provided them with a labor force that could be acquired cheaply and afterwards cost only its upkeep. Some of the slaves from the East were experts in advanced methods of vine and olive culture. The distress of so many small farmers in Italy finally made land available at attractive prices. Thus everything worked together to bring about a profound change in the economic and social structure of Italy.

The production of grain was greatly reduced and replaced by cattle raising and wine and olive growing. Thus Italy, which down to the beginning of the Second Punic War had been, on the whole, self-sustaining, was made dependent on grain imports from abroad. From the last century of the Roman Republic to the late empire the food supply continued to be one of the greatest worries of the Roman government. It was very largely this problem, never completely solved, which led to an ever-tighter supervision of the production and distribution of food in the whole empire, and which produced in the course of centuries a centralized bureaucratic, totalitarian control system which finally tended to strangle all life.[67]

Still more important, however, in the context of our particular problem is the change which this development brought about in the character of a large part of the citizen population. The farmers who had sold their farms settled in Rome, and since there was no industry in which they could have found employment, they formed a rapidly increasing proletariat. Thus a large section of the very men who had conquered the greater part of the world then known became, after some time, its poorest inhabitants.

As a result of this development there was added to the three main population classes (namely the aristocracy with its various subdivisions, the retainers and dependents of this aristocracy, and the independent rural middle class) a fourth class, which was independent inasmuch as its members did not owe any special loyalty or allegiance to anyone; however, the independence of this class was not supported by the possession of property. At the same time these were the people for whom voting in the popular assemblies was easiest. They had not, unlike those who retained their farms, to come from the country to Rome in order to make use of their voting rights, nor did they miss any important business by attending the assemblies. It appears that in this period most of them continued to vote with the tribus to which they had belonged while they had still been living in the country. Thus, unless there was a strong influx from the country on the occasion of an election, or when a bill had to be accepted or rejected, they could outvote their fellow citizens. Therefore, they acquired considerable potential political power which was in sharp contrast to their economic weakness and distress.

With all this it would probably be quite wrong to believe that these people developed from the beginning what may be called a proletarian mentality. The enormous acclaim and support which Ti. Gracchus found for his agrarian reform bills in the city population shows clearly that it was the fondest dream of probably the majority of these people to return to a rural existence. It was only when after some initial success Tiberius' reform program had failed that a proletarian mentality rapidly developed. The former farmers and their descendants who had settled in Rome did not have the traditional and lasting loyalties of retainers, freedmen, or clients. They retained something of the pride and spirit of independence which they or their fathers had had when they had been living on their own property in the country. But they lost their loyalty to the community for which they had conquered the whole known world, and which had given them nothing but poverty in return. Since they could not help themselves, they were looking for leaders who would help them. So they became naturally the material out of which new clienteles could be formed, but clienteles of a very different nature from those of the nobles of earlier periods of the Republic.

This transformation of the character of a large section of the Roman citizen population occurred during a period in which there were no essential changes in the constitutional structure of the Roman governmental system. But it was certainly one of the main reasons why this constitutional system, after a prolonged struggle, broke down and was destroyed. On the other hand, no matter how strong the causes which produced the initial development may have been, one can hardly say that it was strictly necessary, or that it could not have been given a different turn, or could not have been counteracted to some extent if appropriate and sufficient measures had been taken before it was too late—that is, at a time when the mental attitude of the ex-farmers and their descendants had not yet fundamentally changed. Whether such remedial measures are invented, advocated, officially proposed, and ultimately introduced in a given situation depends of course to no small degree on the wisdom of the political leaders. Yet whether it is comparatively easy or extremely difficult to introduce and carry through such measures in a legal way if a majority can be found which favors it, depends again on existing constitutional provisions. Thus it is not possible to arrive at a well-founded judgment concerning the merits or demerits of a constitutional system without paying constant attention to the interplay between constitutional regulations and the underlying social and political forces which may for some time develop quite independently of any change or lack of change in the constitutional rules, and which nevertheless, once they have begun to develop, may to some extent be channeled and directed by a wise use of existing constitutional devices.

X

The Causes of the Downfall of
the Roman Republic

Much has been written about the causes of the downfall of the Roman Republic since Montesquieu wrote the ninth, tenth, and eleventh chapters of his famous *Essay sur les causes de la grandeur des Romains et de leur décadence*, and it will be expedient first to review briefly the main explanations of this historical phenomenon which have been given in the past, and then to see in what way they may have to be supplemented or corrected.

The explanation which was most widely accepted in the second half of the nineteenth century, and which can still be found in many popular books on Roman history, is that the corrupted and rotten Roman aristocracy was no longer able to rule the large empire which the Romans had conquered in the first half of the second century B.C., and that as a result of this the oligarchic regime had to make room for a monarchy. This explanation is somewhat lacking in clarity and neglects to consider those questions which are most important for an evaluation of the merits or demerits of what may be called the Roman constitution. If the explanation means merely that the Roman aristocracy as it was at the end of the Roman Republic was not able to sustain its rulership, the explanation is trivial. For if it had been otherwise, the oligarchic republican regime would not have been overthrown. If, on the other hand, it means in addition that the Roman empire had become too big to be ruled by an oligarchy, the explanation ceases to be trivial; but it is then no longer so certain that it is correct. At least one may ask why the rule of the Roman oligarchy over the empire conquered in the first half of the second century B.C. did continue for about a century, and why, at least in the earlier part of that century, it appears to have been quite effective.

The ambiguity of the explanation becomes even more marked if one considers its second part. If this second part means merely that conditions at the end of the Republican period became such that the result was the establishment of a monarchy, or rather of a governmental system which in the beginning was a slightly disguised monarchy with republican trimmings, but later changed into an openly professed monarchy, the explanation is again trivial and nothing but an application to a particular historical phenomenon of the general law that nothing happens without sufficient cause. If, on the other hand, the explanation is meant to imply that the monarchy solved the problems which the oligarchy of the Republic had left unsolved, it is demonstrably false. For though the principate of Augustus brought peace and a temporary prosperity which produced a great literature, the history of the Roman empire under Augustus' successors is the history of a long-drawn-out agony, and this includes the age of the Antonines, which Gibbon believed to have been the happiest period in the history of mankind.

Still older is the theory that it was corruption of the aristocracy and the factual strife developing within the aristocracy that brought about the downfall of the Roman Republic. But Montesquieu had already pointed out [1] that there had always been factual strife in Rome, both among the different families within the aristocracy and between the aristocracy as a whole and other groups of the population, without its becoming destructive of the republican constitution, and also that if the aristocracy had become so corrupt by the end of the Republic it must be explained why it had not become corrupt at an earlier time, or, if there had been earlier corruption, why it did not at an earlier time become a danger to the republican constitution. Montesquieu, with his absorbing interest in constitutional questions, was also the first to point out, against Polybius, that institutions which had made Rome strong and able to expand were not necessarily best fitted for the preservation of the expanded empire. "C'est une chose," he said, "qu'on a vue toujours que de bonnes lois, qui ont fait qu'une petite république devient grande, lui deviennent à charge lorsqu'elle s'est agrandie; parce qu'elles étaient telles que leur effet naturel était de faire un grand peuple, et non pas de le gouverner." [2]

Thus Montesquieu considered the main reason of the downfall of the Roman Republic to have been its too-rapid expansion. This opinion is of course also implied in the theory that the Roman empire was too vast to be governable by an oligarchic regime. It is likewise implied in the theory that the downfall of the Republic was due to the failure of ancient political theorists to invent a method by which Roman citizenship could have been effectively extended to the population of the whole empire.[3] In a way it is even implied in a theory which has been most carefully elaborated in recent times by a number of scholars, namely, that the main cause of the downfall of the Republic was the depletion of the farming population of Italy with its further consequences, though according to this theory the main direct cause of the final event was only an indirect result of the empire's expansion.

There can hardly be any doubt that the general theory is correct, and especially that the factor last mentioned was of fundamental importance. But historical events can scarcely ever be attributed to a single cause, and Montesquieu's analysis emphasizes, without elaborating, one element which in more modern studies has been somewhat neglected: the role of existing laws and institutional devices. Perhaps modern political theorists are right in putting little faith in the power of institutional devices to influence the course of history, though this opinion appears strange in a period which constantly produces the most elaborate written constitutions. In any case, however, this factor must not be neglected in an attempt to test the truth of this theory as well as the opposite one.

The first indication of a consciousness that something was wrong with the Roman Republic can be found in an observation made by outstanding Romans in the middle of the second century B.C.; they perceived that Rome, after having conquered the whole Mediterranean world, had not become stronger in military power, but weaker, so that it would not be able to accomplish this a second time. This conviction is also the foundation of the controversy between Cato and Scipio Nasica,[4] whether it be historical or fictive, in which Scipio is said to have contended that Carthage must by all means be preserved because Rome would degenerate even more rapidly if her only remaining rival were removed, while Cato contended that, on the contrary, Carthage must not be allowed to exist and to regain some strength since Rome was losing her own strength so rapidly that she would soon be able to cope no longer with her old enemy. Such fears, though perhaps exaggerated, were by no means without foundation; for, since the Roman armies had always been, and still were for the most part recruited from the Italian farmer population, the depletion of this population made it increasingly difficult to maintain the strength of the army. Other indications of a turn for the worse were the laws against corruption and the buying of votes in elections, which were passed about the same time,[5] indicating that—due to the increase in the city proletariat—there were now enough votes which could be bought to have a serious influence on the outcome of an election, and the creation of a permanent law court to deal with extortions committed by Roman governors [6] in the provinces, indicating that such practices had become rather frequent.

These measures were directed against symptoms rather than the disease itself. Yet there were men, especially in the circle around the younger Scipio, who recognized the true cause of the evil and agreed that resettlement of a large part of the Roman city proletariat in the country was the only remedy which would strike at its root. As a result, Ti. Sempronius Gracchus, who had been close to the Scipionic circle though not strictly a member of it, and who had been elected tribune of the plebs in December, 134 B.C., introduced a land-reform bill by which he hoped to solve a large part of the problem.

In the course of the conquest of Italy by the Romans a large part of the land had been made public property (ager publicus). But most of this land had been "loaned" without rent both to communities and to individuals. The land which had been loaned to individuals had been given mostly as a reward for outstanding services, especially in war, and therefore mostly to high-ranking officers, i.e. to members of the noble families. These loans had become hereditary; but officially the land was still considered public property. Ti. Gracchus now proposed that part of this land should be taken back by the state and distributed in small parcels among Roman citizens who had (or whose parents had) lost their farms and wished to become farmers again. He proposed that each of the landowners who had come into the possession of state land should be allowed to retain 500 acres for himself and 250 acres for each of his sons, up to the total of 1,000 acres.

It was at once apparent that the bill would be enthusiastically endorsed by the majority of the voters, but when Tiberius tried to put it to the vote in the assembly, one of his fellow tribunes, Octavius, interceded. Tiberius tried to induce him to withdraw his intercession, but when this was of no avail he asked the people to declare that Octavius had forfeited his tribuneship by acting against the clear wishes of the people, whose representative he was supposed to be; the assembly agreed, and proceeded with the vote. Tiberius' bill was passed by a large majority, and even the Senate accepted it as a *fait accompli*. But his high-handed procedure had aroused violent resentment, and some of his opponents threatened to kill him as soon as he was no longer protected by his inviolability as a tribune. He therefore tried to be re-elected for the next year. Now several tribunes interceded,[7] and when the people began to vote for him in spite of the intercession, the Senate passed an emergency decree.[8] The consuls appear to have refused to take any action, but then a number of senators took the law into their own hands and killed Tiberius and some of his followers in a street battle.

This was the visible beginning of the revolution which after more than eighty years was to end with the destruction of the republican form of government. It is noteworthy, especially if one considers the less visible antecedents, that the movement did not start with riots, strikes, or rebellions of the former farmers who had been reduced to a proletarian existence in the city of Rome, nor with the attempts of demagogues and social prophets to stir up the people against the established government, but with awareness on the part of a group of enlightened statesmen that the proletarization of a large part of the former peasant population weakened the military strength of the state, and with their attempt to remedy the situation by appropriate legislation. The land reform bill which was introduced by Tiberius Gracchus as the result of these deliberations was certainly moderate. No attempt was made to expropriate land that had been purchased by the owners or their ancestors, even though the purchaser might have profited by the distress of the peasants in buying it. Only land legally owned by the state was to be taken away from men to whom it had been given as a loan, and not in outright ownership, and even this land was not to be taken away altogether; a very sizable portion was to be left to the men who had held it.

On the other hand, it is also understandable that many of those whom the bill required to give up land which had been long in their families, and which their ancestors had been "given" as a reward for merit, resented the demand and tried to prevent the bill from becoming law. The easiest way of doing this was by tribunician intercession if a tribune could be found who was willing to intercede. Since the tribunes had long since become members of the new senatorial aristocracy and now had largely the same interests as the other members of the Senate, it is not surprising that such a tribune could be found.

This was the first decisive turning point. Undoubtedly Tiberius was right in his view that, considering the origin of the tribuneship of the plebs, it was not the task of a tribune to oppose the clear wish of the majority of the people; and Polybius, who could hardly have written the sixth book of his work much more than twenty years before the tribunate of Tiberius Gracchus, had stated expressly that the tribunes of the plebs were bound by their office always to act in accordance with the wishes of the people. On the other hand, by Tiberius' time the right of every tribune to intercede even against his fellow tribunes had been for a long time an acknowledged constitutional principle.

Though the details of the development of this principle are not known with certainty, some of its phases are sufficiently clear. That each individual tribune should have the *ius auxilii*, the right of stepping between a plebeian and a magistrate who tried to arrest or punish him, was necessary if the protection of the plebeians by this kind of tribunician intercession was to be effective. One or two tribunes would not have been sufficient. It is also clear that they had to be permitted to use this right at their own discretion if it was to be of any practical value. Because of the danger that a tribune might unknowingly protect a real criminal, the tribunes were given the right of arresting citizens for the sake of an investigation. It is then not quite illogical that a tribune was given the right to intercede against another tribune in order to prevent abuse of the power to arrest. That each individual tribune should have the right to convoke the people and to propose resolutions was equally sensible. Such resolutions might lead to strikes, another kind of indirect intercession. That out of a combination of these two types of intercession there should develop the right of the

tribunes to intercede against any action of a magistrate deemed prejudicial to the interests of the people, and likewise against any senatus
consultum advising such action, is still understandable, though in this
form it meant an enormous extension of negative power. This excessive negative power was for a long time prevented from becoming
too obnoxious by the reconciliation of patricians and plebeians, and
by the incorporation of the plebeian tribunes in the new aristocracy.
But the danger inherent in this prevalence of negative power over
positive power became apparent as soon as a serious dissension developed between two groups both of which were represented by
plebeian tribunes.[9] The result was a clash between what for the lack
of a better name may be called the letter and the spirit of a constitutional principle, though this principle probably did not exist in
the form of a definite law. Clearly it made no sense and was irreconcilable with the original meaning of the office of a tribune that a tribune
should have the right to intercede against a bill which was clearly
favored by the majority of the people and was at the same time certainly in the interest of the community as a whole. Yet Octavius made
use of the literal interpretation of a principle which was generally
considered valid in his time.

It is most interesting to observe the attitudes of the different individuals and groups in this situation. Tiberius Gracchus certainly did not
start as a demagog and a rabble-rouser. His proposal was very moderate. He had obviously given careful consideration to the various
interests involved, and proposed the solution that appeared to him
best for the country. He can hardly have been unaware of the opposition of many of those who were most directly involved, but he
intended to carry through his measure through ordinary legislation.
He does not seem to have made very careful political preparations by
concluding alliances or negotiating beforehand with the opposition.
When faced with the intercession of Octavius he obviously became
indignant over what he must have considered an abuse of Octavius'
tribunician power, and decided to disregard the intercession by opposing the spirit to the letter of the constitutional principle involved.[10]

At this point the roads of Tiberius Gracchus and Scipio Aemilianus
appear to have parted. At least Scipio later declared openly that he
had favored and still favored Tiberius' laws, but that he approved

of his assassination because Tiberius had violated the law and endangered the Republic. This certainly does not mean that Scipio would have abandoned the reform which he considered necessary when meeting with the unexpected obstacle of Octavius' intercession. But he would probably have waited for a better opportunity, and in the meantime would have tried with somewhat less violence to prepare the ground for an acceptance of the law.

Nobody can know with certainty whether Scipio would have been successful in his policy and whether the reform, if it had come later, would have come in time and could have been carried far enough to give history a decisively different turn. But it is significant that the Senate acknowledged Tiberius' law as valid once it had been passed, though it had been voted on in violation of the constitution, for this shows that though the opposition from some quarters was violent, the majority did not lose its head and was ready to carry the reform through once the bill had been passed.

Unfortunately, Tiberius was not able to stop on the road which he had entered. It is impossible to know whether the threats against his life would have been carried out if he had returned to private life. But his second violation of the constitution, though technically the same as the first, was certainly much more serious, for the several tribunes who interceded this time can hardly be said to have violated their trust by interceding against the re-election of a man who during his first term of office had committed an act of doubtful constitutionality. Also, especially since his reform bill had already been passed, it was clear that he now acted in his own interests and not primarily in the interests of the people.[11] It can hardly be denied that a repetition of his act under such different circumstances, and before the issue had been clarified by new rules and regulations, constituted a real danger to the constitution.

When things had gone so far it was extremely difficult, if not impossible, to find a way out that was not fraught with grave dangers for the future. The consul P. Mucius Scaevola, when prodded by Scipio Nasica[12] to take action against Tiberius on the basis of the emergency decree that had previously been passed, is said to have answered: "I shall not start using violence nor shall I put to death any Roman citizen without trial, but if the people will vote in violation of the law, I shall not acknowledge the vote as valid." [13] This was an attempt to prevent a violent solution of the conflict with all the consequences that such a solution was bound to have. But it was also a reversal of the principle followed after Tiberius had disregarded the intercession of Octavius, namely, to recognize the expression of the sovereign will of the people as valid even if it had been elicited in violence of constitutional rules. It is doubtful whether this would have been a better solution than to have Tiberius Gracchus arrested in spite of his tribunician inviolability. In fact, it is hardly possible to say which of three possible courses would have been the best or the worst: to permit Tiberius to violate the constitution a second time, and in all likelihood to proceed on the same road during a second and possibly a third or a fourth tribunate; not to acknowledge him as tribune after he had been elected by an overwhelming majority of the people; or to arrest him while he was still protected by his tribunician inviolability. What actually happened was of course still worse than any of these three possibilities. The action of the senators who killed Tiberius and his followers was covered by the authority of the Senate and there was no trial, but the action not only caused bitter resentment; it did irreparable damage to the dignity and to the authority of the Senate. It was senators who first "in defense of the safety of the Republic" killed "public enemies," with their own hands and very primitive weapons like clubs and the legs of chairs, in the streets of Rome. But it was not so very long afterwards that senators and even the highest magistrates were attacked, beaten, and stoned in the streets of Rome, an occurrence unheard of in the earlier Republic, even in the time of the most violent struggles between the patricians and plebeians.

Everything, therefore, ultimately leads back to that decisive point at which matters had taken a turn for the worse. Obviously there had been a great lack of judgment on both sides: on the part of Tiberius in his refusal to wait when he found that the opposition was stronger than he had believed, and in his disregard for the literal interpretation of a constitutional principle where he believed, not without justification, that the spirit of the constitution was on his side, but even more on the side of his violent opponents, who did not see that the sacrifice of property which Tiberius' land reform required of them was small indeed compared to the evils that neglect in making the necessary reforms in time was bound to bring upon themselves and on their unfortunate descendants. But with all this one must not underrate the importance of the fact that Tiberius' opponents were able to make use of tribunician intercession. It is quite true that the enthusiasm of the richest senators for the rights of plebeian tribunes cannot have been very sincere. But it is a common experience that much stronger emotions can be worked up when the indignation over the violation of very narrow egoistic interests can be connected with the indignation over the violation of most sacred principles, however far fetched, and in the particular case in question it is very doubtful whether Tiberius' opponents would have dared to threaten his life if they had not had the most welcome pretense that he had shown himself an enemy of the state by violating the constitution. It was this threat to his life which more than anything else, according to the ancient authorities, induced Tiberius to proceed on the road of illegality, and so led to all the unfortunate consequences.

It would certainly be ridiculous to say that but for the existence of the principle of unlimited tribunician intercession the Roman Republic would have survived and there would have been no Roman emperors. But it cannot very well be denied, either, that this principle played a most unfortunate role in one of the most decisive turning points of the history of the Roman Republic. This shows at the same time that "naturally grown" constitutions are no more immune than written constitutions from the survival of constitutional rules or principles in a time in which, through the influence of changed circumstances, they may have an effect directly opposite from their original purpose. In fact, when it becomes rigid a naturally grown constitution may be worse in this respect, since its principles are to an even higher degree the product of fortuitous historical circumstances.

Unfortunately the extant ancient tradition concerning the nine years that passed between the tribunate of Ti. Gracchus and the first tribunate of his brother Caius is scanty and often obscure, so that many points in regard to this crucially important period, especially its second half, are controversial. Yet there can hardly be any doubt that the commission for the execution of Tiberius' land-reform bill, in spite of obstructionistic attempts on the part of Tiberius' opponents in the

Senate, worked quite efficiently for some time, and a good deal of land was actually distributed among new settlers.[14] In 130 B.C. the commission ran into some difficulties with noncitizen communities, it is not quite clear for what reasons. Scipio, who had supported Tiberius' land-reform law, now acted as a champion of the Italians, and the Senate appointed a special commissioner to deal with these particular questions. This caused resentment among the adherents of an uncompromising execution of Tiberius' reform, and Scipio was openly attacked. Shortly thereafter he was found dead in his bed, and there was a rumor that he had been assassinated, the extremists on both sides blaming his death upon one another. Thus the political atmosphere was again poisoned.

Within the same period there appears to have been—again for reasons not definitely known but which may have had something to do with the land reform—a great influx of Italian noncitizens or half-citizens into Rome, and in 126 B.C. the plebeian tribune Junius Pennus introduced and carried a bill by which noncitizens were barred from living in Rome.[15] The reason for this harsh measure may have been that, following an old practice, many of the noncitizens, after having lived in Rome for a while, tried to become enrolled in the citizen lists, which were not carefully checked, and that the real citizens who wanted to be considered by the agrarian commission did not wish to share their privileges with these newcomers. On the other hand, the new law naturally created great resentment among the Italians, and the clamor for admission to full citizenship, or at least a share in the advantages of the empire,[16] became very loud. In response to these demands one of the most fervent adherents of the Gracchi, M. Fulvius Flaccus, who was consul in the following year, 125 B.C., proposed a law offering full Roman citizenship to all those Italians who wished to have it, and the privilege of the *provocatio ad populum* [17] to those who did not wish to acquire full citizenship for fear of losing part of their local self-administration. But when he saw that the opposition, both on the part of the Senate and of the majority of the voting population in Rome, was too strong, he abandoned his proposal. Shortly afterward there was an anti-Roman outbreak in Fregellae, one of the most faithful allies of the Romans in the Second Punic War. Thus the second problem of the period, the relationship of Rome with her·

Italian "allies," raised its head, and one can see how an attempted solution of one of the two great problems might aggravate the other.

In December, 124 B.C., C. Gracchus, Tiberius' younger brother, who had served for several years as a member of the commission entrusted with the execution of his brother's reform laws, became tribune of the plebs. His activity appears to have been determined by three main factors: his desire to carry on and complete the work of his brother, his hatred for the men who had opposed and finally killed him, and his realization that it was not sufficient to pursue with determination and intransigence, an aim that was beneficial for the state as his brother had done; he also recognized that it was necessary to prepare the ground by removing possible obstacles of a legal and political nature. He was much more circumspect and astute than his brother Tiberius. Yet he too, unlike Scipio Aemilianus was not a man ready to wait indefinitely until the unreasonable opposition to his reform plans might gradually fade out; and the shortness of a tribune's term of office, combined with the uncertainty of re-election, made it necessary to move quickly if anything was to be accomplished. Perhaps even more important is the fact that the opposition to the Gracchan reforms had also had time to organize. Stirred up to violent resentment by Tiberius' highhanded methods, the opponents of his reforms had not, as Scipio may have hoped, become more enlightened concerning their own true long-term interests, but instead had become more dexterous in the use of political weapons against the hated reformers. As a result of all this the political astuteness of C. Gracchus turned out to be wasted, and his efforts in the end were no less harmful to the Republic than the headstrong straightforwardness of his brother.

The land reforms of Tiberius Gracchus, as far as they had been carried through, were a great step in the right direction. But of course they had not been a complete solution of the problem. In spite of the fact that many of the landless people in Rome had been settled as farmers on public land, the city proletariat had not been sufficiently reduced because there had been a new influx of people into the city, many of them probably distressed farmers who were attracted by the prospect of improving their lot by getting better land plus a sum of money with which to buy the necessary farm implements.[18] The problem of the army was not solved either, partly for the same reason. In addition, the trouble with Rome's Italian allies had shown that it might not be safe to have too large a proportion of the legions consist of non-citizen or half-citizen soldiers. The natural solution of this difficulty would have been the extension of full citizenship to all Italians. But the attempts to do this had been defeated. If it was not quite safe to have too many noncitizen Italians in the army, it was clear that it would be even less practical to recruit too large a part of the army from the provincial population.[19] There then remained two possible solutions of the problem: either to continue the work of Tiberius Gracchus and settle more Roman citizens as farmers, or to draft the citizen proletarians into the army, which of course meant that, contrary to the established practice, the soldiers would have to be equipped and paid by the state. The second course was later followed, but with results destructive to the Republic. The first course had become much more difficult because the land which had become available for resettlement through the agrarian laws of Tiberius was, it appears, almost all allotted, and an attempt to take away more land for that purpose was bound to run into the most violent opposition. Thus nearly all roads seemed to be blocked, and it is interesting to follow C. Gracchus' course as far as this is possible.[20]

From the beginning the measures proposed by him can be divided into those which aimed directly at major reforms and those which were obviously intended to prepare the ground politically and to remove some of the obstacles which had stood in the way of his brother Tiberius. First among these measures appears to have been a bill to debar from future office anyone who had been deposed by the people, and a bill providing that a magistrate who had exiled, or caused to be executed, Roman citizens in violation of constitutional procedure,[21] was to be tried by the people. Ancient tradition says that the first bill was specifically directed against M. Octavius, the second one against Popillius Laenas, under whose chairmanship many of Tiberius' adherents had been condemned by a senatorial court and either exiled or executed.

The two bills, however, can hardly have been introduced merely for the sake of personal revenge. The first bill clearly implied that a magistrate, including a tribune of the plebs, could be deposed by the people before his term of office was over. If passed, therefore, it would, at least indirectly, have legitimized the act by which Octavius had been deposed, because he had used his right of intercession against the will of the people. As applied to plebeian tribunes it would have clarified the constitutional issue that had played such a decisive role in the history of Tiberius Gracchus, and would have given official confirmation to Polybius' view that a tribune of the plebs must always act in agreement with the wishes of the people. This would have been a great advantage for the future. If, on the other hand, as the wording in Plutarch would indicate,[22] the bill was meant to apply not only to plebeian tribunes but to all magistrates, because it implied, if it did not actually state, that any magistrate could be deposed before the end of his term of office for acting contrary to the wishes of the people, it went far beyond anything that had been known in Rome before, and might have led to an anarchic type of democracy worse than Athenian democracy in the last years before the end of the Peloponnesian War. However, the bill was withdrawn before it came up for a vote, according to the ancient tradition, on the pleas of Gracchus' mother Cornelia.

The second bill was passed, and Popillius Laenas went into exile rather than stand trial. Clearly this law also was not concerned merely with revenge for the past, but attempted to create a safeguard against a repetition of the events that had accompanied the death of Tiberius Gracchus.

These were the main preparatory bills.[23] The principle early reform bills introduced by C. Gracchus were the following:[24] (1) a bill to the effect that the state should provide the clothing for the troops; (2) a *lex frumentaria*, or grain bill, fixing the price of corn in the capital through government buying, and probably government subsidies, with the purpose, of course, of keeping the price down so as to relieve the distress of the city proletariat; (3) a *lex agraria*, or land bill, the exact nature of which unfortunately is not quite clear; (4) a law concerning the extension of full Roman citizenship. This list of bills clearly shows that Caius, unlike his brother, tried no longer to remedy all the fundamental ills of the state by one and the same measure, but attacked the evil from different angles. The law concerning the clothing of soldiers made it possible to draft poorer citizens who were not able to buy their own equipment. The lex frumentaria made some provision for the poor people in Rome who could not be settled immediately in the country. The lex agraria tried to enlarge and continue the main work of Tiberius. It is not quite clear where the land for this extended settlement plan was to come from, but it appears that from the beginning Caius meant to supplement the inland agricultural settlements initiated by his brother with colonies or settlements in various places on the sea-coast, where new settlers would not all be confined to agriculture but could also engage in industry and trade, and that he encouraged more substantial citizens to participate in these colonies in order to provide the necessary capital. Such settlement methods were likely to be less offensive to the big landowners in the Senate and at the same time beneficial, since the Romans, in comparison with their allies' towns in southern Italy and in Etruria, were rather backward in the development of industry and commerce. Finally, the fourth bill appears to have proposed the extension of full Roman citizenship to the Latin communities only, and some concessions short of full citizenship to the rest of the Italians; this was obviously an attempt to solve the problem of the Italian allies in steps, since the attempt of Flaccus to solve it in one stroke had failed.

There can be no doubt that this was a well-elaborated plan, and that its peaceful execution would have been greatly beneficial to the state. But the enmity of the opponents of Tiberius Gracchus had not abated but had been aroused anew by the fact that Popillius Laenas had had to go into exile in order to avoid persecution, and by Gracchus' early attempt to have the removal of Octavius from his tribuneship legitimized. Since the people of Rome appeared to be very much in favor of Gracchus and of most of his laws, his opponents did not dare to oppose him openly, but used the good offices of M. Livius Drusus, who was elected tribune of the plebs for 122 B.C., to outdo Gracchus and to undermine his position with the people.

The situation at the time when Livius entered upon his tribuneship appears to have been as follows. Gracchus' bills concerning the clothing of soldiers and the price of grain, and also his first agrarian bill, had been passed. But little progress had yet been made with the execution of the latter; only two small settlements in southern Italy had so far been established. Nevertheless, C. Gracchus had been re-elected to the plebeian tribuneship for 122. With the beginning of the new tribune year Drusus began to lay his countermines. He proposed that twelve new settlements be established at once, thus making the two settlements of Gracchus appear a ridiculously small achievement.[25] He also proposed that the land be given to the settlers as their free property, while the agrarian bills of both Gracchi had contained a clause making the land inalienable. Naturally the actual and prospective settlers were highly pleased with Drusus' proposal, but it was not difficult for an objective observer to see that its acceptance was liable to have an adverse effect on Gracchus' reform. It has never been easy to return, after a long city life, to the life of a small-scale farmer. Since they had been aware of this fact, the two Gracchi had inserted an inalienability clause into their agrarian laws in order to prevent the new settlers from selling their farms as soon as the first difficulties, or the mere hardships of peasant life, were felt. Livius of course was not unaware that his law would probably have the effect which Gracchus had tried to avoid. But this was just what Livius' senatorial supporters wished, for in this way they could hope to buy back the land which they had lost, and to own in the future, as legally acquired private property, what in the past they had possessed only as a loan which at any time could be withdrawn. It may be added that the temptation for the new settlers to sell their farms was all the greater since Gracchus' grain price law made it difficult for a farmer to be financially successful, and at the same time living in the city of Rome was made easier for a poor man. Thus by removing one clause from the agrarian laws of the two Gracchi, Livius Drusus caused Caius' grain law to help defeat the purpose of the agrarian laws.

The fate of Caius' citizenship bill is also interesting. Though it appears to have been restricted to the Latins, it met from the beginning with resistance because the citizen population of Rome did not want to share the advantages of the agrarian grain laws with others. Again, the same phenomenon occurred as in connection with the land and grain bills; though all of Caius' laws were necessary parts of one well-considered reform program, one part of his legislative plan, by arousing selfish interests, had an adverse effect on the realization of the other. Livius Drusus again made a very astute use of this situation. He proposed a bill providing that Latins could not be punished by flogging while serving in the army. This was a privilege that did not take anything away from the full Roman citizens, and therefore was more popular with the assembly than all the previous laws favoring the Italians that had been introduced by Flaccus or by C. Gracchus. Thus everywhere Drusus tried to create the impression that he was doing more for the impoverished Roman citizens than Caius, while in actual fact he tried, for the benefit of the wealthy, to wreck Caius' reform program. As a counterstroke Caius Gracchus induced his colleague in the tribunate, Rubrius, to propose a bill for the settlement of a colony of Roman citizens in North Africa near the former location of Carthage.[26] Since that part of the country had recently been depopulated by an epidemic, land was available which did not have to be taken away from others, and the individual lots did not need to be as small as in Italy. Above all, however, Caius' bill was a bold application to the overseas provinces of a policy which the Romans had followed with great success for more than two centuries in Italy. If it was not safe and feasible to make the provincials Roman citizens so soon after the conquest, it was certainly in the interests of the Romans to settle citizens in the provinces, both in order to have a reliable population on the spot from which soldiers could be drawn in an emergency, and to further the Romanization of the countries in which they were settled. Yet it was on this ground that the bill was furiously attacked by Gracchus' intransigent opponents in the Senate. Carthage, it was said, had been a colony of Tyre as Syracuse had been of Corinth, and both had become more powerful than their mother cities. A colony founded on the site of Carthage, therefore, would be a threat to Rome's future. That these arguments were rather ridiculous in view of the fact that Rome had always maintained control over her colonies, and now ruled over the entire Mediterranean world, including North Africa, while Tyre and Corinth had remained city-states, and from the beginning had retained only loose connections with their colonies, apparently did not impair their effect with some groups. At any rate, Velleius Paterculus, who wrote about a hundred and fifty years later, still repeats the same argument, apparently in good faith and with conviction.[27]

The passage of the bill in spite of this opposition made Caius' enemies even more furious. The rumor was spread that horrible omens had occurred as soon as the commission arrived on the scene of the future settlement,[28] and everything was done to discourage the prospective settlers and to hamper Caius' work. This obstinate and stupid opposition to his most beneficial and moderate reforms gradually changed Caius' attitude. If ancient tradition can be trusted, he had been violent and unsparing of his opponents in his speeches from the beginning. But his legislation at first was well prepared, calculated to conflict as little as possible with legitimate economic interests, and planned in such a way as to provide some measure of temporary relief where most necessary until a better and more permanent solution of the whole problem could be achieved. Now when he saw that nevertheless his plans were thwarted at every point, he looked for other means to defeat his stubborn opponents. Since the clever propaganda of Livius Drusus had alienated some of the poor people in the city, he tried to win the support of the wealthy class outside the senatorial aristocracy, i.e. the equites. One of the means to achieve this was the introduction through one of his fellow tribunes, M'. Acilius Glabrio, of a bill by which the trials for extortion in the provinces were newly regulated and senators were excluded from the law courts dealing with these crimes.[29] Even this bill can be defended on its own merits and regardless of its political implications, since it can be said that it was not good to let senators sit as judges in cases in which senators were the only or the chief offenders. Yet there can hardly be any doubt that the tradition is right when it asserts that one of the purposes of the bill was to win the support of the equites for Caius, and all later authors agree that the bill drove a wedge between the two wealthy classes, creating an enmity between them which later became very harmful to the Republic.

The bill was passed, but the effect was not great or sudden enough to make it possible for Caius to win a final success. It seems that toward the end of his second tribunate he introduced a second bill concerning the extension of citizenship, this time proposing to extend it to all Italians. But the bill was defeated and in the elections Caius was not re-elected tribune of the plebs for the following year. When Caius' term of office was over, an attempt was made to repeal the bill concerning the colony in Africa. Caius made frantic efforts to prevent the repeal and, fearing the fate of his brother, surrounded himself with a bodyguard. A herald or announcer of the consul was killed by one of Caius' overzealous adherents who suspected the man of intending to strike Caius down. When Caius tried to explain what happened to a crowd of people, and to make clear that he disapproved of the deed, he inadvertently interrupted a tribune of the plebs who was addressing the crowd. This was considered a new violation of the constitution. The Senate passed an emergency decree. The consul Opimius summoned

Gracchus before the Senate, and when he did not come, remembering the fate of his brother, but tried to defend himself with the help of his supporters, the consul used force and Gracchus and many of his adherents were killed.[30]

Reflecting on this end of the first act of the drama which terminated with the downfall of the Roman Republic, one comes to the conclusion that its most important single cause was the lack of long-range vision on the part of the majority of the senators which was connected with very considerable skill in playing the game of day-to-day politics in the service of their immediate economic interests. It can also be said that the reform movement began too late, and that when it had finally started, Tiberius acted too hastily and without sufficient preparation. Thus, the fundamental fault was with the leading men on both sides. But the course of events was also very strongly influenced by the existing constitutional order.

Probably the most important factor of this kind was that the Senate represented for the most part a group with very special economic interests and that the counterpart of the Senate, the popular assemblies, had in the preceding decades, gradually come to represent mainly the other end of the social and economic scale, the city proletariat at Rome, while the middle classes, especially the rural middle classes, who were no party in the conflict and therefore might have exercised a moderating influence, were no longer sufficiently represented because of the difficulty of traveling to Rome to attend the assemblies. This latter factor was felt even more severely at times when important legislative assemblies were frequently held, as was the case in the period of the Gracchan legislation. In regard to the particular problem of an equal representation of all economic and social classes in Italy, much more than in regard to the provincial population, it is quite true that the failure of developing something like the representative system, i.e. a device that would have permitted the rural middle classes to make their influence felt, was of crucial importance.

There are still other constitutional factors that may have influenced the course of events. The haste of Tiberius Gracchus in forcing his bills through in violation of constitutional rules may have been partly due to the restriction of his term of office to one year, connected with the customary rule against re-election. Though this difficulty might have been overcome by a group of political friends working together over a longer period of time—still a difficult undertaking where the incumbents of office changed so frequently—it is interesting to observe that here again, rules originally adopted in order to prevent any individual from becoming too powerful helped to start a development which ended with the establishment of monarchy, a result diametrically opposed to the effect intended.

Finally, it has been shown earlier that the excessive negative power of the tribunes of the plebs played a not unimportant part in giving the reform movement of the Gracchi a wrong start. All these deficiencies of the Roman constitution are beyond the scope of Polybius' inquiry and are not covered by his explanation that a naturally grown mixed constitution will ultimately deteriorate through democratization. Yet inasmuch as it was Polybius' aim not only to predict the inevitable, but also to show how what is avoidable and undesirable can be avoided, an analysis of the factors just discussed appears necessary in order to determine exactly both the merits and the deficiencies of his theory. In evaluating these factors, then, it will hardly be necessary to add that the best constitution could not have prevented the inevitable results of rashness, stubbornness, and lack of long-range vision on the part of both of the opposing parties, just as on the other hand a community of wise men, or men of somewhat greater wisdom than the Gracchi and their contemporaries, could have saved the Republic in spite of the shortcomings of its constitutional order. Considering the fact that there was a considerable party in the Senate favoring the reform, and that Tiberius' agrarian law was largely carried through, one can, however, hardly deny that deficiencies in the technical rules of the Roman political order did play a part in the unfortunate turn of events in the first phase of what became the Roman revolution, and that this might have been avoided by greater attention to constitutional questions.

The next phase in the development, which extends from the death of Caius Gracchus to the conquest of Rome by Sulla, appears to have been determined by three or four main factors. The first of these was the bitter resentment which the outcome of the Gracchan struggle left in the hearts of the opposing factions. The second was the increasing dissatisfaction of the Italian allies which finally resulted in open civil war.

The third, and perhaps in its ultimate consequences the most important one (though this was not realized in the beginning) was the gradual transformation of the Roman army from a citizen army to an army of professional soldiers.

The opposition between the surviving adherents of the Gracchi and the reactionaries in the Senate crystallized in the formation of two parties which were later known as populares and optimates. It has often been said, especially in recent publications, that it is misleading to speak of parties in Rome, and that one should rather speak of factions, since ideological parties were unknown in antiquity, and since what did exist were rather loosely formed political alliances between aristocratic leaders, each of them supported by the various family ties which he was able to form, and by his clients and followers. This is true almost without qualification of the period from the end of the Second Punic War to the time of the Gracchi, and true again, with some qualifications and restrictions, of the period between the consulate of Cicero and the downfall of the Roman Republic. But it does not apply without very serious qualifications to the period between the Gracchi and the conquest of Rome by Sulla. Even in this period, it is true, there was no party organization that could be compared with the party organizations that have been developed since the second half of the nineteenth century, and there were no elaborate party ideologies like that of the Communist party today. Yet the ideological element was by no means missing; and, as in modern times, it was exactly this ideological element which made the struggle so bitter and so destructive. For a conflict between selfish interests may be unscrupulous and harsh, but if coupled with a modicum of insight and long-range vision it also sets its own limitations through the realization that too ruthless a pursuit of such interests may defeat its own ends. It is where the struggle for interests becomes coupled with ideological elements and with the conviction that the opponent is morally wrong and represents an evil element, that all restrictions are abandoned and the struggle may become destructive to the whole political order. This was the case with the most fervent representatives of the two opposite parties in the period between the Gracchi and the dictatorship of Sulla. Certainly Tiberius Gracchus had not been motivated by selfish interests in introducing his legislation, but by the sincere conviction that it would be beneficial to the state. Tribunician intercession against his bill appeared to him mere chicanery and an abuse of a constitutional principle. In his indignation he had no scruple against using every means to defend what he considered the spirit of the constitution against its letter, and when his life was threatened, in an attempt to safeguard himself he committed another violation of the letter of the constitution, and in the end was killed. His brother Caius took up his reform work with greater circumspection, but again met with the same kind of opposition and finally with violent death. It is certainly not surprising that the adherents and admirers of the Gracchi considered their opponents as men who would stop at nothing in the defense of selfish interests which were directly contrary to the best interests of the community as a whole. Yet it is clear that after Tiberius' highhanded action against his fellow tribune, Octavius, there were many men inside, and also outside, the Senate, who with equal sincerity considered the Gracchi dangerous revolutionaries who aimed at the destruction of the inherited public order through which Rome had become great and who appealed to the lowest classes of the population for support in the pursuit of their sinister aims.

It is characteristic that this bitterness between the two parties also affected foreign policy. In the early Republic the plebeians had not infrequently engaged in military or civic strikes in order to force through their demands; but whenever serious interests of the community were at stake the two conflicting parties arrived at a compromise, and unity was restored so that they could face the common enemy. Now it happened that the populares set free a captured Numidian king because they wished to use him as witness in a public trial to discredit their domestic enemies.[31] The result was that the Romans had to fight another costly war in Africa in order to subdue the king a second time and, by an irony of fate, it was in this war that both Marius and Sulla, who later were to fight with Roman armies against Romans, earned their first great glory.

The political career of Marius had begun some ten years before the Numidian War, and his whole development is of fundamental importance for the period between the Gracchi and the dictatorship of Sulla. He had done military service under Scipio Aemilianus, after whose death he was politically supported and pushed by the family of the Caecilii Metelli, who at that time were leading among the conservative elements in the Senate. This shows that Marius, though not from a senatorial family, had conservative leanings in the beginning: the Metelli probably favored him because they considered it expedient to make use of a man of the people with great talents. Thus Marius was elected tribune of the plebs for the year 120/19. He showed his conservatism by opposing and preventing a corn bill which was considered ruinous to the treasury,[32] and which he also may have considered harmful because the cheap distribution of grain in Rome was bound to increase the proletariat in the city. But he was not the man to follow slavishly the wishes of his aristocratic supporters. Since he believed that the vote in the popular assemblies should be free from influence and pressure he proposed a law intended to insure the secrecy of the ballot (introduced twelve years before by the Lex Papiria of 132) by making it difficult or impossible to approach voters on their way to the voting urn. This bill was naturally most distasteful to the great nobles who feared to lose by its acceptance the influence on legislation which they had still been able to exercise through their dependents and clients. One of the consuls, Cotta, summoned Marius before the Senate to be called to account for his action, and when Cotta was supported by the other consul, Metellus, Marius attempted to have the latter arrested for disregarding the will of the people.[33] As a result the Senate gave in and withdrew its opposition. Again the two parties in the dispute were indignant with each other, Metellus because the man whom he had made and whom he had intended to use as an instrument of conservative policy had dared to introduce a reform bill without consulting him, and Marius because Metellus considered himself entitled to direct and call to account a constitutionally elected tribune. As a result Marius was started on a course at the end of which he was to become a savage enemy of the optimates and a revolutionary, though he had entered upon his political career as a conservative with moderate reformist aspirations.

After having been praetor in 115 B.C., Marius served under Metellus as a legate in the Numidian War and was slighted by him when he asked for support in his candidacy for the consulship for the next year.[34] But he was elected and entrusted with the continuation of the Numidian War. In making his preparations, he for the first time enrolled in the army considerable numbers of city proletarians, who of course had to be equipped and supported by the state. When the war was over, this created a problem which continued to plague the Roman state to the end of the Republic. When the soldiers came back victorious, some provision had to be made for those who owned no property on which they could live, and since large-scale "employment," as in modern states, did not exist, the only possible way was to find land on which to settle them. But this meant a renewal, after each war, of the agrarian legislation of the Gracchi, which, even in its beginnings, had been so distasteful to the majority of the Senate. In fact, one may say that the Gracchi had merely tried to do before the war and, as far as possible, for all time what later had to be done piecemeal after each war; and since the Senate was ever reluctant to approve such grants of land to veterans, the former general of the discharged soldiers naturally became their advocate and champion and they his followers. This gave rise to a new type of clientship most dangerous to the state.

The next years were characterized by a reversal of the events of the first years of the Second Punic War. Then the progressives and reformers, when acting as generals against Hannibal, had been defeated and the representatives of the old families had restored the military fortunes of the Romans. Now, when two Germanic tribes appeared at the northern borders of the Roman territory, the generals who had been elected to the highest offices in the state because of their noble birth suffered one disastrous defeat after the other, and it was Marius, the man of the people, who had several times come into conflict with the conservative leaders, who saved Rome. He was elected consul for 104 B.C., and then every year until 100. In 103 he concluded an alliance with the tribune Appuleius Saturninus, one of the leading populares of the time, and it was through his help that he obtained land for his veterans, probably those from the Numidian War. For the year 100 Saturninus was again elected tribune and the political alliance between him and Marius, now consul for the sixth time, seems at first to have been renewed.

Unfortunately both the chronology and many details of the legislation introduced by Saturninus are anything but clear. But what is known shows that it had become even more difficult than at the time of the Gracchi to reconcile the different interests. The city proletarians of Rome needed and demanded land and, as long as sufficient land was not forthcoming, they needed cheap food to sustain themselves and their families. Marius' veterans also needed and demanded land, and a large section of the Italian allies wanted Roman citizenship, partly also in order to be able to participate in the expected distribution of land. Thus a large settlement plan was elaborated; it envisaged settlements in Cisalpine Gaul, in Sicily, in Greece, and in Macedon.[35] The land in Sicily, Greece, and Macedon was to be bought from the booty of the Spanish War of 106 B.C. But the new farms in Cisalpine Gaul were to be created from land that the Cimbri had devastated and that the Romans had reconquered in the recent war. The theory obviously, then, was that this land had become the property of the Cimbri when they conquered it and killed or drove away its owners, and that it became the property of the Roman state when the Romans took it away from the Cimbri. It is doubtful whether the native inhabitants of Cisalpine Gaul were pleased with this theory and its application in practice. The bill provided further that Marius, who was to be entrusted with its execution, was to have the right to "make a number of Roman citizens for each colony," [36] obviously as a concession to the Italian allies. But while the plan concerning the settlements in Cisalpine Gaul offended the Roman allies in that region, the citizenship plan in its turn was displeasing to the city proletariat, who wished to keep the advantages to be drawn from Roman citizenship for themselves.[37] In order to satisfy the city proletariat Saturninus introduced a grain bill providing for the distribution of grain at a nominal price.[38] The Senate declared that this bill was contrary to the interests of the state because of the intolerable burden it would lay on the public treasury, and induced some tribunes to intercede. Following the example of Tiberius Gracchus, however, Saturninus continued with the voting procedure, and in a tumultuous vote the bill, plus a provision requiring all senators to swear to abide by its decisions, was passed. This was not to Marius' liking. After first having refused to take the oath, he subsequently agreed to take it subject to the reservation that it would be binding only "if the law was a law," [39] assuming of course that the validity of the law could be questioned because of the way in which it had been passed.

The final break between Marius and Saturninus, however, came towards the end of the former's consulate. Saturninus had succeeded in being re-elected as tribune for the following year, but hoped in addition to be able to have his political friend, Glaucia, elected to the consulship. While the elections were in progress a rival of Glaucia, who appeared to be winning, was slain. The Senate passed an emergency decree, with the execution of which Marius as consul was entrusted. So he had to arrest his former political ally, who was charged with having instigated the murder; soon after, Saturninus was lynched by a mob that broke into the Senate house where he was imprisoned.

The whole episode of the second tribunate of Saturninus and the sixth consulate of Marius is especially interesting because it shows to what the highhanded methods of Tiberius Gracchus in dealing with constitutional rules were bound to lead when used by an unscrupulous politician. For the rest, the agrarian and colonial laws of Saturninus seem to have fallen by the wayside. There is no evidence that any great efforts were ever made to implement them, except that some Italians received the Roman citizenship through Marius. Marius himself withdrew for some years from political life after having obscured, by his failure as a political leader, the military glory he had earned in defeating the Numidians and the Teutonic tribes of the North.

In 91 B.C., M. Livius Drusus, the son of the political opponent of C. Gracchus, made another attempt to solve all the great problems. He had been elected tribune of the plebs with the support of the optimates, and tried to find a solution that would satisfy all the conflicting groups.[40] The Senate was to get back a share in the public law courts. A considerable number of knights selected according to merit were to become senators, the city proletariat was to be satisfied by an extensive agrarian legislation and a new grain law, and the Italians were to be admitted to Roman citizenship. He hoped to overcome the resistance of the Roman voters to the citizenship bill by carrying through the agrarian reform before bringing in a bill concerning the citizenship of the Italians, so that the proletarians would not have to be afraid of having to share the advantages from the agrarian reforms with the Italians. In fact, there is some evidence to indicate that he tried to induce those Italians who were in the possession of land which might have been considered for distribution under the agrarian bill to give up such land in return for full Roman citizenship, which he promised to obtain for them as soon as the rest of his reform legislation would have been passed. In this way he tried to reconcile the conflicting interests of the different groups and parties. But he was no more successful than his predecessors. His agrarian bill and his grain bill were passed, but later declared invalid by the Senate because they violated a law of the year 98 B.C., which forbade *leges saturae*, i.e., bills with riders, or rather bills combining in one law matters that were not related to one another.[41] He was not able to carry a bill giving Roman citizenship to the Italians. Toward the end of his tribuneship he was assassinated, but the murderer was not discovered.

The failure and subsequent assassination of their champion, Livius Drusus, brought the dissatisfaction of the Italians to a head. A large part of the allies rose in rebellion against Rome, and the Roman armies sent out to subdue them were at first defeated. When, in consequence, the rebellion was about to spread, the Romans passed a bill offering Roman citizenship to all those Italians who had not yet rebelled, or who were willing to lay down their arms immediately. From then on the civil war took a more favorable turn, and by the end of the year 89 B.C. the rebellion was, to all practical purposes, over. The main results of the war were as follows. In various successive steps Roman citizenship was granted to all Italians willing to apply for it. Marius had come back from his eclipse and again proved his ability as a general, but even greater renown had been won by Sulla. Another general who profited greatly by the war was Pompeius Strabo, the father of the famous Pompey. He owned large estates in Picenum and was entrusted with the conduct of the campaign against the rebels in that region. After an initial rebuff he combined military success with diplomatic skill in such a way as to win the good will and gratitude of the Picentini, and in a way became their patron. He also won the gratitude of the towns of upper Italy or Transpadane Gaul by a law giving them Latin rights. Thus he acquired a clientele of a nature and extensiveness not known in the earlier Republic; this was to play an important role in the rise of his famous son.[42]

With all this the question of the citizen rights of the Italians still continued to cause trouble, for though nominally they had the right to become Roman citizens, they were enrolled in only eight tribus,[43] so that the influence of their vote was greatly reduced. One of the tribunes of the year 88 B.C., Sulpicius Rufus, again a man who originally appears to have been a conservative and to have enjoyed the support of the optimates, took up their cause and prepared a bill providing that the new citizens and the freedmen be equally distributed over all thirty-five tribus. In order to overcome the opposition he tried to win the support of Marius, who had again become very popular, and since Marius wished to renew his military glory, Rufus introduced a bill entrusting him with the war against the King of Pontus, Mithridates, though this task had already been assigned to the consul L. Cornelius Sulla. In order to prevent this bill from being passed Sulla declared a suspension of all public business.[44] There was a riot among the adherents of Marius and Sulpicius, and Sulla had to flee. He left Rome and went straight to the army that was assembling to be led by him to the East. Soon after, the other consul arrived to support Sulla, but also two military tribunes with orders to take over the army in the name of Marius. The soldiers, however stoned the tribunes and obeyed the consuls. They marched on Rome and the city was for the first time conquered by a Roman army. Intimidated by the soldiers, the popular assembly repealed the laws of Sulpicius and passed a number of laws destined to put an end to tribunician legislation and to restore the authority of the Senate. The most important of these laws provided that no bill could be introduced without previous approval of the Senate, and that laws could be passed only by the Comitia Centuriata. This was essentially a restoration of the conditions existing after the Lex Publilia of 338 B.C., but before the Lex Hortensia of 287 B.C.[45] After having made the consuls for the following year swear that they would not attempt to have his laws repealed, Sulla left for the East to conduct the war against Mithridates.

Almost immediately after he had left a conflict broke out between the two consuls; Octavius wished to retain the order established by Sulla, while Cinna opposed it and tried to reenact the laws of Sulpicius.[46] In an armed clash Cinna was driven from Rome and the Senate declared him an enemy of the people who could no longer hold the consulship. But in southern Italy he found troops whom he was able to persuade of the justice of his cause, calling also on the famous name of Marius. At their head he returned to Rome, conquered it together with Marius, whom he had recalled from Africa whither he had fled from Sulla, killed the consul Octavius, and forced the intimidated Senate to revoke the decree against him, and to declare Sulla instead an enemy of the Republic. There followed a regime of terror during which Cinna was regularly re-elected consul by the terrorized voters, first together with Marius, then, after the latter's death, with various other men of his choice as colleagues, until, in the spring of the year 84 B.C., he was assassinated, and his last associate in the consulship, Cn. Papirius Carbo, remained sole consul. In the meantime preparations had been made to meet Sulla, who threatened to come back from the East at the head of a victorious army and to take revenge upon his enemies. In the spring of 83 B.C. Sulla set out from Greece and landed in Italy. The rest of the year was spent in fighting. Only the following year, with Carbo and the son of Marius as consuls, brought a decision. After having defeated the main armies of his opponents, Sulla entered Rome, where the younger Marius in the last days before the conquest had killed a great number of the leaders of the conservative party, among them the Pontifex Maximus, Scaevola. Sulla's revenge was terrible. The younger Marius killed himself when captured while trying to escape from Rome, and 4,700 men, many among them senators, were placed on proscription lists to be hunted down and killed by anyone willing to execute Sulla's orders.

Looking back on the events of this period, one can discern a fourth very important factor in addition to the three mentioned at the beginning of this section (p. 272), and this factor, as will be seen, is, unlike the other three, directly connected with deficiencies in the Roman constitution. The secessions of the plebs in the fifth century and in the third century B.C., and to a minor extent, the military and civil strikes that had occurred in the interval between the great secessions, were open revolts against the existing political order. But all of them ended in compromise, and each time the result of the compromise was incorporated in new constitutional laws, which from then on were most scrupulously observed. The *sacrosanctitas* or inviolability of the tribunes of the plebs, for instance, first established by a one-sided resolution of the plebeians, but then, through the Valerio-Horatian laws, acknowledged as a *lex sacrata*,[47] continued to be respected without exception down to the time of the Gracchi.

The development, on the other hand, which ended with the complete anarchy and lawlessness which characterized the rule of Cinna and the two Marii from 87 to 83 B.C., began not with an open rebellion against the existing political order, but with a mere dissension concerning the interpretation of an accepted constitutional rule, or rather with the attempt of a strong party in the Senate to use the constitutional device of tribunician intercession for a purpose for which it certainly had not been originally intended. When Tiberius Gracchus successfully, but through rather highhanded methods, resisted this attempt, the problem was not solved through either a change or a reinterpretation of the constitutional rule. The two opposite interpretations remained, causing deep bitterness between the parties, each of which believed itself to be in the right.

The first introduction of the *senatus consultum de re publica defendenda* was another case of this kind. Again the starting point was a deficiency in the constitution which, when the institution of the temporary dictatorship became obsolete, had lost its most important constitutional device for dealing with emergencies.[48] Certainly a substitute had to be found; and something may even be said in favor of using the prestige and the authority of the Senate in creating such a substitute. But it was not good that the Senate should try one-sidedly to set up its own authority as the ultimate criterion of when and where it was necessary and justified to overstep the limits of ordinary law in order to save the Republic. Or perhaps even such one-sided action might still have turned out for the good if it had been taken on an occasion when both its necessity and its justification were beyond doubt. If this had been the case, and if the same device had been used again, but sparingly and wisely, it might in the course of time have become an acknowledged constitutional custom. But neither the necessity nor the justice of the first *senatus consultum ultimum* was beyond doubt, and the method by which it was carried out was certainly not likely to increase the dignity and the authority of the Senate.

As a result, the *senatus consultum ultimum* remained a two-edged weapon. There appears to have been no trial of the men who slew Tiberius Gracchus. The consul Opimius, who executed the second *senatus consultum ultimum*, was tried, but acquitted.[49] Thus in both cases the device had proved formally effective. By an irony of fate it turned out to be ineffective some fifty years later when its application was clearly justified, on the occasion of the Catilinarian conspiracy, and again in 49 B.C. at the time of the last struggle for the preservation of the Republic. The first of these cases, it is true, was technically not clear, for Cicero did not put the conspirators to death simply on the basis of the *senatus consultum ultimum* which had been passed some time before they were captured, but asked the Senate again whether they should be executed, and when the vote seemed to lean to the negative side, made a speech advocating their execution.[50] Therefore, when he was on trial, his accusers were able to say that the Senate had no right to condemn anyone to death, and that if Cicero had been sure that the death of the conspirators was necessary for the safety of the Republic, he would not have consulted the Senate. But though Cicero's ill-advised attempt to strengthen his cause, while actually weakening it, complicated the case, the fundamental issue is no less clear. An emergency decree, based not on legal competence of the agency issuing it but merely on its authority or prestige, can fulfill its function truly only if it is pronounced with near unanimity and by an agency which acts clearly as the guardian of the political order. This unanimity was lacking altogether in the case of Cicero; and while the majority voting for the two first *senatus consulta ultima* was probably great, it was not clear how far the Senate was really acting as the champion of the fundamental law of the country and how far in the defense of narrow, selfish interests of a group.

This is the salient point. In the case of Octavius' intercession against Tiberius Gracchus it was still possible to argue that complete freedom of every individual tribune in the exercise of his right of intercession had been a long-established custom. In the case of the first two *senatus consulta ultima* there had been a previous violation of constitutional rules, so that it could be argued that the Senate had to act to safeguard the constitution, though in both cases it was easy for a discerning eye to see that the use made of these devices was somewhat abusive. But when Sulla and his colleague announced a long series of religious holidays in order to prevent passage of legislation disagreeable to them, even the most dim-witted individual could see that this was a flagrant abuse of a privilege of the consuls. It is this use of constitutional devices contrary to their true intent and meaning and as weapons against political adversaries that created within less than fifty years an attitude of complete disregard of constitutional rules and laws in a nation that for centuries had been famous for its strict adherence to legal principles. While this was undoubtedly not the only cause of the downfall of the Roman Republic, it must certainly be considered as a most important factor.

After Sulla had conquered Rome he had himself appointed *dictator rei publicae restituendae et legibus scribundis* without time limit, i.e., dictator for the restoration of the Republic and legislator to give the restored Republic a new constitutional foundation. In other words, an attempt was now finally to be made to change the constitution in such a way as to adapt it to altered conditions. And in fact, Sulla abdicated voluntarily after having accomplished to his own satisfaction the work that he had promised to do, though everybody agreed that he would have had the power to retain his dictatorship indefinitely.

What Sulla tried to do, essentially, was to restore, on a firm basis of definitely formulated constitutional law, those powers of the Senate which this body had possessed, as the result of a historical development and without clear legal foundation, in the first half of the second century B.C. In that period the legislative initiative of the tribunes and their power of intercession had been more or less at the disposal of the Senate.[51] Since the tribuneship of Tiberius Gracchus, however, the legislative initiative had again and again been used against the Senate, and the intercession of other tribunes, still at the command of the Senate, had not always been effective. To restore by legislation the relation between Senate and plebeian tribunes that had existed in the first half of the second century B.C. was clearly impossible. Hence the power of the tribunes had to be curtailed. Thus Sulla deprived the tribunes of the legislative initiative, or made it dependent on the previous agreement of the Senate.[52] Tribunician intercession was not completely abolished, but made subject to various restrictions.[53] Only the *ius auxilii*, the right to protect a plebeian against coercive action by a magistrate, and the personal sacrosanctitas of the tribunes—the earliest privileges which the tribunes had acquired in the beginning of the struggle between patricians and plebeians—remained intact. In addition, Sulla tried to make the tribuneship unattractive for any able and ambitious politician through the provision that a man who had been tribune became ineligible for all time for any other public office. This might have become a dangerous rule, since it tended to free an incumbent of the tribuneship from all restraints that ambitions for other political offices might have imposed upon him. But the law, as will be seen, did not remain in force long enough for this danger to be realized.

With the partial or complete elimination of the legislative initiative of the plebeian tribunes this very important function naturally reverted solely to the curule magistrates, especially the consuls, from whom, of course, it had never been taken away, but who in the period immediately preceding had made much less use of it than the tribunes. The next task then was to curb the curule magistrates under the will of the Senate. Sulla tried to achieve this end by two groups of laws. The first group concerned the ordinary city magistracies, including the consulship. Its laws provided that nobody could be elected to a higher magistracy without first having held certain lower magistracies; i.e., he could not become consul without first having been praetor, and could not become praetor without first having been quaestor, while ten years of military service were required of candidates for the quaestorship. So far this was merely a renewal of an earlier law.[54] Sulla added, however, the provision that nobody could be elected to the quaestorship before he had reached the age of thirty, the praetorship before the age of thirty-nine, and the consulship before the age of forty-two. He also renewed the provision that no one could be elected to the consulship again before an interval of ten years had elapsed since his first consulship.[55] The purpose of this part of Sulla's constitutional legislation is clear. To have attempted by legal regulations to make the consuls dependent on the Senate in every decision would have been a hindrance to any effective administration. By a provision which aimed at the result that no one could become consul unless he had previously been a member of the Senate for at least twelve years, and, after having held the highest office, could not be re-elected to it for another ten years, he could hope to restore the fundamental conditions of the early Republic when the consuls had felt as senators or as members of the senatorial aristocracy first and as highest magistrates of the community second. Thus they would naturally tend to follow the wishes of the Senate always, even though not compelled to do so by detailed legal regulations.

The second group of laws, which concerned the governors of the provinces, tried to achieve the same end in a somewhat more direct way. Its most important provisions were the following.[56] A provincial governor was not permitted to leave his province during his term of office without permission from the Senate, and specifically he was not to lead an army beyond the confines of his province, to wage a war, or to invade the kingdom of a client king without senatorial authorization. Furthermore, he had to leave his province within thirty days after the arrival of his successor.[57] By these laws Sulla tried to prevent anyone from doing in the future what he himself had done when he had come back from the war against Mithridates and had conquered Rome with his victorious army. He also gave the Senate by law a right which this body had claimed since the end of the third century B.C. without having a definite legal basis for this claim,[58] namely, to designate the consular provinces.[59] This, however, as pointed out before, now no longer meant the fields of activity of the consuls during their regular terms of office, for, barring special emergencies, the consuls and the praetors were now to attend to the central administration and the administration of justice in Rome. But it meant the provincial governorships which the consuls were to take over as proconsuls after their regular terms of office. There was also a new order: The Roman territory outside Italy was divided into ten provinces, and the election of eight praetors for the jurisdiction in Rome and for occasional extraordinary military tasks, in addition to the two consuls, was to make it possible to fill all ten provincial governorships annually with the consuls and praetors of the preceding year. In this way repeated prorogations of office such as had occurred in earlier times were generally to be avoided, though a longer prorogation of a command, or a governorship in case of special need, was not prohibited by law. Clearly the whole system was designed to prevent any individual from becoming too powerful and to make it impossible for any magistrate or promagistrate to become independent of the Senate. As a special safeguard a law was added making any violation of the Sullan constitution—especially of the provisions concerning the provincial governors—treasonable; [60] i.e., a *crimen laesae maiestatis populi Romani.*

Sulla made many more laws which cannot all be discussed here. What has been mentioned is sufficient to demonstrate the general character and purpose of Sulla's legislation. The ambiguities in the constitutional rules and principles that had existed, and which had been the cause of so much violence and bitter party strife since the conflict between Tiberius Gracchus and his fellow tribune Octavius, were eliminated. A great part of what had been customary law was either abolished or clearly formulated and incorporated in the new written constitution.[61] The selection of the old rules which were retained and the new provisions which were added was made in such a way as to make the Senate the dominant factor in the state.

It might then appear that the rule of the senatorial aristocracy had been firmly established as never before. But events were to prove otherwise. What happened is very illuminating. In the century from 350 to 250 B.C., in which legislation had deprived the Senate of its most important legal powers and prerogatives, the actual power of the Senate had constantly grown, and had continued to grow for another hundred years, during which no legislation was passed giving greater powers to the Senate. On the contrary, after the dictatorship of Sulla, who had given the Senate the most far-reaching legal powers by an elaborate system of constitutional laws, these powers vanished rapidly, and a little more than thirty years later the Republic and the senatorial regime gave way to the monarchy of Caesar.

The first cracks in the imposing building erected by Sulla were soon shown. In the year 80 B.C. Sulla had completed his legislation. Soon afterwards he laid down his extraordinary powers and early in the year 78 he died.[62] In the same year trouble broke out between veterans of Sulla who had received land grants in upper Italy and the former owners of the land given to them, a conflict in which the latter appear to have been supported by a large part of the population. The consuls were sent out with troops to suppress the threatened rebellion. But one of them, Lepidus, when the task had been fulfilled, did not come back, but continued to levy troops. When finally urged to return for the elections, he came with troops and demanded to be allowed to be a candidate for the consulship for the following year, contrary to the Sullan constitution. He also demanded introduction of a bill to restore the powers of the tribuneship, obviously because he knew that this would win him popular support. Therefore it was only a few months after Sulla's death, and less than two years after the completion of his legislation, that a direct attack was made on some of the most fundamental provisions of his constitution.

The senate passed a *senatus consultum de re publica defendenda*, and called upon the other consul, Catulus, to deal with this threat to the constitution, but they needed a general more appealing to the soldiers. Thus they called on young Pompey, who had distinguished himself as a lieutenant of Sulla and enjoyed great prestige with the army. He consented to serve as legate under the command of Catulus, but it was he who appears to have won the decisive victory over Lepidus' legate Brutus, the father of the murderer of Caesar. Thus the danger threatening from Lepidus was averted. But when Pompey came back as the real victor, he did not, on the order of the consul, disband his army until he had been entrusted with a new and much more important mission—the war against Sertorius who, in 83 B.C., had been sent as governor to Spain by the anti-Sullan government in Rome, and who ever since had refused to submit to Sulla and the new order he had established. This time Pompey did not have even a nominal superior in command, though he had held none of the positions which were normally the prerequisite for a provincial governorship. He was to be the equal in command of Metellus Pius, the governor of one of the two Spanish provinces.

It took Pompey and Metellus more than five years to subdue Sertorius, one of the greatest Roman generals of all time. Or, to put it more exactly, they did not succeed in ending the war until Sertorius was assassinated in 72 B.C. In 71 they returned to Italy after having accomplished their mission. In the meantime a slave rebellion under Spartacus had broken out and, after various vicissitudes in the war against the rebellious slaves, Crassus had succeeded in driving them into the southeastern tip of the Italian peninsula. But when a large number succeeded in breaking through the cordon which Crassus had drawn around them, the frightened Senate called on the help of the returning Pompey. In actual fact the danger was much less great than had been feared, and Pompey succeeded without difficulty in putting out the last embers of the rebellion.

On the basis of these new victories Pompey asked to be allowed to be a candidate for the consulship for the year 70 B.C. He was neither of the age prescribed for that office by the Sullan constitution, nor had he held any of the offices prescribed by the cursus honorum. But he did have the great fame which he had acquired through his military exploits and the support of the victorious army that he had brought home from Spain and of the clientele of his father Pompeius Strabo in

Picenum,[63] and in addition he promised to introduce a bill revoking the curtailment of the powers of the tribunes by the Sullan constitution, a promise that was sure to win him the support of the majority of the voters in Rome. In view of these overwhelming assets the Senate gave up its opposition, Pompey was released from the constitutional restrictions, and was duly elected with Crassus as his colleague. Thus, the man who had defeated Lepidus' attempt to violate the Sullan constitution became consul through a still greater violation of this constitution, and by using the same method, though with greater skill, which Lepidus had tried to use. As consul he had to act as chairman of the Senate of which he had never been a member, so that Terentius Varro in all haste had to write a little booklet for him from which he could familiarize himself with the rules of procedure. He kept his promise to introduce a bill to restore the full powers of the tribunes, and the bill was passed. Thus one of the cornerstones of the constitution of Sulla was removed without much opposition.

From then on Pompey was the man to be called upon in emergencies. For years piracy had been rampant in the Mediterranean, and the Roman commanders sent out to suppress the pirates had not been equal to their task. Thus in January, 67, one of the tribunes of the plebs, Gabinius, introduced a bill asking for the election by the people of a general *contra praedones* with sweeping powers, and everybody knew that the man to be elected was Pompey. The optimates, who were afraid of the growing power of one man, did everything in their power to prevent the bill from being passed, including intercession by a tribune of their party. But Gabinius, imitating Tiberius Gracchus, asked the people to vote upon whether a tribune interceding against such a law could retain his tribuneship, and when the vote was clearly going against him, the objecting tribune withdrew his intercession. This time there was no *senatus consultum ultimum,* and Pompey, after having been duly elected, took over his command with still greater powers than the bill of Gabinius had originally envisaged.

Pompey accomplished his task brilliantly within a year. He had hardly finished it when he was entrusted with the conduct of the war against Mithridates, the king of Pontus, who had inflicted a crushing defeat on the legate Valerius Triarius. For this purpose Pompey received the governorship of the provinces of Cilicia and Bithynia and, in addition, the supreme command over all armies east of the Adriatic. The task which he faced this time was not a purely military one. The forces at Pompey's disposal were much greater than those which the enemy was able to put in the field. But Pompey soon realized that military victories were not sufficient, and that only a reorganization of the Roman administration in the conquered countries of the East could bring a real pacification of that part of the Roman empire. This gigantic organizational task required a good deal of time, and it was therefore not before the year 62 that he returned from his mission.

In the meantime the Catilinarian conspiracy had broken out in Italy, and there are indications that Pompey expected, and in fact hoped, that the conspiracy, or rather the revolution planned by the conspirators, would be successful, so that he, like his master Sulla, could then come back from the East as the savior of the state. Cicero, however, during his consulate in 63 B.C., succeeded in suppressing the conspiracy, and public order had been restored before Pompey was ready to return. Many people expected that Pompey nevertheless would use his armies to make himself master of Rome. But to the great relief of the Senate, Pompey, when landing with his army at Brundisium toward the end of the year 62 B.C., dismissed his soldiers, asking them only to return for the triumph which he expected to celebrate in Rome. He did not wish to make himself master of the state by force, but he wanted and expected, on the basis of his extraordinary accomplishments, to be able to assume and hold a position outside and above the political factions and their daily struggles. He expected above all, as a reward of his act of self-abnegation, that the Senate would promptly approve and ratify the new arrangements he had made and the new order he had established in the East. He also needed land for his veterans, and he expected that the very moderate and sensible laws which he wished introduced with that end in view would likewise get the support of the Senate.

It soon became clear that he was mistaken in these expectations. He became involved at once in factional conflicts, and the optimates in the Senate, who were afraid of his extraordinary position, refused to approve of his regulations in the East and opposed the agrarian legislation which Pompey introduced through the tribune L. Flavius. In the ensuing struggle there were once more used all the tricks that were made possible by a constitution which, since the restoration of the powers of the tribunate, had again become contradictory. For the moment Pompey gave in. He did not call on his veterans and start a civil war, as he might have been able to do with some hope of success. But the unwise opposition of the optimates forced him to conclude a political alliance with men and forces much more dangerous to the state, and with which he would hardly have had allied himself if the Senate had made reasonable concessions. The result was the so-called first triumvirate, a private political alliance of Pompey with Crassus, the richest man of Rome with a large following in the capitalist class of the equites, and with Caesar, who had become an influential leader of the populares. In spite of strong opposition the allies succeeded in getting Caesar elected to the consulship for the year 59 B.C. In this year Caesar, as a loyal ally, after many difficulties finally succeeded in placing before the assembly, which passed it, the agrarian bill previously introduced by Flavius according to the wishes of Pompey. A law was also passed which gave Caesar the province of Cisalpine Gaul for five years; later in the year, Transalpine Gaul was added, thus giving Caesar the opportunity of conquering a little empire for himself.

The alliance between Caesar and Pompey was not natural, and whenever the optimates showed an inclination to satisfy Pompey's ambitions, his relations to Caesar cooled. But renewed difficulties for Pompey from the same quarter led to a renewal of the alliance after a conference between Pompey and Caesar at Lucca in 56 B.C. The coalition succeeded in getting Pompey and Crassus elected to the two consulships for the year 55 B.C. Then laws were passed giving Caesar the governorship of Gaul for an additional five years, and to Pompey the governorship of Spain for the same period. This gave Caesar the opportunity to consolidate the new empire he had conquered and to create the armies, absolutely loyal to him, with which he was later to conquer Rome, while Pompey did not go into his province but remained in Rome in order to keep watch on the Senate and all the forces of the opposition. It appears that in this period Pompey gradually formed the plan of letting Caesar grow to become a danger to the state so great that the men who saved the Republic from this danger would be assured for all time of the position which Pompey had coveted from the beginning, and which he had hoped to attain ten years earlier when the Catilinarian conspiracy was about to come into the open while he was finishing the war in the East.[64] As to his ability to save the state at the last moment he had no doubt. But he underestimated Caesar, and when early in 49 Caesar crossed the Rubicon and led his legions against Rome, he was not only able to conquer the capital (an initial success which Pompey had expected), but, after having conquered Spain, he followed the new Sulla to the East and defeated him in a decisive battle in Greece. This was the end of the Roman Republic.

Roman history from the death of Sulla to the end of the Roman Republic shows clearly that the example set by Sulla when, coming home from the East, he had conquered Rome and, for two years, had become the absolute master of the state, was much more powerful than his constitution. Into this constitution he had seemingly incorporated every conceivable safeguard to prevent anyone in the future from imitating his example. Yet it was only a few months after his death that the first attempt was made to do just this, and the history of the next three decades is full of similar attempts, until in 49 B.C. the republican order was finally destroyed. The reason was clearly that Sulla had merely cured the symptoms of the disease, but had done little if anything to cure the disease itself. But in order to understand fully the process of the final decay of the Roman political system, and to distinguish between what is essential and what is not essential, it is necessary to return once more to its beginnings.

The causes of the downfall of the Roman Republic have now been discussed for about two thousand years, and ever since Montesquieu have again become the subject of the most intensive study. As a result of these studies the following causes have been pointed out: The rapid expansion of Roman domination since the beginning of the second century B.C. and the consequent exclusion of a very large part of the population of the territory thus included in the Roman Empire from active citizen rights; the ruin of a large part of the peasant population in Italy and the consequent growth of a numerous proletariat in Rome on the one hand, and of large latifundia in the remainder of Italy on the other; the change in the recruiting system and consequently in the composition of the Roman armies; the corruption of the Roman

aristocracy through the acquisition of too much uncontrolled or in-
sufficiently controlled power, when consuls, praetors, proconsuls, pro-
praetors, or even simple emissaries of the Republic became great lords,
considering themselves not only the equals of kings, but their supe-
riors; the corrupting influence of foreign ideas and customs on a community hitherto kept together by strong traditions, and of the sudden
influx of enormous riches into a society accustomed to frugal living;
the factional strife within the Roman aristocracy; and, finally, the
inability of this aristocracy to handle efficiently the many big tasks
which arose in consequence of the extension of the empire and which
required the attention of one man with far-reaching powers extending over a long period, while the republican order, and especially the
Sullan constitution, placed very narrow limits on the powers and the
term of service of the highest functionaries of the state.

Unquestionably all these causes, which have been pointed out in
the course of centuries of investigation, contributed to the downfall
of the Roman Republic. But for the present study it is not sufficient
to state them nor even to discuss their relative importance or their
mutual interrelations, as has been done in a number of recent works.
It will be necessary to ask and answer a number of very precise and
specific questions.

The downfall of the Roman Republic was a change from one kind
of government to another; but it was also a phase in a historical process
extending over a much longer period of time and ending with the
disintegration of the Roman Empire. The statement that the Roman
oligarchy was unable to cope with the problems of the large empire
that had come under Roman domination since 200 B.C. and that therefore "an emperor was needed," [65] a statement which in one form or
another has been repeated by nearly all the historians who have
written on the period within the last two hundred years, tacitly implies that a monarchic regime was better suited for such an empire
and better able to cope with its problems. It may even appear to imply that the development would have been a much more favorable
one if Rome had been a monarchy at the time when it started on the
conquest of the Mediterranean world. But the fact that—after a short
respite during the later years of the rule of Augustus—the process

294 CAUSES OF DOWNFALL

of internal disintegration continued under the emperors raises serious doubts concerning the accuracy of the assumptions implied in the prevailing theory.

But even granting that the process of disintegration which began even before the conquest of the empire was fully completed was to some extent promoted by the political order prevailing at that time at Rome, there still remains the question: Which aspect of that political order hastened the disintegration? Was it promoted by the fact that Rome was really ruled by an oligarchy and the fact that the system of checks and balances, which Polybius describes, no longer existed or no longer functioned? Or was there a system of checks and balances and was it this system which was unsuitable for the empire? If so, would any system of checks and balances have been unsuitable, or was the political disintegration promoted by certain deficiencies peculiar to the particular system of checks and balances prevailing at that time in Rome and not inherent in systems of checks and balances as such? Finally, though it is quite unfashionable with present-day historians to ask the question, what would have happened if in a given situation a different decision had been made, it is still true that sometimes the course of history is decisively influenced by individual decisions. Since the ability of individuals to make such decisions depends to a large extent on the prevailing political system, it will be necessary to ask such unfashionable questions.

In trying to answer these questions, then, in regard to the various causes of the downfall of the Roman Republic mentioned before, comparatively little has to be added to what has been said concerning the lack of integration of the large population of the empire in the political system as one of these causes. Clearly the integration of the population of Italy and the integration of the population of the provinces present different problems.

It has been pointed out that an integration of the enormously large and utterly unhomogeneous population of the many provinces in the political system would have required a long period of time under any circumstances, and that no kind of regime could have speeded up this process very considerably. The exploitation of the provinces by the Roman aristocracy was certainly a very great evil and might have led to serious disturbances in the course of time. But it can hardly be considered to have been one of the immediate causes of the downfall of the Republic.

The emperors tried, to some extent successfully, to stop the exploitation of the provinces for the benefit of individuals, and some of the early emperors, especially Augustus and to a lesser degree Tiberius, attempted to promote local self-administration. But this beneficial attempt of the earliest emperors soon gave way to a tendency toward ever tighter control of the political, communal, and economic life of the provinces by the central government. This central control, which, by an irony of history, increased much more rapidly under the so-called good emperors in the second half of the first century and in the second century than it had ever done under the "rotten oligarchy" of the Republic or under so-called tyrants like Caius and Nero,[66] gradually strangled all life, and, because it was systematic and continuous, was much worse in its consequences than the irregular exploitation of the provinces by governors or tax-farmers in the Republic.

The integration of the population of Italy in the political system, in contrast to that of the provincial population, was both possible and highly desirable, in fact necessary, if the political order was not to fall apart. This integration was achieved, though with great difficulty and after violent civil disturbances, some time before the downfall of the Roman Republic, at least to the extent that all Italians were granted full Roman citizenship. Because of the lack of a representative system the citizen rights remained to some extent ineffective. This may be called a defect in the existing political system. But it is clearly a defect in the particular system of checks and balances existing in the Roman Republic and not one inherent in systems of checks and balances as such. It is also clear that the exclusion of a large part of the Italian population from Roman citizenship was not one of the immediate causes of the final downfall of the Republic, since at that time they were no longer excluded. But the struggle of the Italians for citizen rights since the last decades of the second century and the civil disturbances which accompanied this struggle may be counted among the indirect causes of the decay of the Republic because of the stresses which they caused in the political and constitutional system. Since these struggles were closely connected with the struggles for a new distribution of land in Italy and the restoration of a larger peasant population, it will be convenient to consider these two matters together.

That the decrease in the peasant population of Italy and the change in the recruiting system and the composition of the Roman armies necessitated by this decrease were among the most important causes of the Republic's downfall cannot be doubted. But the problem of the relation of this development to the particular constitutional system prevailing in Rome in the last century of the Republic is twofold. No political system, whether it be an oligarchy, a monarchy, a democracy, or a mixed constitution, or a system of checks and balances can survive for long if a very important part of the population, and especially that part which through discipline, organization, and the possession of arms has the greatest power, has no interest in its preservation. Such was the case when the armies of the early Republic, which consisted of independent peasants, were replaced by soldiers who, while serving in the army, were fed, clothed, and paid by the state, but who had no place to go to when dismissed from the army. Since the state was not willing to make sufficient provision for them after their term of service was over, they naturally followed any military leader who promised to take care of them. This then was one of the major immediate causes of the downfall of the Republic and the establishment of a monarchic regime.

Yet not even in this respect can one say that the monarchy cured the disease that had destroyed the Republic. For some time, it is true, the danger threatening the whole public order in consequence of the dissociation of the army from the civilian population was, to some extent, overcome through the loyalty of the troops to the person of Augustus, a loyalty so great that for half a century after his death it was transferred to the most incapable and vicious rulers if they could only claim some family relation to him, or rather to his wife, Livia. After the death of Nero, the last representative of this strange dynasty, some very capable generals like Vespasian and Trajan successively succeeded in establishing for some time new dynasties and in keeping the armies under their control, though even they had to make great concessions, especially in the form of the ever-increasing extraordinary payments or donatives which had to be made on various occasions. But the fundamental problem was not solved; the armies were not reintegrated with the rest of the population. After Marcus Antoninus the armies got completely out of hand and plunged the empire into a state of military anarchy combined with an ever-increasing totalitarian control of civil life, until Diocletian succeeded in creating a new but very oppressive order.

But though it is clear that the emperors did not cure the disease which had developed during the last century of the Republic, it may very well be said that the development of the disease could have been prevented or at least arrested if appropriate measures had been taken in time, and that these were not taken was due to some faults of the constitutional system prevailing at the time. For the agrarian legislation of the Gracchi obviously had the purpose of curing the disease while this appeared still possible; and while one may doubt whether Ti. Gracchus' program was sufficiently extensive, a later gradual extension of this program to the provinces, as envisaged by his brother Gracchus, combined with an extension of Roman citizenship first to the Italians and later, likewise gradually, to the provincial population, might very well have given history an entirely different turn and prevented the development of one of the greatest evils that plagued the Roman state for several centuries.

The agrarian legislation of the Gracchi was bound to arouse the antagonism of a large part of the Roman senatorial aristocracy. But the history of Ti. Gracchus and of his legislation shows that large-scale reforms might very well have been carried through without revolutionary disturbances if it had not been for the fact that his opponents in the Senate were able to use tribunician intercession in order to obstruct his legislation and to brand him as a revolutionary and a violator of most sacred constitutional principles when he put his bills to the vote in spite of the veto of his colleague. Here then it can be said that a deficiency in the constitutional system prevailing in the second century B.C. actually played a decisive role in starting a development which led to the destruction of the republican order. Yet again it was a particular defect of the particular system of the time and not a defect inherent in any system of checks and balances that played this role. Nor can it be truthfully said that the Roman state had simply become an oligarchy with merely the trappings of a system of checks and balances when in the course of the rise of the new patrician-plebeian senatorial aristocracy the Senate obtained control over the tribunician veto. In this connection it is instructive to consider some phases of the struggle of the Italians for admission to full Roman citizenship. Though the agents of the senatorial aristocracy frequently used obstructionist tactics against legislation favoring the aspirations of the Italians, the reason for this was not so much a genuine opposition of the aristocracy to the extension of citizen rights as their desire to make trouble for the Gracchi. The genuine opposition to this legislation came from the city proletariat, and this opposition was effective because the proletarians could outvote the much more numerous inhabitants of the countryside since the latter could not regularly come to the city in order to participate in the assemblies. In the first case, then, the senatorial aristocracy, in the second case the city proletariat had gained control over constitutional instruments which had not been designed to be controlled or (in the first case) even to be used by them. In both cases this had not been the result of deliberate changes in the constitutional developments but of extra-constitutional developments. In both cases the results which proved so harmful to the political order might possibly have been prevented by a timely change of the constitutional provisions, aiming at the restoration of the original function of the constitutional instruments in question.

The corruption of the Roman aristocracy through the acquisition of too much uncontrolled power in the administration of the outlying districts of the empire, and the corrupting influence of foreign ideas and customs as causes of the downfall of the Republic need hardly be discussed in the present context since they have but little to do with the constitutional system. Apart from this it is very doubtful whether these factors alone, important as they were, would have sufficed to destroy the republican order if it had not been for the other factors mentioned in the survey above.

The same may be said concerning the factional strife within the Roman aristocracy. Unquestionably this factional strife in the form which it assumed in the last decades of the Republic greatly contributed to its downfall. Yet there had been factual strife within the aristocracy for several centuries before it became a serious danger to the republican order. The reason for this is easy to see. All through the first four centuries of the Republic no individual and no family was ever able to muster all by itself a sufficient number of clients or supporters to become a danger to the state. Factions were formed by coalitions between families or gentes. But the gentes were very jealous of one another. Whenever there was any danger that one gens might become too powerful a regrouping took place and the danger was easily overcome. Thus the factual strife became dangerous only when in the last century B.C. new forms of clientship developed, when the populations of whole districts (like the Picentini in regard to the Pompey) [67] or whole armies became, in a way, clients of great military or political leaders and when this made it possible for individuals rather than for families to form new sorts of political coalitions in which each participant tried to outwit the others and to win a position above the legal and constitutional order.

The question of whether and how far the inability of the aristocracy to handle efficiently the big tasks arising from the expansion of Roman domination contributed to the decay of the political order and necessitated the replacement of the republican by a monarchic regime, requires a somewhat more detailed answer. It has been pointed out at an earlier occasion that in the course of the expansion of Roman domination the consuls became increasingly incapable of fulfilling their task as chief executives of the state, because, in addition to their civil duties, they had to command the Roman armies in actual warfare, and because they had no cabinet. Of the first handicap they were to a considerable extent relieved after the middle of the second century, when major wars became less frequent. But the second handicap continued to the end of the Republic. As pointed out earlier the resulting inability of the consuls to attend to all the tasks of a chief executive produced a great shift of power and influence from the consuls to the Senate. But it did not in itself mean that the tasks could not be handled efficiently. One can hardly say that the administrative tasks resulting from the conquest of the whole Mediterranean world were considerably greater in the period after this conquest had been completed than in the period when it was in rapid progress. Yet in the first half of the second century the Senate managed to solve ever new and ever more complicated problems with a truly astonishing efficiency. It was able to do this only by constantly delegating great powers to many of its individual members. But these powers in that period did not become dangerous to the state.

The reason for this is not simply that the aristocratic leaders of that time were not yet corrupted by foreign ideas or by the possession of too much power. A man like the elder Scipio Africanus had been no less haughty and ambitious than Sulla or Pompey. Yet none of the great men of the earlier Republic had ever tried to march on Rome with his victorious army in order to force the Senate and the people of Rome to change the constitution in his favor or according to his wishes. The most daring deed of the elder Scipio in defiance of the government was to tear to pieces his accounts of his expenditures when called upon to produce them because he was suspected of mismanagement. Again the reason for this fundamental difference is very simple and obvious; Scipio's soldiers would have ceased to obey his commands instantly if he had ordered them to march against Rome, while the legions of Sulla, of Pompey, of Caesar, and even of a man like Lepidus, were ready to follow their generals wherever they wished to lead them.

The change in the composition of the Roman armies made it dangerous to the state to entrust anyone with the command of a large army. Hence the Sullan constitution aimed at keeping the commanders of armies under strict control of the Senate and at preventing them from acquiring more military power and prestige than the Senate considered reconcilable with the safety of the political order. But many occasions arose on which a unified command of large armies was a practical necessity. In consequence the Sullan constitution broke down within less than a year, and this was the beginning of the end of the Republic.

Thus everything appears to lead back to the one great decisive cause of the downfall of the Roman Republic, frequently pointed out by modern historians of the period: the change in the nature of the Roman armies in consequence of the decrease of the Roman farming population. Undoubtedly this factor was of the greatest importance. But there is one other, perhaps hardly less important, factor that has been much less frequently considered. It has been pointed out above that the dissociation of the Roman army from the civilian population with all its dire consequences might possibly have been avoided if the legislative program of the Gracchi had been fully carried out in its three main points: the restoration of a more numerous farmer population in Italy, the establishment of overseas colonies of Roman citizens, and the gradual extension of Roman citizenship, especially if the program had later been suitably supplemented and expanded. The opponents of the Gracchan reforms used tribunician intercession and later other constitutional devices to prevent the execution of most of the planned reforms. That they were able to do so has been called a defect in the Roman constitutional system, though a defect that had developed in consequence of extraconstitutional changes in the political structure of the population. But though this defect made it possible to use certain constitutional devices for the obstruction of highly desirable legislation, it did not follow that these devices inevitably had to be used for this purpose.

The temptation to use them was certainly very great. But if Polybius, who lived for more than a decade beyond the day when the tribune M. Octavius for the first time tried to prevent a vote on Tiberius' bills by his tribunician veto, took it as self-evident that it was the very purpose of the office of the tribunes to promote actively what the majority of the people wanted, then many of the senators who persuaded Octavius to use his tribunician power to prevent legislation fervently desired and demanded by an overwhelming majority of the popular assembly must certainly have been aware of the fact that this was an abuse of these powers. Here, then, is a point at which an individual human decision had a very great influence on the future course of history: the decision to use a constitutional device, in agreement, it is true, with acknowledged rules, but clearly contrary to its original intent and purpose. The action taken by Octavius in execution of this decision provoked Ti. Gracchus to violate the constitution, and this in its turn marked the beginning of the embittered struggle which first led to the violent death of Tiberius and in its later course to the destruction of any true respect for constitutional law.

Yet it would be wrong to say that the whole later development was the inevitable consequence of the decision taken by a reactionary group in the Senate in the year 133 B.C. and of the action taken by the agent of this group, M. Octavius. After the violent death of Tiberius his agrarian legislation was carried through to a considerable extent; and there was a breathing spell in which the struggle appeared somewhat to subside. There also was a not quite uninfluential group led by the younger Scipio which worked for a compromise between the two opposite parties and above all for a restoration of a true respect for law. Though ancient tradition, as far as it has come down to us, tells only that Scipio blamed Tiberius for having formally violated the constitution, a man of Scipio's intelligence can hardly have been unaware of the fact that Octavius' use of the tribunician veto was a violation of the spirit of the constitutional order, and, as the honest man that he was, he must then have disapproved of Octavius' action no less than of that of Tiberius Gracchus. Thus in the interval between the tribuneships of Tiberius and Caius Gracchus it might conceivably still have been possible to repair to some extent the damage that had been done in the year 133 B.C. It might even have been possible to amend or to reinterpret the rules governing the use of tribunician intercession in such a way as to make a recurrence of the events of that year impossible. But Scipio died a premature death—he was possibly assassinated by a fanatic belonging to one of the two extremist groups between which Scipio tried to effect a compromise. His death took the strength out of the party of moderation and gave new impetus to the extremist groups, who accused each other of being responsible for Scipio's death. In the tribuneships of Caius Gracchus the struggle was taken up again with methods very similar to, even if not identical with, those used in its first phase at the time of Tiberius. Caius also suffered a violent death and during the following decades the two parties vied with one another in using constitutional and legal devices to fight one another with utter disregard for the true purpose and meaning of these devices. When later Sulla changed the constitution so as to make abuse of the tribunician power impossible it was too late because through five decades of misuse the respect for law had been utterly destroyed. The history of the thirty years from the death of Sulla to the invasion of Italy by Caesar's troops gives ample evidence that this destruction of the respect for law was at least as potent a factor in the decay and ultimate downfall of the Republic as was the dissociation of the army from the civilian population.

This part of the inquiry, then, appears to lead back to the old explanation that the "rottenness" of the Roman oligarchy was one of the main causes of the downfall of the Republic. But an unprejudiced evaluation of the evidence shows very clearly that this time-honored explanation, even though largely true, is nevertheless rather misleading, for it conceals very effectively the fact that the misuse of constitutional rules and regulations which started in 133 B.C. and had such disastrous consequences, had but little to do with the oligarchic or democratic character of the political order. It is self-evident—and illustrations from recent history are not lacking—that a destructive development of that kind can just as easily be started in a system of checks and balances that rests on a democratic basis as in a system of checks and balances that is connected with a socio-political order characterized by strongly oligarchic features.

There can be no doubt that the development was greatly favored by certain conspicuous deficiencies of the particular system of checks and balances prevailing at Rome in the second century B.C. The abuse of the tribunician veto was so easy, in fact, that the temptation to misuse it in a situation like that of 133 B.C. was almost overwhelming. But it is more than doubtful whether it is possible to devise a constitution that is completely immune to any abuse of this kind. Where a politically influential group is fully determined to use every legal trick to defeat their domestic opponents by misusing constitutional regulations with complete disregard of their true intent and purpose and the majority of the people is too cowardly or too negligent to stop such practices, any constitutional order will in the end be destroyed. It is an equally great error to believe that it is possible to create a political constitution so perfect that it will uphold itself without any effort on the part of the citizens as to believe that it makes no difference what constitutional rules are adopted because there are no rules that cannot be misused. But the history of the Roman Republic shows that such abuse, though in the beginning it may appear to be a minor matter, has in the long run more destructive consequences than even a temporary outbreak of open violence, and that in the end these consequences will fall most heavily on those who started the abuse or, if like Sulla they have died in time, on their unlucky descendants.

The consequences of the pernicious development which had started with the misuse of constitutional principles in the time of the Gracchi continued to be felt far beyond the downfall of the Republic. In this respect also the monarchy did not cure the evils that had caused the change in the form of government. In spite of his most strenuous and persistent efforts Augustus was not able to overcome the most basic evil, the disappearance of a general respect for constitutional law. On the one hand the assassination of Caesar had shown that the republican tradition in the abstract was still strong enough to make the open introduction of a purely monarchic regime impossible or inadvisable. On the other hand the constant abuse of constitutional principles had destroyed the very foundations of the republican order. Thus Augustus found it expedient to conceal the monarchy under republican trappings and to establish what Mommsen and others were later to call the dyarchy of emperor and Senate. But this dyarchy was anything but a mixed constitution or a system of checks and balances, since it was never doubtful for a moment which of the two participants in this mixed government, the Senate or the emperor, would be the stronger in the case of any conflict between them.

During Augustus' lifetime it may have been possible to uphold to some extent the fiction that the princeps excelled all other citizens in personal prestige but had no more power than his colleague in whatever magistracy he might hold at a given time.[68] After the death of Augustus nobody could believe in this fiction any more. It was the tragedy of Tiberius that during the first part of his principate he sincerely tried to deal with the Senate as if the fiction had been true, though he was neither willing, nor, if willing, would have been able to restore an equal distribution of actual power, which alone could have turned the fiction into reality. The sickening atmosphere of insincerity which pervades the whole principate of Tiberius is due to this discrepancy between fiction and reality, which Tiberius, at least in the beginning, did not desire, but could not prevent. Nothing could illustrate the continuation of this discrepancy under Tiberius' successors better than a comparison between the speech, written by Seneca, which Nero, according to Tacitus,[69] made in the Senate on his accession to the throne and in which he promised to leave the government of the empire to the Senate, reserving for himself only the command of the armies, on the one hand, and, on the other hand, the same

Seneca's treatise *De clementia*, written shortly thereafter, in which he beseeches the young emperor to make a mild use of his absolutely unlimited powers.

The simple truth is that, whatever efforts might be made to conceal the fact, political power after Augustus rested no longer on constitutional law. The Senate, it is true, continued to enjoy considerable prestige in spite of everything, not only with the aristocracy, but also with the population of Italy, and later increasingly even in the provinces, where in the beginning it had been lowest. But this prestige gave the Senate no longer a kind of power that could be of avail where the wishes of this body might disagree with those of an emperor, or, at times when the succession was open, with those of the army. The real prop of the public order in the first part of the imperial period was the loyalty of the army to the emperor. But the loyalty of an army alone is not a very solid foundation for a state, and in later times this loyalty also became precarious for a long time. As a supplement there developed, in the later phase of the empire, a bureaucracy which exercised an ever more oppressive control over the civilian population and continued to function even through the period that has been called the military anarchy, when emperors were continually assassinated by the army.[70]

All this, of course, proves no more that a monarchy was unsuited for the Roman Empire than the downfall of the Roman Republic proves that a system of checks and balances was unsuited. It merely shows that the same evils which had destroyed the Republic continued to plague the empire of the Caesars in somewhat different forms. It is therefore necessary to distinguish these specific evils and their specific causes (even in so far as they may have been the results of that specific kind of system of checks and balances that developed in the late Roman Republic or the specific kind of monarchy that followed upon the former) from the merits or demerits of a system of checks and balances or of a monarchy as such.

CONCLUSIONS

POLYBIUS had defined the mixed constitution as a mixture of monarchy, oligarchy, and democracy. He had described it as a system of checks and balances in which each of the three elements has an equal share in the political power, and in which the political powers are interlaced in such a way that none of the three elements can make use of its powers without constantly being checked by the other two. For this mixed constitution, or system of checks and balances, Polybius had claimed three fundamental advantages over all other kinds of constitutions or political systems: that it was more stable, that it made a country stronger than those countries or states having a different political order, and that it guaranteed the liberty of the citizens participating in the system. In respect to the first of these advantages Polybius had tried to show that all "simple constitutions" are of necessity unstable; for, he contended, since in any simple political order one of the elements of which a state is necessarily composed has all the power, or nearly all the power, and since unlimited power has a corrupting influence, the ruling element will inevitably deteriorate until it is overthrown by a revolution, after which, if the revolution gives unlimited power to one of the other elements, the same process of deterioration will start again. Thus there will be a cycle of constitutions or political orders.

In setting off the mixed constitution against the simple constitutions Polybius had distinguished two types of the former: a mixed constitution created in a single act and according to the plan of a legislator or political reformer, and a "naturally grown" mixed constitution, which comes into being when political changes of the kind characteristic of the cycle of constitutions result in a compromise instead of a complete overthrow of the government, so that the new kind of political order is added to and mixed with the preceding one instead of replacing it, until a perfect mixture of the three fundamental types of political order is achieved. Polybius had tried to show that of these two types of mixed constitutions the first is not subject to the kind of change characteristic of the cycle of constitutions, but that under certain circumstances it may be destroyed through a fault in its construction. In regard to the second type Polybius had come to the conclusion that it may to some extent be subject to the mechanism of the cycle of constitutions, though to a lesser degree than the simple constitutions; as one element is added to the others it always may become more powerful than the others until in the end the delicate balance is destroyed and the vicious cycle of simple constitutions may start again. This part of Polybius' theory emphasizes again the importance of an equal distribution of powers in a mixed constitution or a system of checks and balances. Finally, Polybius had tried to show that Sparta and Rome had possessed the most perfect examples of mixed constitutions in history down to his own time, and especially in regard to Rome he had tried to show how extremely well balanced its constitutional system had been at the time of its greatest perfection.

An analytical survey of the functioning and development of the Roman political order in the period in which, according to Polybius, it came very close to the ideal of a mixed constitution, has revealed several aspects not mentioned by Polybius. Thus Polybius did not distinguish between legal competences and actual powers, and it has been shown that the actual powers of the Senate, for instance, grew in a period in which its legal powers were reduced, while its actual powers vanished rapidly after they had for the first time been secured by an elaborate body of laws.[1] To this observation Polybius might conceivably have answered that he had expressly stated at the beginning of his analysis of the Roman constitution that it was not his intention to deal in detail with all the aspects of this constitution, but only with those which were relevant for his theory, and that it was irrelevant whether the powers of the three elements of the state had a foundation in formulated law or not, as long as their actual powers were in balance with one another. This answer, however, can hardly be accepted as sufficient if one accepts Polybius' principle that political analysis has the purpose of teaching future statesmen how to act in a

given situation. For in order to apply the theory of the mixed constitution or the system of checks and balances in practice, the statesman
would have to know under what circumstances the attempt to check
the power of one political agency, or to enhance that of another, is
likely to be effective and in what circumstances it is not. But it has
been shown that the attempt to check the power of a political agency
by legislation may have little or no effect if the concentration of power
is necessary for the performance of certain necessary tasks, or that,
if it is effective, the same concentration of power will merely turn up
unexpectedly in some other place where it may be even less desirable.
What is more, the rapid breakdown of the Sullan constitution has
shown that the attempt to prevent by elaborate legislation the concentration of power in anyone's hands while there are urgent tasks
which require such concentration of power, will lead to a rapid disintegration of the whole political system.

On the basis of these observations it might even appear at first sight
as if the whole idea of the system of checks and balances, and the
claims made in favor of it, were altogether wrong, and that all the
arguments which have been set forth against the validity of the theory
in recent times were completely justified. On closer inspection the
historical facts do not appear to support such radical criticism. However, one criticism is certainly warranted. If, as Polybius seems clearly
to imply, though he does not state it expressly, it is essential for the
functioning of a system of checks and balances that the distribution
of power between the various main agencies of the state be nearly
always equal, then a system of checks and balances would be the most
fragile, and not the most stable, of all political systems. This concept
of equal distribution of power is a fundamental fallacy which has crept
into many theories directly or indirectly dependent on Polybius. Considering the constant changes in foreign relations and in internal economic and social conditions from which no state is exempt, it is impossible for any state to preserve over a long period of time a perfect
balance of power between its various components or political agencies.
In fact, the analysis of the Roman political order attempted in the
preceding chapters has shown that enormous shifts of power took
place in Rome within the four hundred years from the publication of
the Twelve Tables and the acceptance of the Valerio-Horatian laws

to the downfall of the Republic. Yet throughout the greater part of this period the Roman political order possessed certain fundamental characteristics of what is called a system of checks and balances, nor was the basic stability of this political order or the strength of the Roman state seriously affected by those shifts of power. If this is correct, it follows that Polybius (though much of his theory may still be correct and of great practical value) has placed the emphasis on the wrong point, and that his theory presents a number of problems of fundamental importance of which he appears to have been unaware, and which he did not touch in his discussion.

Another objection that can be raised to Polybius' political theory in connection with the history of the Roman constitution is that the downfall of the Roman Republic did not follow very closely the pattern of the cycle of constitutions as applicable to a naturally grown mixed constitution. In a way, of course, Polybius might contend that the events did follow the prescribed pattern. During the later part of the Second Punic War and during the greater part of Polybius' own lifetime, as he himself points out, the oligarchic element in Rome, represented by the Senate, prevailed, though even then, in Polybius' opinion, the system was on the whole still extremely well balanced. With the so-called Gracchan revolution, with the rise of the populares, and with Marius and Cinna, the democratic elements raised its head in opposition to the oligarchic element which, towards the end of Polybius' life, had begun to abuse its powers, and finally the whole process ended with the establishment of an increasingly absolutistic monarchic regime, in perfect agreement with the theory of the cycle of constitutions as applied to the naturally growing and developing mixed constitution.

Yet it does not require very deep insight to see that such an attempt to explain the development of the Roman Republic from the middle of the second century B.C. to the conquest of Rome by Caesar in terms of Polybius' theory would be extremely superficial. It is not very relevant that the Gracchan revolution and the first rise of the "party" of the populares was followed by the Sullan reaction. For Polybius' cycle is a gross oversimplification anyway. But it is of great importance that the success, or lack of success, of the Sullan reaction cannot be evaluated in Polybian terms since Polybius does not provide any criterion by which to measure the effectiveness of the legal provisions of Sulla's constitution. Still more important is the fact that most of the major reasons for the downfall of the Roman Republic find no place in Polybius' theory, for some of these causes are not of a purely incidental nature, as Polybius believes the cause of the ultimate destruction of the Spartan constitution to have been, but touch the very essence of the theory of the mixed constitution. They show clearly that it is not sufficient for a just evaluation of this theory to look merely on the purely political agencies like the magistrates, the Senate, and the various forms of popular assemblies and the distribution of political power between them, but that it is also necessary to consider the social groups by which this political order is sustained, and their relations to the various official political agencies, to one another, and to the community as a whole. Only when this is done is it possible to show whether a system of checks and balances can produce the results which Polybius claims for it, and if it can, what general conditions are required for those results. But this leads to a still more basic question.

The most fundamental objection to the theories of the mixed constitution and of the system of checks and balances has been raised on the basis of the theory of sovereignty, which has found its classical expression in the works of Thomas Hobbes but which has been formulated in various slightly different ways by Hobbes' numerous modern admirers. According to this theory any true commonwealth must have a sovereign, and it is of the utmost importance that there be no doubt as to who within the commonwealth has the sovereign power. This sovereign power can be vested in one man, so that there will be a monarchy; in an assembly in which only part of the people participate, when it will be an aristocracy; or in an assembly "of all that will come together," when it will be a democracy.[2] But the sovereign, whoever he may be, is above the law. For the law can neither make nor defend itself. Therefore he who makes and defends the law cannot himself be subject to the law. His sovereignty, in other words, can in no way be restricted. According to Hobbes (who, in contrast to some of his modern followers, believes in natural law), the sovereign, it is true, is subject to the laws of nature; i.e., to the laws of equity, since such laws are divine and cannot be abrogated by any man or any commonwealth.[3] Yet, even so, Hobbes believed, the sovereign, if violating the natural law, cannot be called to account by his subject or subjects, but is accountable only to God. Finally, since according to this theory the sovereignty is indivisible, absolute monarchy appears to be the most perfect form of a commonwealth, since in absolute monarchy the indivisibility of sovereignty finds its clearest and most unmistakable expression.[4]

On the basis of this theory of sovereignty Polybius' ideal, the mixed constitution, must necessarily appear as a most imperfect political order. And in fact, Hobbes states expressly that it was one of the greatest deficiencies of the Roman Republic that it was not clear whether the sovereignty was vested in the Senate or in the people, and it was this, which in Hobbes' opinion, "caused the seditions of Tiberius Gracchus, Caius Gracchus, Lucius Saturninus, and others, and afterwards the wars between the Senate and the People, under Marius and Sulla; and again under Pompey and Caesar, to the extinction of their democracy and the setting up of monarchy." [5] Though Hobbes does not call the constitution of the Roman Republic a mixed constitution, it is perfectly clear that he considers the Roman Republic a political order in which sovereignty was divided, or at least in which it was not clear in whom the sovereignty was vested, and that he considers this a great weakness of the constitution of the Roman Republic. To Hobbes' argument drawn from Roman history, Polybius might reply that though the Roman republican system did decay and finally was destroyed in a process which started in the last years of his life, sovereignty had been divided in the Roman Republic long before, and that nevertheless the Republic had continued to enjoy remarkable internal stability and external strength over an unusually long period.

In attempting to evaluate the strength of this counterargument it will be expedient to look at what Hobbes has to say about the other constitution which Polybius considers a model of a mixed constitution: the political order of Sparta. In this case Hobbes does not say that this order was weakened by divided sovereignty, but he points out that the sovereign power in the Spartan kingdom was not held by the kings, but by the ephors.[6] At this point, however, Hobbes comes clearly in conflict with his own theory, according to which the sovereign cannot be limited by civil law in regard to his term of office.

Yet the sovereign power of the Spartan ephors was strictly limited by civil law to one year. Nor can it be said that the ephors at the end of every year imposed this limitation upon themselves, for they patently had no power to circumvent it, since if they had tried to continue to exercise the powers of their office beyond that limit of time, they would simply have ceased to be obeyed. If, then, Hobbes, in some Socratic *dialogue des morts,* could be questioned concerning his statement about sovereignty in the Spartan state, he might conceivably answer that he had been mistaken and that the sovereignty was vested in the apella, an answer according to which Sparta, strangely enough, would appear to have been a democracy. But how could the apella have been the sovereign, since it had no executive powers whatever and not even the legislative initiative? That the kings were not sovereign in Sparta has rightly been pointed out by Hobbes himself. The gerousia, which had less power than either the kings, the ephors, or the apella, can certainly not be considered the sovereign of the Spartan commonwealth. Thus it is obvious that in Sparta the sovereignty cannot be clearly located anywhere. Or shall one say that the kings, the ephors, and the gerousia together were the sovereign, since, according to one tradition, they could, if agreed among themselves, make laws without consulting the apella, and since between them they also had the executive power. But what a strange sovereign who, it seems, never was able to make a law since he was never in agreement with himself! Yet the Spartan state, it cannot be denied, proved to be more stable internally and to have greater strength externally, in proportion to its size and population, than many ancient states which corresponded more nearly to Hobbes' notion of well defined sovereignty. A similar analysis could be made of the Roman Republic of the fourth, third, and second centuries B.C. Thus the theory of Hobbes clearly breaks down in the face of the historical evidence provided by these two states. But this conclusion is only the first step to a solution of the problem, since it is necessary to show where the error in Hobbes' reasoning is to be found, and also whether important parts of his theory cannot still be saved from the debacle.

The further inquiry may then start with the very simple question of who it was in Sparta who protected the law setting a time limit to the sovereign power of the ephors. The answer again is extremely simple: all Spartan citizens did, since, at least under normal conditions, all of them simply ceased to obey the ephors when their term of office was over. In other words, assuming that the ephors in Sparta were the sovereign, as Hobbes believed, it is simply not true that "the power of the sovereign cannot, without his consent, be transferred to another." In fact, on the face of it, the observation made concerning the ephors in Sparta and the limitations imposed on their sovereign power might appear to lead to more far-reaching conclusions. It would seem that the commonwealth itself—i.e. the individual members of the commonwealth, both together and individually—could protect the law. Yet Hobbes is quite right when he begins that section of his main work which deals with the commonwealth by pointing out that generally speaking this is not possible, and that the members of the commonwealth must delegate this power.[7] For, as Hobbes says, "if the actions [of the multitude] be directed according to their particular judgments and particular appetites they can expect thereby no defense nor protection neither against a common enemy nor against the injuries of one another." In other words, the protection and application of what Hobbes calls the natural law (assuming that such a thing exists) and of whatever civil laws, in addition to laws derived from the natural law, are necessary to regulate the intercourse of the members of the commonwealth with one another, the organization of the defense of the country, the conduct and foreign affairs, and many other things, must by necessity be entrusted to special agencies. These agencies, in order to be able to perform their tasks, must be invested with specific powers—i.e., with the right to demand obedience, since the multitude, as Hobbes points out correctly, is not able to perform these tasks directly. But it is easy to see that this does not apply to those laws or rules by which the power of political agents is restricted in time, in extent, or in any other fashion, since rules of this kind, as has been shown, can be protected directly by the multitude or by all individual members of the commonwealth. They have merely to cease to obey whenever a political agent oversteps the limits of his competence; and this is no mere theory but what actually happens in any well-ordered community in which sovereign powers are limited. Thus the apparent stringency of Hobbes' arguments when he contends that the power of the sovereign cannot be limited since he is by necessity the protector of all law, and thus cannot be restrained by law, is simply the result of a lack of distinctions in his premises.

It is, however, not sufficient to demonstrate that what applies to positive law does not apply to laws and rules whose only purpose is to limit political power. It is much more important to inquire into the sources of political power and to see how sufficient power can be produced and retained where it is needed in spite of constitutional restrictions. The simplest case is indeed absolute monarchy, in which the legislative, judiciary, and executive powers and the supreme military command are all vested in the person of the monarch. What Hobbes says about this type of government is largely true where it appears in the form of kingship. If and when the king is placed so high above every individual, and also every social or economic group within the country, that he does not ally himself with any group against any other, he may indeed appear not only as the protector of the law but also as its very incarnation, and may be readily obeyed, if not by every individual member, yet by the great majority within any group of the population. In other words, the interest which most, if not all, the members of the commonwealth have in the preservation of a rule of law and justice is, so to speak, transformed into personal loyalty to the monarch.

In Hobbes' opinion this is the very essence of all absolute monarchy. But if the restriction "if and when" appearing above is justified, this may indicate that here again Hobbes' analysis is somewhat defective. Even kings have sometimes allied themselves with one group of the population against another, and when this happens the king ceases to be the protector of the law, pure and simple, though he may try to retain, and to a large extent may actually retain, this function. Hobbes, it is true, distinguished between a commonwealth by institution, in which the sovereign power is acquired by covenant, and a commonwealth by acquisition, in which the sovereign power is acquired by force, but he insists that, apart from the method of acquisition, the position of the sovereign is exactly the same, since in both cases men choose their sovereign from fear, though in the first case they choose him from fear of one another (since they need a protector of the law which protects them against injury that they may suffer from one another), while in the second case they subject themselves to him because they are afraid of him.[8] This argument, however, is clearly sophistic, since the two cases would be analogous only if in both cases the sovereign was obeyed from fear of his own power, and not from fear of someone else. Now it may be true that in any monarchy the ruler is largely obeyed from fear. But it is equally clear that no ruler of any kind can ever be obeyed from fear alone, for no monarch is by himself strong enough to keep his people subjected to his will. He is strong and feared only through the knowledge that his executive organs will obey him and execute his commands.[9] Hence there must necessarily be some power of command that precedes fear, or is at least not based upon it entirely. It is the origin of this power that makes all the difference between various types of monarchy, and also has a very great influence on the actual function of the monarch.

When Hobbes speaks of sovereign power acquired by force he has primarily in mind sovereignty by conquest from the outside. Where sovereignty rests on this basis the conquered may obey the sovereign simply from fear. But the conquest could not have been made nor retained unless the conquering monarch had been able to command the obedience of his own native subjects, and especially of his army, not merely from fear but from loyalty. Such a monarch, and even more the kings of the dynasty that he founds, may in the course of time become true sovereigns of all their subjects. But the conquering king will have difficulty in achieving such a position from the beginning. Or to put it more clearly, he may in a way fulfil the task of a true sovereign in regard to his conquered subjects by protecting them from injury that they might inflict upon one another, and he may fulfil the same function in regard to his original subjects, but in the beginning at least he will have difficulty in establishing a body of civil law incorporating the natural law, or in protecting such law where established, in regard to the interrelations between his conquered and his conquering subjects. For to the extent that he has to use the loyalty of his conquering subjects in order to obtain, through fear, the obedience of his conquered subjects, he will be dependent on, and will have to make concessions to, the desires of the former.

Sovereignty by conquest, however, is only one of the possible types of sovereignty acquired by force. In very primitive conditions the military force of a community is generally identical with the male adult population. Similarly, in many of the most advanced states the army is essentially nothing but a selective group of citizens doing military service. Yet, on the other hand, history shows many examples of communities in which the army was, or is, more or less separated from the rest of the community. The most frequent cases of this kind are armies of foreign mercenaries such as have been used by many sovereigns in many wars, and also to subdue and keep their own subjects under control. As the example of Rome shows, armies formally composed of citizens can come to play a similar role if the soldiers become separated from the general civic body, either because they have no place in civil life, or because they have stayed together long enough to feel as a separate group outside the community, or for both reasons. Where such is the case the loyalty of the troop will be to its leader rather than to the community, and this may enable the military leader to conquer the state from within and to establish himself as an absolute ruler. This kind of monarchy is usually called Caesarism, though those who conquered or sustained their rule with the help of foreign mercenaries have usually been called tyrants, because the tyrants in the proper sense—i.e., absolute rulers come to power as leaders of a party—in antiquity often used mercenary armies or bodyguards as an additional prop to their rule. But if applied to rulers whose power is not primarily based on party leadership, the designation of tyrant is somewhat misleading. A ruler who has acquired his power through the support of an army can become a true sovereign to the extent to which he succeeds in winning the allegiance of the civilian population and, at the same time, is able to make himself independent of his supporters. This is especially true if after having come to power he succeeds in narrowing the gulf that separates the army from the rest of the population. Otherwise (that is, if the army remains the sole or the basic foundation of his power), he is in danger of becoming the puppet of his army even though his arbitrary power over the rest of the population (but not his power to protect the natural law) may be increased at the same time. This is what happened in the Roman empire after Commodus, though the beginnings of a situation of this kind can be observed as early as the reign of Tiberius. That the full evils of Caesarism developed so late in Rome shows how difficult it is to convert a Caesarian regime into a system resembling kingship. A survey of historical examples would also show that this conversion is much more difficult than the transmutation of a kingship by conquest from without into a kingship by (tacit) covenant.

A third type of monarchy acquired by force is tyranny, concerning which not much need be added here since it has been discussed at some length earlier.[10] It may, however, be emphasized again that tyranny, i.e. monarchy acquired through leadership of a party which has won a complete victory over all other parties and thus has gained absolute power, not only can never form an element in a mixed constitution, but is also most difficult to convert into kingship, if this is not altogether impossible. Since the aims and desires of a party are much more clearly defined, and much more far reaching, than those of a conquering race or an independent army, it will be more difficult for the leader to free himself from the control of his adherents. Also, since the party or parties that have been subdued will not forget that they have been fellow citizens with equal rights, or even greater privileges, they will not submit to the new rule without feeling the most violent resentment. Therefore a full reconciliation will be nearly impossible, especially since the inevitable expressions of such resentment will force the tyrant to take very oppressive measures, even against his will.

Finally there is one more aspect of monarchy which must be considered. Except in the most primitive conditions it is not possible for a monarch to exercise all his various functions directly. Where such conditions do exist the power of the monarch rests exclusively on the loyalty of the majority of his subjects. On the other hand, wherever the size or the differentiated composition of the community requires a more complicated organization, the monarch will have to delegate most of his power to executive organs, and it will then be the function of the monarch to supervise and control these organs and at the same time to represent, in the eyes of his subjects, the source and fountain from which all the powers of these subordinate organs ultimately spring. Where these subordinate organs are numerous and organized in a well-ordered system, it may be possible for the monarch to support himself largely through the loyalty of these organs, even against a majority of his subjects, since the former are organized and the latter are not, though a monarchy supported exclusively by the loyalty of a bureaucracy will hardly last long. But one of the most frequent forms of power is that which is exercised through control over an organized minority which, by being organized, and especially if at the same time it has a monopoly or near monopoly of the more effective weapons, can keep a much greater multitude in check. Such an exercise of power is a common feature of monarchies by conquest, of Caesarism, of tyranny, and of rule through a controlling bureaucracy, the organized minority in the first case being represented by the conquerors as against the conquered, in Caesarism by the army as against the civilian population, and in tyranny by the conquering party if the latter is organized. Occasionally some of these systems may also be combined. It may even be possible to base control over such a controlling organization to some extent on mutual fear and distrust among its members. But it is not possible to retain power by fear alone.

It remains then to inquire briefly into the origin and nature of political power in the two other forms of government in which the ultimate seat of power, i.e. sovereignty, can be more or less clearly determined: oligarchy and democracy. (Here, of course, these terms mean pure oligarchy and pure democracy, not oligarchy or democracy within a mixed constitution or coupled with a system of checks and balances.) About these forms of government Hobbes has very little to say. But what he does say is rather significant. He defines an aristocracy or oligarchy as a political order in which the sovereignty is vested in an assembly to which a part of the people only are admitted, and a democracy as an order in which the function of the sovereign is exercised by an assembly "of all that will come together." [11] Then he tries to show that though the sovereignty of aristocratic and democratic assemblies is just as absolute and indivisible as the sovereignty of a monarch, nevertheless the aristocratic and democratic systems are "less apt to produce the peace and security of the people" than a monarch, since a monarch cannot disagree with himself but an assembly can (the absence or presence of a few may result in a majority for opposite resolutions so that the assembly may "undo today all that was concluded yesterday," etc.).

This part of Hobbes' theory is again significantly lacking in clarity.

If one accepts Hobbes' definition of an aristocratic system as a system in which the sovereign power is vested in an assembly of certain persons nominated or otherwise distinguished from the rest, then a state in which a parliament, elected directly by the people without class distinction, has the sovereign power would be an aristocracy. In another passage, it is true, Hobbes says that "it is absurd to think that a sovereign assembly inviting the people to send up their deputies with power to make known their advice or desires, should therefore hold such deputies rather than themselves for the absolute representative of the people," and adds, "so it is absurd also to think the same in a monarchy." By this argument he tries to prove that a parliament can have no sovereign power in a monarchy. But this does not solve the problem of the position of a parliament in what we call a parliamentary democracy. Such a parliament is not "sent up by a sovereign assembly," but is elected by the voters. In this case are the voters then the "absolute representatives of the people," i.e., in Hobbes' terminology, the sovereign? Obviously such an assumption would be in complete disagreement with Hobbes' own theory, since the voters have neither the legislative nor the judiciary nor the executive power which in his opinion are inseparable from the indivisible authority of the sovereign. Or is an elected representative body actually an aristocracy? Aristotle would probably agree that in a way it is, but then another essential distinction is lacking which Aristotle makes,[12] for he distinguishes between aristocracy and oligarchy, and between various types of oligarchy, while Hobbes does not. Yet there is a most essential difference between what is usually called an aristocracy and a parliamentary democracy.

What is more, an elected representative assembly cannot perpetuate itself indefinitely, and if it tries to, as has happened a few times in history, it will after some time run into trouble. Yet such perpetuation, according to Hobbes, is an essential attribute of sovereignty. Hence, though it would be wrong to say that a parliamentary democracy is necessarily a system of checks and balances, it must be admitted that, in the terms of Hobbes, an elected representative body in a parliamentary democracy has but an imperfect sovereignty. But the further discussion of imperfect and divided sovereignty can be reserved for the final analysis of the theory of the mixed constitution.

For the present it will be sufficient to have demonstrated that, Hobbes' specious arguments notwithstanding, imperfect and divided sovereignty does exist.

But the analysis of the origin and source of political power in the different political systems must be carried still further. The source of the power of a popular assembly is clear. Under the most primitive and simple conditions, where the whole adult population can actually come together, the majority has the power by the nature of things. The same is true where the assembly consists of the warriors, or of those warriors who have the most effective weapons. Where the geographic extension is greater and conditions more complicated, so that many of the people are prevented by various circumstances from attending the assembly, the assembly of those who do come is then by tradition nevertheless considered the true representative of the people as a whole, and so may have the sovereign power. In a way, then, an elected representative assembly may be considered nothing but a body so constituted by the mode of its election that it is a fairer representative of the population as a whole than is a primary assembly in which everybody is allowed to participate, but from which a large section of the population may have to stay away because of geographical or other circumstances. From this point of view an elected representative body appears as a democratic and not an aristocratic institution. In actual fact, of course, an elected representative body need not be a true representative of the people because party organizations may manage the elections in such a way that the people have a choice only between candidates whom they dislike. It is therefore possible that a representative body might be mistrusted by a large section of the people. Even in this case, however, it still has its power through the belief of the majority (or at least through the acceptance by the majority of the fiction) that it is truly representative of the population as a whole.

The question of the origin of the power of an oligarchic assembly or council is more difficult to answer. In the first place it must be emphasized again that an aristocracy in the full sense of the word is always prior to, and usually larger than, any political council or assembly that can be called aristocratic in the narrower sense of the word. Generally speaking, one can say that an aristocratic council or assembly has the same relation to the aristocracy that a popular assembly has to the people, which is also prior to its assemblies, though in the most primitive conditions the participants in the assembly may comprise the whole adult male population. An aristocratic council which is primarily the political representative and political instrument of the aristocracy may then at the same time be willingly obeyed by, and have authority with, that part of the population which does not belong to the aristocracy, because it is accepted as the true protector of the legal and political order and the interests of the community as a whole. Within a mixed constitution the Roman Senate appears to have enjoyed something like an authority of this kind for some time towards the end, and during some decades after, the Second Punic War. But since an aristocracy is always a group set off from the rest of the population and has interests which are different from and often opposed to those of the people, such a position as representative of the people, freely acknowledged by an overwhelming majority, will much more rarely be granted to an aristocratic council than to a monarch. Hence, almost always its powers must be supported by other means. The most important of these means historically derives from the nature and origin of aristocracies. Aristocracies consist of individuals and families who are more powerful than others because they have, through economic or other means, control over other people; i.e. because they have clients and retainers in the widest sense of these words. Each member of the aristocracy therefore contributes the power which he individually controls to the power of the aristocracy as a whole and also to the power of its political instrument, the aristocratic council. The power of an aristocracy may be further increased by its constituting an organized group in contrast to the unorganized rest of the population. It may also support its power through its control over military bands or groups. Thus, most of the different sources of power found in the various forms of monarchies recur also in oligarchies. But here they are very seldom, if ever, as clearly separated from one another as is often the case with kingship, Caesarism, tyranny, and so on. In oligarchies these different types are usually mixed with one another, yet fundamentally the actual sources of power are the same.

It has been necessary to make a brief survey of the origin and nature of political power in those political orders in which the seat of the sovereignty (in Hobbes' sense) can be clearly determined in order to understand fully the purpose and essential nature of a system of checks and balances, whose fundamental characteristic is that the sovereignty in such a system cannot be clearly located anywhere. According to Hobbes [13] it is the great advantage of monarchy over all other forms of government that in a monarchy "the private interest is the same with the public, for in monarchy the riches, power, and honor of a monarch arise only from the riches, strength, and reputation of his subjects, and no king can be rich nor glorious nor secure whose subjects are either poor or contemptible, or too weak through want or dissension to maintain a war against their enemies." This is quite true of kingship, though it is not (or not to the same extent) true of Caesarism or tyranny. The same truth could also be expressed by saying that the king is not a party, while both in an aristocracy and in a democracy it is always a party, even if in a democracy not necessarily an organized party, that rules. This is quite correctly pointed out by Hobbes when he says that "in a democracy or aristocracy the public prosperity confers not so much to the private fortune of one who is corrupt or ambitious as does many times a perfidious advice, a treacherous action, or a civil war." All this is perfectly true, and it can hardly be denied that absolute monarchy in the form of kingship has been historically one of the most successful, one of the most stable, and not infrequently even one of the most equitable forms of government. But this form of government involves also great dangers, for in making the public interest identical with the private interest of the monarch, it does not guard against the possibility that the king may take care of the public interests as badly as some people take care of their private interests, even though they may believe otherwise, and this danger is greatly increased by the corruption through the possession of unlimited power to which the absolute monarch is exposed, and of which so many philosophers from Plato to Lord Acton have spoken.

It is then the purpose of a system of checks and balances to avoid these dangers by making the law supreme. In this respect absolute monarchy and a system of checks and balances are at opposite ends of the scale. In an absolute monarchy the king is the absolute representative, the incarnation, so to speak, of the law and of the legal order, and all the respect for the law and the legal order assumes the form of loyalty to the king. This contrast is very well illustrated by Greek and Roman history and by the Greek historians, and all the more strikingly because they illustrate it unconsciously. The law is constantly emphasized in Sparta and Rome, the two communities which Polybius mentions as models of mixed constitutions. But it is significant that the law is also emphasized, though not quite so much, in other republican states —in Athens, for instance—and that even those Greek writers who dream of a monarchy because they hope that a monarch might restore the influence of the aristocracy and re-establish a hierarchic society speak of the law and not of personal loyalty.[14] The historians who write after Alexander in the monarchies of his successors, on the other hand, emphasize loyalty to a sovereign and not the law.[15]

In a system of checks and balances, then, it is the law that is supreme, not an individual or a group of individuals. But the law cannot defend itself. Hence, just as in states with other systems there must be someone to protect and to apply it. In this respect there is no difference between the two forms of government. But the means by which the same end is reached are different. In a system of checks and balances the respect for the law is not converted into loyalty to a person but into respect for an office, and for an individual only in so far as he is the holder of the office. This may appear to be a mere play on words since, it may be argued, the king also has his dignity only as holder of his office. But any serious reflection on the nature of kingship will reveal that this argument is not valid. This is especially clear where kingship forms part of a mixed constitution. The authority and dignity of an office-holder, including a judge, are strictly limited to the functions connected with his office and do not go beyond it, either in time or in field of competence or in any other way. Hence the fewer or the less important the functions connected with an office, the less the dignity of the holder of the office. This does not apply at all to a king in a constitutional monarchy. As pointed out on another occasion a king can be deprived of nearly all functions and legal power and still not lose at all in dignity. Nor is the loyalty or the allegiance of the people to the king affected by the fact that he has very little legal authority in particular matters. In fact, it might be said that while a magistrate or a public official without function and power is nothing, a king, paradoxically, is perhaps most useful under a constitution that gives him hardly any but ceremonial functions and little or no power. For in a constitutional monarchy which gives the monarch important functional powers there may be great temptation for the monarch to make use of the loyalty which the majority of his subjects feel towards his person in order to overstep the limits of his legal authority. In a system in which the king has few if any specific functions the possibility, and therefore the temptation, of overstepping the limits of his legal authority are greatly reduced. Yet it will always remain the function of the king to supplement the respect for the law and its public administrators by the loyalty which he inspires in his subjects and which can be felt only towards a person.

It is then of the essence of a system of checks and balances that the law is supreme, and that the respect and the obedience due and given to individuals in office, and also to public assemblies with political powers, are subject to certain limitations. These limitations are of a threefold nature, namely, limitations in time, limitations in regard to a field of competence, and special limitations specifically defined by law.

The first of these limitations presents the least difficulty. It does not apply to kings. In some states with systems of checks and balances it does not apply to judges. It may or may not apply to political councils or assemblies—that is, these may be either permanent and self-perpetuating or subject to elections after a fixed period of time.

But with the exceptions mentioned, all individual incumbents in office on the highest level in systems of checks and balances are subject to limitations in time, i.e., in regard to their terms of office. This limitation has the twofold purpose of preventing an individual from acquiring too much power through the favors that his office may enable him to distribute, and of making it possible to replace an incumbent in office by someone else when for some reason it becomes desirable. Where re-election is prohibited or permitted only after the lapse of considerable time, the first of these aspects is emphasized. Where there are no such restrictions, the second aspect is stressed, since under such a law it is possible to continue the same man in office as long as no better man can be found to replace him. It is the great advantage of this first type of limitation that generally, and even where no definite date is fixed by law, the limit is clearly and unmistakably defined for everybody so that no special executive organs are required for the protection and execution of such limiting laws, except that it is very important that careful provisions be made for the replacement in time of any incumbent after his term of office is over, so that the office will not be vacant and its functions will not lapse.

The two other types of limitations present much greater difficulty, both practical and theoretical. An attempt to give a history of the various limitations of this kind that have been established in practice or advocated in theory at different times and in different places would require a voluminous work of its own. But it is possible to illustrate with examples from Greek and Roman history some important general points. It will be expedient to begin with special checks, since they present the comparatively simpler problem.

In Rome in the earlier period of the Republic the coercive and judicial powers of the consuls were subject to the limitations of the ius auxilii of the tribunes of the plebs and of the *provocatio ad populum*. It was the purpose of these limitations to prevent the consuls from abusing their legal powers while in office. Since these two limitations were technically effective regardless of whether the consuls had actually abused their power or not (as all such limitations necessarily must be, because the question of whether there has been an abuse or not cannot be decided in a moment), they weakened the power of the consuls even where they made legitimate use of it. Thus we find that the plebeians, when they had grievances against the patricians, sometimes resisted the draft, each individual being confident that a tribune would come to his aid if a consul tried to arrest him, and that even if he were arrested he could appeal to the assembly, in which the majority might vote in his favor. If we can trust the tradition, in such cases the patricians sometimes called upon the consuls to appoint a dictator who was not subject to the two limitations mentioned. "The dictator," the patricians on such occasions are said to have threatened, "can have executed without appeal any one of you who will refuse to do his duty, and he will do it." According to the tradition [16] this method was sometimes successful to a certain extent, though this may appear strange in view of the fact that the soldiers who were strong enough to defy the consul would certainly also have been strong enough to resist the executive organs of the dictator if they had banded together against them. Yet the story is not altogether incredible if one considers the modern analogy that workers on strike not only against a private firm but against their government have performed, when drafted and under military orders, the same services which they refused to perform as private citizens. Obviously it was ultimately the law, when appearing with all the paraphernalia of its majesty, that enforced obedience.

Yet in Rome this obedience was often given reluctantly, and it was very often under the dictators appointed to overcome the resistance of the plebeians, or immediately afterward, that the patricians, or later the Senate, had to make the necessary concessions to satisfy the demands of the plebeians if they did not wish to lose even that last resort of the power of the state and have to face open revolution. At this point the adherents of Hobbes will undoubtedly claim that what has been described here is a state of anarchy or near-anarchy, and that this shows the grave dangers inherent in any system in which sovereignty is not clearly defined, one and indivisible. But history does not support this claim. It is exactly the elasticity of the Roman legal and constitutional order that made it possible, in the face of violent antagonisms, to arrive at adjustments without a revolution. That the legal order had been strained to the utmost, but was not ultimately broken in the process of adjustment, had the result that, after the adjustment had been made, respect for the law was not destroyed, but if anything increased, and that it was neither necessary nor possible for one part of the population to force a completely new order of its own liking on the reluctant other half of the citizenry. Polybius therefore is quite right when he considers the middle of the fifth century as the decisive turning point in the history of the Roman constitution, if the tradition is correct which says that it was through the Valerio-Horatian laws of 449 B.C. that the tribunes of the plebs received a definite position in the political order which enabled them to fight for constant new adjustments, in bitter struggles to be sure, but without ever destroying the foundations of the legal order. It was only when the right of tribunician intercession had become both excessive and rigid, when in this excessive form it was made a shibboleth of constitutionality, and in addition was used for purposes for which it had never been intended, that it became dangerous and harmful to the state. The salient point is that in the tribunes an agency was created to which the individual plebeians could turn to find protection from and redress against the abuse of power by the regular magistrates, and which, through the tribunes' position within the legal order, could work for necessary reforms and adjustments.

The third type of limitation, the limitation of fields of competences, presents very complex problems of which only the most essential can be discussed in the present context. Since Montesquieu the theory of the separation or division of power—i.e., the theory that the executive, the legislative, and the judiciary power should be entrusted to three different and independent branches cf the government—has been in the foreground among theories as to how such a limitation of fields of competences can best be achieved. In fact, the separation of the judicial power from the other two powers has a very great advantage, both because the judicial function alone gives hardly enough power to allow the agents or agencies entrusted with it to become a danger to the fundamental political order, and because the judiciary is perhaps best able to prevent other agencies from abusing their political competences.[17] But the example of the Roman constitution shows that the same end can be achieved, though perhaps less well, by entirely different means, for in Rome these three powers were never assigned to three different branches of the government, but each of the different branches had some share in each power. On the other hand, it may be observed that even the fathers of the American constitution, which was perhaps the most consistent attempt ever made to apply Montesquieu's theory, did not succeed in achieving—or rather, wisely refrained from trying to achieve—a pedantically perfect separation of the three powers.

In the Roman Republic such limitations of competences and powers were not established as part and parcel of one definite over-all plan. As a consequence the Roman constitution reveals more clearly than most other constitutions a danger of which no system of checks and balances is completely free, and which, it could be shown, some modern constitutions, especially of the twentieth century, have not escaped. This is the danger of creating too narrow and rigid limitations of power. Nobody, whether he makes an over-all plan for a new constitution or whether he introduces changes in an existing one, can foresee what new functions and what new powers to take care of these functions may become necessary in the future, nor is it always possible to change the fundamental law quickly enough to provide for such contingencies. It is therefore of the utmost importance that it be possible for such new functions to be taken over either by existing or newly created governmental organs without great difficulty. This will inevitably give the agency which assumes such new functions additional power, and this in its turn will bring about a shift of power within the political order. Such shifts, however, are not harmful as long as there remains the possibility of checking the abuse of power; i.e., as long as a responsible agency or agencies whose task this is retain the authority to step in and stop abuses if the need arises.

At this point there reveals itself again from another side what is perhaps the greatest deficiency in Polybius' theory of the mixed constitution. When he says that in the absence of the consuls Rome appears to be an oligarchy and during their presence in the capital a monarchy, he does, it is true, implicitly admit that there are temporary shifts of power. But these shifts of power are of an extremely short-range character; and, apart from this, he emphasizes the absolutely equal distribution of power between the three main elements of the Republic—the consuls, the Senate, and the people. What is more, in the second half of his analysis Polybius tries to show that none of these parts can move at all without the constant concurrence of the others. If that was really the essence of a system of checks and balances it would not only be the most fragile, but also the most inefficient, of all forms of government. But it has been demonstrated that the assumption that this is the essence of mixed government, consciously or unconsciously widely accepted ever since Polybius, is erroneous.

It is now also possible to point out the source of the error. Polybius had observed quite correctly that the Roman political order included something that might be called a system of checks and balances, and connected this with the greatness of Rome. The intrinsic logic of the observation then seemed to demand that a system of checks and balances was the more perfect according to the degree to which everything was constantly perfectly balanced and checked. But as so often happens with theories not verified by further observation, the apparent logic proves fallacious. Actually, a system of checks and balances is the more perfect according to the degree to which it leaves room for constant and easy shifts of power, in such a way, however, that the movement becomes more difficult as it approaches certain limits, that it can be stopped when it goes beyond an ultimate point, and that a certain equilibrium can then be restored by a renewed shifting of weights without breaking the mechanism. Thus the enormous shifts of power that took place in the Roman Republic from the middle of the fifth century to the middle of the second century B.C. did no serious damage to the machinery of the Roman state in spite of violent conflicts. But when the power of tribunician intercession had become excessive and rigid, and was used in such a way as to make it impossible for the mechanism to adjust itself without breaking, the constitutional machinery did break, and from then on it disintegrated rapidly.

Since this point is of fundamental importance it is worth while to illustrate it somewhat further by a more detailed analysis of the various possibilities which existed at the time when tribunician intercession was used by the reactionary majority of the Senate through the medium of the tribune M. Octavius against Tiberius Gracchus' proposed agrarian legislation. Obviously there were two ways in which the immediate difficulty could have been solved. Tiberius Gracchus could have given in and accepted Octavius' intercession as valid; from the point of view of formal legalism this would undoubtedly have been the correct attitude. The reforms would then have had to be given up for the moment. But—and this was probably Scipio's plan—the proposals could have been introduced again and again by different tribunes (or by curule magistrates, in later years) until it was possible to bring them to a vote because no tribune could be found who would intercede against them. Or M. Octavius could have withdrawn his intercession, as Tiberius Gracchus in fact tried to induce him to do. In this case the agrarian legislation would have been passed without a formal violation of a constitutional principle, and a great step forward would have been made. Yet it is clear that neither Tiberius' laudable submission nor the moderation of Octavius would have permanently removed the fundamental difficulty. As long as unrestricted tribunician intercession remained an acknowledged and sacred principle, and especially as long as this dangerous weapon remained at the disposal of majority or minority groups in the Senate, it was bound to be abused again, whether in the near or distant future. If successful, such methods were bound to be repeated more and more frequently, and since it is unthinkable that they could have been tolerated indefinitely, the clash which might have been avoided at the time of Ti. Gracchus would inevitably have occurred at some later date with hardly less disastrous consequences. Clearly the difficulty could be solved only by a revision of constitutional law and a reasonable restriction of the tribunician veto. Yet any such constitutional revision could be made legally impossible by tribunician intercession itself, against which, after the dictatorship had become subject to it, there was no legal remedy whatsoever. It is, one may say, a perfect example of a system of checks and balances tying itself up in a knot. Yet, in order to understand fully all the implications of the development which led to this result, it is necessary to carry the historical analysis still somewhat further.

It has been observed on an earlier occasion that the grave dangers inherent in the excessive extension of the right of tribunician intercession would have become apparent much earlier if it had not been for the fact that the tribunes became members of the senatorial aristocracy and so had no reason to make an obstructive use of their excessive negative powers as long as the direction of public affairs was almost exclusively in the hands of the Senate, and as long as this body handled these matters to the satisfaction of the great majority of the senatorial aristocracy and in a manner at least not intolerable to the majority of the rest of the population. This is quite true of the period from the Second Punic War to the middle of the second century B.C. But it naturally ceased to be true as soon as great new social problems arose which had to be solved if the social and political body was to remain sound, but which were of such a nature that their reasonable solution was contrary to the short-range interests of the vast majority of the senatorial aristocracy. As soon as such a contingency arose it became apparent that the possession of the weapon of tribunician intercession by the Senate gave the reactionary majority in this body the power to prevent all necessary reforms. This is of deep significance from the point of view of constitutional analysis, for it shows that the conflict between Ti. Gracchus and M. Octavius merely brought into the open a fundamental change in the political order which, since it was not connected with any institutional changes, appears to have escaped everybody's notice up to then, and which certainly escaped the notice of Polybius. Potentially—though for a long time this had not become apparent in practice—the flexible system of checks and balances which had existed in earlier centuries was destroyed from the moment when the Senate or groups of the Senate became able to use tribunician intercession to prevent the passing of legislation laid before a popular assembly and desired by the people. This is the reverse aspect of the apparent advantage that for a long time tribunician intercession had not been used to obstruct the government because the tribunes had become members of the governing class.

It is then highly instructive to reflect what would or might have happened if the tribunes of the plebs had not become members of the senatorial aristocracy but had remained true representatives of "the people," i.e. of the majority of the citizen population, and their champions against the ruling aristocracy. There can not be the slightest doubt that the unrestricted power of every one of the ten tribunes of the plebs to intercede against any action of a magistrate, and in addition to intercede in advance against any action that a magistrate might take in execution of a senatus consultum, would have been a great hindrance to effective government in any case, whether used as a weapon in the struggle of the "people" for greater political power or for the special aims of individual tribunes. Yet it would probably have been much less dangerous than it was when it became a weapon in the hands of the Senate.

The danger that an individual tribune would use his constitutionally unrestricted right of intercession for his own private purposes, without strong backing by a powerful group, was probably never very great. In fact, such an attempt, if it had been made, might have had a very salutary effect, since it would have made visible to everyone the absurdity of the principle of unrestricted veto power vested in each one of ten annual counter-magistrates. As the result of such an experience a reform of the constitution in this respect might have been accepted easily, and could have been carried through without a violation of constitutional principles, since the term of office of an individual tribune was only one year.

Unrestricted use of tribunician intercession as a weapon of the people in a struggle for greater political power might indeed have been much more dangerous and a great hindrance to effective government. But it is doubtful whether the effect would have been much worse than the effect of the various secessions and military strikes of the plebeians which filled the period from the first secession of the early fifth century to the last secession in the year 287 B.C., and from which, after all, the tribunician right of intercession in its later form had taken its origin. Tribunician intercession, if used against the senatorial aristocracy, would of necessity have had to be used against the executive. But the executive cannot be stopped permanently, nor even for very long, since it is in the very immediate interest of everybody that the administration of public affairs should continue. Like the strikes and secessions of an earlier period, tribunician intercession might therefore have been used to wring concessions from the Senate and the magistrates. But as soon as reasonable concessions had been obtained, it would always have had to subside for urgent practical reasons, however unrestricted the power of intercession was from the point of view of constitutional principles. It was in the hands of the Senate that tribunician intercession became really dangerous, because the attempt could be made to prevent necessary legislation altogether, and so in effect the Senate could try to deprive the popular assemblies of their share of power within the system of checks and balances. If, then, the interested group was determined not to give in and could find tribunes to support it, there was no solution of the difficulty but an open break and violation of an accepted constitutional principle, with all the consequences which such action was bound to have for respect for law in general.

This is not to say that a solution of the immediate conflict might not have been possible if Ti. Gracchus had given in when faced with Octavius' unyielding attitude. Nobody can know whether the obstructionists would always have been able to find a tribune to support them by his power of intercession if the agrarian bills had been introduced again and again in the following years. But this is not the point in the present context, for it has been shown that even a withdrawal of his intercession by Octavius himself would not have removed the essential difficulty.

It is highly significant that Polybius obviously was unaware of all these aspects of the problem. He saw merely that the plebeian tribunes were officially the representatives and champions of "the people" and not members of the Senate, an interpretation of their function and position which found visible support in the fact that they sat on lowly benches separated and different from the seats or *sellae* of the senators. He did not see that, in spite of these appearances, they had actually,

as individuals, become members of the senatorial aristocracy and that
this fact was at least as important, if not more important, than their
official function and position. This demonstrates again the second great
deficiency of Polybius' approach, his tendency to see everything only
on the institutional level and to neglect the very important question of
the ultimate source of actual political power and of its distribution
among social groups which cannot simply be identified with the political agents and agencies by which they may be officially represented.

The deficiency of Polybius' approach in this respect becomes even
more apparent if an attempt is made to analyze once more the constitution of Sulla in the light of this fundamental problem. The Sullan constitution removed the obstacle presented to any reasonable functioning
of government by the excessive veto power of the tribunes. Yet Sulla
did not try to re-establish a system of checks and balances according to
Polybius' ideals. His constitution was clearly designed to give the decisive power to the Senate. But the essential question in the present context is not whether this was desirable or undesirable, but whether Sulla's
constitution was workable, and if not, why. Sulla tried to support the
power of the Senate by an elaborate system of constitutional law. But
the law cannot defend itself. It could not be defended by the Senate
either, a small body of a few hundred men. It could be effectively defended only by a majority of the population or by the organized executive organs of the state who were in possession of weapons, i.e., by the
army or armies. The population or the armies might have defended
the Sullan constitution at the orders and under the direction of the
Senate if there had been a strong tradition of respect for the established
law. But this tradition had been thoroughly destroyed, both by the
flagrant abuse of constitutional rights and principles of which the Senate
and Sulla had both been guilty repeatedly ever since the conflict between T. Gracchus and M. Octavius in 133 B.C., and by the open violations of constitutional law which had occurred again and again
in the same period. In both respects Sulla, in fact, had been the
worst offender. How, then, could it be expected that Sulla's constitution would be defended through a tradition of respect for established
law?

A traditional respect for law could have been replaced by a genuine
interest of the population or of the armies in the preservation of the

established public order. But the majority of the soldiers had no interest whatever in the preservation of a political order which made it so difficult for them to obtain the most basic necessities of human existence once their term of military service was over. Finally, the armies might have obeyed the Senate regardless of any respect for the law as such, or interest in the preservation of the public order, because they felt a special allegiance to that body, because they regarded the Senate as their protector and bread-giver, or simply because they had no one else to whom they could turn. But the soldiers had no reason whatsoever to feel a special allegiance to the Senate. It was the Senate which, after Sulla as well as before him, constantly turned against anyone, whether he was a tribune or a general, who tried to make provision for the needs of the veterans; and their generals were usually the only persons to whom the soldiers could look for help in their predicament. Considering all this, it is amply clear that this constitution could not have lasted even if it had not had the additional fault, pointed out above, that its limitations on the functions and powers of individuals were much too rigid to make it possible, without violation of its provisions, to take care of the many emergencies which were bound constantly to arise in so vast and unhomogeneous an empire. Thus to the student of constitutional theory the Sullan constitution and its fate provide the most perfect illustration of the utter uselessness of the most consistent, elaborate system of constitutional law where the necessary moral and social foundations are lacking.

It is also illuminating to compare the process in the course of which the Roman Republic and the system on which it was based gradually disintegrated with the process through which the system of checks and balances which Polybius admired came into being. At the beginning of this latter process nearly all the political power was in the hands of the patrician aristocracy and of the political body representing it, the Senate. Though there existed at that time no elaborate code of constitutional law, this power had a much firmer foundation than the power of the Senate under the Sullan constitution, since it rested on the allegiance to their patrons of the clients of the individual gentes and on a strong tradition of respect for established law and institutions in the rest of the population.

The plebeians had their grievances against the patrician regime: the wealthy resented their total exclusion from political office and influence; the poor were oppressed by the unequal distribution of conquered land, and possibly by the high rate of interest and the harsh treatment of debtors by their patrician creditors; both the wealthy and the poor felt the harsh and high-handed attitude of the patrician magistrates towards the plebeian citizens. Yet the majority of the plebeians, and certainly those who were potentially most powerful because they constituted the core of the army, were not deprived of the most basic needs of human existence. Consequently they wanted a better place in the present political order, but did not desire its complete overthrow. At the same time the memory of the oppression under the last Tarquin king (or kings, according to some modern historians, who consider Tarquinius Superbus a symbol of a longer period of oppression), and the respect for the order of law which had replaced the monarchy, made it more difficult for ambitious leaders to use the discontent of the plebeians for their own private ends. Still, even so, if ancient tradition can be trusted in this respect, the danger that a plebeian leader might overthrow the Republic and set himself up as a tyrant was not altogether absent.[18] The decisive fact, then, was that the patricians gave in while there was still time, and the leaders and representatives of the plebeians were given a place within the legal order so as to be able to work continuously for the redress of grievances as they arose again and again in the course of centuries.

Yet for a long time the tribunes of the plebs had no active share in the government whatsoever. For more than a century they did not have even the right to introduce legislation except indirectly, inasmuch as they had the right to have the plebeians vote in so-called plebiscites, which, however, as has been shown, in the earlier period of the Republic represented merely demands for specific legislation, but in themselves did not have the force of laws. In spite of this, their position, as it was formally acknowledged by the Valerio-Horatian laws, enabled them to fulfil two functions most essential for a system of checks and balances: to protect individuals against the abuse of legal power by the official functionaries of the state, and to press for changes in the legal order whenever such changes appeared necessary or desirable. This second factor may also be expressed by the statement that it was one of their functions to keep the political order open and adaptable to changing conditions.

It is not difficult to see that in many respects the situation in the last century of the Republic was exactly the reverse. Officially and legally the popular assemblies and the plebeian tribunes had in the meantime acquired much greater and more active powers. But tribunician power, which had been partly snatched away from the people by the senatorial aristocracy, was now used to make the legislative powers of the popular assemblies ineffective and to prevent necessary changes instead of promoting them. This perpetuated the existence of an increasingly large group of citizens which had no interest in the preservation of the present order, and it was this group which was given the greatest physical power when it became customary to draw the core of the armies from it.

It remains to apply the results of the historical analysis to the most fundamental problems presented by the theory of Polybius. It has been shown that the concept of a system of checks and balances and the concept of a mixed constitution are not identical, though they are closely related to one another. In Greek political theory before Polybius the mixed constitution, or mixed political order, had been in the foreground of the discussion. Polybius retained this term but actually applied it to a system of checks and balances. By identifying the purely functional consulship with the monarchic element, and the Senate with the aristocratic or oligarchic element in the state, he demonstrated that he was not aware of the difference. This is obviously one of the main causes of the two great deficiencies of his analysis which have revealed themselves repeatedly in the course of the present inquiry. But several points are still in need of further clarification.

A king and an aristocracy, in contrast to a functional head of the government or a functional council or representative body, have this in common, that their position and power in the state are prior to whatever specific functions they may have or may acquire within the machinery of government. But apart from this their position and function in a mixed constitution are by no means the same. It is of the very essence of kingship, in contrast to tyranny or Caesarism, that the king is above the parties. Where the king, as has often happened in history, has to assert his power against an aristocratic *fronde* or a popular movement, the king, it is true, with his adherents may for some time form a party of his own. But unless the monarchy is overthrown in the process of such a conflict, the end result will always be either the establishment of an absolute monarchy in which all functions and powers emanate from the king and are ultimately united in his hands, or of a constitutional monarchy in which the king has but few, if any, specific functions and powers, but nevertheless remains the representative of the political order as a whole. From this point of view it becomes apparent that a system of checks and balances and absolute kingship (though in one respect, as shown before, on opposite ends of the scale) have one very essential thing in common. They are the only forms of government whose purpose and effect it is to prevent as far as possible, through a true rule of law, the oppression of one section of the people, whether this be the majority or a minority, by the other. It also becomes apparent that it is not the function of a king in a mixed constitution to be one of the forces which keep one another in a movable balance of power, but to supplement the respect for law which is the indispensable foundation of a system of checks and balances by the loyalty which his subjects feel for him as the representative of the whole legal order.

This factor should not be underestimated; for history shows that the transition from a tradition of respect for the law and its public functionaries to a tradition of loyalty to a person representing the law, and vice versa, is extremely difficult and fraught with great dangers. That the attempt to convert the Caesarism of the Roman emperors into a monarchy somewhat resembling what we have called kingship was unsuccessful for more than three hundred years was certainly due mainly to the fact that the army remained separate from the civilian population. But indubitably it was also an important factor that a large section of the population, especially the heirs and successors of the ruling aristocracy of an earlier period, was never able to forget the Republic. Though there was much submissiveness, servility, and fawning adulation for the princeps, and later, especially under Trajan and the Antonines, sincere admiration among some of the best representatives of the aristocracy for the person of the princeps, no genuine feeling of loyalty for the emperor *as* emperor can be discovered in this class for centuries. This is much more important for an evaluation of the development than are the conspiracies of some die-hard republicans in the early empire. It is also significant that it was in the main Christian writers who first developed the idea of the emperor as a universal monarch in about the same sense in which the early Stoics had spoken of a universal king.

The transition from a tradition of loyalty to a king as the personal representative of the legal and political order to a respect for the law as guaranteed by a system of checks and balances is no less difficult than the reverse process, and a country upon which such a system is imposed from the outside is apt to fall prey to the first usurper or tyrant because of its desire to return to a tradition with which it is familiar and which it understands. There are not many examples from antiquity to illustrate this fact, since there are very few cases in which an attempt was made to impose from the outside a republican regime on a country with a monarchic tradition. But the four Macedonian republics which the Romans established after the capture of King Perseus in the hope that a republic would be less warlike than a monarchy are a striking case of this kind. The modern examples are too obvious to be in need of mention. Generally speaking a transition from monarchy to a rule of law through mere functionaries of the law, instead of a person incorporating or representing the law in its entirety, has been successful only where it was a long and gradual process, or where it was the result of a genuine revolt of a large majority of the people against an intolerably oppressive regime in the course of which the rule of law was set up as the remedy of the ills suffered. Even in such cases, however, it takes a long time for the new form to take firm root.

The position of an aristocracy in a mixed constitution is clearly different from that of a monarch. The example of the position enjoyed by the Senate in the first half of the second century B.C. shows that it is possible for the representative body of an aristocracy to have, for a certain period of time, a genuine authority which comes very near to the authority that a king may have in a monarchy. Yet there remains a fundamental difference in two respects. A client or retainer may feel as great or even greater a loyalty to his lord than a monarchist to his king. But it is not possible to feel for a composite body, like the Roman Senate, the same kind of loyalty that an individual may feel for the person of a king. What is even more important, an aristocracy will always be a party since it inevitably has its own economic and other interests different from, and to some extent in conflict with, those of the rest of the population. It therefore can never be the representative of the whole to the same extent as a king, though this fact may for some time be concealed by special services rendered to the community and by good and skilful government.

An aristocracy, furthermore—and this is the most important factor —is not identical with any governmental agency by which it may be more or less officially represented. Its powers and influences are larger, may come from many and varied sources, and therefore may appear in unexpected places. Hence, a system of checks and balances on the purely governmental level provides no guaranty against the possibility that an aristocracy, or in fact any kind of social or economic group, may gain actual control over all the governmental and political agencies which are supposed to check and balance one another. This is what actually happened in the Roman Republic of the second century B.C. when the senatorial aristocracy acquired control over tribunician intercession and thus, in fact, over the legislative initiative. The situation resulting from this development was much more dangerous than the open control of the government by the patricians in the early fifth century, for then the issues and the fronts were clear, and when the two parties had measured their strength against one another they could conclude a compromise, the results of which were incorporated in law. In the second half of the second century, on the contrary, it could be claimed speciously that resistance to tribunician intercession, over which the senatorial aristocracy had gained control, was a flagrant violation of a sacred constitutional principle and of a principle guaranteeing the rights of the people and not the supremacy of a class. Thus the fronts were confused, the situation in regard to the law was not clear, and the ensuing conflict led to general disrespect for the legal order.

All this shows once more that the problem of the position of an aristocracy in a mixed constitution cannot be determined simply in terms of a functional system of checks and balances. It also shows that in a community which is not socially homogeneous it is not sufficient that there be a flexible system of checks and balances on the governmental level to secure an equitable distribution of political power.

Though in the particular course of events which started the Roman Republic on the way to its destruction the rigidity of the principle of tribunician intercession played an important role, it is clear that an aristocracy can get control of all governmental agencies, even if less easily, where the balance of power between these agencies is freely movable and where there is no rigid device by which this movement can be stopped, as was the case in the late Roman Republic. It is therefore of the utmost importance that, quite apart from existing agencies, newly forming social groups be permitted to organize, and not be prevented from exercising their influence within the limits of the legal order so that they may find their place in the social system and be able to attain or preserve an existence worthy of human beings. In fact, this is more important for the internal stability of a state than the existence of a well functioning system of checks and balances, for as the example of the tribunes of the plebs in the earlier period of the Roman Republic after the middle of the fifth century shows, the most important checks and balances can be provided by agencies or agents which have no active share in government, provided they have an acknowledged position within the law which makes it possible for them to make their influence felt where necessary.

The problem of the relation between democracy and a system of checks and balances is different from that of the position of a democratic factor or element in a mixed constitution. It is by no means analogous either to the problem of the position of a monarchic element or to that of the position of an aristocratic factor in a mixed constitution, and it has been shown that these two problems are also quite different from one another. Least of all is it sufficient for the establishment of a stable political order to advocate an even mixture of monarchic, oligarchic, and democratic elements, as Polybius has done.

An indication of the nature of the difference may perhaps be found in the fact that in recent times little distinction has been made between a democracy and a system of checks and balances. In fact, it has become quite common to call democracies certain countries whose governmental system is clearly a system of checks and balances. It is easy to see that this linguistic habit has created a good deal of confusion. Especially in the many cases in which, after the overthrow of a tyrannical regime, democracy was to be restored and to be supported by a constitution, there were not infrequently two groups, one of which advocated a system of checks and balances, while the other advocated a constitution favoring simple majority rule. Since both groups wanted a restoration of "democracy," it is obvious that their concepts of democracy were different from each other.

In order to clarify the issue it is necessary to consider the problem from more than one angle. Of fundamental importance is again the distinction between a purely functional system of checks and balances and a mixed constitution. The different branches of government in a functional system of checks and balances can of course be elected more or less directly by "the people" in such a way that all citizens have an equal vote. In this case it can be said that the system of checks and balances rests on a democratic basis, though an equal vote of all adult citizens does by no means guarantee that "the people" can elect whom they wish, since this depends largely on the way in which candidates are presented, and since there are also other ways in which the vote can be influenced by socially and economically powerful groups. Yet where social and economic contrasts are not too great, and where the citizens can freely associate to break the dominance of established political groups and organizations, it can be said that the governmental system of checks and balances is democratically controlled, and it is therefore not quite unjustified to call such a political order a democracy.

There is still another reason why democracy and systems of checks and balances often are not clearly distinguished. Except in the most primitive conditions a pure majority rule is hardly feasible. Even in ancient Athens, which probably represents the most consistent attempt to realize the ideal of pure and simple democracy, there were certain checks on the regulation of all matters by plain and direct majority decisions in the popular assemblies. Only during a very brief period between the death of Pericles and the end of the Peloponnesian War can one discern a strong tendency to decide everything merely by a decree of the majority of the assembly, regardless of whether the decision was in conflict with existing laws or not. This tendency culminated in the demand of the assembly in 406 B.C. that the commanders of the Athenian fleet in the battle of the Arginusae be condemned to death by a mere decree of the ecclesia without a trial in a law court. At that time Socrates refused to put the proposal to a vote because he claimed it was against the law to condemn a man without due process of law, but the crowd shouted that it would be terrible if the sovereign people of Athens should not have the right to do as it pleased.

This example illustrates very well the difference between pure democracy in the sense of undiluted majority rule and a rule of law on a democratic basis which always implies some form of checks and balances. But the protest of Socrates and the institution of the γραφὴ παρανόμων indicate that even in Athens in the period of the democracy there had always been some checks on the sovereignty of the popular assembly, though for a moment the doctrine that the assembly was the absolute sovereign, having no law above it, gained the upper hand.

When after the overthrow of the so-called Thirty Tyrants the democracy was restored, the dangerous implications of the doctrine of absolute democracy were realized, and the new constitution placed severe checks on changes of the fundamental law and made proposals for decrees contrary to established law punishable. Yet the system of checks—one can hardly speak of balances—incorporated in the new constitution was still very imperfect. Thus one may say that the terminological confusion is understandable because absolutely uncontrolled majority rule has hardly ever existed in history, except perhaps under very primitive conditions, and because most historical democracies have held a place somewhere between a system of pure majority rule and a democratically controlled but otherwise well-elaborated system of checks and balances. But the difference in the two concepts of democracy is no less clear.

The problem of the position and function of a democratic element in a mixed constitution is quite different from the question of the relation between a democracy and a system of checks and balances as governmental systems. It has been shown that though a monarchic element in the proper sense of the word was missing in the Roman Republic, one may speak of a mixed political order in Rome in the sense that ever since the middle of the fifth century B.C. there was a certain balance of political power between a ruling aristocracy and the rest of the people. This mixed constitution had come into being through a compromise, and for some time developed further through ever-new compromises between an aristocracy which, in the beginning, had ruled supreme and other classes which asserted themselves against this aristocracy and acquired ever-increasing political powers until a new aristocracy was formed and the process was to some extent reversed.

A mixed constitution in this sense, i.e. in the sense of a balance of political power between two or more social classes, is clearly not identical with a system of checks and balances of a purely functional nature and on the governmental level. For the latter can be either democratically controlled or be connected with a mixed constitution of the kind just defined, or even with a constitutional monarchy. Yet, though for the sake of clarity it is necessary to make this distinction, which Polybius failed to make, the two systems are historically and practically not quite unrelated to each other.

Ever since the very first beginnings of political thinking in ancient Greece the existence of different social and economic groups and classes side by side with one another has been considered a cause of trouble, and ever since Hippodamus of Miletus and Phaleas of Chalcedon in the fifth century B.C.,[19] many schemes have been invented in efforts to find a lasting solution of this problem. So far these schemes have not been found to be effective, at least not in so far as they aimed at the permanent removal of class differences, and the most recent attempt to apply a scheme of this kind in practice has merely led to the emergence of a party aristocracy ruling in a still more oppressive fashion than any hereditary aristocracy or aristocracy of wealth had ever done in the past. But here again the internal history of the Roman Republic is of the greatest interest.

It took a long time: but once some kind of balance of political power between the plebeians and patricians had been established, the plebeians did not cease in their struggle until the gulf between themselves and the patricians was bridged. By working for a juster distribution of land they also, for a considerable time, prevented the two ends of the economic scale in the population from drifting too far apart. A new aristocracy, it is true, came into being in the course of this process. But this new aristocracy was not so exclusive as the older aristocracy had been, and at the beginning of the Second Punic War a still greater equalization of the classes seems to have been in the making.

Then the trend was reversed as a consequence of external circumstances. But in the second half of the second century new forces arose which might have brought about an adjustment of the social and economic balance if the political system had not in the meantime become rigid through the development of tribunician intercession and the conquest of this constitutional device by the senatorial aristocracy. There can hardly be any doubt that if the political conditions had still been the same as at the end of the fourth or the beginning of the third century B.C., the agrarian legislation of Ti. Gracchus would have either been carried or forced through without the disastrous consequences for the whole political system which it had under the changed conditions of the late second century.

It appears, then, that the formation of social and economic groups and classes cannot be prevented, since this is a natural historical process. If nevertheless an attempt is made to stop this process altogether, it can be done only through the constant application of force and the most oppressive controls; and even then the social and political cleavage will simply reappear in a different guise. Yet those early Greek theorists were not wrong who pointed out that such cleavages, if allowed to widen beyond a certain limit, are the cause of great evils and may ultimately turn out to be destructive of the very foundations of the legal order.

On the basis of these complementary observations Aristotle, and others before him, developed the theory of the middle-of-the-road social and political order. The early history of the Roman Republic shows how such a middle-of-the-road social order is promoted by the existence of a certain balance of political power between different social groups, which gives free play to forces which counteract the process by which social differences are created without stopping it altogether. The same history shows also that such a balance of political power must find its expression in political institutions if the process of constant readjustments is to be prevented from assuming violent and tumultuous forms. While, therefore, a middle-of-the-road social order, a mixed constitution in the sense of a balance of political power between different economic, social, and political groups, and a functional system of checks and balances are by no means identical with one another they are to some extent complementary, and it is doubtful how far they can exist completely separated from one another, though a system of checks and balances which becomes rigid instead of remaining flexible can also become a hindrance to the creation or preservation of the two other political forms.

Looking back on the results of the preceding analysis one may perhaps acknowledge that in a way Mommsen's judgment is not too harsh when he says that there can be hardly a more absurd political speculation than Polybius' explanation of the Roman constitution as an even mixture of monarchic, oligarchic, and democratic elements, though this explanation is exactly what many of Polybius' readers have found most brilliant in his work. Yet, paradoxically, there is also some truth in Schwartz' opinion that Polybius' evaluation of the Roman political order showed a deep understanding of what was most essential, and in a way unique, in the Roman state; and perhaps what Schwartz had in mind when making this statement is more important than what Mommsen pointed out. What Polybius did see is that the greatness and the power of Rome was an historical phenomenon of the first magnitude, that the greatness of Rome had something to do with its internal order, and that this internal order in its turn was in some relation to what earlier Greek theorists had had in mind when they spoke of the preferability of a mixed constitution or a mixed political order. But when Polybius tried to elaborate in detail what he believed he had discovered, he was carried away by the apparent intrinsic logic of the general theory and described the Roman state as a perfect mixture of monarchy, oligarchy, and democracy, in which none of the three elements can move without the concurrence of the two others, a picture which has but little relation to reality.

If, therefore, the attempt is to be made to answer the question of whether the claims which Polybius makes for his mixed constitution are justified or not, the answer must be given in respect to the political order which he meant to describe and not in reference to his oversimplified description. The first of his claims had been that a mixed constitution is more stable than any simple constitution. In order to decide whether this claim is warranted, it is necessary to define stability. Obviously, if the claim is to have any validity at all, stability cannot mean freedom from change, for it has been shown that the Roman constitution (which according to Polybius was the greatest model of a mixed constitution) underwent very great changes indeed in the period during which, in his opinion, it continued to be excellent. But when Polybius speaks of the instability of simple constitutions he means the violent overthrow of the whole political order and its replacement by an entirely different one; revolution, in other words, ending with the complete defeat of one party and the complete victory of the other, often connected with the banishment of large groups. Of such violent changes of the political order, so frequent in Greek states, Rome and Sparta in fact remained free for a remarkable length of time. In this sense, then, Polybius' claim appears to be justified by history.

It is most remarkable that the political systems of Rome and Sparta enjoyed such stability in spite of the fact that their systems of checks and balances, and what may be called their mixed constitutions, applied only to the citizens, who during the major part of the history of the two states constituted a minority in respect to a much larger subject population. The reason for the stability of these two states in this respect is of course quite different from the reasons for the internal stability of their political systems as far as the citizens were concerned. In relation to their noncitizen subjects, or "allies," the Spartans and the Romans constituted a highly organized minority as against unorganized majorities. They were therefore in a position to concentrate their organized force at any moment on any point at which a rebellion might start and to subdue it before it could spread and so become dangerous. But the history of both communities shows also that there is a limit to such a rule. With its extension over the southern and southwestern part of the Peloponnesus, enlarged and supplemented to some extent by a system of alliances with other Peloponnesian communities under Spartan leadership, Spartan domination had reached a point beyond which it could not safely go. The system was then very strong in defense but it could not expand any farther without destroying itself. When, through Sparta's victory in the Peloponnesian War, it had to expand nevertheless, the system began to crack. This victory and the inevitable extension of political engagements which followed it mark the beginning of the process of the decay of Spartan power, though two more centuries were to pass before the Spartan political system had disintegrated completely.

Polybius believed that the Roman system was better suited for expansion, and in fact the Romans not only conquered an enormous territory, far beyond anything that the Spartans had ever held under their political influence, but the empire which they conquered remained under Roman control for centuries. Yet the extension of Rome domination in the beginning of the second century B.C., by which the non-citizen population became many times more numerous than the citizen population, was also closely connected with the development which led to the downfall of the Roman Republic, though this became apparent only some time later. In both cases, however, the disintegration of the political order was not directly caused by a revolt of non-citizens. All the revolts of the allies of the Romans in Italy, of the Roman subjects in the East, and so on, were ultimately subdued through the organized power of the Roman armies. It was the strain which the rule over large subject populations caused within the political and social systems of the ruling nations that promoted the disintegration of their political systems.

The external strength of a state (other factors, as, for instance, its material resources being equal) is closely related to its internal stability, though by no means identical with it. In recent times it has often been argued that a system of checks and balances, both in the wider sense in which it includes elements of what the Greeks called a mixed constitution and in the sense of a purely functional system of checks and balances, weakens a state because it makes it very difficult, if not impossible, to make clear-cut and quick decisions and to maintain a consistent policy, since each of the elements hinders the others. But historical evidence does not support the observation in this general form, since many communities with mixed constitutions or systems of checks and balances, both in antiquity and in modern times, have shown a much greater strength and staying power than communities with simple constitutions but with comparable, or even greater, material resources. In actual fact the problem cannot be settled in such general terms. A government which is constantly checked and hampered in its actions by groups or parties controlling it cannot move, and is therefore likely to fall in emergencies. But the same may be true of an absolute democracy with changing majorities. On the other hand, historical analysis has shown that it is essential to a well-constructed and well-functioning system of checks and balances that it permit considerable shifts in the balance of power, and very considerable concentrations of power in various governmental agencies. It is not the purpose of such a system that the various agents and agencies of government be constantly hampered in every action, but that there be institutions making it possible to check them when they abuse their power. Now it is true that the power and possibility of checking the abuse of power can also be abused, and that no system of checks and balances, however well constructed, will be free of such abuse. Hence it is true that, generally speaking, communities with systems of checks and balances are usually slower in reaching decisions and are more hampered in the consistent execution of a long-range policy than are communities in which the sovereignty is clearly and permanently located in one man or in a small group. But they have an advantage which more than compensates for such disadvantages. Since in a system of checks and balances in the wider sense, which includes social balances, there are no oppressed classes, such a system has a staying power that no community in which one class or section of the population rules over the other can have.

This fact is very well illustrated by Roman history. In the early Republic there were many military strikes when the plebeians tried to wring new concessions from the patricians, but once the concessions were made, or even if an immediate emergency arose before the concessions were made, the plebeians fought for the community to the last man, because, in spite of existing antagonisms and unsolved problems, it was a true res publica, a community belonging to all. In the late Republic, when it was a res publica only for a small minority, it was still strong enough to ward off attacks from the outside, and even to make new conquests, but everybody realized that it would no longer have been able to stand a test like the Second Punic War. It was under the early emperors, who are supposed to have solved the problems which the rotten oligarchy of the Republic could not solve, that a wall, the limes, had to be built to defend the empire against the barbarians, and some time later this enormous empire had become so weak that it was overrun by barbarian tribes whose actual manpower was ridiculously small in comparison to the resources of the Roman state. Yet the cities of the empire flourished economically under the early emperors, and under Caracalla citizenship was given to all the inhabitants of the empire with the exception of the so-called *dediticii* and, of course, slaves. All this was of little avail. The decisive fact is that Rome was no longer a res publica, and the history of Rome shows clearly that no organization, however efficient, can in the long run replace the genuine allegiance of the population to the political order in which it lives. It need hardly be pointed out again that such allegiance can exist in a monarchy—for where the king is truly the representative of the legal order, this legal order can in a sense be a res publica—but not in a Caesarian monarchy, and even less in a tyranny.

The third claim which Polybius makes for his mixed constitution is that it protects the liberty of the citizens. Since it is the very purpose of a system of checks and balances to protect the individual citizen from the abuse of power, and any kind of arbitrary action on the part of any functionary of the state, by making it possible for him to appeal to some other clearly designated agent or agency of the state to find redress against such action, it seems clear that Polybius' claim is justified. It need hardly be stated expressly that where the system of checks and balances applies only to citizens, and the larger part of the population consists of noncitizens, as was the case in Sparta and in the later Roman Republic, what Polybius claims applies to the citizens only.

However, it is necessary to be very clear as to what is meant by liberty in this case. If liberty means freedom from arbitrary interference, then a system of checks and balances, as long as it functions properly, is a guaranty of liberty. Essentially liberty in this sense means nothing but a rule of law. This is very beautifully expressed in the famous dialog between the Persian king Xerxes and the Spartan king Demaratus in Herodotus.[20] "How can you think," asks Xerxes, the Spartan king, "that these people, who are always quarreling with one another, will fight against such overwhelming odds, when they do not even have a king who could force them to fight against their will?" "O king," answers Demaratus, "though they have no master, they are not entirely without a master. In fact they have a master whom they obey much more than your subjects obey you. This master is the law; and this master says always the same thing, while you say one thing one day and another thing the next day."

Liberty, then, here means nothing but the rule of (self-imposed) law: autonomy in the etymological sense of the word. In this sense the Spartans were actually the freest of the free, and they always considered themselves as such. No Spartan could be arbitrarily punished or ordered around either by a king or an ephor, or the gerousia, or even the apella. Any command that was given had to be strictly within the fundamental law, and there was always the possibility of appeal. Yet we do not think of Sparta as a liberal country. It is doubtful whether there ever was a country in which the life of the individual, almost from the cradle to the grave, was more tightly controlled by the state than in ancient Sparta. In this sense Sparta was a model of totalitarianism.

We are inclined to consider as more or less synonymous the terms tyranny (i.e. absolute rule of one party with a monarchic or semimonarchic head over the rest of the population), despotism (i.e. arbitrary rule of one man), and totalitarianism (i.e. tight control of the state over the lives of the individual citizens), because within our personal historical experience these three phenomena have most often appeared in close connection with one another, but history shows that this is by no means always the case. Investigating the causes of totalitarianism and the possible means of preventing it is outside the scope of the present book.[21] But it is necessary to point out that while a system of checks and balances, as long as it functions, is a safeguard against despotism and tyranny, it has nothing to do either negatively or positively with totalitarianism. As the example of Sparta shows, such a system is certainly not a safeguard against totalitarianism, though it does not of course promote it either.

In conclusion it may then perhaps be said that a system of checks and balances or a mixed constitution is no political panacea. There are no more panaceas in politics than there are in medicine. Nothing certainly could be more wrong than the belief that a well-constructed constitution incorporating a system of checks and balances is all that is needed in order to insure the internal stability of a country and to make it secure against any kind of violent internal upheaval. Perhaps this fact is acknowledged by most political scientists. Yet it may not be superfluous to stress it again in a time in which the universal belief dominating practical policy seems to be that one merely has to give a country a new constitution according to some accepted model, and to add a few years of "re-education" in order to set it on the right path, on which it will then continue for the foreseeable future. There are many different types of mixed constitutions and systems of checks and balances, and which of these types will be suitable in a given situation depends on many circumstances, not the least important of which are the prevailing traditions, which cannot be eradicated in a few years and replaced by new ones. Yet in the course of time conditions and even traditions change, and it will be necessary to adapt the political system to these changed circumstances. One might therefore be tempted to say that the spirit which produced mixed constitutions and systems of checks and balances where they existed in history is more important than the existence of such system. But the spirit has little power unless it can express itself in and through definite institutions, just as the institutions are of little avail when the spirit is lacking.

From all this it follows that it is wrong to reject the mixed constitution and the system of checks and balances as political devices because, like everything that man has invented, they do not work if they are applied in the wrong form or are not handled properly. In advocating certain forms of government as against others, political theory can only give the most general outline. All the details have to be filled in according to varying circumstances. But in combination with the study of history, political theory can also show what consequences and results certain measures are likely to have in connection with certain circumstances, and specifically that these results very often are apt to be very different from what a superficial observer would expect them to be. This latter kind of inquiry is by its nature endless, since there is an infinity of possible combinations. The same is true of medicine; yet any inquiry, however restricted, that shows what influence on the human body or the body politic a certain treatment is likely to have under certain conditions is not quite without value.

According to Polybius it is the task of the pragmatic historian to make history predictable and to enlighten future statesmen. The first claim presupposed a causal mechanism of which the cycle of constitutions is an example. The enlightened statesmen of Sparta and Rome interrupted the mechanism. So they made history less predictable, since it is hardly possible to predict where and when such enlightenment will make itself felt. Nevertheless it is not necessary to go into the metaphysics of freedom and causality in history to solve the problem, for insight and enlightenment can enter as causal factors into history, even if it is not predictable when and where. The occasions on which statesmen or legislators can help to create a new legal order are rare, and such an order will not live unless its spirit is kept alive. This is not in the power of a few men, however exalted their position may be. The contribution which the historian can make is therefore very modest. All he can do is to make public whatever little truth he believes himself to have found, and to see where it will fall.

APPENDICES

FROM THE FIRST AND THIRD BOOKS

I, 64, 1: Some readers may perhaps wonder for what reason the
Romans, now that they have conquered the whole world and have
a power many times as great as formerly, are no longer able to man
so many ships nor to put to sea with equally large fleets. It will, however, be possible to see the reason for this paradoxical state of things
quite clearly when we come to the analysis of their political system.

III, 2, 6: At that point [i.e., at the end of Polybius' account of the
140th Olympiad, the years 220–216 B.C.] I shall interrupt the narrative and give the [promised] account of the Roman constitution,
by which I shall show, through a systematic analysis, that it was the
peculiar form of their political constitution which did most to enable
the Romans, first to win the supremacy over the Italians and the
Sicilians, then to add to this the rule over the Iberians and the Celts,
and finally, after they had defeated the Carthaginians in war, to en-
visage the conquest of the whole world.

III, 118, 11: When, at the end of my account of Greek affairs in that
Olympiad [the 140th], I shall have reached that same date [i.e., the
date of the battle of Cannae], then, as an introduction to what will
follow, I shall give a special and separate account of the political
system of the Romans, since I believe that an analysis of that system
not only belongs properly to a historical treatise on the period but will

also be of the greatest value for those eager to gain a deeper insight and to make use of this insight in practice when dealing with the task of reforming a political order or of instituting a new one [as for instance in the foundation of a colony].

FROM THE SIXTH BOOK

Introductory Remarks

VI, 2: I am quite aware that some people will wonder why I have reserved my analytical account of the aforementioned political system [i.e., the Roman constitution] for insertion at this point, though this makes it necessary to interrupt the continuous flow of my narrative. However, that this section was from the beginning planned as an integral part of my whole enterprise I believe I have made perfectly clear on many occasions and, above all, in the introductory remarks about the purpose of my history, where I said that it was the highest aim and would be the most useful result of my undertaking to make the readers of my work understand clearly how and in consequence of what political system it came about that, within a period of less than fifty-three years the whole of the inhabited world fell under the domination of the Romans, an event the like of which had never occurred before. Well, then, this point being decided, I could not see a more fitting occasion than the present one [i.e., immediately after the narrative had been carried down to the end of the period in which the Romans suffered the crushing defeat at Cannae] for taking up what I intended to say about the Roman political system and for testing the truth of my opinion concerning it. For just as in the case of private individuals, those who try to distinguish between worthless characters and men of quality and who try to put the matter really to the test do not look upon the uneventful and quiet periods of the lives of those individuals but on those periods in which they suffered misfortune or had an unusual streak of good luck, since they believe that the real test of a perfect man is his ability to bear with a high mind and with perfect poise the most complete reverses of fortune, exactly in the same way one should look upon and test a political system. Hence, since I did not see how anyone could find a more violent or a greater reverse of fortune in our times than that which was experienced by the Romans at that time, I reserved my political analysis for the present occasion.

What is most interesting and fruitful for students of history is the investigation of causes and the selection of what is best in every field. The greatest cause of success or failure in all matters, however, is obviously the political order of a state. For it is a fact that all plans and all beginnings of political actions spring from this as from a fountain-head and that their completion likewise is dependent on the political order.

On the Different Forms of States

VI, 3: In regard to those Greek states which have often risen to strength and power and then have again suffered complete reverses of fortune, it is easy to give an account of their fate in the past and to predict their future. For to explain what is known is easy and to predict the future where one can draw one's conclusions on the basis of what has happened in the past is not too difficult. In regard to the Roman state, however, it is not altogether easy to give an account even of its present condition because of the complicated character of its political order, and it is difficult to predict the future because of a certain lack of knowledge in regard to the peculiar character of their public institutions and their private habits. An uncommon degree of attention and a very careful analysis are therefore required if one wishes to obtain a clear and comprehensive insight into the distinctive characteristics of these institutions and traditions.

The majority of those who have tried to give a methodical account of these matters speak of three types of constitutions, the first of which they call kingship, the second aristocracy, and the third democracy. It seems to me, however, that one might very well ask these theorists whether they introduce these three types as the only ones possible or rather as the three best forms of constitutions. In either case it seems to me they are mistaken. For it is obvious that one must consider as the best that political order which is a compound of all the three aforementioned types, since this has been demonstrated not only in theory, but by actual experience, Lycurgus having been the first to organize the Spartan state according to this principle. Likewise it must be emphasized that one cannot accept the three forms of constitutions mentioned as the only ones possible. For we have witnessed monarchies and tyrannies that were most remote from true kingship, although they seem to have some kind of resemblance to it; which is the reason why all monarchs as far as possible apply the name of kingship to their rule, even if they may have little or no justification for doing so. Likewise there have been an even greater number of oligarchies that seemed to have some resemblance to aristocracies and yet in fact were as different from a true aristocracy as possible. It is the same with democracy.

4. That what I have said is true becomes quite clear through the following observations. One cannot call every kind of monarchy kingship, but only that which is based on the consent of those who are governed and which appeals to reason rather than to fear and force. Likewise one must not consider every kind of oligarchy as an aristocracy but only that kind in which the government is in the hands of a selected body of citizens distinguished by justice and insight. Similarly, that state is not a true democracy in which any kind of chance majority can do anything it pleases. Only when it is traditional and customary in a community to worship the gods, to honor one's parents, to have respect for older people, and to obey the laws, and when in a community of this kind the political decisions are made by the majority; only in this case are we entitled to call such a state a democracy. Hence one must speak of six different types of political orders: three that are in everybody's mouth and of which we have just spoken, and three [sc. depraved ones] that correspond to them, namely monarchy, oligarchy, and ochlocracy [1] or mob rule.

The first of these forms to come into being without any deliberate planning and through a natural process is monarchy. Upon this follows kingship, which is produced by deliberate improvement of the former. When this changes into the corresponding evil type of government, namely tyranny, aristocracy arises out of the overthrow of the latter. When in the natural course of things aristocracy degenerates into oligarchy and the common people finally rise in anger against the injustice of their rulers, democracy is born. Again, when democracy falls into license and lawlessness the final result in the course of time is mob rule.

That what I have said about these matters is true will be seen most clearly by anyone who looks attentively upon the natural beginnings, developments, and changes of the various political constitutions. For only he who has observed how each of these different types of government comes into being and develops will be able to see how they come into being, grow, reach their peak, and turn from one form into another, and finally also when and how this will happen again. I consider this kind of analysis especially appropriate in regard to the Roman constitution since it came into being and developed in a perfectly natural way.

5. Perhaps the theory of the natural transition from one type of constitution to the other is more thoroughly explained in the works of Plato and of some other philosophers. But, since there the theory appears in a very complicated form and is made the subject of very lengthy discussions, it is accessible in this form to only a few readers. Hence I shall try to expound in a somewhat more summary fashion just so much of it as belongs to pragmatic history and is not beyond the reach of common intelligence. For if something should appear to be missing in my general exposition the detailed analysis which will be given in the following chapters will make up fully for anything that now may seem to remain an unsolved problem.

What, then, do I consider as the beginnings and from what origin do I say that political organizations have first come into being? When through a deluge, a plague, a famine, or some other cause of this kind great destruction has come upon mankind, the like of which according to tradition has happened in the past and hence is probably likely to happen again many times in the future, and when consequently all social customs, all arts and crafts have perished also, and when from the few survivors, as if it were from seeds, in the course of time a greater number of human beings have grown up again, then they will flock together—for it is plausible that they should associate with their own kind because of their natural weakness—and when this has happened it is inevitable that, just as in the case of animals living in flocks, he who stands out among all others through physical strength and boldness of character will be the leader and ruler. For that this is truly the work of nature can be seen by observing the animals, which are not endowed with reason and among whom we see admittedly the strongest rule; I mean bulls, boars, cocks, and the like. It is therefore probable that such were the beginnings and the original life of men, namely that they flocked together like animals and followed the strongest and boldest. The extent of the rule of the latter in such circumstances is determined by their strength, and if one wishes to give a name to this kind of rule he may call it a monarchy or one-man rule. When, however, in the course of time, within such conglomerations of men, social feelings and social habits develop, this is the beginning of kingship; and it is then that human beings first begin to conceive the notions of a moral good and of justice, and likewise of their opposites.

6. The way in which these notions are first formed and then developed is as follows. All human beings have a natural drive toward sexual relations and the result of this is the birth of children. Now when one of the children who have been reared does not, after having reached maturity, pay back his gratitude to his parents, by whom he has been brought up, and does not support them, but on the contrary treats them badly in words and deeds, then it is natural that the people who witness this and who have also witnessed the care and the pains with which their parents have nursed them and have brought them up will be displeased and take offense. For since it is the distinctive characteristic of human beings in comparison with other animals that they are capable of reason and of drawing logical conclusions, it is not likely that the significance of the difference in the behavior of the young will escape them as it escapes other animals, but they will take what is happening as a symptom and will be displeased with it because they foresee the future and draw the conclusion that the same thing may happen to any one of themselves. Then again, when one man has received help and support from another man in a difficult or dangerous situation and then does not show his gratitude toward the man who has saved him, but is even ready to harm him, the people who know of it will naturally be displeased and take offense: they share the resentment of their neighbor and they apply what is happening to him by analogy to themselves. From this there develops in every human being a notion of the practical importance and the nature of decent behavior, and this is in fact the beginning and the end of morality.

Now again, in a similar manner, if a man stands out among all others as a fighter and helper in common dangers and, for instance, stands up bravely against the attack of the fiercest beasts, it is natural that he should be honored with marks of favor and distinction by the other people, while he who does the opposite will be despised and reproved. From this there arises naturally among men a perception of what is base and what is noble and of the difference between the two, and the noble will be admired and taken as a model because it is advantageous, while the base causes repulsion. When, then, the chief or he who has the greatest power always gives his support according to the sentiments of the majority and when it appears to his subjects that he gives everybody what is due to him, then they will obey him, not so much because they fear his strength or power but because they have a high opinion of him and they will then support his rule even when he has become quite old and weak, and will defend him as one man and fight for him against those who wish to deprive him of his rule. In this way, by insensible steps, the monarch becomes a king, as reason instead of daring and strength becomes the decisive quality in the choice of a leader.

7. This, then, is the first and natural origin of the notion of the moral good and of justice among men, and this is the way in which true kingship originates and develops. For the people retain as rulers not only those first kings themselves but also their descendants; for they believe that, being born and bred by such men, they will be similar to them in their conduct. When, on the other hand, they are dissatisfied with the descendants of the rulers, they elect new magistrates or kings but now no longer according to their physical strength and their boldness but rather on account of their practical and theoretical intelligence, since they know by experience what a difference it makes whether a man has these qualities or not. Now in the old times those who had once been elected kings and had come into the possession of this power retained it unto their old age and continued to fortify suitable places with walls, and to acquire new lands, the first for the safety of their subjects, the second in order to provide them with ample food. While this became the main occupation of their lives they nevertheless escaped attacks caused by jealousy or envy, since they did not distinguish themselves through their dress or table and lived, both in regard to consumption and in regard to their personal habits, very much like the common people. But when, generation after generation, they took over

their rulership from their ascendants, when everything was ready for them and secure without effort and more food was provided than they possibly needed, then, in consequence of this superabaundance, they yielded to their desires and began to think that rulers must distinguish themselves from their subjects by different clothing and by the variety, the refinement, and the splendor of their table, and that nobody should dare to object to their sexual escapades, even if most illicit. Thus, as their luxury caused envy and offense and their license burning hatred and passionate resentment, kingship was converted into tyranny, and this was also the beginning of the downfall of monarchy since it led to the formation of conspiracies among their subjects. These conspiracies, however, did not originate with people of the lowest class, but, on the contrary, with the most high-minded and intrepid members of the most distinguished families, since men of this kind are always least willing to submit to the insolence of princes.

8. Because of the reasons mentioned, however, the people, once they had found leaders, joined forces with them against their rulers, and thus kingship and the monarchic form of government were completely destroyed, and aristocracy began to develop. For the common people paid, so to speak, without delay their debt of gratitude to those who had freed them from their tyrants by choosing them [i.e., their liberators] as their political leaders and entrusting their affairs to them. In the beginning, then, these new administrators accepted their trust with great eagerness and cared for nothing more than for the common good, watching like parents over the interests of their fellow citizens and of the community as a whole. But when the children and the children's children of these men took over this power from their fathers, they, who had been brought up in positions of power and influence inherited from their ancestors, and consequently knew nothing of the hardships of life and had no notion of political equality and civil liberty, then became corrupt and either tried to accumulate wealth by improper means or abandoned themselves to drinking and table luxury, or began to rape women and young men. In this way they converted what had been an aristocracy into an oligarchy and aroused the same resentment in the common people as the tyrants formerly had done, so that ultimately they brought about their own ruin in a similar fashion.

9. For when, in such a situation, a man who sees the resentment and hatred which they [i.e., the oligarchs] have evoked in their fellow citizens takes courage to attack the rulers in words or deed, he has at once the eager support of the whole mass of the common people. Then, when they have killed some of the oligarchs and driven the rest into exile, they neither dare to make a king their ruler, since they still think with terror of the wickedness of the kings of former times, nor do they have the courage to entrust the state to a selected group, since they have the results of their former mistake before their eyes. Thus they naturally turn to the only hope that has not yet been disappointed, namely the hope that they place in themselves. This is the reason why the people turn from oligarchy to democracy and take the administration and the trust of public affairs upon themselves. Then as long as some of those who had a taste of the evils of privilege and oligarchic rule are still alive, people in general are quite content with the present state of things and value equality and freedom of speech more than anything else. But when new generations grow up and democracy is handed down to the children of the children of its founders, people have become so accustomed to liberty and equality that they do not think very much of them any more and it becomes an ambition to rise above the common crowd, and the people who are distinguished by more than ordinary wealth are most prone to such ambition. Then, when such people strive for political power and prove unable to attain their ends through their own strength and genuine ability they squander their money in their attempts to bribe the common people and corrupt the people in every possible way. Finally, when through their insane ambition they have accustomed the people to accept gifts and have whetted their appetite for more and more, democracy is replaced by a rule of violence.[2] For once the common people have become accustomed to eat what they have not earned and expect to live at the expense of others, they merely have to find a bold and daring leader, a man whom only his poverty has prevented from attaining a high political position; as soon as such a leader appears, violence breaks out and the result is anarchy during which the rabble bands together and kills the rich or drives them into exile, dividing up their estates, until in the last stage of savagery they again find a master and a monarch.

This is the cycle of constitutions and this is the natural law according to which constitutions change, are converted from one form into another, and finally return to the point from which the whole development started. A man who has seen this clearly may perhaps be mistaken in his estimate as to the exact time at which a certain change in a given state will occur in the future, but he will hardly go wrong in regard to the point in growth or decay which that state has reached [at a given moment], nor in regard to the form into which it will ultimately change, at least when he draws his conclusions without prejudice or passion. This kind of investigation will also give us the best insight into the way in which the Roman constitution originated, developed, and reached its peak, and likewise concerning the way in which someday it may be converted into its opposite. For, as I said before, if there is any political system which originated and developed in a perfectly natural way it is that of the Romans. Hence one may conclude that in any change in the opposite direction that it may undergo in the future it will also follow the general laws of nature. But this will be seen more clearly in the following part of my discussion.

10. Now I shall give a brief account of the legislation of Lycurgus. For such an analysis is not at all unrelated to my subject. Lycurgus saw clearly that all the aforementioned changes and revolutions are natural and inevitable and drew the conclusion that every simple political system—that is, every system in which political power is vested in only one definite element of the state—is insecure because it quickly degenerates into the corrupt form of government which corresponds to it, and naturally follows upon it. For just as rust is the congenital corruption of iron, and worms and grubs the congenital disease of wood, so that these substances, even if they escape all injury from external causes, are nevertheless destroyed by these inbred blights, in the same way each form of government has a congenital disease which breaks out in due time. In this way kingship degenerates into despotism, aristocracy into oligarchy, and democracy into anarchy: and for the reasons given all the aforementioned forms of government must inevitably in the course of time undergo a change for the worse.

Lycurgus foresaw this and therefore did not make his political system simple and one-sided. Instead he tried to unite all the advantages and characteristic features of the best governments so that none of the elements could grow unduly powerful and so be converted into its evil counterpart, since the power of each would be counteracted by that of the others. In this way, he thought, no element could outbalance the others and the political system would for a long time remain in a state of equilibrium like a boat sailing close to the wind. For the monarchic element would be prevented from becoming arbitrary and overbearing by its fear of the common people, who were also given an appropriate share in the government, while the common people would not dare to be irreverent to the kings because they would be kept in awe by the Council of Elders who, since they were to be selected from the best citizens, would always be on the side of law and justice so that, whenever one of the elements mentioned was in danger of being oppressed by the other, it would always gain strength and power through the support and the authority of the Council of Elders because of its adherence to tradition.[3] It was the result of the introduction of this political system by Lycurgus that the Lacedaemonians retained their liberty for a much longer time than any other people we know of.

Lycurgus then very capably established the political system mentioned because sound reasoning enabled him to foresee from what causes and in what way political conditions grow and develop. The Romans, on the other hand, have arrived at the same result in regard to the political order of their country, not by simple reasoning but in the course of many struggles and troubles, always choosing the best solution through the insight gained in the critical moments of their history. In this way they arrived at the same result as Lycurgus, namely the best political order yet realized among men.

From Polybius' Account of the Development of the Roman Constitution before It Became Well Balanced

Lucius [Tarquinius], the son of Demaratus of Corinth, came to Rome placing great confidence in himself and in his resources and convinced that he if any one [literally: no less than anyone] had what a man needs to make a good start in politics. He brought with him a wife who was a great help to him in every respect and showed the greatest natural talent in supporting him in his political ambitions. When he had settled in Rome and acquired Roman citizenship he at once assumed an attitude of great obsequiousness toward the king.

Through his show of wealth, his inborn tact and skill, and not the least through the excellent education which he had received from his earliest childhood, he soon won great favor with the sovereign by ingratiating himself with him and attained a position of great trust. In the course of time his credit with the king reached a point where he became the assistant, almost the associate, of [Ancus] Marcius in all his royal functions. In this position he was helpful to everybody, collaborated and shared in the distribution of favors to supplicants, and made the most generous use of his own personal wealth, and this always to the best purpose and at the right moment. In this way he acquired a great claim to the gratitude of many, everybody's good will, and the reputation of a most noble character. In the end this helped him to become king.[4]

The Roman Political Order in Its Prime

VI, 11: After, starting from the time of Xerxes' crossing over into Greece and thirty years later, from this moment onward the details of the Roman political order had steadily continued to be ever more well arranged,[5] this order was most excellent and perfect at the time of the Hannibalic War, within the description of which I have entered upon my present digression. Now, therefore, after having given an account of the way in which it came into being, I shall try to make clear in detail what the Roman political system was like at the time when, in consequence of the defeat suffered at Cannae, the Romans faced complete disaster.

I know very well that to those who have spent their lives under this system my account of it will appear somewhat defective since I have disregarded some of the details. For, since they have a perfect knowledge of it and are familiar with every part of it from personal experience, having been brought up in these traditions and institutions from their earliest childhood, they will not be impressed by the positive information which I give but will look for what I have omitted; they will not assume that the author has omitted the less important points of detail on purpose but that it was his ignorance which made him pass over those special features which in their opinion are of fundamental importance and hold the whole system together. However, if I had mentioned these things they probably would not be impressed either and would consider them as small and unessential; but now that

I have omitted them they will look out for them as for something very important since they wish to appear better informed than the historians. A good critic, however, should not judge an author by his omissions but by the positive information that he imparts and if he finds any mistake in this then he may judge that he [sc. the author] left out the rest through ignorance, while if everything that he [sc the author] says is correct then he [sc. the critic] must concede that the remainder has been omitted on purpose and not from ignorance. So much may be said against a kind of criticisms which are not made in order to evaluate the work of the author correctly but in order to demonstrate the superiority of the critics. . . .

Any critical judgment, whether positive or negative, is sound if it views the matter in its proper setting. But when circumstances have changed and the matter is considered in connection with these changed conditions, then the most pertinent and true remarks of a historian may appear not only unacceptable but even utterly unsound.

. . . .

All the three types of government which I have mentioned before were found together in the Roman Republic. In fact they were so equally and harmoniously balanced, both in the structure of the political system and in the way in which it functioned in everyday practice, that even a native could not have determined definitely whether the state as a whole was an aristocracy, a democracy, or a monarchy. This is indeed quite natural. For if we fix our attention on the power of the consuls the government appears quite monarchic and seems to resemble kingship. If we look upon the power of the Senate, it seems to be aristocratic, and, finally, if one regards the power of the people, it seems clearly a democracy. What share in the government each of these elements had at that time and, with the exception of a few minor changes, still has at the present, will be explained in the following chapters.

12. The consuls, before they lead the armies into the field and while they are present at Rome, are in control of the administration of all public affairs. For all the other magistrates, with the exception of the tribunes, are their subordinates and subject to their orders. It is they who introduce foreign embassies to the Senate. In addition they bring all urgent matters for deliberation before the Senate and it is entirely their task to carry out the opinions rendered by that body.

It is also their duty to prepare all that part of public business which is to be transacted by the people, to convoke the public assemblies, to lay the proposals before them, and to direct the execution of the decisions reached by majority vote. They have almost absolute authority in regard to the preparation for war and the management of everything that pertains to the armies in the field. For they have the right to impose on the allies whatever contributions they see fit, to appoint the military tribunes, to levy soldiers and to select those who are fit for service. In addition they have unrestricted power to inflict punishment on any one of those who are under their command, as long as they are in the field. They have authority to spend whatever sums they propose from the funds of the public treasury, and they are accompanied by a quaestor who is always ready to execute their orders. Hence if one looks at this part of the system it is quite natural to conclude that the constitution is monarchic and in fact a kind of kingship. I should, however, like to add that if in regard to any of the points that I have mentioned or shall mention later there should be a change either now or in some future time, this will in no way be an argument against the truth of my statements.

13. The Senate has above all the control of the treasury, that is, it controls all public revenue and expenditure. For, with the exception of the money expended in the service and at the direction of the consuls, the quaestors cannot make any payments for special and particular purposes without authorization by a placet of the Senate. Even the most comprehensive and largest item of expenditure, the construction and repair of public works, provision for which is made every five years by the censors, is under the control of the Senate, and it is through the Senate that the necessary appropriations are made to the censors. Likewise all those crimes committed in Italy which require a public investigation, as for instance treason, conspiracy, poisonings, and assassination, are a concern of the Senate. Furthermore, if in the public interest it is necessary to settle a dispute between private persons or communities in Italy, or if a party must be rebuked or assistance or protection must be given, all such matters are taken up by the Senate. When embassies have to be sent to countries outside of Italy in order to bring about a reconciliation of conflicts, to admonish the recalcitrant party or, if necessary, to impose a settlement, to accept submission, or to make a

denunciation of war, the Senate makes provision for all this. Likewise when foreign embassies come to Rome the Senate determines how they shall be received and what answer is to be given to them. The people have nothing to do with these matters. Thus to anyone who happens to make his sojourn in Rome while the consuls are absent the political order will appear completely aristocratic. This is also the impression of many Greek states and foreign monarchs, since the Senate transacts nearly all the business and conducts all the negotiations into which they have to enter with the Roman state.

14. At this point everybody will naturally ask what share is left to the people in this political system where the Senate controls all the various matters which I have mentioned and, what is most important, handles all the revenue and expenditure while the consuls have complete control of all preparations for war and have absolute authority in the field. And yet there does remain a part of the government which is reserved for the people, and this in fact the most important. For the people alone have the power to bestow public honors and to mete out punishment, the two devices by which monarchies and republics, and in fact all human societies, are held together. For where this distinction is not understood or, if understood, is not applied in the best way, no existing political system can function well. And how indeed could this possibly be the case when the good and the bad are held in equal esteem?

To take up this point in more detail: the people often decide cases in which the result is the imposition of a fine, especially when the fine is considerable and the accused are men who have held one of the highest offices. They are the only court that can impose capital punishment. In this respect they have a custom that is laudable and worthy of being recorded. For their custom permits those who are on trial for their lives to leave the country openly while the vote is in progress, as long as one single tribe of those which pass the judgment has not yet voted, and so to impose voluntary exile on themselves. Such exiles find asylum in Naples, Praeneste, Tibur, and any other of the cities with which the Romans have entered into a confederacy.

Again it is the people that bestow the political offices on those who are most worthy of them, and this is the most noble reward for civic virtue in a state.

The people have the power of approving and rejecting laws, and, what is most important, they deliberate over war and peace and have the final decision. Likewise in regard to alliances, peace terms, treaties, and the like it is again the people who ratify them or reject their ratification. Thus, again, taking all this into consideration one might easily say that the people have the greatest share in the government and that the political system is democratic.

15. In what way the administration of the state is distributed among its several parts has now been described. I shall therefore proceed to explain in what way these parts can either counteract one another if they wish to do so, or then again cooperate. When the consul, invested with all the power I have mentioned, leads his army into the field he appears to have absolute control over everything that is necessary for the completion of his undertaking: and yet in fact he is dependent on both the people and the Senate and cannot, without their support, carry through his plans to a successful end. For, as everybody knows, armies are in need of constant supplies. But without the will of the Senate neither food nor clothing nor pay can be provided for the soldiers, so that the projects of the commanders cannot be executed if the Senate chooses to be deliberately negligent and obstructive. It also depends on the Senate whether or not a commander can bring the execution of his plans and designs to completion, since it has the power to send him a successor when his term of office is over or to continue him in command. The Senate, furthermore, has the power of exalting and magnifying the successes of the military commanders and again of obscuring and depreciating them. For the so-called triumphs by which the generals bring the glory of their achievements visibly before the eyes of their fellow citizens cannot be celebrated with the proper magnificence, and sometimes cannot be held at all, unless the Senate gives its consent and grants the money for the necessary expense.

As to the people, it is indispensable for the consuls to do everything to retain their favor even while they are very far from home. For, as I mentioned before, it is the people who ratify or annul all terms of peace and other agreements and, what is most important, when they lay down their office the consuls must give account of all their actions to the people. It is, therefore, in no way safe for the consuls to think lightly of the approval of the Senate or the favor of the people.

16. The Senate, again, which possesses so much power, must first of

all pay attention in all common affairs to the sentiment of the masses and try to avoid disagreement with the people's will.[6] Furthermore, it is not able to carry through completely the investigation and correction of the gravest crimes against the state, namely those that are punishable by death, unless the conclusion reached by the Senate is confirmed by the people. The same is true of matters that concern the Senate itself. For if anyone introduces a law with the purpose of depriving the Senate of the authority that this body enjoys according to custom and tradition, or of abolishing the privileges and public honors of the senators, or even of reducing their private possessions, the people alone have full power either to pass or to reject all measures of this kind. Finally, to top it all: if one single tribune intercedes, the Senate is not only unable to carry out its deliberations, but it cannot even hold a meeting or assemble. The tribunes, however, must always do what the people want and must try to act in agreement with the people's wishes. For all the reasons mentioned the Senate is afraid to conflict with the feelings of the masses and pays close attention to their wishes.

17. In like manner, again, the people are dependent on the Senate and must try to be on good terms both with the Senate as a body and with its individual members. There are a great many public enterprises all over Italy, contracts for which are given out by the censors, such as the construction and repair of public works, too numerous to be easily counted; furthermore, river navigation, harbor installations, public parks or plantations, mines, public lands, in a word everything that belongs to the public domain: all these things are managed by the common people and one may truly say that nearly everybody has something to do with these enterprises, either as a businessman and contractor or as a laborer. Now some people negotiate these contracts with the censors in their own names, others act as partners of those first mentioned, still others stand surety for them or pledge their own fortunes to the state for this purpose. Now the final authority in all these matters is again the Senate. For the Senate can prolong the time in which the contract is to be fulfilled, revise the terms of the contract in the case of unforeseeable difficulties, and release the contracting party entirely from its obligation if the execution of the contract becomes impossible. There are, in a word, a great many ways in which the Senate can either benefit or injure those who work for the state, since all the aforementioned

matters are referred to the Senate. The most important point, however, is that the judges in the most important lawsuits, whether private or public, are taken from the Senate. In consequence of this, nearly all people are dependent on the good will of the Senate or its members, and since they are uncertain as to when they may be in need of it they are very cautious in opposing or obstructing the wishes of the Senate. Likewise they will not lightly oppose the projects of the consuls, since all of them together and individually are under the authority of the consuls when in military service.

18. This, then, is the power which each one of the several elements of the state has either to hamper the others or to cooperate with them. The result, however, is that they are so aptly fitted together for all possible emergencies that it is hardly possible to find a better political system than this. For whenever the fear of some common danger from abroad compels them to forget their disagreements and to cooperate with one another, the internal strength of the state becomes so great that nothing that is necessary to cope with the situation is neglected, since all the parts of the state vie with one another in concentrating all their thought and efforts on the present emergency, and their decisions will always be executed with the greatest promptness because everybody cooperates in public and in private in the speedy execution of their plans. In a word, the peculiar character of this political system is such that a state of this kind is nearly irresistible and can attain anything that it has set as its aim. On the other hand, when they are freed from the fear of external dangers, when they live in the prosperity and abundance which are the consequence of their success and, in the enjoyment of their good fortune, become vainglorious, frivolous, overbearing, and insolent, then it is especially noticeable how the political order finds in itself a remedy against its own disease. For whenever one of the elements of the state exceeds its natural bounds, tries to encroach upon the domain of the others, and assumes more power than is due it, then, since none of them, as explained before, is able to carry anything to its conclusion without the others and since therefore the designs of each of them can be counteracted and obstructed by the others, the result is that in actual fact none of them can really exceed its bounds and overlook the others. Thus every part remains essentially in its once established position, partly because it is checked by the others

when trying to extend its power, partly because, from the outset, it is afraid of the reaction of the others.

From the Third Book

On Dictatorship
III, 87, 7: The dictator is distinguished from the consuls in the following way. The consuls are attended by twelve lictors each, while the dictator has twenty-four, and while the consuls need the cooperation of the Senate in many respects in the execution of their projects, the dictator is a commander with absolute powers, and as soon as the dictator is appointed all the other magistrates in Rome with the exception of the tribunes of the plebeians lose their power. But I shall give a more accurate account of these matters in another part of my work.[7]

From the Sixth Book

Comparison Between the Roman System and Similar Political Systems
VI, 43: Nearly all the authors who have written about these states mention the reputation for excellence enjoyed by the constitutions of the Lacedaemonians, the Cretans, the Mantineans, and the Carthaginians. Some authors include also the constitutions of Athens and Thebes. But I leave these constitutions aside. For I do not think that the Athenian and the Theban constitutions require a very long discussion, since they did not grow by natural steps, did not long remain in a state of prosperity when they had reached it, and did not change gradually from one phase to another, but through a sudden wind of good fortune had a short moment of brilliance and glory and then, while they still seemed to be at their peak and to have the best prospects for the future, experienced a complete reversal of fortune. Thus the Thebans, making use of the political errors of the Lacedaemonians and the hatred of their allies toward them, earned a reputation of superiority among the Greeks through the superior qualities of one or perhaps two of their citizens who had discovered the aforementioned weaknesses of the position of the Spartans. And that the reason for the success of the Thebans was not their political system but the excellence of their politi-

cal leaders became quite clear through the bad fortune that followed immediately afterward. For the power of the Thebans clearly grew, reached its peak, and ceased with the lives of Epaminondas and Pelopidas. The obvious conclusion is therefore that not their constitution but these two men were the cause of the temporary eminence of the Theban state.

44. About the same can also be said about the Athenian constitution. For though Athens had more than one period of prosperity and glory —the most brilliant one through the excellence of Themistocles' political leadership—she, too, experienced a complete reversal of fortune because of the lack of balance in her political system. For the Athenian people always resembles to some extent a ship without a master.[8] When in such a ship the fear of the disturbed sea or of a threatening storm makes the sailors act in concert and compels them to pay attention to the orders of the pilot, they do their duty exceedingly well. But as soon as they take courage because the danger has passed they begin to show contempt for the officers and to quarrel with one another, since they no longer have the same aim and purpose: one party will wish to continue the voyage while another party will urge the pilot to go to port, some will unfurl the sails and others will hold them back and tell them to take the sails in, so that with their disagreement and quarreling they will be a sorry sight for anyone who looks at the ship from a distance and a danger to themselves and to all those aboard; thus often, after having escaped the greatest perils of the sea and the most terrible storms, they suffer shipwreck in the harbor or when they are near the shore. This in fact happened more than once to the Athenian state. For several times after having come safely through the greatest and most dangerous crises, and this through the strenuous efforts and the capability of the people and their leaders, it has then in times of undisturbed prosperity come to harm without apparent reason and against every expectation. Therefore it is not necessary to discuss the state of the Athenians or of the Thebans any further, since in both of them it is the multitude which decides everything according to its unenlightened impulses, and since this multitude in the one case is congenitally rash and ill tempered, and in the other traditionally prone to violence and outbursts of passion.

45. If, then, we pass on to the Cretan constitution, two points would

be worthy of investigation: namely, how the most learned of the early writers, Ephorus, Xenophon, Callisthenes, and Plato, could say that this constitution was similar to that of the Lacedaemonians, and how they could declare it praiseworthy. In my opinion, at any rate, neither assertion is correct. This can be shown in the following way. First, its dissimilarity to the Spartan constitution. The following features are said to be peculiar to the Lacedaemonian political order: First, the rules concerning landed property, of which nobody has a larger share than another, since all citizens must have an equal share of the land belonging to full citizens; [9] secondly, their customs in regard to the acquisition of money, which is altogether looked down upon among them so that any pride in having more money than others and any competition in this respect is completely eliminated in their social system; thirdly, the fact that in Sparta the kings are perpetual and hereditary rulers and that the so-called *gerontes* or members of the Senate are elected for life, these being the two political agencies through which or with the collaboration of which all public affairs are managed.

46. With the Cretans it is just the opposite in all respects. The law permits them to acquire, without any limit whatsoever, as much landed property as they can buy, and money is held in so great esteem that its acquisition is considered not merely one of the necessities of life but as the one thing by which a man can attain the greatest distinction. In fact sordid greed for money and the desire to distinguish oneself by wealth are so much a native characteristic of the Cretans that they alone among all nations of the world consider no kind of gain dishonorable. Finally they select their magistrates on an annual basis and by a democratic procedure. So I have often wondered how those writers could talk about two political and social systems which are the very opposites of one another as if they were related and similar. For they not only overlook these most important differences but add for good measure all sorts of general reflections, saying that Lycurgus was the only one who saw deeper reasons for the stability or instability of governments. For, they say, since there are two things by which a state is preserved, bravery against the foreign enemy and concord among the citizens at home, Lycurgus, by making impossible any attempt to become more wealthy than others, eliminated all civil strife and discord, so that the Lacedaemonians, being freed from these evils, had of all the Greeks the most

perfect order in their civil affairs and lived together in concord. Having emphasized these points and then seeing on the other side how the Cretans, because of their innate love for gain, most frequently suffer disturbances through private and public dissensions, murder, and civil war, these writers nevertheless do not seem to think that this has any bearing on their argument and dare to talk as if the Cretan and Lacedaemonian political orders were similar to each other. Ephorus even uses, apart from the proper names, the very same words when speaking of either of the two constitutions, so that, unless one pays attention to these proper names, one is not even able to make out of which of the two he is speaking

This, then, in my opinion is the difference between the political and social systems of the two countries. Now I shall go on to make clear why I believe that the Cretan system is not praiseworthy and should not be imitated.

47. I believe that there are two elements in every political order which determine whether the structure and the functioning of this order can serve as a model to be imitated, or the opposite. These are the customs and the laws. Those laws and customs that are worthy of being adopted tend to hold the private lives of individuals within the bounds of decency and wise moderation and to promote a spirit of gentleness and justice in all public affairs within the state, while laws and customs that have the opposite effect are undesirable and should be rejected. Now, just as when we see that in a nation the customs and laws are excellent, we do not hesitate to say that as a result the citizens and the political life in that nation will also be of a high order, so when we see that in some place the private conduct of individuals is characterized by their immoderate desire for gain and that there is no regard for justice in public transactions of the state, we are clearly entitled to say that in such a nation the laws, the customs, and the political system as a whole are bad. At the same time it is hardly possible to find, apart from perhaps a few very rare cases, more treacherous conduct on the part of private individuals and more immoral political scheming in public life than among the Cretans. Therefore I cannot consider the Cretan constitution similar to that of the Spartans, or praiseworthy or desirable in any other respect, and consequently I am going to exclude it completely from my further discussion.

It would not be appropriate either to draw Plato's Republic into the discussion, though it has been praised so highly by some philosophers. For just as we do not admit to athletic contests untrained and untested athletes, so we must not admit Plato's Republic to the contest for the first prize among constitutions as long as a test has never been made as to how it would work in actual practice. This being the case up to the present moment, to talk about Plato's Republic in comparison with the constitutions of Sparta, Rome, and Carthage would be about the same thing as to take a statue and to compare it with living and breathing human beings. For even if the former happened to be an excellent work of art a comparison between an inanimate thing and living beings would still appear very deficient and in fact quite incongruous to those having these different objects before their eyes.

48. For all these reasons I set aside the constitutions last mentioned and return now to the Spartan constitution. It seems to me that in regard to the promotion of concord among the citizens, the safety and defense of the Spartan territory, and the establishment of effective safeguards for the liberty of the Spartan people, Lycurgus has chosen his laws so wisely and shown such admirable foresight that his wisdom appears almost divine and superhuman. For the equal distribution of property and the frugality of their way of living, in which everybody shared, were apt to make them simple and self-controlled in their private lives and to keep the state free from civil strife and violent dissension, while the training in hardships and dangerous exercises had the effect of producing brave and high-minded men. Now when both these virtues, bravery and self-control, come together in one soul or in one city, such a man and such a city will not easily be subdued by their neighbors. Lycurgus, therefore, having built his whole state on these two principles, gave to the whole Laconian country a high degree of safety against dangers from abroad and to the Spartans in particular the best guaranty for the long-lasting preservation of their liberties. But in regard to the acquisition of neighboring territory, the aspiration to a position of political leadership or supremacy and, generally speaking, the conduct of an ambitious foreign policy, Lycurgus does not seem to have made any provision whatsoever, either in his constitution as a whole or in any part of it. What remained, then, for the lawgiver was to incorporate in his state some compelling factor or some institution

apt to create a nonexpansionist spirit and a tradition of self-restraint in the state as a political entity in the same way in which he had made the individual citizens simple and contented in their private lives. In reality, however, he made them the most unambitious and sensible people in regard to their private lives and to the laws of the state, and yet at the same time let them remain the most ambitious, the most power-hungry, and the most aggressive of all states in their relation to the other Greeks.

49. Who does not know that the Spartans were probably the first of all Greeks to start a war merely because they coveted the land of their neighbors and attacked the Messenians with the purpose of making them their slaves. Who has not heard the story of how out of sheer obstinacy they bound themselves by an oath not to raise the siege of the city before they had taken Messene by force. And this too is known to everybody, namely, that in their desire to rule supreme among the Greeks they took it upon themselves to do the bidding of the very people whom they had formerly defeated in battle. For when the Persians invaded Greece they [sc. the Spartans] vanquished them fighting for the liberty of all the Greeks. But when the Persians had withdrawn and fled they [sc. the Spartans] left, through the peace of Antalcidas, the Greek cities of Asia Minor to their [sc. the Persians'] mercy in order to obtain money with the help of which they could establish their own supremacy over the rest of the Greeks. In this way a defect in their system of laws and traditions was revealed for everybody to see. For as long as they strove merely for supremacy over their immediate neighbors or even the Peloponnesians as a whole they were able to manage with the native resources and supplies of Laconia alone, and they had everything which they needed near at hand and could quickly return to their base or send for supplies or reinforcements from there. But when they started undertaking expeditions overseas and to wage war with land armies outside the Peloponnesus it became clear at once that neither their iron currency nor the exchange of the annual products of their country for those necessities in which they were lacking, as provided by the laws of Lycurgus, were sufficient for their needs. For these enterprises required internationally recognized currency and supplies from other countries. In consequence the Spartans were compelled to beg the Persian court for subsidies, to impose tribute on the

islands, and to exact money from the Greeks everywhere. Thus they found out that they could not strive for supremacy over all the Greeks or even conduct a vigorous and aggressive foreign policy while keeping strictly within the Lycurgan institutions.

50. Why, then, did I enter upon this digression? In order to make it clear by a simple presentation of the facts that the legislation of Lycurgus made quite sufficient provision for the security of the country and the preservation of the freedom of its citizens. Anyone, therefore, who considers this the supreme purpose of a state must admit that there does not exist and never has existed a political system or order superior to that of Sparta. But if someone has greater aspirations and considers it more glorious and more sublime to rule over many, to be their lord and master, and to have everybody pay attention to him and do his bidding, then he must admit that in this respect the political order of the Spartans is deficient and that that of the Romans is superior and more suitably constructed for expansion. This is quite evident from the actual course of events. For when the Lacedaemonians set out to gain supremacy over the other Greeks they very soon jeopardized their own liberty, while the Romans, once they had won control over Italy, in a very short time subdued the whole inhabited world. One of the contributory causes of this success, and certainly not the least important one, was the fact that they had always an abundance of supplies ready at hand where they were needed.

51. The Carthaginian constitution also appears originally to have been well contrived, at least in regard to its more general characteristics. For there were kings, the Senate represented the aristocratic element of political power, and the people also had their appropriate share in political decisions. In a word, generally speaking, the structure of the state was very similar to that of the Romans and of the Lacedaemonians. But at the time when it entered upon the Hannibalic War the Carthaginian system was less good and the Roman system was better. For everybody and every state and every enterprise has its natural growth, then has its prime and, following that, gradually declines, and all of them have their period of greatest strength when they are at their prime. It is exactly this which made all the difference between the two states at that time. For Carthage had attained great power and prosperity earlier than Rome, and it was just by that length of time that she

had already passed her period of greatest perfection while Rome had at that very moment just reached her prime in regard to the development of her political system. This difference expressed itself also in the fact that Carthage had already reached a stage in which the people had the decisive power in regard to political decisions, while in Rome the Senate was in the period of its greatest strength. Since, then, in one case the deliberations of the common people were decisive and in the other those of the most outstanding men were, the political decisions of the Romans were superior to those of the Carthaginians, and this is the reason why the Romans, even though they had suffered the most crushing defeat, nevertheless through the wisdom of their counsels in the end proved victorious in the war against Carthage.

52. To come then to more special matters, as for instance preparedness for war, the Carthaginians are naturally better trained and better equipped for naval warfare, since experience in this field is a very old tradition with them and since they are the most assiduous seafarers of all men, while the Romans are much better trained for land warfare than the Carthaginians are. For they concentrate all their efforts on this matter, while the Carthaginians neglect their infantry altogether and do not make very farsighted provisions for the training of a good cavalry either. The reason is that they use foreign mercenaries while the Romans have an army consisting of native citizens. Therefore in this respect also the Roman system appears preferable as compared with that of the Carthaginians. For the Carthaginians rely for the preservation of their freedom on the bravery of foreign troops, while the Romans rely on their own valor and on the support of their allies. Hence the Romans, even if they suffer a severe setback in the beginning, always come back in full force, while with the Carthaginians it is just the opposite. For the former, since they are fighting for their country and their children, can never slacken in their fighting spirit but continue to fight with all their strength until they have won the victory over their enemies. Although therefore, as I have pointed out above, the Romans are far behind in experience in naval warfare, the final balance nevertheless is in their favor even in this field because of the bravery of their men. For though familiarity with the sea is of no small importance in facing its dangers, the victory in a naval battle depends for the most part on the bravery of the soldiers on board the ships.[10] Furthermore,

all Italians are naturally superior to the Phoenicians and Libyans in physical strength and personal courage, and in addition they do everything by upbringing and training to promote these qualities among their young men. It will be sufficient to give one example to show what efforts the Roman state makes to produce men who will do and endure everything in order to attain a reputation for valor among their fellow countrymen.

53. When in Rome an outstanding man dies it becomes, in addition to the usual ceremonies, part of his funeral that he is carried to the market place to the so-called *rostra*, sometimes conspicuous in an upright posture, rarely reclined. Then, while all the people stand around in a circle, either his son, if he has a grown son who is present, or some other member of his gens mounts the rostra and speaks about the virtues of the deceased and the great deeds that he has done. The result is that the people in general are reminded of his accomplishments, and have them vividly placed before their eyes so that not only those who in one way or another had some share in his exploits but even those who had no personal relations with him whatsoever are so strongly affected that his death appears a public misfortune rather than a loss suffered merely by his relatives and friends. Then after he has been buried and the traditional funeral rites have been performed, the image of the deceased, surrounded by a wooden shrine, is set up in the most conspicuous place in the house. This image is a facial mask which is made to reproduce with the greatest possible accuracy the form and features of the face of the deceased. On the occasions of public festivals they uncover these images and decorate them with the greatest care, and when an outstanding member of the family dies they carry them [the masks] in the funeral procession by putting them on the faces of men who have the greatest similarity in size and appearance to those whom the masks represent. Furthermore, if the deceased had been a consul or a praetor, the man who wears his mask dons a toga with a purple border; if he had been a censor, a purple toga, and if he had had a triumph or received some similar honor, a toga embroidered with gold. In this apparel they drive in chariots preceded by the fasces, axes, and other insignia to which each one was entitled in his lifetime in accordance with the public office which he held, and when they have arrived at the rostra they sit down in a row on ivory chairs. It would not be

easy to find a spectacle more apt to arouse the enthusiasm of a young man eager to win true distinction. For who would not be affected by the sight of the images of so many men, famous for their true accomplishments, all of them brought together in one place and as if they were still alive and breathing? And what more glorious spectacle could there be than this?

54. Besides, the person who makes the funeral speech, after having come to the end of the memorial in honor of the man about to be buried, recounts the accomplishments and deeds of all the others who are present in their images, beginning with the most ancient among them. Since in this way the reputation that outstanding men have won through their great qualities is constantly renewed, the fame of men of great achievements is rendered immortal, and the glory of those who have done a great service to their country is fresh in the memory of everybody and handed down from generation to generation. The most important result of this custom, however, is that it is a great incitement for young people to dare and endure everything for the common good in the hope of attaining the fame that is the certain reward of all men who distinguish themselves in serving the community. That this is actually so is also confirmed by the following facts. Many Romans have volunteered for single combat in contests concerning the whole nation, and not a few have even chosen certain death, some of them in war in order to save the lives of their comrades, others in peace in order to save the whole state from destruction. Some Romans, when holding an office of high authority, have even, against all human custom and tradition, put their own sons to death because they had a higher regard for the interest of their country than for the natural bonds that tie a man to his closest relatives. A great many examples of such men and such actions can be found in Roman history. In order to illustrate and prove my point it will however suffice for the present to give one example with all the details and the names of the persons involved.

55. The story is told that Horatius Cocles, when he was engaged in combat with two enemy soldiers at the farther end of the bridge across the Tiber which leads out from the city, and when he saw a greater number of soldiers rushing to the assistance of his adversaries, was afraid that they might force the bridge and penetrate into the city, and that therefore he turned around calling out to those behind him that

they should withdraw and destroy the bridge as fast as possible. When his comrades did as he had told them he stood his ground though he suffered many wounds, and held out against the onrush of the enemy until the bridge was destroyed, the soldiers of the enemy being taken aback not so much by his physical strength as by the daring with which he withstood their attack singlehandedly. Finally, when the bridge had been completely torn down and thus the enemy were barred from rushing into the city, Horatius Cocles hurled himself into the river with all his armor and so deliberately sacrificed his life, since he valued the safety of his country and the glory which would attach to his name in the future more highly than his present life and the years which he might have continued to live. Such, it appears, is the incentive to distinguish themselves by great deeds which these customs provoke in the young men of Rome.

56. Moreover, the Romans have better customs and rules in regard to the acquisition of wealth than the Carthaginians have. For the latter consider nothing disgraceful that leads to material gain, while the former hold nothing more shameful than to accept bribes and become rich by improper methods. For while they have a high regard for wealth acquired by the most honorable methods, they have an equally great contempt for riches acquired by improper means. An indication of this difference in attitude can also be found in the fact that in Carthage the candidates for political offices openly bribe the voters, while in Rome this is considered a capital crime. Since, then, in the two nations the rewards due to virtue are granted under conditions that are the very opposite in the two cases, it is nothing but natural that they should also differ widely in their efforts to gain these rewards.

The one thing, however, in which it seems to me the superiority of the Romans reveals itself most clearly is their system of beliefs in regard to the gods. In fact, what among other people is an object of reproach, namely superstition, appears to be the very mainstay of the Roman Republic. For in Rome these matters are shrouded in such impressive pomp and ceremony and play such an enormous role both in the lives of individuals and in public affairs that it seems impossible to go farther. This may perhaps appear strange to many people. But I believe that they have introduced these customs for the sake of the common people. For if it were possible to bring together a commonwealth consisting of nothing but wise men, such customs would perhaps not be necessary. But since the common crowd everywhere is fickle, full of lawless desires, prone to irrational passion and violent of temper, there is no other way of restraining it except by fear of the unknown and by impressive ceremony. In my opinion, therefore, it was not by chance and not without good reason that the ancients introduced among the common people certain notions of the gods and certain beliefs about life in the other world, and I consider it, on the contrary, rather rash and inconsiderate on the part of the moderns that they try to extirpate such superstitions. For, not to mention other consequences, it is a fact that in Greece the people who have to handle public funds are unable to preserve their integrity, even if they are entrusted with no more than one talent and have to have ten countersignatures and as many official seals and twice as many witnesses for every transaction, while in Rome the men who, because of the positions that they hold as magistrates or ambassadors, have to handle huge sums of money, perform their duty with absolute honesty because they have pledged themselves by an oath. Thus, while in other countries it is a rarity to find a man who refrains from robbing the public treasury and has a clean record in this respect, it is equally rare to discover in Rome a man who has been caught in committing such an action.

Conclusion of the Discussion of the Roman Republic

57. That everything that exists is subject to decay and change is a fact which hardly requires any further proof or discussion. For the invariable course of nature is quite sufficient to impress this truth upon us. There are two types of causes by which any kind of state in the natural course of things can be destroyed, one coming from the outside, the other originating in the state itself, and while it is impossible to bring the causes of the former kind under the head of one general and consistent theory, this is quite possible in regard to the second kind. Now what type of state, in the natural course of things, was the first to come into existence, and what kind of state followed upon it, and how then, after this, the state is continually transformed from one type to another —all this I have explained before so that anyone who is able to connect the beginning and the end of the present inquiry will now also be able to predict the future all by himself. This much, I believe, is clear: when

a state has weathered many great dangers and then has attained over-whelming power and undisputed supremacy it is manifest that under the influence of a prosperity that has lasted so long as to have become habitual, life will become more luxurious and the rivalries of men in the pursuit of high political positions and similar aims will become more violent than is good for the state. As this trend becomes stronger the desire for political power and distinction, the disgrace connected with obscurity, and, in addition, the spreading of snobbism and ex-travagance, will mark the beginnings of a change for the worse. But then the common people become the actual initiators of the change, namely when they feel wronged by the greed and insolence of one group of people and at the same time are puffed up by others who flatter them in order to get their votes in the elections. For once the people get thoroughly stirred up in this fashion, they follow only their passions and are no longer content to obey the authorities or even to have an equal share with them in the government, but claim absolute and un-limited sovereignty for themselves. When this happens the state will change to a condition that is given the most high-sounding name, namely freedom and democracy, but in actual fact is the worst possible of all, namely mob rule.

Since, then, I have now given a complete account of the first estab-lishment and the further development of the Roman constitution and likewise of its prime and its present condition, and since I have further-more shown in detail how it compares both favorably and unfavorably with other constitutions, I may conclude my discussion of this constitu-tion at this point.

58. But taking up my narrative of the historical events at the point at which I left it in order to enter upon this digression, I may perhaps briefly mention one special occurrence in order to demonstrate not only by an abstract description but by a concrete example what this political order, at those times when it had reached its prime, was able to achieve in actual practice, just as the power of a great artist is best demonstrated by displaying one of his works.

When Hannibal, in consequence of his victory at Cannae, had cap-tured the eight thousand Romans who were left to guard the fortified camp, he permitted them to send a delegation to Rome in order to take up negotiations concerning their ransom and release. After the captives had selected ten of their most distinguished men for this purpose he allowed these men to depart after having made them take an oath that they would return to him. But one of the men so nominated, after having left the camp, came back under the pretense that he had forgotten something and then left again after having taken with him what he had left, thinking that through his return he had fulfilled his promise and satisfied the condition of the oath.

When they arrived in Rome they begged and entreated the Senate not to begrudge the prisoners their release but to allow them to pay three *minae* each and so to earn their release and to return to their families. They said that Hannibal had agreed to this condition and that they themselves were worthy of being released. For, they said, they had not acted in a cowardly way in battle and had not done anything unworthy of Rome. But they had been left behind to guard the camp and when all the others had perished in the battle they had been overwhelmed by the force of circumstances and this was how they had fallen into the hands of the enemy. The Romans at that time had suffered crushing military defeats, were deserted by practically all their allies, and expected that at any moment immediate danger for the very city might be right upon them; but nevertheless, when they listened to the delegation, they did not, under the influence of misfortune, forget for one moment what they owed to their dignity and did not overlook in their deliberations anything that had to be considered, but saw clearly that Hannibal had a double purpose in this proposed transaction, namely to obtain an ample supply of money and at the same time to deprive the soldiers of his enemy of their fighting spirit by showing them that even if defeated they might still hope to get off safely. In view of this they were so far from granting the request that they did not permit themselves to be decisively influenced by their pity for their fellow countrymen or by the fact that these men might be of service in the future, but demonstrated to Hannibal that his calculations and the hopes which he had based on them were vain. They refused to pay a ransom for the men and at the same time made a law for their remaining troops by which they were ordered either to conquer or to die fighting, since no hope of escaping safely would be left for them if they were defeated. In agreement with this attitude and after having reached this decision, they dismissed the nine delegates to return voluntarily in agreement with their oath. The one man, however, who had invented a trick to free himself from the oath was put in chains and handed over to the enemy, so that Hannibal's joy over his victory in the battle was less than his consternation over the steadfastness and highmindedness of these men in their counsels and decisions.

The use which Polybius makes in his histories of the concept of Τύχη, which may be variously translated as Chance, Luck, or Fortune, has always been very puzzling to his readers. Apparently Polybius does not always use this concept in the same way.

There are a great many passages in his work in which Tyche appears as a half-personalized and semidivine power that bends everything to its will. Thus, when Polybius speaks of the terrible cruelties perpetrated by both parties in the rebellion of the Carthaginian mercenaries and during its subsequent suppression, he says "it was as if Fortune on purpose gave both belligerents in turn cause and opportunity for inflicting the most cruel punishments on one another."[2] When describing how the Aetolians suffered a crushing defeat at a moment when they were so sure of success that they had already been quarreling among one another as to which of their generals should have the honor of the victory, Polybius adds: "It was as if Fortune on purpose had tried to show her power."[3] In speaking of the last struggles of the Achaean League he says that "it was as if a very clever and skilful Tyche counteracted the folly and insanity of the Achaean Leaders of that time, since she wanted to save the Achaeans by all means, and so, after having been thwarted in every possible way by the stupidity of the leaders, like a well-trained wrestler made use of the only means still available for their salvation."[4] He speaks of Tyche as putting a tragedy on the historical stage.[5] He talks of the fickleness of Fortune and affirms that if she has ever helped anyone and put her weight into the scale in his favor, she will surely, as if she repented of her former attitude, make compensation for it and spoil what he has achieved.[6] He says that those who abuse their success to persecute others should know that it is the business or custom of Fortune to make people suffer the application of the same laws and rules of conduct that they have used in regard to others,[7] but on another occasion he says also [8] that Fortune must be blamed for having permitted a particularly wicked man to die a most honorable death. He speaks of the jealousy of Fortune and says that she shows her power especially when someone appears to have reached the summit of prosperity and success.[9] There are many more passages in which similar ideas are expressed.

On the other hand, one finds a not inconsiderable number of passages in Polybius' work in which he inveighs against those who explain certain historical events as the result of luck, chance, or fortune, and says that the historian must not indulge in any such facile explanation but should try to find the true causes of everything. Thus he says [10] at the end of his narrative of the First Punic War that the history of this war bears out what, from the outset, it had been his intention to show, namely, that the success of the Romans was not due just to good luck and had not come about by sheer accident, "as many of the Greeks think," but that "it was perfectly natural that by training themselves in such great enterprises they should not only acquire the courage to strive for the dominion of the whole world, but should actually attain this end." Similarly, he says [11] that one should not deprive the younger Scipio of the full glory due to his great achievements by ascribing them to good luck out of ignorance of the true causes of each one of them.

Such utterances are, of course, not necessarily at variance with the belief that some events are the result of chance; in fact, Polybius himself, on several occasions, has given an account of his concept of the role of chance in history and its relation to historical causality. On one occasion Polybius says [12] that if someone is overtaken by some great disaster against all reasonable expectation, one must not blame this man but his bad luck, or those who have caused the disaster, but if he became involved in it through his own lack of judgment, then he himself is to blame. Chance, then, here is simply what a person cannot reasonably foresee. But on another occasion the concept is given a somewhat wider application. "In regard to those things or events," Polybius says here, "the causes of which are difficult to grasp for a human being, it is perhaps justified to attribute them to a god or to Chance, as for instance exceptionally heavy snow, or rainfalls of long duration, or severe droughts, or frosts that destroy the crops, or long-lasting epidemic diseases, or similar things, since in all such cases it is not at all easy to detect the cause. In such matters it is more or less natural to follow the belief of the common crowd, since one is at a loss to find a better explanation . . . but wherever it is possible to find out the cause of what is happening one should not have recourse to the gods, as for instance in the following case: In recent times there was a low birth rate and a decrease of the population in Greece, in consequence of which whole cities were deserted and agricultural production ceased [in some districts], though there were no continuous wars or epidemic diseases. Yet it would be absurd to appeal to the gods in such circumstances and to ask for their advice, since the cause is quite clearly to be found in the avarice and indolence of men who no longer wish to marry, or if married to bring up children . . ." [13] These passages show clearly that in Polybius' concept of history there is room for chance, but that, in his opinion, not everything should be attributed to chance. Whatever is accessible to human insight and foresight or subject to human control is outside the field within which it is legitimate to speak of chance.

Yet this passage does not solve the whole problem. There are cases in which Polybius appears to attribute the same event in one section of his work to chance and in another section to foreseeable and controllable causes. For, even within the same book, he says in one section [14] that in his time Fortune has forced all the affairs of the inhabited world into one direction, and that this was one of her finest and most beneficial accomplishments, while, a little later,[15] he criticizes those who ascribe the unification of the known world under Roman rule to chance, and affirms that it was clearly due to the Romans' superior effort and training. Since from the context it is perfectly clear that in the first instance also he refers to the unification of the world under Roman domination, there seems to be a direct contradiction. What is more, in a passage of the second book Polybius appears to reject the notion of Tyche as a force in history altogether,[16] saying that it is unbecoming for the historian to speak of chance or fortune, but that the historian should always look for the cause of everything since neither those things which happen according to reason, nor those which happen against all

reasonable expectation, can come about without a cause. While, therefore, in some of the passages quoted above Polybius says that it is legitimate to speak of chance in regard to events which cannot be foreseen
and which happen against all reasonable expectation, he appears here
to express the opinion that, even in regard to events of this latter kind
the historian should not talk of chance but try to find out the causes.

It is quite understandable that various attempts have been made to
solve the difficulties presented by these apparently contradictory passages by the assumption that they represent different stages in the development of Polybius' thought. Thus it has been said [17] that one can
clearly distinguish three phases, a first phase in which Polybius spoke
of the influence of Tyche everywhere, even where definite specific
causes can be determined; a second phase in which he considered it
legitimate to speak of Tyche wherever definite causes are not recognizable or where events are in no way foreseeable or controllable by
human beings, but not legitimate wherever definite causes can be
found; and a third phase in which he rejected altogether any reference
to Tyche by a historian. But it has also been argued [18] that the sequence
of these phases must have been different, that a phase of unrestricted
belief in Tyche was first followed by a complete and radical rejection
of this notion, while the last phase of Polybius' development is marked
by a compromise between these two attitudes and a distinction between
the cases in which reference to Tyche is legitimate and those in which
it is not.

Neither of these theories, however, is tenable, for the simple reason
that the passages in which Tyche appears as a force that governs everything are scattered through the whole work,[19] including the last
books,[20] and that it appears hardly possible that within the very last
decade of his life Polybius should twice have changed his fundamental
views of the role of chance in history, so that the evidence of his later
opinions would be found only in some revisions and additions to the
original text that he made when he was more than seventy years old.
On the basis of the purely external evidence one might much more
readily come to the conclusion that Polybius began with rejecting
Tyche as an explanation of historical events and that he was later converted to a belief in chance as a ruling factor in history. Nobody, as
far as I can see, has made the suggestion that this was the true sequence

of the different phases in Polybius' thought, probably because such a development appeared too unlikely on general grounds. But there are other compelling reasons why such a suggestion would have to be rejected; for it appears quite impossible to assume that all the many passages in the first two books in which Fortune appears as a half-personalized and semidivine power [21] are late insertions.

Thus, it is clearly impossible to solve the problem presented by the apparent or real contradictions and inconsistencies in Polybius' use of the concept of Tyche through the assumption that there were different phases in the development of his ideas. The solution therefore must be sought in an analysis of Polybius' concept of Tyche itself and of his way of thinking.[22] Where Polybius distinguishes between the cases in which it is legitimate to make reference to Tyche or to a divine power, and those cases in which it is not, the distinction, as we have seen,[23] is based on the difference between what is accessible to human foresight and subject to human control and what is not. Specifically, therefore, everything that is the result of human foresight, training, effort, or of the excellence of political institutions created by human beings, or, on the other hand, the natural consequence of human folly, vices, or other avoidable human deficiencies, should in his opinion not be ascribed to Fortune but to these ascertainable causes, while events that are clearly beyond human control or foresight, like storms, droughts, epidemics, and also sudden inroads of tribes or nations that had lived beyond the horizon of the known political world of the time, and their effects, may very well be ascribed to Fortune or to some divine force.[24] But the very passage in which this distinction is most elaborately discussed with many examples has a strange sequence. Polybius had affirmed that one must *not* attribute the decrease of the birth rate in Greece to Fortune or to the gods, since it is all too apparent that it is due to the avarice and indolence of the majority of the Greeks who do not wish to undergo the expense and trouble of raising children. Then he gives an example [25] of a case in which in his opinion it *is* legitimate to attribute an event to Fortune or to a divine power. This is the case of the Macedonians who, when fighting under their legitimate kings, were several times defeated by the Romans, but later when they had no legitimate kings, but were ruled by a most contemptible and tyrannical usurper, fought so well that they defeated the Romans, and this at a time when they could have lived in perfect comfort under the free republican constitution which they had had to adopt after the battle of Pydna. Such utter folly, Polybius says, can hardly be explained except on the assumption that the Macedonians were stricken with madness by some divine power. Obviously this passage cannot be explained as a later insertion since it represents the necessary counterpart to the first example. Yet, on the face of it, it may appear to be in complete contradiction to the whole theory that it serves to illustrate; for according to this theory the results of human wisdom or folly should not be attributed to Fortune or to the gods, yet in the example given it is exactly the foolish behavior of the Macedonians that is to be explained by divine interference.

The solution of the problem—and in this case it is even a logical solution—is, of course, not difficult as soon as the problem is stated in this way, for it is the *results* of human wisdom or folly that should not be attributed to Fortune or some other divine power, but to human wisdom or folly, while the folly itself may be of such a kind that it can be explained only by the assumption of divine intervention. In a somewhat wider formulation the same principle can also serve to eliminate some other apparent contradictions. The success of the Romans, which enabled them to conquer nearly the whole inhabited world within less than fifty-three years after their greatest defeat, must, according to Polybius, not be attributed to chance, but to the excellence of the Roman constitution, and the virtues, the training, the unrelenting efforts, and the unity of purpose of the Romans. But that the Romans should acquire a superiority in these qualities over all other nations sufficient to enable them to conquer nearly the whole inhabited earth, and that this conquest should be completed exactly at the time when Polybius had reached the age and acquired the political experience enabling him to write an adequate history of this great event, may then still be called "a wonderful achievement of Fortune." There is no logical contradiction between this statement and the claim that the success of the Romans was not due to their good luck but to their superior qualities.

It is not too difficult to see that this solution of the problem can be made still more comprehensive. If the unpredictable and uncontrollable may be attributed to chance or fortune, but the predictable and controllable should be attributed to its specific and knowable causes, it can be shown on the basis of Polybius' own examples that the explanation in terms of chance or cause must change with the aspect of a given event that is under consideration. The conquest of Greece by Macedon in the seventh decade of the fourth century B.C. can no more be ascribed to the good luck of Philip and Alexander than can the conquest of Greece and Macedon by Rome in the second century to the good luck of the Romans.[26] But that in the fourth century it should be the Macedonians who had the superior qualities to conquer the East, and in the second century the Romans who had the qualities to conquer the East *and* the West, was not predictable; therefore it is quite legitimate to speak of Tyche in regard to these events, if they are considered under this aspect. Yet, on still a higher level of historical contemplation, it can be predicted on analogy that in all likelihood no nation will ever be able to retain indefinitely the superiority that makes it the master of the world, and that therefore the Roman empire will come to an end just as other empires had done before.[27] To that extent history becomes again predictable, though not in the sense that one can predict, centuries in advance, which nation will be the dominating power of the future, though one can predict that the dominating nation will not always be the same one. Thus a good part of the apparent contradictions in Polybius' treatment of the concept of Tyche can be resolved.

The fact, however, that such a "logical" resolution of some of the most striking apparent contradictions in Polybius' use of the concept of Tyche is possible does not prove that he had consciously elaborated his theory in this fashion. If this had been the case, he would, with his propensity for general discussions, hardly have neglected to discuss it at length in the chapter in which he explains when reference to Chance or Fortune is legitimate and when it is not.[28] In order to attain a full understanding of Polybius' way of thinking one has to understand him on his own terms, and this is often possible only by looking for the concrete and, so to speak, historical origin of the opinions that he expresses. In the case of his utterances about Tyche these historical origins are not very difficult to find. Both after the conquest of Greece by Alexander and later after the conquest of Greece by the Romans, many Greeks tried to console themselves and to escape a feeling of humiliation by the assertion that these events were entirely attributable to luck. One of the results of this widespread belief, in the case of Alexander, was the century-long controversy in the rhetorical schools over the question of whether Alexander owed his success to his superior qualities or to his phenomenal good luck.[29] In the case of the Roman conquest the argument assumed, among other variations, the form of the claim that if Alexander, who now appeared as a representative of Greek culture as against the Roman barbarians, had not, by mere chance, happened to die so young, he would have conquered the West, and Rome would have become subject to Greek kings. It is against such foolish complacency that Polybius revolts when he asks his readers to look for the real reasons for what has happened to them. But it is hardly a mere coincidence that the one passage in which he rejects in the most absolute and uncompromising fashion all reference to Tyche is concerned with the causes of the success of the Achaean League during the first decades of Aratus' leadership.[30]

The origins of the very extensive positive use that Polybius makes of the concept of Tyche throughout his work are somewhat more complex. Most Greek historians of the Hellenistic age liked to emphasize the sudden and unexpected turns of fortune in order to make the narrative more dramatic, and though Polybius disliked the dramatizing type of historiography [31] he does not seem to have escaped its influence altogether in this respect. On the other hand, there can be hardly any doubt that, quite apart from such literary influences which account for the frequency of the use of the term Tyche in his work, he was on occasion struck by the wholly unexpected turns that events had taken, both in his own time and in the past. Where this is the case he says so, and obviously does not always reflect on the relation of his statement to his theory of historical causality.

There is, however, still another factor involved which is of great importance for a full understanding of Polybius' way of thinking. Polybius very often uses the expression, "It is as if Fortune had done this or that on purpose." This is in essence not very different from our popular way of saying, "It is as if the bus was late on purpose every time when we are in a special hurry, while it always arrives on time when we are late," though Polybius uses the expression in reference to events of a somewhat higher order. But this usage is also in agreement with Aristotle's definition of Tyche as the coming together of two unrelated chains of causes in such a way as to produce a result that might have been brought about by purposeful action, as for instance, when a man goes to the market place in order to buy something, and there meets a friend whom he wanted very much to see but whom he did not expect to find there.[32] At any rate, this way of speaking does not imply any belief in Fortune as a divine force, but rather—at least in its strictly philosophical formulation—excludes it. Yet in the main passage on Fortune and historical causality [33] Polybius speaks of Fortune and divine powers as equivalent terms, and even expresses the opinion that in regard to completely unpredictable things it may be reasonable to consult oracles or to pray to the gods, but that where cause and effect are known and controllable, one should not appeal to the gods, but act on the basis of one's own insight. This may, of course, be a concession to popular notions in which Polybius did not share, though what he says about the causes of the extreme folly of the Macedonians does not support such an interpretation. But there are not a few passages in which the expression of a feeling that there must be some divine power appears to be quite sincere.[34] In fact, this inconsistency is characteristic of his attitude toward religion in general. In a famous passage of the sixth book [35] Polybius expresses the opinion that religion and a belief in gods and another world would not be necessary in a community consisting entirely of wise men, but that such beliefs were introduced by wise men who saw that only in this way could the common crowd be prevented from acting foolishly and wickedly, and that therefore religion should be carefully preserved. Yet in many other parts of his work Polybius shows such a spontaneous and unreflecting disgust at any kind of offense against the gods [36] that it is difficult to believe that this is altogether due to purely political considerations of the kind expressed in the passage quoted. Traces of such a discrepancy between strictly theoretical convictions and spontaneously expressed sentiments can be discovered in Polybius' treatment of other matters also, especially in his political philosophy.

All this shows clearly that Polybius was not a philosopher for whom nothing is more important than absolute consistency in his terms and concepts. It is equally clear that the many fluctuations in his use of the concept of Tyche cannot be explained by the assumption that they represent several definite phases in the development of his philosophy of Chance. He took his philosophical concepts partly from popular philosophy, partly from individual philosophers [37] or other writers, developed and changed them through his own meditations, but used them at no time with complete consistency. He rather made use of them on each occasion as they seemed to serve best his purpose of elucidating an historical event in a given context. It is, therefore, also safe to say that Polybius, if he had lived long enough to elaborate a completely revised edition of his great work, would not have eliminated all the apparent and real inconsistencies in the use of the concept of Tyche which modern scholars have discovered. Vice versa, it follows that similar discrepancies in other concepts cannot, without the greatest caution, be used to distinguish different phases in the elaboration of the work. This does not mean that on some points Polybius' later opinions did not definitely and consistently differ from his earlier ones, and that traces of both the earlier and of the later opinions cannot in such cases still be found in the work as we have it. In regard to the question of the excellence of Roman rule, this is certainly the case. In other cases, however, the reasons for such inconsistencies may be of an entirely different nature. They may be due to the fact that Polybius derived various elements of his theoretical philosophy from different philosophers or different philosophical schools without being quite able to integrate them with one another. They may be due to a clash between theoretical concepts taken over from others with his own natural way of thinking. They may be due to the inherent difficulties in certain concepts that he was not quite able to resolve, or to a discrepancy between his theoretical convictions and his natural sentiments. All these possibilities must be taken into consideration. It is not possible to evaluate the merits and demerits of Polybius' political philosophy correctly by means of the theory of a straight development easily reconstructable through an analysis of the composition of his work.

APPENDIX III: POLYBIUS' CRITICISM OF THE IDEALIZATION OF CRETAN POLITICAL AND SOCIAL INSTITUTIONS

ACCORDING TO THE TEXT given in the extant manuscripts, Polybius mentions [1] four admirers of the Cretan political institutions: Ephorus, Xenophon, Callisthenes, and Plato, in that order. No other extant ancient work mentions a work or even a passage of a work of Callisthenes dealing with the Cretan constitution. But no conclusions can be drawn from this fact, since only fragments of the works of Callisthenes have survived. The case of Xenophon is different. A catalog of his works has been preserved by Diogenes Laertius,[2] and this catalog indicates that everything that Xenophon published is still extant. Nevertheless no reference to Cretan political institutions can be found in his works. It has, therefore, been suggested that the name of Xenophon in the Polybius manuscripts might be due to a copyist's error, and that Polybius actually named Xenion, an author who, probably in the late third century B.C., wrote a special history of Crete, some fragments of which have been preserved.[3] Against this suggestion it has been rightly pointed out [4] that Polybius appears to have no knowledge of the special histories of Crete (by Xenion, Dosiadas, Sosicrates, Laosthenes, etc.) which were published in the Hellenistic age. It is therefore most likely that Polybius trusted to his memory and credited the fervent admirer of Sparta, Xenophon, with a similar admiration for Crete, because in the time of Xenophon it had actually been very common for admirers of Sparta to extend their admiration to Cretan institutions also.

As mentioned earlier, Plato in his *Republic* uses the Cretan constitution along with that of Sparta as an example of a timocracy. By timocracy he means a state in which it is the principle of honor that holds the society and the state together. This does not exclude the existence of a mixed constitution or of a system of checks and balances, but does not imply it either. In the *Laws*, in which the Cretan Cleinias is one of the chief interlocutors, together with the Spartan Megillus, Cretan educational and social customs and institutions are likewise treated as similar to those of the Spartans. There is just one passage [5] in which the political order of the Cretan city of Cnossus appears to be characterized as a mixed constitution, though only indirectly. For, after the Spartan Megillus has described the Spartan constitution and has come to the conclusion that it can be neither called monarchic nor aristocratic nor democratic (but, one must understand, a mixture of all of these forms of government), the Cretan Cleinias chimes in with the remark that the political order of Cnossus cannot be identified with any of the simple constitutions either. Apart from this one passage, however, the emphasis is on social, religious, educational, and military institutions. These institutions are generally praised by the chief interlocutor, who obviously expresses Plato's own views. But the Cretans are severely criticized for having made war rather than peace the guiding principle of their lives.

By far the most interesting discussion of the relation between Spartan and Cretan political and social institutions from a truly historical point of view is found in a long extract from the historical work of Ephorus, which has been preserved by the geographer Strabo.[6]

Ephorus is especially interested in establishing the priority of either Crete or Sparta in regard to those customs and institutions that are common to both of them. Most people, he says, believe that the Cretan institutions were derived from Sparta; in order to prove this they point out that the Spartan variety of these institutions is better than the Cretan one, and that the better institutions are not very likely to be derived from less good ones. They also point out that the Cretan city of Lyttus, whose institutions are most similar to those of Sparta, is known to be a Spartan colony. These arguments, according to Ephorus, are not valid. He tries to show that Lycurgus lived much later than the time when Lyttus was founded as a Spartan colony, so that the institutions of that city cannot very well be derived from the constitution of Lycurgus. There are also other indications to show that the Cretan institutions are older than those of the Spartans. The "knights" (ἱππεῖς), for instance, are still serving on horseback in Crete, which accords with the original meaning of the name, while in Sparta they form an elite corps in the heavy armed infantry. Some institutions common to both nations have been given a new name in Sparta, but that the Cretan term is the older one can be proved by the fact that it was formerly used in Sparta also. Thus the common meals which are now called *syssitia* in Sparta were known as *andreia* in the old Spartan poems of Alcman; in Crete the designation *andreia* has never been changed. For all these reasons Ephorus believes that it was the Cretans who invented the institutions common to Crete and Sparta. He explains the fact that in later times they were much more vigorously applied in Sparta than in Crete by the assumption that the Cretans after some time began to neglect their ancestral laws and allowed them to fall into desuetude, while the Spartans took them over and improved on them. He thinks that it was Lycurgus who brought the Cretan institutions to Sparta but applied them much more rigidly, and also added a number of new features, partly copied from Egypt, partly invented by himself.

Polybius' criticism of Ephorus' theories must then clearly be considered under three heads: (1) Are there actually striking similarities between Cretan and Spartan institutions as Ephorus contends? (2) If so, is his historical interpretation of these similarities correct? (3) Have the existing similarities any importance in the context of Polybius' general political theory?

There can be hardly any doubt that a good many of Ephorus' observations concerning similarities between Cretan and Spartan institutions are well founded [7]—as for instance what he says about the institution of common meals and about the fact that originally these meals were designated by the same term in both countries—furthermore, what he observes concerning the institution of the knights or horsemen, what he later adds about the division of the boys into flocks (ἀγέλαι) or bands,[8] and about the harsh training which they received, about the role of the love of grown men for boys in the education of the latter, about similar war dances, etc., finally—and this is especially important for constitutional theory—what he says in the last sentence of the excerpt about the important functions of a council of elders (γέροντες), obviously corresponding to the Spartan gerousia. The original identity of the regulators (κόσμοι) in Crete with the Spartan ephors which Ephorus claims is less certain. But there are enough similarities to require an explanation.

In recent times it has been pointed out [9] that some of the institutions common to the Cretans and the Spartans, as for instance the famous andreia, syssitia, or phiditia, have parallels outside Crete and Sparta, and even outside preponderantly Dorian settlements, and that analogies to the division of the boys into "flocks" or bands can also be found elsewhere. It has also been argued [10] that some of the similarities might be due to similar developments under similar conditions rather than to direct borrowing. This assumption is in all likelihood at least partly correct. Yet the similarities between Cretan and Spartan institutions are too numerous and too close to be explained altogether on such a basis. It must also be taken into consideration that those Spartan institutions and customs which are most similar to the Cretan appear for the first time in Greek history after the conquest of the southern Peloponnesus by the Dorian ancestors of the later Spartans, and that their counterpart in Crete appears for the first time after the Dorian conquest of that island. It seems logical, therefore, to assume that the Dorian conquerors in both cases brought at least the germs or beginnings of those institutions with them and developed them further in a similar fashion under similar circumstances.

Thus Ephorus was clearly right when he contended that many of the similarities between Cretan and Spartan institutions were so striking that they required a historical explanation. But the explanation which he gives is clearly untenable. Though the assumption that the Laconian institutions were borrowed from Crete is very old and mentioned as a Lacedaemonian tradition by as early an author as Herodotus,[11] it has been rightly rejected by practically all modern scholars,[12] so that it is not necessary to refute it again. In actual fact there can be hardly any doubt that the institutions of the two countries had a common origin but, under the influence of different conditions, developed in different directions.

There remains, then, the question of whether the existing similarities have any importance within the context of Polybius' political theory. A perusal of the extract from Ephorus' work that has come down to us

shows clearly that the problem of the mixed constitution can hardly
have played a major role in Ephorus' discussion of the relations between Crete and Sparta. His reference to a council of elders (*gerontes*)
corresponding to the Spartan gerousia is the only point even remotely
related to this problem.

Yet Polybius does not attack Ephorus on the ground that he had
failed to notice the fundamental difference between Crete and Sparta,
namely that the latter developed a "mixed constitution" while the
former did not, or certainly not to the same extent, though he might
very well have done so. On the contrary, he emphasizes the difference
in the distribution of wealth in the two countries and the concomitant
differences in the attitude of their populations towards money.

Here for once, then, Polybius shows an interest not only in political
power relations that can be expressed in clearly defined competences,
but also in underlying social and economic conditions. But he does not
pursue the analysis of the political significance of these conditions any
farther. He argues that the Cretans cannot have had a good political
constitution because there is too great a difference of wealth and because money is all-important. Yet he praises the Spartan constitution as
the best constitution next to that of Rome, in spite of the fact that
not only Aristotle,[13] whose *Politics* he had not read, but also Xenophon, in his *Constitution of the Lacedaemonians* and in his *Hellenica*,[14]
had pointed out that in Sparta also after the middle of the fifth century
the difference in wealth became excessive, to the great detriment of the
stability of the political order. Thus here again Polybius did not make
use of an excellent opportunity to study in two closely related historical objects the interrelation between economic and political factors.

NOTES

Notes

Chapter I: Polybius' Life and Political Background

1. The most probable date of his birth is 201 B.C. The arguments by which various scholars have tried to prove that Polybius was born as early as 208 or even 210 B.C., or as late as 198 B.C., have been refuted by Konrat Ziegler in his article on Polybius in Pauly-Wissowa, Vol., XXI, Part 2, pp. 1445 ff.

2. For a detailed discussion of the constitution of the Achaean League see André Aymard, *Les Assemblées de la Confédération achaienne* (Bordeaux, 1938). Concerning some major points of controversy, see the reviews of this work by M. Cary in the *Journal of Hellenic Studies*, LIX (1939), 154–55, and by J. A. O. Larsen in *Classical Philology*, XXXVI (1941), 406–9, and, above all, the excellent article by Larsen, "Representation and Democracy in Hellenistic Federalism," in *Classical Philology*, XL (1945), 65 ff.

3. Polybius II, 37.

4. According to Livy (XXXV 36, 8 ff.), a boy seems to have been made king after the death of Nabis and immediately before Sparta was taken into the League. From the context one might assume that he remained (nominal) king of Sparta within the League. But the whole story is rather obscure, so that no certain conclusions can be drawn.

5. Polybius II, 38, 6.

6. *Ibid.*, 38, 1 ff.; see also II, 39, 4 ff., where it is shown how an imitation of the Achaean principles produces excellent results in southern Italy.

7. Since a very large part of the sixth book has been preserved and since in the existing excerpts the comparison between the Roman constitution and other examples of mixed constitutions plays a very large role, it is most improbable that the absence of any reference to the Achaean League in the extant parts of the sixth book is due to mere chance and that Polybius actually discussed the Achaean constitution in the lost parts of that book.

8. Polybius II, 43, 7 ff.

9. See, for instance, Polybius II, 57, 3 ff.

10. *Ibid.*, V, 11 ff.

11. *Ibid.*, II, 44, 2 ff.

12. For an excellent detailed analysis of these events see Elias Bikerman, "Notes sur Polybe II," *Revue des études grecques*, LVI (1943), 287 ff.

13. Polybius II, 47 ff.

14. *Ibid.*, 47, 10.

15. See also Elias Bikerman, "Notes sur Polybe II," *Revue des études grecques*, LVI (1943), 298.

16. *Ibid.*, p. 302, note 4.

17. Polybius II, 46, 1; II, 48, 1.

18. *Ibid.*, 51, 4.

19. Plutarch, *Cleomenes*, 3–5; 12; 14–16; *Aratus*, 35 ff.

20. Plutarch, *Cleomenes*, 15.

21. Plutarch, *Cleomenes*, 16; *Aratus*, 38.

22. There can be no doubt whatever that Polybius knew of Cleomenes' offer, since it was mentioned and discussed in the work of Phylarchus, which Polybius knew exceedingly well. If there had been any doubt as to the historicity of Cleomenes' offer, Polybius would certainly have mentioned it and would have accused Phylarchus of having distorted the truth, as he has done on other occasions.

23. See text, pp. 12 ff.

24. *Catalogue of Greek and Latin Papyri in the John Rylands Library*, III, No. 491; see W. Hoffmann, "Ein Papyrusfund zum Frieden von 203," *Hermes*, LXXVI (1941), 270 ff.; A. Körte, in *Archiv für Papyrusforschung*, XIV (1941), No. 974, pp. 129 ff.; M. Gelzer in Vogt, *Rom und Karthago*, 195 ff.; H. Bengtson in *Historische Zeitschrift*, CLXVIII (1944), 486 f.; M. Gigante, "Una fonte antiromana sulle trattative romano-cartaginesi del 203 a.C.," *Aegyptus*, XXX (1950), 77 ff.; and, above all, M. Treu, "Der Papyrus über die Friedensverhandlungen des Jahres 203 v. Chr. (Ryl. Pap. III, nr. 491)," *Aegyptus*, XXXIII (1953), 30–56.

25. For a recent discussion of Polybius' occasional lack of objectivity in his criticism of other historians, see M. Gigante, "La crisi di Polibio," *La Parola del Passato. Rivista di Studi Classici*, XVI (1951), 38 ff.

26. Livy XXXVIII, 32, 6–8.

27. *Ibid.*, XXXIX, 36–37.

28. Polybius XXVII, 2, 11.

29. *Ibid.*, XXVIII, 6, 9.

30. *Ibid.*, XXVIII, 3, 7.

31. *Ibid.*, XXVIII, 6, 1–7.

32. *Ibid.*, XXVIII, 12–13.

33. *Ibid.*, XXVIII, 13, 1–11.

34. See text, pp. 24 f.

35. See Pausanias VII, 10, 11 f.

36. Polybius XXX, 6–9.

37. According to Pausanias (VII, 10, 7–9), one of the Roman ambassadors whom the Senate sent after the battle of Pydna to bring order into the affairs of Greece, at the instigation of Callicrates, announced in the Achaean assembly that "the most influential Achaeans" had given money to the Macedonian king Perseus and demanded that the Achaeans decree the death penalty for these men. But it is doubtful whether Polybius was among the men indicted or to be indicted on this occasion. At any rate the demand of the Roman ambassador was declined, and the Senate did not back it up.

38. Polybius XXXI, 23–24.

39. In Book XXXI, 26–27, Polybius tells an amusing story of how the un-Roman generosity in financial affairs, which the young Scipio adopted under the influence of Greek ideas about the proper conduct of a nobleman, caused a considerable shaking of heads among some of Scipio's uncles, though they themselves, or rather their wives, were the ones who on that occasion profited from Scipio's unwonted generosity.

40. Polybius XXXI, 11, 5.

41. *Ibid.*, XXXIII, 18, 10.

42. *Ibid.*, XXXVI, 11, 3–4.

43. *Ibid.*, IX, 25, 4.

44. Pliny the Elder, *Historia naturalis*, V, 1, 1.

45. Polybius XXXVIII, 22.

46. *Ibid.*, XXXIX, 2 ff., especially 5 ff.; see also Pausanias VIII, 30, 8–9.

47. For further details see H. M. Werner, *De Polybii vita et itineribus* (Leipzig, 1877); Otto Cuntz, pp. 50–59 and 75–78; and the article on Polybius by K. Ziegler in Pauly-Wissowa, Vol. XXI, Part 2, pp. 1453 ff.

48. [Pseudo-] Lucian, *Macrobioi*, 22 (225).

49. Concerning Polybius' training in mathematics see Polybius IX, 20, 4 ff. An attempt to determine the extent of Polybius' education and knowledge in detail, especially his acquaintance with earlier and contemporary philosophy, has been made by Rudolf von Scala (see bibliography). Unfortunately his otherwise extremely useful book is somewhat marred by his

tendency to make Polybius appear directly dependent on some definite, in most cases little known, author, where Polybius merely reflects ideas which were generally current among well-educated people of his time.

50. See Polybius IX, 22–26; XXIII, 13; XI, 19; XV, 6 ff., and *passim*.

51. *Ibid.*, I, 62, 3–4 and 64, 6.

52. *Ibid.*, XXXVI, 9 ff.; see also XXXVI, 6–7 and XXXI, 21, 6.

53. XXXIX, 2; see also XXXVI, 9, 7 and XXXI, 21, 6.

CHAPTER II: THE COMPOSITION OF POLYBIUS' WORK AND ITS PRESENT STATE OF PRESERVATION

1. Codex Urbinas, 102.
2. Palimpsestus Vaticanus, 73.
3. See text, Chapter VI.
4. Polybius I, 1 ff.
5. Polybius III, 4, 1 ff. In an article published recently, after the first chapters of the present book had been written, H. Erbse (*Rheinisches Museum*, New Series, XCIV [1951], p. 57 ff.) has tried to prove that the whole work of Polybius was written in one sequence and the whole of it after 146. Thus he considers all the various theories concerning later additions and revisions as completely wrong. He is also of the opinion that Polybius from the beginning intended to carry his work down to the year 145 or even 144 B.C. and argues (p. 176) that the passage in the first book (I, 1, 4) in which Polybius speaks of a period of approximately fifty-three years does not mean that he did not intend to carry his work beyond that period, but merely that these were the years in which Rome suffered its greatest defeat, recovered from it, and completed the conquest of the major part of the Mediterranean world.

Quite apart from the very serious difficulties which this interpretation of the first chapters of the first book presents in itself, Erbse appears to have overlooked the words κατὰ τὴν ἐξ ἀρχῆς πρόθεσιν, "in accordance with my original intention," in the passage quoted above in the text. For in the context in which they appear (ἐνθάδε που λήγειν ἂν ἡμᾶς ἔδει καὶ καταστρέφειν ἅμα τὴν διήγησιν καὶ τὴν πραγματείαν ἐπὶ τὰς τελευταίας ῥηθείσας πράξεις κατὰ τὴν ἐξ ἀρχῆς πρόθεσιν), the last words must be connected with λήγειν, "I could stop," and cannot possibly be taken to refer only to the words τὰς τελευταίας ῥηθείσας πράξεις, "the last-mentioned events." Nobody in his right mind will say "I could bring my work to an end with the last mentioned events in accordance with my original intention, but for certain reasons I shall continue," and then expect his reader to understand that the continuation was also intended from the beginning.

But though Erbse's theory is utterly untenable in regard to the main point, his analysis is not without merit. Most scholars had assumed that the fourth chapter of the third book was a later insertion, and there cannot be the slightest doubt about this if one considers the passage just quoted. But Erbse has rightly pointed out that the whole prooemium of the third book is a unit and presupposes the experiences of the year 146 B.C. and of the period immediately thereafter. This proves, however, merely that the whole prooemium and not only its second part is a later insertion. As pointed out above in the main text (pp. 36 f.), the summary of the description of the events down to the year 167 B.C. clearly indicates that the description of these events was already completed or nearly completed when the summary was written, just as the summary of the events between 167 and 145 B.C., which follows in the fourth chapter and is of a completely different character, indicates that Polybius had not yet written the history of that period when he wrote the prooemium of the third book.

There are other valuable sections in Erbse's article, e.g. his criticism of the exaggerated importance attributed to Stoic influence on Polybius by many modern scholars (see Erbse, p. 158 f., and *text*, pp. 54 ff.). But it is a pity that, when a theory has been carried to absurd lengths, the tendency with so many scholars—and scientists—is not to bring it back to the truth but to carry the opposite theory to equally absurd lengths.

6. Polybius III, 5, 7.

7. See, for instance, Polybius XXXII, 6, 4–6; XXXI, 22; XXXIX, 6.

8. For instance, Polybius XXXI, 10, 7; XXXIX, 6; see also XXX, 31, 3–20.

9. *Ibid.*, XXXVI, 9.

10. *Ibid.*, XXXI, 25, 2 ff.

11. *Ibid.*, III, 2–3 and 5.

12. Cicero, *Ad familiares*, V, 12, 2.

13. See text, p. 38.

14. M. Gelzer, "Die Hellenische προκατασκευή im zweiten Buch des Polybius," *Hermes*, LXXV (1940), 27–37, and "Die Achaika im Geschichtswerk des Polybius," *Abhandlungen der preussischen Akademie*, 1940, phil.-hist. Kl., No. 2.

15. Polybius III, 59, 3 ff.

16. *Ibid.*, 48, 12.

17. *Ibid.*, X, 10. Concerning the special problems connected with this insertion see O. Cuntz, pp. 8 ff. In the following chapters of his book Cuntz also discusses a number of demonstrable or probable later insertions on points of geography.

18. Polybius III, 39, 8; see Cuntz, pp. 20 ff. For a refutation of later theories concerning these passages see K. Ziegler in Pauly-Wissowa, Vol. XXI, Part 2, p. 1446.

19. Polybius III, 32, 2.

20. R. Laqueur, *Polybius* (Leipzig, 1913).

21. For a detailed refutation of one of Laqueur's typical arguments see E. Mioni, pp. 41 ff.

22. A striking example of this kind is Laqueur's contention (p. 15) that "the Carthaginians" in Polybius II, 36, 3 does not mean the Carthaginian government and people, which is the natural meaning of the word in the context, but the Carthaginian army in Spain, which largely consisted, not of Carthaginians, but of foreigners, and that therefore Polybius here contradicts another passage in his work, in which he attributes the same action to the Carthaginian government and people, and not to the army. In actual fact there is, of course, no discrepancy whatsoever between the two passages.

23. For a discussion of this assumption see K. T. Neumann, "Polybiana," *Hermes*, XXXI (1896), 519–29, and Mioni, 36 ff.

24. In the fourth chapter of this book an attempt will be made to show that many of the real or apparent contradictions in Polybius' sixth book (that is, in his political theory), which modern scholars tried to explain by the assumption that different passages of that book were written at periods widely separated from one another, must actually be explained in a different way. It is obvious that the explanation given in that chapter will greatly gain in probability if it can also be shown that difficulties in other books which have been explained by the assumption of later revisions can be solved in a much more convincing fashion by an explanation analogous to that applied in our Chapter IV to the sixth book of Polybius. A case of this kind is provided by Polybius' use of the word *Tyche* or Fortune. This notion of Fortune plays an important part in Polybius' general concept of history and must therefore be mentioned in our third chapter. But a detailed analysis of the difficulties inherent in Polybius' use of this notion does not fit into the framework of that chapter. I have therefore dealt with this problem in Appendix II.

CHAPTER III: POLYBIUS' PRINCIPLES OF HISTORIOG-
RAPHY AND HIS THEORY OF THE ORIGIN OF THE STATE

1. Polybius I, 2, 8; IX, 2, 4, and *passim.*
2. *Ibid.,* II, 56, 10; IX, 1, 2 ff., and *passim.*
3. See E. Schwartz, *Fünf Vorträge über den griechischen Roman,* 2d ed. (Berlin, 1943), pp. 45 ff.
4. Aristotle, *Poetics,* 5, p. 1451b, 5 f.
5. See B. L. Ullman, "History and Tragedy," *Transactions and Proceedings of the American Philological Association,* LXXIII (1942), pp. 25 ff.
6. Polybius XXIX, 12, 2 ff.; XII, 12, 3; XII, 15, 10–11; II, 56, 10 ff.
7. *Ibid.,* XII, 25e to 25i; 26 ff.
8. *Ibid.,* XII, 28, 2–3.
9. *Ibid.,* I, 1, 2.
10. See Appendix II.
11. Polybius V, 97, 5 ff.; cf. also IX, 17.
12. See, for instance, Polybius II, 68; III, 116, 7 ff.; IV, 11 ff.; XI, 14 ff.; and *passim.*
13. See, for instance, Polybius II, 58, 4 ff.; V, 9 ff.; and *passim.*
14. Polybius VI, 9, 11.
15. *Ibid.,* IX, 2, 5.
16. *Ibid.,* III, 6, 6 ff.; cf. also Thucydides (I, 23, 6), whose distinction, however, is somewhat different.
17. Polybius III, 10, 4–6.
18. *Ibid.,* I, 1, 5; I, 64, 1; II, 38, 4 ff.; III, 2, 6; VI, 48, 5 ff.; VI, 51, 3 ff.; and *passim.*
19. *Ibid.,* VI, 10; VI, 48, 2 ff.
20. *Ibid.,* VI, 9, 10 ff.
21. *Ibid.,* VI, 2, 3 ff.
22. *Ibid.,* VI, 3, 5 ff.
23. Plato, *Politicus,* 291d ff.
24. Plato, *Laws,* III, 677a ff.
25. Plato, *Republic,* II, 369b ff.
26. Aristotle, *Politics,* I, 2, 8 ff., p. 1252b, 27 ff.
27. Aristotle, *Politics,* I, 2, 8, p. 1252b, 29–30.
28. Aristotle, *Nicomachean Ethics,* X, 1 ff.; p. 1172a, 11 ff.
29. Aristotle, *Nicomachean Ethics,* X, 9, p. 1181b, 20 ff.

NOTES TO PAGES 48–50

30. See W. W. Jaeger, *Aristoteles* (Berlin, 1923), pp. 271 ff.

31. Concerning certain intrinsic difficulties in Aristotle's theory concerning "the good life," especially in its relation to his theory of human society and of "the best state," see E. Kapp and K. von Fritz, pp. 46 ff.

32. To see the intimacy of Polybius' acquaintance with Plato's *Republic*, compare Polybius IV, 35, 15 with Plato, *Republic*, II, 363d and Polybius VII, 13, 7 with *Republic*, VII, 566a. See also Polybius VI, 5, 1 and VI, 47, 7. The last-mentioned passage, in which Polybius says that he is not going to consider Plato's utopia on the same level with constitutions that have actually existed, has been regarded by many scholars as a criticism of Aristotle, who, in the second book of his *Politics*, discusses Plato's ideal state side by side with the actually existing states or political orders of Lacedaemon and Crete. If this opinion was correct it would, of course, prove that Polybius knew Aristotle's *Politics*. But it is obvious that Polybius may just as well have had in mind one of the many Hellenistic treatises on political theory which are now lost. It would be very strange indeed if this were Polybius' only reference to Aristotle's great work, if he knew it at all; and it would in fact be completely incomprehensible in this case that he did not mention Aristotle among those who likened the political order of Crete to that of Sparta (see Appendix III and Chapter V, note 3). In actual fact it is most unlikely that Polybius knew of Aristotle's *Politics*, which, like most of the other *pragmateiai* of Aristotle, was not in general circulation at the time of Polybius.

33. Plato, *Republic*, II, 372d.

34. See text, p. 47. One might also say that Polybius tries to reconstruct the point of transition in an evolutionary process from man as a kind of herd animal to man as a real human being, while Plato and Aristotle from the beginning speak of man as a member of a society that permits him to develop fully his abilities and potentialities as a human being.

35. In this connection it may perhaps be pointed out that the term "the state" in its political sense is of comparatively recent origin, having been developed first in Italy in the period of the Renaissance. Its more remote ancient origin may be found in expressions such as *optimus status rei publicae* ("the best state of public affairs," or "of the community"), or *statum rei publicae movere* ("to try to change by force the existing state [or order] of the body politic"). For the further development of the concept in Italy in the period of the Renaissance, see also J. Burckhardt, *Die Kultur der Renaissance in Italien*, I, 1, where he says: "Die Herrschenden und ihr Anhang heissen zusammen *lo stato*, und dieser Name durfte dann die Bedeutung des gesamten Daseins eines Territoriums usurpieren."

36. This, at least, is the prevailing meaning of the term, especially as it is used by Polybius. In Aristotle's *Politics* it is also used to designate a specific kind of political order. For a more detailed analysis of the terms *Polis* and *Politeia*, see also H. Ryffel, pp. 3 ff.

37. Plato, *Republic*, 361d and 368e; Aristotle, *Politics*, 1252b, 30, and *Nicomachean Ethics*, X, 1177a, 12 ff.

38. Polybius VI, 47, 7.

39. Aristotle, *Politics* V–VI, 1301a, 20 ff.

40. See text, Chapters IX and X.

41. Polybius VI, 4, 7 ff.

42. Herodotus I, 96–101.

43. Both Polybius' construction and Herodotus' story are, of course, strong oversimplifications, but that their constructions are not quite unsound, if taken with several grains of salt, seems to be proved by evidence so widely apart in space and time as the inquiries into legal processes among the Cheyenne Indians in the excellent book by K. N. Llewellyn and E. A. Hoebel, *The Cheyenne Way* (Norman, Okla., 1941), pp. 72 ff., and in the inferences drawn by R. von Ihering from Roman legal institutions to the role of the arbitrator in the earliest development of Roman law, in his famous book *Vom Geiste des römischen Rechts auf den verschiedenen Stufen seiner Entwicklung*, I, C, 12.

44. For the life of Panaetius, see M. Van Straaten, *Panétius, sa vie, ses écrits et sa doctrine avec une édition des fragments* (Amsterdam, 1946), pp. 3 ff.

45. Cicero, *De officiis*, I, 4, 11: "Homo autem, quod rationis est particeps, per quam consequentia cernit, causas rerum videt earumque praegressus et quasi antecessiones non ignorat similitudines comparat rebusque praesentibus adiungit atque adnectit futuras, facile totius vitae cursum videt ad eamque degendam praeparat res necessarias."

46. See Epicurus, ΚΤΡΙΑΙ ΔΟΞΑΙ, 31–33 and 37 (see *Epicurus, The Extant Remains, with Translation and Notes* by Cyril Bailey, Oxford, 1926, pp. 110–11); see also the Epicurean Hermarchus as quoted by Porphyrius, *De abstinentia*, I, 7–12.

47. See, for instance, Polybius III, 4, 1, where it means the external success *in contrast* to moral merit or achievement, and *passim*. A collection of passages in which Polybius uses characteristically Stoic terms in a non-Stoic sense has been made by R. Hercod, p. 15 ff.

48. Cicero, *Ad Atticum*, XVI, 11, 4.

49. Polybius XXI, 32c.

50. For instance, Polybius IV, 16, 2 ff.; 18, 9 ff.; 67, 1 ff., and *passim*.

51. In this connection one may perhaps mention the theory of Rudolph von Ihering, *Der Geist des römischen Rechts auf den verschiedenen Stufen seiner Entwicklung,* I, 1, 9–10, that the notion of justice developed first not at all from rational calculations but from the strong feeling of the individual of being wronged, and from the gradual extension of that feeling to cases in which it was not the individual himself, but those near to him, his children, his family, his fellow tribesmen, etc., who were wronged, a feeling that gradually can become extended to all human beings.

52. Polybius XXXVIII, 1, 7 f.

53. Polybius III, 4, 1 ff. See also the text, p. 34.

CHAPTER IV: THE CYCLE OF CONSTITUTIONS AND THE MIXED CONSTITUTION

1. Polybius VI, 7, 5 to 9, 11.

2. Herodotus III, 80–83, 1. An attempt to collect all the material on the change of constitutions in Greek political thought down to Polybius and to reconstruct a good deal that has not been preserved has been made by H. Ryffel in his ΜΕΤΑΒΟΛΗ ΠΟΛΙΤΕΙΩΝ. This book should be read together with a review of it by H. Strohm in *Gnomon*, XXIII (1951), 144 ff., where the attempt has been made to show that Ryffel's reconstructions of the political ideas of the early Sophists do not always rest on very solid ground. Strohm's criticisms perhaps go somewhat too far in several respects, but they are very valuable as a warning not to accept Ryffel's conclusions without thorough examination.

Ryffel (pp. 14 ff.) tries to show that the idea that extreme or simple constitutions must necessarily deteriorate and finally be overthrown by a μεταβολή goes as far back as Solon, who worked for a good order, an εὐνομίη, in which both the wealthy and the poor would get what was due them, but no more. Now it is true that the political order which Solon created was to some extent a mixture of oligarchy and democracy and that, as his poems show, he consciously worked for a compromise between the wealthy and the poor both socially and politically. It is also true that Solon warned that he himself could have used the existing party strife to set himself up as a tyrant, as others had done under similar conditions elsewhere. But with all this he has nowhere expressed the idea that certain types of political orders or "constitutions" must naturally deteriorate in the course of time and be replaced by different orders. In fact he could hardly have thought in such terms at a time when the most advanced Greek communities had just begun to develop somewhat higher forms of political life. It required the experiences of another century and a half before such an idea could be conceived, and in extant Greek literature we find it for the first time in Herodotus.

Strohm (p. 146), on the other hand, points out that the emphasis in the dialog in Herodotus is at first not on the inevitable change of constitutions, but, as he formulates it, on a "phenomenology" of the three forms of constitutions which could be found in the realm of Greek experience, a phenomenology in which the different interlocutors successively contemplate the good and the bad aspects of each type of constitution. This is quite correct. One might even add that the contention of Darius at the conclusion of the dialog—that both an oligarchy and a democracy must inevitably end by being converted into a monarchy—is a piece of special pleading conditioned by the fact that monarchy must come out victoriously if the actual historical result is to be explained. But all these considerations, however pertinent, cannot change the simple fact that here for the first time in extant Greek literature we find clearly expressed the idea that certain forms of government must deteriorate naturally and inevitably, not only under special conditions, and in the end will be overthrown and replaced by specific kinds of different political orders.

3. The Oriental elements in the story are emphasized and discussed by F. Altheim, II, 159 ff.

4. F. Altheim, II, pp. 174–75, tries to show that Herodotus' story presupposed an older tale containing the idea of the cycle of constitutions and that in the story as told by Herodotus the cycle "was straightened out to form a straight line" in order to comply with the requirement that the development must come to a stop with monarchy. It is, however, doubtful whether this assumption is correct. Only this much is clear: the story contains elements of the later cycle theory.

5. On the different meanings of the word "tyrant" and their importance for the theories of the cycle of constitutions and of the mixed constitution, see the text, Chapter VIII.

6. Plato, *Republic*, VIII, 544a–569b.

7. *Ibid.*, 547b–c.

8. *Ibid.*, 550c ff.

9. *Ibid.*, 552c ff.

10. *Ibid.*, 557b ff.

11. *Ibid.*, 565a ff.

12. *Ibid.* 566d/e ff.

13. Aristotle, *Politics*, V, 10, 3, p. 1316a, 25 ff.

14. Plato, *Laws*, IV, 709e–710e; see also his *Seventh Epistle*, 327a ff.

15. See, e.g., R. von Scala, p. 250: "Die Erwägung, dass diese umfassende philosophische Bildung, diese tief eindringende Verarbeitung früherer philosophischer Gedanken sich nirgends findet als in diesem VI. Buche, genügt, um dem Soldaten Polybius die freie Schöpfung einer Staatstheorie, die von stoischem Geiste erfüllt ist und platonische Gedanken in freier Umgestaltung verwertet, abzusprechen." The further course of our inquiry will show that nearly every detail in this sentence is wrong. For Polybius' relation to Stoicism and other philosophical systems see also the text, pp. 54 ff.

16. An attempt to do this has been made by Ryffel, pp. 198 ff. See also the text, pp. 82 ff. and 92 ff.

17. See Chapter III, note 32.

18. Polybius VI, 5, 1.

19. See Appendix III, note 3.

20. Herodotus V, 92.

21. Plato, *Republic*, VIII, 548d ff.

22. See Xenophon, *De re publica Lacedaemoniorum*, 14; Aristotle, *Politics*, 1270a, 21 ff.; Plutarch, *Agis*, 5; Polybius VI, 45, 3.

23. Aristotle, *Politics*, 1270a, 21 ff.

24. See Heracleides (Lembos), *De rebus publicis excerpta* (from Aristotle's histories of constitutions), II, 7; (Pseudo-) Plutarch, *Instituta Lacedaemoniorum*, 22; Plutarch, *Agis*, 5.

25. Plutarch, *Agis*, 5.

26. Xenophon and Aristotle, who mention the law in the passages cited in note 22 above, do not say anything about its revocation.

27. Aristotle, *Politics*, 1270a, 19–34. Concerning the whole problem see also our Chapter V, pp. 107 ff. with notes, especially note 28.

28. Xenophon, *Hellenica*, III, 3, 5–6, who calls the impoverished citizens ὑπομείονες, seems to imply that they no longer had full citizen rights and were not even counted as Spartiates. But it is difficult to know exactly how much their status was reduced. See V. Ehrenberg in *Hermes*, LIX (1924), 38 ff.

29. See Xenophon, *Hellenica*, III, 3, 4–11, and Aristotle, *Politics*, 1306b, 34 ff.

30. Concerning citizen rights in Sparta see the text, pp. 107 ff.

31. See Diodorus XIII, 2 ff. (from Ephorus); Plutarch, *Lysander*, 24–26; Aristotle, *Politics*, 1301b, 19 ff.

32. Aristotle, *Politics*, 1304b, 20 ff., especially 1305a, 3 ff.

33. *Ibid.*, 1301a, 19 ff.

34. Plato in the third book of his *Laws* (695a ff.) gives examples of the transition from a patriarchic kingship to a despotic regime in an Oriental environment. These examples resemble Polybius' description of the transition from kingship to tyranny so closely that it is extremely likely that Polybius was influenced by the passage from Plato's *Laws* quoted above, especially since for other reasons also there can be no doubt that he had read this work of Plato. It is then all the more significant that in Plato's work there is no further transition to an oligarchic regime as in Polybius' sixth book—and here again it is Plato, not Polybius, who is in agreement with actual history.

35. Aristotle, *Politics*, 1316a, 29 ff.

36. See the text, pp. 63 ff.

37. Polybius VI, 10, 2 ff.

38. See W. J. Woodhouse, *Solon the Liberator* (Oxford, 1938), and K. von Fritz, "The meaning of 'ΕΚΤΗΜΟΡΟΣ," *American Journal of Philology*, LXII (1941), 142 ff., and "Once more the 'ΕΚΤΗΜΟΡΟΙ," *ibid.*, LXIV (1943), 24 ff.

39. See Aristotle, *Constitution of Athens*, 5 ff.

40. See Solon, frgt. VI and VIII, 7 ff. (Greek with an excellent prose translation in I. M. Linforth, *Solon the Athenian*, University of California Press, 1913, pp. 134–37), and Aristotle, *Constitution of Athens*, 12 ff.

41. See Ernst Kapp and K. von Fritz, *Constitution*, p. 155, note 19.

42. See also Gustav Grossmann, *Politische Schlagwörter aus der Zeit des peloponnesischen Krieges* (Zürich, 1950), p. 12 ff.

43. See Aristotle, *Constitution of Athens*, 29 ff. and 35 f. Most interesting, however, in this connection is what Thucydides (VIII, 97) says about the regime that followed immediately upon the oligarchy of 411 B.C., namely: καὶ οὐχ ἥκιστα δὴ τὸν πρῶτον χρόνον ἐπί γε ἐμοῦ ᾿Αθηναῖοι φαίνονται εὖ πολιτεύσαντες· μέτρια γὰρ ἥ τε ἐς τοὺς ὀλίγους καὶ τοὺς πολλοὺς ξύγκρασις ἐγένετο κτλ. Here the two terms are combined: *the mixture* (σύγκρασις) and *the middle* or, as it is expressed here, the right measure (τὸ μέτριον). Yet, and this makes it so significant, the right mixture between oligarchy and democracy here does not at all mean a complicated system of checks and balances the like of which Polybius finds in the constitutions of Sparta and Rome. It means simply that it was not a small minority that monopolized the political power, but that the political power rested on a reasonably broad basis. Thus, then as now, the same political terms and slogans were used to designate very different things, and it is essential for an understanding of these matters to orient oneself not by the terms but by what they designate in the individual case.

44. See Aristotle, *Politics*, II, 1266a, 39 ff.

45. *Ibid.*, II, 1267b, 22 ff.

46. Concerning Archytas, see the text, p. 83.

47. Plato, *Statesman*, 292a ff., especially 294a–c.

48. *Ibid.*, 301d–e; cf. 298a ff., 300b–c.

49. Plato, *Laws*, III, 691c–d; 713c.

50. *Ibid.*, III, 683d ff.

51. *Ibid.*, III, 691d ff.

52. *Ibid.*, VI, 756e–757a.

53. Aristotle, *Politics*, 1266a, 5–7.

54. Concerning these functions see the text, pp. 190 ff. and 336 ff.

55. Aristotle, *Politics*, 1320a ff.; for a similar remark concerning monarchy or tyranny, see 1314a, 34 ff.

56. *Ibid.*, 1294b, 14 ff. and 34 ff.

57. *Ibid.*, 1266a, 4 f.

58. *Ibid.*, 1294a, 30 ff.

59. *Ibid.*, 1295b, 39 ff.; see also 1295b, 2 ff.

60. For a more detailed analysis of Aristotle's discussion of these problems, see also T. A. Sinclair, *A History of Greek Political Thought* (London, 1951), pp. 214 ff.

61. See Fritz Wehrli, *Die Schule des Aristoteles, Texte und Kommentar*, Heft I: *Dikaiarchos* (Basel, 1944), pp. 28 ff. and 64 ff.

62. Diogenes Laertius VII, 1, 66, 131.

63. Stobaeus, *Florilegium*, XLIII, 134, ed. Meinicke (or I, 138 ed. Wachsmuth-Hense [Vol. IV, Part 1, p. 85]).

64. See E. Zeller, *Die Philosophie der Griechen*, 5th ed., Vol. III, Part 2, pp. 115 ff.

65. Rudolf von Scala, pp. 114 ff.

66. See text, p. 78.

67. See text, pp. 54 ff.

68. Polybius VI, 10, 2 ff.

69. *Ibid.*, VI, 9, 12–14.

70. *Ibid.*, VI, 51, 6.

71. *Ibid.*, VI, 57, 5–9.

72. This is, for instance, the interpretation given by V. Pöschl (p. 51), who speaks of the "einheitliche biologische Entwicklungsverlauf" of the Roman constitution according to Polybius, but also by F. Taeger (pp. 15 and 39 and *passim*); by E. Kornemann (*Philologus* LXXXVI [1931], pp. 175 ff.); and by H. Ryffel (pp. 208 ff.), who adduces a great number of other biological cycle theories as possible models of Polybius, among others

a treatise περὶ τῆς τοῦ παντὸς φύσεως, which has come down to us under the name of Ocellus Lucanus and which its editor, F. Harder (*Neue philologische Untersuchungen*, I [Berlin, 1926]) attributes to a "pythagoreisierenden Peripatetiker" of the second century B.C., i.e., of the time of Polybius.

73. Because a correct interpretation of what Polybius says and means in every instance is absolutely essential for an understanding of his methods and his way of thinking, and specifically also for the reconstruction of his history of the development of the Roman constitution, which will be attempted in Chapter VI, it is necessary, at least by way of a note, to make an attempt to disentangle the various misunderstandings which are found in the works of the modern commentators of Polybius' sixth book.

F. Taeger (*op. cit.*) had tried to show that in Polybius' opinion the Roman constitution in a way followed the cycle of constitutions, with the difference, however, that in the case of Rome the constitutions did not follow upon one another but were added to one another, or rather grew into one another, so that first an oligarchic, then a democratic, element was added to an original monarchy until in the end a mixed constitution resulted. As I shall try to show in Chapter VI, Taeger was essentially right in this respect. Believing, however, that Polybius must be consistent in his similes or in the use which he makes of them, he insisted that the whole process of the cycle of constitutions from monarchy to monarchy must also correspond to the biological process of growth and decay, just like the process from the beginnings to the future decadence of the Roman Republic. In this respect Taeger was clearly wrong and so gave Pöschl (pp. 50 ff.) an opportunity to attack his whole interpretation of Polybius' theory. For—so runs the argument of Pöschl—the cycle with its three summits can correspond neither to the biological process from birth to death nor to the development of the Roman Republic, since both of them have only one high point of maturity and greatest perfection. Hence, according to Pöschl, it cannot have been Polybius' intention to make the naturally grown mixed constitution of Rome go through the same cycle as the simple constitutions, even in a somewhat different way.

Pöschl's first argument is quite correct. There can be no doubt that Taeger was wrong in his belief that Polybius' simile of biological growth must apply to the cycle of simple constitutions also. No further conclusion, however, can be drawn from the fact that the simile does not apply to the cycle, since Polybius is not consistent in his similes. Therefore Pöschl's second argument is not valid. It is not permissible to conclude that Polybius cannot have made the Roman constitution go through a process similar to the cycle because the biological simile applies only to Rome but not to the cycle. We just have to accept the fact that he is not so consistent.

Apart from this the difficulty at this point is a rather minor one. Leaving aside the simile of biological growth, there is no contradiction in the assumption that a mixed constitution may go through a development similar to that of the cycle of simple constitutions, though in this case the development is much slower and has only one summit, since the constitutions do not follow upon one another but grow into one another. If there is some awkwardness in the way in which Polybius suggests that the growth of such a mixed constitution has a certain analogy to biological growth, though this does not truly apply to the cycle, this awkwardness is not greater than the awkwardness of using the simile of rust in regard to the Spartan constitution and then having this rust prevented by a construction. It is certainly not comparable even to Polybius' awkwardness in making the reader expect that he will speak of the stability of the Roman constitution and then pointing out that its future downfall can be predicted. Yet this is what Polybius unquestionably does and, as has been shown above, not merely by making a later addition to an existing text. Hence it is not possible to interpret Polybius correctly by starting from the assumption that he must always have been perfectly logical and consistent.

In actual fact there cannot be the slightest doubt that Polybius made the naturally grown constitution of Rome go through the cycle essentially in the way in which Taeger has explained it. For what else could he have meant when he said (VI, 51, 6) that Carthage at the time of the Second Punic War was farther advanced in the process of growth and decay than Rome, as shown by the fact that in Carthage the people (whose rule, as we know, represents the last stage in the cycle) *already* ($\mathring{\eta}\delta\eta$) participated in the councils of the state (which, as we learn from the analysis of the Roman constitution, is the proper domain of the aristocratic or oligarchic element in a mixed constitution). The word "already" in this context makes it absolutely clear that Polybius refers to the cycle and not merely to an undesirable "Verschiebung der Kompetenzen" within a mixed constitution, as Pöschl (p. 52) claims. The argument (*ibid.*, p. 55) that democracy in the cycle of constitutions is not inferior to oligarchy has no validity in this context either. For this is not the point which Polybius tries to make when he compares Carthage and Rome. What he tries to show is rather that in the development of the naturally growing mixed constitution there comes a point when, one element having been added to another, and the democratic element last, these elements are equally balanced and each of them has its proper function. As long as this state of affairs lasts the political order has a great internal strength which will make itself felt also in the military field and in the field of foreign policy. But then the element last added—and in the cycle this is always the democratic element—may acquire power and influence beyond what it should have and invade a domain rightfully belonging to one of the other elements. This, so Polybius believed, at the time of the Second Punic War was *already* the case in Carthage but *not yet* so in Rome, where the aristocratic element, which comes in in the middle of the process, was just at its summit, but was counterbalanced on the one side by the monarchic element with which the process had begun and on the other side by the democratic element, which had started to make its power felt but had not yet surpassed the desirable limits of its power.

Pöschl's main error—which in a way is very understandable since it is, so to speak, a natural tendency of the philological commentator to try to make his author perfectly logical and consistent—has further consequences. For, with an author like Polybius, the penalty for attempting to make him perfectly consistent may be that one has constantly to make him say the opposite of what he actually says. Thus Pöschl says on p. 54: κατὰ φύσιν ist die Entwicklung Karthagos, Spartas und Roms . . . weil diese Staaten sich in einem natürlichen Lebensprozess entwickelt haben." But this, in regard to Sparta, is the very opposite of what Polybius says. There is not a word about a *natürlicher Lebensprozess* by which Sparta became a mixed state. On the contrary Polybius says in no uncertain terms that it was all a rational construction of Lycurgus. It is true that, as I have tried to show in the text, this causes difficulties with the similes that he has used immediately before. But these are the facts.

In conclusion it may be observed that it is instructive to read Ryffel's discussion of the problem (pp. 187 ff. and 221 f.), for he starts by accepting Pöschl's arguments and conclusions, because at first sight they are so perfectly convincing and plausible, but in the course of the discussion he is constantly forced to modify them, because he comes into conflict with the clear evidence of what Polybius says.

74. E. Mioni (p. 51), through an excellent analysis quite different from the one made above, but supplementary to it, has shown that the various sections of Polybius' sixth book (9, 10 to 10, 14) are interdependent, so that it is quite impossible to remove one or another passage on the grounds that it is a later insertion without leaving a gap which in no way can be filled, and so destroying the whole.

75. Polybius VI, 2, 5 ff.

76. *Ibid.*, VI, 43.

77. *Ibid.*, VI, 43, 398: the expression actually used is "a ship without a

master." But since Polybius later says that in such a boat the crew will obey the captain when a storm is threatening, he obviously means "a ship without a master" in the sense that the ship nominally has a captain but that this captain, while the sky is serene and the sea quiet, has no authority and thus is really not the master of the ship.

78. Polybius VI, 18.

79. *Ibid.*, VI, 57.

80. Plutarch, *Cato Maior*, 27; see also Diodorus XXXIV, 33.

81. See F. Jacoby, *Die Fragmente der griechischen Historiker*, II A (Berlin, 1926), 87 F 112, and Jacoby's commentary on the fragments in II C, pp. 159 and 210. Since the dispute is assumed to have taken place within the period of time which Polybius describes in his histories, the suggestion has also been made that Polybius reported it in one of the lost sections of his work. But Diodorus mentions the dispute not when describing the events preceding the Third Punic War, but in connection with a discussion of the character and the merits of Scipio Nasica's grandson, who was consul in 111 B.C. For this and other reasons it is much more likely that Diodorus followed Poseidonius, who wrote a continuation of Polybius' historical work.

82. Plato, *Republic*, VIII, 526a.

CHAPTER V: POLYBIUS' ANALYSIS OF CONSTITUTIONS
OTHER THAN THE ROMAN

1. Polybius VI, 45 f.

2. For a more detailed analysis of Polybius' criticism of the admirers of Cretan political institutions, see Appendix III, pp. 398 ff.

3. That Polybius did not know Aristotle's *Politics* (see the text, Chapter III, p. 49, and note 32) is by no means so strange as some recent commentators on Polybius' political theory appear to believe. The story that Aristotle's *pragmateiai* survived only in one copy in a cellar of the house of his friend Erastos at Skepsis and were rediscovered there by Apellico in the first century B.C., it is true, deserves no credit. But the very fact that this story was widely believed shows clearly that these works of Aristotle, in contrast to his dialogs and some other published works which are now lost, were not read by the educated public before the time of Apellico and that it must have been very difficult to obtain copies of them. See also, on this point, W. W. Jaeger, *Studien zur Entwicklungsgeschichte der Metaphysik des Aristoteles* (Berlin, 1912), pp. 131 ff.

4. See also H. Van Effenterre, pp. 288 ff.

5. Polybius XIII, 6.

6. See Appendix III, pp. 398 ff.

7. Polybius VI, 10, 6 ff.

8. See Appendix III, pp. 400 f.

9. H. T. Wade-Gery (in *Classical Quarterly, XXXVII* [1943], 66) has pointed out that the word "apella" seems never to occur in the singular, and has drawn from this and other indications the conclusion that the word does not designate the Spartan popular assembly as an institution, but rather its convocation at a given time. But the conclusion is not certain and the question is of minor importance. For convenience's sake I have therefore retained the word "apella" as a designation of the Spartan popular assembly. See also H. Michell, p. 140, note.

10. This is the opinion of U. Kahrstedt (p. 246). Others, like Michell (pp. 64 ff.), are of the opinion that the poorer Dorians were reduced to perioecic status, with the consequence that they lost the right to vote in the apella. There would then, however, have been no difference whatever in the political status of various groups among those who retained full citizen status. All the latter would always have had an equal chance to be elected to the gerousia. For reasons which I have explained in some detail in my review of Michell's book (in the *American Journal of Philology*, LXXIV [1953], pp. 429 f.), I consider Kahrstedt's opinion much more likely. In other words it appears very probable that at some time in the early history of the Spartan community an aristocracy arose among the Spartan citizens, just as it did in nearly all other Greek cities or tribes. Through the effects of the Second Messenian Wars, however, political equality among the Spartiates appears to have been restored. This appears to be the most probable theory. But the evidence is too scanty to permit any certain conclusions.

11. This view has been presented especially by H. Berve, in an article in *Historische Vierteljahrsschrift* (XXV [1929], 5 ff.), and also in his *Griechische Geschichte* (Freiburg im Breisgau, 1931), I, 155 ff.

12. K. M. T. Chrimes (pp. 345 ff., pp. 412 ff., and pp. 475 ff.) dates the reforms of Lycurgus much earlier than the Second Messenian War. She even considers it possible (p. 413) to assign the year 809 B.C. as a definite date to this reform through which, she believes, the number of kings was increased from one to two, the number of members of the gerousia from twenty-seven to twenty-eight, and that of the ephors from four to five. After this, in her opinion, there was no break in the constitutional development of Sparta down to the reformer king Cleomenes in the second half of the third century B.C. These are very bold constructions, to say the least, based partly

on speculations which A. J. Toynbee had published in the *Journal of Hellenic Studies*, XXXIII, 255 f. But Toynbee is much more cautious; and no one, so far as I can see, has up to the present accepted Miss Chrimes's constructions.

13. See Appendix III, p. 400.

14. For instance S. Luria (in *Klio*, XXI [1927], 413 ff.), and H. Berve (in *Historische Vierteljahrsschrift*, XXV, 7). A very pertinent argument against the assumption that the functions of the ephors had originally been essentially religious can be found in Michell's book on Sparta (p. 120).

15. See also J. Hasebroek, p. 205.

16. This comparison was made for the first time in antiquity in Cicero's *De re publica*, II, 33, 58. He stresses, however, merely the fact that the ephors in Sparta constituted a check on the power of the consuls and the other curule magistrates. In modern times the comparison has been stressed especially by Max Weber, *Wirtschaft und Gesellschaft* (Tübingen, 1922), pp. 567 ff. He extends the comparison far beyond what Cicero had in mind and beyond what is justified by the historical facts. The comparison between the ephors and the Roman quaestors made by K. M. T. Chrimes (p. 412) is even more misleading.

17. See text, pp. 200 ff.

18. See K. von Fritz, *Reorganisation*, pp. 21 ff.

19. The conjecture that it was Chilon who was the driving force in the reorganization of the Spartan state some time after the Second Messenian War has been made and defended, especially by V. Ehrenberg (pp. 46 ff.). Ehrenberg dates the reform in the middle of the sixth century, which is probably somewhat too late. But the date of Chilon is also somewhat uncertain; for a story told by Herodotus (I, 59) presupposes that he lived in the very beginning of the sixth century. Diogenes Laertius (I, 3, 1, 68), who quotes as his authority Sosicrates, who in his turn probably used the chronicle of Apollodorus (see Jacoby II B, 244 F 335) says that Chilon was ephor in 556/55 B.C.; and a papyrus fragment published by F. Bilabel, *Die kleinen Historikerfragmente (Lietzmann's kleine Texte* 149), No. 1 (cf. Ehrenberg, p. 125, note 14), says that he helped to overthrow the tyranny of Hippias in Athens in 511, which is of course irreconcilable with the anecdote told by Herodotus and its chronological implications.

Berve (in *Historische Vierteljahrsschrift*, XXV, 27 ff.) believes that the reformer and lawgiver was probably a certain Asteropus, who, according to Plutarch (*Cleomenes*, 10) had been the first to raise the ephorate to a position of great political influence and power. But all this is quite uncertain. The only thing that can be asserted with some confidence is that the reform can hardly have been gradual but must have been the result of a decisive act, and that the result of the reform, which of course preserved many institutions inherited from a much earlier period, was later generally known as the Lycurgan constitution. See also Wade-Gery in the *Cambridge Ancient History* (III, 557 ff.) and more specifically in *Classical Quarterly* (XXXVII [1943], 62 ff., and XXXVIII [1944], 1 ff.).

20. This is what Plato actually says in his *Laws*, IV, 712d. In this connection the word "tyrant" is used simply to designate a strict and harsh ruler. One might also say that it designates the totalitarian character of the Spartan political order, since it was through the ephors especially that the Spartan state exercised its strict control over the lives of its citizens. Thus the word tyrant does not here, as with the Greeks of the sixth and fifth centuries (see text, pp. 187 ff.), primarily designate a ruler who has come to power through the support of one party against another section of the citizens; for the ephors certainly represented the whole body of the Spartiates. Yet since the Spartans ruled over the subject population of the Helots, who had no civil rights, and since the totalitarian control of the ephors over the citizens had been introduced in order to make it possible to keep the Helots subdued, one may say that in a way the ephors can also be considered as tyrants in the original sense of the word. This shows the complexity of the problem. See also K. von Fritz, *Totalitarismus*, 48 ff., where the relations between totalitarianism and tyranny are discussed.

21. For a full discussion of these problems, see especially U. Kahrstedt, *Griechisches Staatsrecht*, I, pp. 119 ff. (plus the literature quoted in notes 7–9, *ibid.*), and H. Michell, *Sparta*, pp. 93–164.

22. See Thucydides I, 87, 2 and Xenophon, *Hellenica*, IV, 6, 3. H. Michell (*Sparta*, p. 126) says: "Certainly the final decision on war, peace, and the making of treaties rested with the gerousia and ecclesia [i.e., apella] sitting together." But I cannot find any conclusive evidence to support this opinion, and the passage in Thucydides quoted above shows clearly that the final decision lay with the apella alone, even if, as is likely, the gerousia was present. Thucydides (V, 77) proves further that international treaties were concluded in the name of the ecclesia, no mention being made of the gerousia.

23. See K. von Fritz, *Totalitarismus*, pp. 48 ff.

24. Aristotle, *Politics*, II, 1720a, 15 ff.; see also Polybius VI, 48 and Xenophon, *Constitution of the Lacedaemonians*, 6–7.

25. The problem of the iron money in Sparta has been discussed at some length by H. Michell, *Sparta*, pp. 296 ff. Unfortunately he has made a difficult question worse confounded by misinterpreting an important passage

in Plutarch's *Lysander*, 17. He translates the passage as follows: "[an ephor] declared they [the Spartans] ought not to receive any gold or silver into the city, but to use their own coin which was iron. . . . But Lysander's friends being against it and endeavoring to keep the money within the city it was resolved to bring in this sort of money to be used publicly, enacting at the same time that, if anyone was found in possession of any privately he should be put to death, as if Lycurgus had feared the coin and not the covetousness resulting from it." After the words "this sort of money" in the second sentence of this quotation Michell inserts the word "iron" by way of an explanation. Yet from the context it is crystal clear that "this sort of money" (in Greek simply τὰ χρήματα) means foreign gold and silver money and not iron money, since the Spartans could hardly have been punished by death for possessing iron money. If correctly interpreted, the passage, then, does not at all imply that the possession of gold and silver had *not* been forbidden to private citizens before, but merely that a more severe penalty was decreed for its possession.

On p. 304 Michell quotes Xenophon's statement that private persons in Sparta were forbidden to possess gold and silver, and then continues: "This is a curious statement to make after he had lived there for some time and must have known that money was used there as freely as anywhere else in Greece." One might rather say that this is a perfect example of the attitude of the modern scholar, who not only knows everything better than ancient historians describing events at which they were not present (in which case they may of course be mistaken), but even better than direct eyewitnesses as honest as Xenophon. Michell's main proof for his assumption that gold and silver money was used as freely in Sparta as elsewhere seems to be that high-ranking Spartans were frequently accused of embezzling foreign money which they should have handed over to the public treasury. It is hardly necessary to discuss the validity of this argument. The law may quite probably have been violated as frequently as was the Eighteenth Amendment in this country, and there may have been periods in which no very strong efforts were made to enforce it. But there can be hardly any doubt as to its existence.

26. See Herodotus I, 65, 2.

27. See Thucydides I, 18, 1.

28. See Aristotle, *Politics*, VI, 1319a, 11. The problem of land tenure in Sparta is one of the most difficult problems of Spartan history. It has been discussed very thoroughly by Michell, *Sparta*, pp. 205 ff. His conclusions, however, are not very convincing. All we can say with some confidence is

that originally each Spartan was assigned a lot and that this custom was restored and reemphasized through the "Lycurgan" reforms, but that nevertheless by the end of the fifth century many Spartans had fallen into great poverty while others had become very wealthy. See also the text, Chapter IV, pp. 70 f., and the passages quoted in Chapter IV, notes 22 and 24.

29. See Strabo, VIII, 4, 365; Pausanias, III, 20, 6, 261–2; (Pseudo-) Xenophon, *Constitution of the Athenians*, I, 11. K. M. T. Chrimes (p. 41) asserts that Strabo and Pausanias are mistaken and that the earlier Helots "were in no way public slaves but were owned by individual Spartans." She fails, however, to prove this on pp. 301 ff. of her work, to which she refers.

30. Polybius VI, 10, 11, and VI, 48, 5; cf. also VI, 50, 1.

31. See (Pseudo-) Xenophon, *Constitution of the Athenians*, I, 11.

32. Polybius VI, 48, 7 ff.

33. E. Schwartz in his famous book, *Das Geschichtswerk des Thucydides* (2d ed., Bonn, 1929), has tried to show that Thucydides originally believed that the Spartans were driven into the war against Athens by their allies, but later came to the conviction that they had considered a war against the rising power of Athens a necessity even before the complaints of the Corinthians provided them with a direct cause or pretext. Even then, however, it remained Thucydides' belief that it was the *fear* of the growing power of Athens that *compelled* the Spartans to wage a war before it was too late, and not any desire for expansion (see Thucydides, I, 23, 6).

34. Aristotle, *Politics*, II, 1270a, 20; see also the testimonies quoted in the text, Chapter IV, note 24.

35. See the text, Chapter IV, pp. 70 f.

36. See the text, p. 107.

37. Plato, Laws, III, 684a ff. and 691d ff.; see also the text, Chapter IV, p. 80.

38. Polybius VI, 10.

39. *Ibid.*, VI, 45–50.

40. *Ibid.*, VI, 45, 5.

41. See Ephorus F 149 (Jacoby); Plato, *Laws*, I; Aristotle, *Politics*, 1272b, 24 ff. (who also mentions, however, the changes that had taken place in the course of time, the factional strife, and the rather anarchic conditions that prevailed at the time when he was writing).

42. Aristotle, *Politics*, II, 1272a, 13 ff.; see also the text, Chapter IV, p. 27 and notes 25–27.

43. The problem of the *hypomeiones* is discussed by Michell, *Sparta*, pp. 88 f. He fails however to mention that it is the combination of the two

NOTES TO PAGE 113

passages (Xenophon, *Hellenica*, III, 3, 6 and Aristotle, *Politics*, 1271a, 13 ff.) which almost inevitably leads to the explanation of the term given by Busolt and accepted above in the text.

44. The problem of the nature and status of the *neodamodeis* is another vexed problem of the history of the Spartan social and political organization. It has been discussed at some length by Kahrstedt, *Staatsrecht*, I, pp. 46 ff.; K. M. T. Chrimes, *Sparta*, pp. 40 ff., 216 ff., and *passim*; H. Michell, *Sparta*, pp. 90 ff. and 251 f.; and most thoroughly by V. Ehrenberg in the article "Neodamodeis" in Pauly-Wissowa, XVI, 2396 ff. The most extreme solutions of the problem on opposite sides are those presented by Kahrstedt and K. M. T. Chrimes. Kahrstedt believes that the *neodamodeis* had full citizen rights and were separated from the old-time Spartiates only by being organized in separate syssitia because the latter did not wish to associate with them on an equal social footing, though there was no difference whatever in their political status. Miss Chrimes, on the contrary, contends that the *neodamodeis* were still slaves or serfs, or at least certainly not wholly free, and that the liberation of six thousand Helots by king Cleomenes reported by the ancient authors was in actual fact a liberation of *neodamodeis*. This theory, however, is quite untenable and altogether contrary to the testimony of a good many contemporary ancient authors. The opposite theory of Kahrstedt certainly comes much nearer to the truth. But Ehrenberg has shown that there are various factors that make it difficult to believe that the *neodamodeis* should have had absolutely equal rights with those Spartans who were *homoioi* by birth. The *neodamodeis* must however have had a status at least equal to that of the Perioecs, and were associated with the Spartiates more closely than the latter, both geographically, through the location of the landed property which was assigned to them, and through their organization in the military service. Their name also appears to indicate that they enjoyed some kind of citizen rights.

Quite recently, and long after the present chapter and note had been written, R. F. Willets, "The Neodamodeis," *Classical Philology*, XLIX (1954), 27 ff., has taken up the question again. He has come to the conclusion that the *neodamodeis* "were newly admitted to the demos but not to the citizenship," and explains this to mean that they enjoyed the usufruct of their land without paying tribute to a Spartan master and assumed "the same military obligations to the state as the Spartiates themselves, equipping and financing themselves as hoplites." He adds that "they would have the means to do so if, in default of heirs, they too could hold land in fee tail, exonerated from tribute because there was no point in exacting that tribute in kind. Tribute would thus be transformed into hoplite service." If this explanation is correct the status of the *neodamodeis* would have been very similar to that of the Perioeci. The demos would then presumably have been that of the Lacedaemonii in contrast to the Spartiates. But the available evidence permits at most a more or less plausible guess.

45. Polybius VI, 51–56.

46. *Ibid.*, VI, 48.

47. *Ibid.*, VI, 51.

48. The expression used by Polybius (τῶν καθηκόντων αὐτῷ) appears to suggest that the people are master over those things over which they ought to be master under a good constitution, though it can be understood also to mean that they are master over those things which concern them most directly.

49. The expression used by Polybius (τὸτ᾽ εἶχε τὴν ἀκμήν) can mean either that at the time in question the Senate reached the highest power that it ever reached within the course of the entire development, or that it was at that time the most influential of the three elements or factors sharing the political power in the state. It is likely, however, that the second of these assertions expresses what Polybius meant to say, both because it is the logical supplement to what he has said before, and because the first assertion would be historically correct only in regard to the development which took place in the course of the third century B.C., but not in regard to the whole course of Roman history down to the time of Polybius.

50. The general description of the Carthaginian constitution as it had been of old (ἀνέκαθεν) is clearly contrasted with the state in which it found itself at the time of the Punic Wars.

51. Isocrates III, 24.

52. Apart from the extant discussion of the merits and demerits of the Carthaginian constitution in his *Politics*, Aristotle also wrote a history of the Carthaginian constitution within the framework of his collection of constitutional histories. Furthermore, there existed in antiquity a work in at least two volumes on the Carthaginian constitution by a certain Hippagoras, which is quoted by Athenaeus XIV 630A. But nothing of importance has survived of these works.

53. Aristotle, *Politics*, II, 8, 1272b, 24 ff.

54. *Ibid.*, 1272b, 36 ff. The text in our manuscripts is not quite easy to understand; it runs as follows: τοὺς δὲ βασιλεῖς καὶ τὴν γερουσίαν ἀνάλογον τοῖς ἐκεῖ βασιλεῦσι καὶ γέρουσιν, καὶ βέλτιον δὲ τοὺς βασιλεῖς μήτε κατὰ τὸ αὐτὸ εἶναι γένος μήτε τοῦτο τὸ τυχόν, εἴ τε διαφέρον ἐκ τούτων αἱρετοὺς μᾶλλον ἢ καθ᾽ ἡλικίαν. μεγάλων γὰρ κύριοι καθεστῶτες ἂν εὐτελεῖς ὦσι, μεγάλα βλάπτουσι, καὶ ἔβλαψαν ἤδη τὴν πόλιν τὴν τῶν

Λακεδαιμονίων. Many editors have tried to emend the text or have assumed a lacuna, so that the end of the first sentence would not refer to the kings but to the gerousia. (For a detailed discussion of these suggestions see W. L. Newman in his annotated edition of Aristotle's *Politics*, II [Oxford, 1887], pp. 362 ff. and O. Meltzer, *Geschichte der Karthager*, II [Berlin, 1896], pp. 11 ff.) But Jowett seems to be right when, in his translation of Aristotle's *Politics* in *The Student's Oxford Aristotle*, VI (Oxford, 1942), he suggests that the text can be understood as it stands if one understands εἴ τε διαφέρον as referring back to μήτε τοῦτο τὸ τυχόν, as if this was followed by ἀλλὰ διαφέρον. The meaning then is: And the kings and the gerousia correspond to the kings and the gerousia there (i.e. in Sparta). But there is this advantage, that (in Carthage) the kings are not always of the same family nor, on the other hand, taken from any family (but from an outstanding one), and if it is only an outstanding family (i.e., if this condition is fulfilled) then they are selected from it and not appointed according to seniority. This is better because the kings have great power and can do great harm if they are of little worth (for the meaning of εὐτελής in Aristotle see, for instance, *Poetics* 22; 1448b, 26), as they have actually done in Sparta.

55. Concerning possible meanings of this strange statement see Gsell, Vol. II, p. 209, note 2, and A. Heuss in J. Vogt, *Rom und Karthago*, pp. 111–12, note 4.

56. At first sight Aristotle's statement that the highest magistrates were elected and that the highest office could be bought (*Politics*, 1273a, 36: τὰς μεγίστας ὠνητὰς εἶναι τῶν ἀρχῶν) would seem to indicate that the electorate could be bribed. It is, however, possible that Aristotle alludes to a custom found in many African communities of a later period, namely that the elected magistrate legally had to pay a certain sum for his office. See Gsell, p. 198.

57. Concerning the consuls see the text, pp. 151 ff.

58. See Justinus (XIX, 2, 5), who says that when at the time of the expansion of the Carthaginian empire in Africa in the middle of the fifth century B.C. the descendants of Mago became too powerful for the liberty of the Carthaginian republic, a new high court of a hundred men, chosen from among the senators, was created to pass judgment on the conduct of the generals in war after their return from the field, and to see to it in peacetime that the generals stayed within the law. This law court is in all probability identical with the Council of One Hundred and Four mentioned by Aristotle. Concerning the probable characteristics and functions of this council see also Heuss, pp. 111 ff. and notes.

59. Aristotle, *Politics*, 1273a, 15.

60. See Heuss, p. 111, note 5.

61. Polybius X, 18, 1 and XXXVI, 4, 6.

62. Justinus XIX, 2, 6 (see *supra*, note 58).

63. Livy XXX, 16, 3 speaks of *triginta primores seniorum* who were sent in 203 B.C. to negotiate a peace with Rome. It has been conjectured that these thirty men were identical with the narrower council within the Senate, i.e., with Polybius' gerousia. This is not impossible, but is by no means necessarily so, since commissions of thirty and also of ten are not infrequently recorded on Carthaginian inscriptions and elsewhere (see Heuss, pp. 113 f.). The assumption that the number of the members of the Senate was three hundred rests on even more uncertain ground. The assertion in some recent publications that the numbers of three hundred for the Senate and thirty members for the gerousia are "attested" for the fifth century B.C. is totally unwarranted.

64. Livy XXXIII, 46.

65. See Gsell, II, 279; Lenschau, "Karthago," in Pauly-Wissowa, X, 2236; and others.

CHAPTER VI: TRACES OF POLYBIUS' ACCOUNT OF THE DEVELOPMENT OF THE ROMAN CONSTITUTION

1. The first, second, and fourth of these sections are enumerated by Polybius himself in VI, 57, 10, where he draws the summary of his discussion. The reason why he does not mention the third section, the most important part of which was obviously a description of the Roman military system, is clearly that he considers it as part of the second one. This is quite correct from his point of view, since the discussion of the military institutions of the Romans as they existed at the end of the third century B.C. is clearly meant to be part of his analysis of the Roman state at the height of its internal strength. Yet it is not strictly a part of the analysis of the Roman constitution as a mixed constitution, and since this is our main concern, it appears justified to consider the discussion of the military institutions as a separate section.

2. See the text, p. 31. The fourth section has largely been dealt with in Chapter V and still earlier (see, for example, p. 85). We shall therefore not come back to it for an extensive discussion, though reference to it will occasionally have to be made in the discussion of the second section, which is, of course, the most important of all.

3. See the text, pp. 109 f. and 115 f.

4. Polybius III, 87, 7–9.

5. There can be no doubt that the dictatorship was mentioned in the first section. But that does not exclude the possibility that there was also a more systematic discussion of the institution after the second section, as some scholars have assumed. See also Appendix I, note 6.

6. See the text, p. 31 f.

7. The most important contributions to this question are the following: E. Ciaceri, "Il trattato di Cicerone De Republica e le teorie di Polibio sulla costituzione romana," in *Rendiconti della Reale Accademia dei Lincei*, 1918, pp. 236–49, 266–78, 303–15; F. Taeger, *Die Archaeologie des Polybius* (Stuttgart 1922); V. Pöschl, *Römischer Staat und griechisches Staatsdenken bei Cicero* (Berlin, 1936; Neue deutsche Forschungen, Vol. 5). Further literature is quoted by Taeger, pp. VII–VIII, and Pöschl, p. 7 and *passim*.

8. The question, for instance, of whether the discussion of the chronology of Pythagoras and of his possible influence on the Roman king Numa, in *De re publica* II, 15, 28 ff., goes back to Polybius or was added by Cicero is certainly of some interest in considering Polybius as a historian, but is not of crucial importance for our main problem.

9. See Pöschl, pp. 73 ff.

10. Polybius VI, 10, 13–14.

11. Cicero, *De re publica* II, 1.

12. See text, p. 74.

13. See the text, pp. 87 ff., and Chapter IV, note 73.

14. The curiae constituted the oldest division of the Roman army into larger units. Since the popular assemblies in early times were essentially assemblies of the warriors, the army units were naturally also the voting units. The curiae were probably led by noble clans or families and consisted mostly of their followers.

15. The authority (*auctoritas*) of the Senate means here the influence which this body possessed because of the esteem which the populace had for its members on account of their dignity and their outstanding qualities. It is contrasted with the power and domination of the king. Concerning other meanings of the term *auctoritas* see the text, pp. 133, 174, and 232 f., with notes.

16. Cicero, *De re publica,* II, 7, 13–9, 16.

17. *Ibid.,* II, 12, 23–24.

18. Since the command of the army was one of the most important, if not the most important, of the functions of the king in early times, it does

not make very much sense that immediately after his election a king should ask the same assembly which has elected him to give him a power which is of the very essence of the dignity to which he has just been elected. In actual fact, the custom of giving the chief magistrate the command over the army by a special *lex curiata de imperio* undoubtedly originated in a different fashion. See K. Latte, "Lex Curiata und Coniuratio," in *Göttinger gelehrte Nachrichten, Fachgruppe Altertumswissenschaften*, Vol. I (1934–36), pp. 59 ff.

19. Cicero, *De re publica*, II, 13, 25–14, 27.

20. *Ibid.*, II, 17, 31.

21. See F. Taeger, p. 52.

22. See also the text, p. 139.

23. Cicero, *De re publica*, II, 18, 33.

24. See also the text, p. 269.

25. Cicero, *De re publica*, II, 20, 35–36.

26. *Ibid.*, II, 21, 37–38.

27. The figures given by Cicero do not agree with those given by Dionysius of Halicarnassus and Livy. But the problems arising from this discrepancy are of no importance for the present subject. See Taeger, pp. 63 ff. and the present text, p. 238 and Chapter IX, note 52.

28. Cicero, *De re publica*, II, 22, 40.

29. *Ibid.*, II, 23, 42–43.

30. *Ibid.*, II, 25, 45.

31. Livy I, 49, 3: "ut qui neque populi iussu neque auctoribus patribus regnaret."

32. Cicero, *De re publica*, II, 24, 44 and 25, 46.

33. *Ibid.*, II, 26, 47 and 27, 49.

34. *Ibid.*, II, 28, 50 and 29, 51.

35. *Ibid.*, II, 30, 52.

36. *Ibid.*, II, 31, 53.

37. Augustinus, *De civitate dei*, V, 12.

38. In the period of the Republic the term *imperator*, which is used by St. Augustine, means the supreme commander of an army. But in the time of St. Augustine the term *imperator* had acquired the meaning of "emperor," i.e., head of the state. St. Augustine therefore can use the same term to designate both functions, which would not have been possible for an author of the republican period.

39. See text, pp. 130 and 238.

40. Concerning the decemviri see the text, pp. 134 ff.

41. This means probably no *ordinary* magistracy, for the emergency

magistracy of the dictatorship was, according to the unanimous testimony of the ancient sources, exempt from the *provocatio ad populum* down to the second half of the fourth century B.C. See Livy II, 18, 8; II, 30, 5; III, 20, 8; Dionysius Halicarnassensis V, 75; VI, 58; Zonaras VII, 13.

42. Here, in contrast to an earlier passage (*supra,* note 15), *auctoritas* is used as a technical term designating the approval of the Senate which was *added* to the bill passed by the assembly of the people, giving it legal validity.

43. Cicero, *De re publica,* II, 32, 56.

44. In one of the English translations of Cicero's *De re publica* most widely used in this country in university courses on political theory, Cicero's words *cedente populo* (the people giving way) are translated "being granted by the people" and are understood to refer to the authority of the senators which has been mentioned before. This is a most flagrant mistranslation, which converts Cicero's meaning into its very opposite. It is linguistically wrong, since *cedere* means "to give way" and not "to grant." It makes nonsense of the context, since Cicero does everything to show that in the early period the people had very *little* power. It is completely at variance with the history of the Roman constitution, and it makes no sense if applied to auctoritas, since auctoritas, in none of the senses in which it is used of the Senate, can possibly be granted by an act of the people.

What Cicero actually says, on the other hand, agrees in this case perfectly with the historical evidence. The dictator, as pointed out above (note 41), was exempted from the *provocatio ad populum* (i.e., he could have a citizen put to death without permitting him to appeal to the popular assembly), and he was exempt from tribunician intercession (see pp. 211 ff.). In other words, the main safeguards by which the individual was protected against arbitrary use of the power of the consuls did not apply against the dictator. This is what Cicero means when he says that the people had to give way (to the power of the dictator). Furthermore, the Livian tradition on the early history of the Republic has one story after another of how the patricians, when hard pressed by the demands of the plebeians, used the appointment of a dictator with his extraordinary powers to curb the people under their will. Only in later times, when the resistance of the patricians was about to be broken, do we hear of dictators who tried to mediate between the two classes and were no longer simple tools in the hands of the aristocracy. This is unquestionably the tradition which Cicero followed. See also Appendix I, note 6.

45. Cicero, *De re publica,* II, 33, 57; II, 34, 59.

46. Concerning the privileges and powers of the *tribuni plebis,* which are no more described by Cicero in this connection than the extraordinary powers

of the dictator are defined in the preceding chapter, see Polybius VI, 16, 4 and the text, pp. 200 f., 208.

47. The expression used by Cicero is "voluptatibus erant inferiores nec pecuniis ferme superiores." This phrase is usually understood to mean that the senators did not even surpass the rest of the population very much in wealth. If this was the meaning, the sentence would, however, be in flagrant contradiction with what Cicero has said shortly before. For if the plebeians were so hard pressed by debts that the only remedy left to them was a secession from the community, who were their creditors? Since the secession was directed against the patricians, i.e., the senatorial families, obviously the latter were. From this it follows that the patricians in general and the senators in particular must have been very much more wealthy than the majority of the population. The same conclusion can be drawn from the division of the population into five property classes of which Cicero had spoken shortly before.

But there is no such self-contradiction in Cicero's statements. For the sentence quoted above must be interpreted in the light of a parallel passage in his De legibus. In the beginning of the third book of this work, Cicero, in laying down the fundamental rules for his ideal Roman state, says of the ordo senatorius "is ordo vitio vacato, ceteris specimen esto" ("This class or order shall be free from faults. It shall be a model to all other citizens"). Later in the same book this prescription is illustrated more in detail. In this context Cicero tells the following story (De legibus, III, 13, 30–31): Somebody reproached Lucullus for the extreme luxury which he displayed at his villa at Tusculum. Lucullus' reply was "look at my two neighbors. One of them is a freedman. Yet what luxury do they display. Should I then not be permitted to do the same or a little more?" But Cicero answers that Lucullus as a man of superior rank should have been a model to the others through simplicity. If that was the way in which senators acted a lowly freedman would not dare to display the luxury that he now shows to the world.

The point then is clearly that senators, though wealthy, should not display their wealth but live a simple life of model virtue. It is Cicero's romantic belief that in the good old times of the early Republic all senators actually lived according to this ideal. There can be hardly any doubt that this is also the meaning of the phrase in the De re publica quoted above; that is, it means "they hardly made themselves superior through the use which they made of their money," or "they did not display their wealth but lived almost as simply as their poorer fellow citizens." If the sentence is understood in this way there is no contradiction with what Cicero has said in the preceding chapters.

48. Cicero, *De re publica*, II, 35, 60.

49. This is obviously the meaning of the words *cedente populo* ("the people giving way" or "the people conceding it") in this context. The assembly of the people was not a law court. But when appeal was made to the people against the death penalty they could either prevent this punishment by voting against it or "concede" it by agreeing to (or "giving way to") the demand of the magistrate who wished it to be inflicted.

50. Cicero, *De re publica*, II, 36, 61; II, 37, 63.

51. The expression is again similar: *populo patiente atque parente*, i.e., "the people suffered it and obeyed": they did not rise up in rebellion against the creation of a commission exempted from observation of all the safeguards of the rights of the people that had been created in the first years of the Republic. It is noteworthy that this is the point which is emphasized by Cicero, since other ancient and modern authors consider the creation and publication of a law code as one of the most important steps in the process by which the people became gradually more independent of the aristocracy, the knowledge of the law up to that time having been a privilege of the patricians. The notion, on the other hand, that the lawgiver must be above the law is very widespread in antiquity. While he acts as lawgiver, therefore, he must of necessity also be at the head of the government, since he can have no government above him. He must also be exempt from previously existing constitutional limitations of the governing power. All this, however, is not mentioned by Cicero, who emphasizes again and again that the decemviri represented the uncontrolled and absolute power of an aristocratic or oligarchic body.

52. See Livy III, 55 ff.

53. Polybius VI, 11, 1; see also Appendix I, note 4.

54. Cicero, *De re publica*, II, 2, 4.

55. Taeger, pp. 29 ff.

56. Diodorus VIII, 4.

57. See Polybius VI, 4, 2 and 5, 9-10; see also the text, pp. 52 ff.

58. This is obviously the meaning of the custom in Cicero's opinion (and in all likelihood in Polybius'). But see *supra*, note 18.

59. Cicero, *De re publica*, II, 23, 56.

60. *Ibid.*, II, 9, 15.

61. *Ibid.*, II, 23, 42-43.

62. *Ibid.*, II, 28, 50.

63. V. Pöschl, pp. 80 ff.

64. See Beloch, *Griechische Geschichte*, Vol. III, Part 2 (2d ed., Leip-

zig, 1923), pp. 107–12, and V. Ehrenberg in Pauly-Wissowa, IV A, 645 ff.

65. See the text, pp. 118 f.

66. The relation of the early Athenian aristocracy to their *pelatae* was entirely different, and there seems to be no analogy to the Roman patron-client relation anywhere in ancient Greece.

67. See the text, pp. 200 ff.

68. See *American Journal of Philology*, LXIV (1943), 24 ff., and the text, pp. 200 ff.

69. See *supra,* note 47.

70. See Krister Hanell, *Das römische eponyme Amt* (Lund, 1946).

71. Livy II, 28 ff. and III, 52 ff.

72. K. von Fritz, *Reorganisation*, pp. 22 ff.

CHAPTER VII: POLYBIUS' ANALYSIS OF THE ROMAN CONSTITUTION AT THE TIME OF ITS GREATEST PERFECTION; LEGAL, TRADITIONAL, AND FACTUAL FOUNDATIONS OF THE DISTRIBUTION OF POWER IN THE ROMAN REPUBLIC

1. Polybius VI, 12.

2. *Ibid.*, VI, 13.

3. *Ibid.*, VI, 14.

4. What Polybius means here is of course the *provocatio ad populum,* concerning which see the text, p. 132.

5. Concerning the legislative power of the popular assemblies, see the text, pp. 174 and 203 f.

6. Polybius VI, 15.

7. *Ibid.*, VI, 16.

8. Concerning the powers and functions of the tribunes of the plebs see the text, pp. 200 ff. and 208; see also pp. 257 ff.

9. Polybius VI, 17.

10. *Ibid.*, VI, 51, 5.

11. See the text, pp. 174 and 204.

12. Polybius VI, 16, 5.

13. *Ibid.*, VI, 13, 3.

14. Concerning the relation between the consuls and the Senate in the early Republic, see the text, pp. 169 f. and 197 f.

15. See Dio Cassius XLI, 17, and the story told by Polybius (XXIII, 14), and Livy (XXXVIII, 55), about the elder Scipio. Mommsen is, of

course, right in placing this story in the second consulate of Scipio. The version of Valerius Maximus (III, 7, 1)—that Scipio held the keys of the treasury while he was *privatus*—is clearly impossible and due to a complete misconception of Scipio's position.

16. Cf. the stories told by Plutarch (*Regum et imperatorum apophthegmata*, p. 201 A–B); Livy (XXVIII, 45, 13–14); and Plutarch (*Fabius*, 25); concerning the latter story see the text, p. 169.

17. There are of course other reasons why the opinion of the Senate always carried great weight and why it was not easy for a consul to disregard a *senatus consultum* (concerning this aspect of the question see the text, p. 197). But this is not the point here. On the one hand Polybius indicates clearly that the consuls were not obliged to consult the Senate when they wanted to spend money from the public treasury. On the other hand we shall find a considerable number of instances in which the consuls actually did refuse to act in other matters in accordance with a *senatus consultum* that had been made. See the text, pp. 167, 169, and 257. Concerning the "authority" of the Senate see the text, pp. 232 f.

18. See Livy XXXI, 6, 3 ff.

19. See Livy VIII, 23, 12.

20. Concerning the force of "opinions" of the Senate see the text, pp. 232 f.

21. Livy X, 24.

22. *Ibid.*, XXVI, 29.

23. *Ibid.*, XXVIII, 40 ff.

24. *Ibid.*, XXVIII, 40, 5 ff.

25. *Ibid.*, XXVIII, 45.

26. Concerning the relations between the Senate and the tribunes of the plebs in various phases of the history of Rome see the text, pp. 228 f.

27. See Livy XXV, 3. The year is 212 B.C.

28. See Sallust, *Jugurtha*, 27; Cicero, *De provinciis consularibus* 2, 3 and 7, 17.

29. Cicero (*De domo sua*, 9, 24) points out triumphantly that even C. Gracchus did not take away this right from the Senate but rather confirmed it by his law.

30. Concerning the condemnation to the death penalty by the Senate of the participants in the Catilinarian conspiracy in 63 B.C., see the text, pp. 282–83.

31. The ancient tradition concerning this law is very confused and contradictory. Appian (*De bellis civilibus*, I, 22); Tacitus (*Annales*, XII, 60); Diodorus (XXXVII, 9); and Plutarch (*C. Gracchus*, 5) attribute the law

to C. Gracchus, and the quotation of the law as *rogatio Sempronia* by Tacitus seems to indicate that a law of this kind was actually known under Gracchus' name. But Plutarch says that Gracchus merely added 300 equestrian jurors to 300 senatorial jurors, and did not eliminate senators from the Juries. Appian and Tacitus, on the other hand, say simply that the juries were transferred from the senators to the equites. However that may be, the *Lex Acilia de Repetundis* of Gracchus' fellow tribune Acilius Glabrio, the major part of which is extant, did exclude senators from the juries in trials *de repetundis* (see *Fontes juris Romani*, 7, 13 [p. 61, Bruns; p. 89, Riccobono]: "[dum nei quem eorum legat quei] . . . queive in senatu siet fueritve"), whether this was a new provision or merely an incorporation in this new law of a provision which had been part of an earlier law introduced by C. Gracchus. See also Scullard's note in Marsh, 409–10, and our text, Chapter X, note 23.

32. See Livy VIII, 12. I do not distinguish here between the patrum auctoritas and the auctoritas of the Senate. For though on the basis of certain passages in Livy it has been argued that the "patres" in this formula meant the patrician part of the Senate only, there can be no doubt that at the time of the Publilian laws it was for all practical purposes the Senate, and not the patrician senators only, who decided whether a law should be ratified or not, though some scholars try to solve the difficulty by the assumption that the Senate as a whole decided whether its patrician part should give its approval or withhold it.

33. The belief is still widely held that plebiscites required the auctoritas of the Senate either before or after they had been passed by the Concilium Plebis. In an article in *Historia*, I (1951), 25 ff., I have tried to prove that the assumption in this form is erroneous, and I have also discussed at some length the probable interrelation between the Valerio-Horatian, the Publilian, and the Hortensian laws. That in the period after 287, when plebiscites had the same validity as laws passed by the Comitia Centuriata, plebiscites did not require any approval of the Senate either before or after they were passed by the popular assembly seems to me to be proved by three facts: (1) that Livy in his history of that period always mentions it as a special point when a plebiscite is introduced *ex auctoritate senatus*, which in this period clearly means "on the initiative of the Senate" and not merely "with the approval of the Senate"; (2) that the Gracchi could never have introduced their laws in a popular assembly if they had had to obtain the previous approval of the Senate; (3) that Sulla in 87 B.C. (see Appian, *De bellis civilibus*, I, 59) made the assembly pass a law prohibiting the introduction of laws without previous approval of the Senate. Obviously there would have been no point

in forcing the assembly to pass such a law if the same law had been in force all the time.

34. See, for instance, *Festi fragmenta e codice Farnesino*, LXIII, p. 318M.

35. Isidorus (*Etymologiae*, II, 10, 2) defines *mos* as "vetustate probata consuetudo sive lex non scripta," adding: "nam lex a legendo vocata quia scripta est." In this sense a very large part of the Roman "constitution" was undoubtedly based on *mos* or *mos maiorum*. Later (V. 3, 2) Isidorus defines *mos* as *longa consuetudo*, which raises the question of how old a custom or habit must be to become an unwritten law in the fullest sense.

36. It should perhaps be pointed out in this connection that the first of the two kinds of *mos maiorum* or *mos* distinguished here corresponds to the first definition given by Isidorus, since it is in the fullest sense an unwritten law with the same validity as a written law. Yet in Roman literature this kind of constitutional rule is hardly ever referred to as derived from *mos* or *mos maiorum*. It is the second type which is not infrequently designated by that name. For the evidence see Hans Rech, *Mos Maiorum, Wesen und Wirken der Tradition in Rom* (Marburg, 1936), pp. 35 ff.

37. Mommsen and other modern scholars have tried to prove that the early quaestors of the consuls are identical with the quaestores parricidii, which are also mentioned in the tradition on the early history of the Republic, and that therefore one of the earliest special tasks with which the quaesters were entrusted regularly was the investigation of crimes, especially capital crimes. But K. Latte, in the article "The Origin of the Roman Quaestorship" in *Transactions of the American Philological Association* (LXVII [1936], 24 ff.), has shown conclusively that there is very little ground for this assumption, and that the quaestores parricidii in all likelihood were not permanent magistrates but temporarily appointed special commissioners.

K. Latte has further tried to prove that the quaestorship in actual fact did not exist before the year in which it became elective; i.e., that the tradition according to which the quaestors were originally appointed by the consuls is erroneous and was caused by the same mistaken identification of the quaestors with the quaestores parricidii that has misled modern scholars. His main argument is that there could have been no heads of the financial administration or administrators of the public treasury before there was a building to harbor the treasury, and before a fixed relation between the value of cattle and a pound of copper was established, which according to ancient tradition was done in the year 454 B.C. These arguments, however, though very ingenious, are hardly quite convincing. The temple of Saturnus, which housed the public treasury, was built in 495 B.C., nearly fifty years before the quaestorship became elective. The attempt to fix a definite relation between the value of cattle and a pound of copper, which is a very artificial measure, seems to indicate that payments in copper had been made along with payments in cattle for quite some time, so that difficulties did arise from the lack of a fixed relation between the two. Finally, as pointed out before, there are indications that even after the quaestorship had become elective the quaestors for some time were still not restricted to financial affairs but continued to be the helpers and substitutes of the consuls in general. For all these reasons it appears unnecessary to question the tradition that in the early Republic the quaestors were appointed by the consuls and that the quaestorship existed before it became elective.

38. The two censors, acting together, could strike a man from the voting list for conduct unworthy of a Roman citizen. Through a Lex Ogulnia of uncertain date, but certainly earlier than the last decade of the fourth century, the censors also were given the right to strike a senator's name from the Senate role for improper conduct. Such a decision remained valid without appeal for five years; i.e., until the new censors entered upon their term of office. If the new censors did not then confirm the decision of their predecessors, the persons concerned were automatically reinstated in their former positions.

39. See Livy IV, 7 ff.

40. See Tacitus, *Annales*, XI, 22.

CHAPTER VIII: MIXED CONSTITUTION, SEPARATION OF POWERS, AND SYSTEM OF CHECKS AND BALANCES; CHECKS BEYOND BALANCES AND EMERGENCY PROVISIONS

1. See, for instance, C. H. McIlwain, *The Growth of Political Thought in the West* (New York, 1932), p. 100.

2. According to the Solonian constitution the archonship had been reserved for the highest property class, the so-called *pentakosiomedimnoi*. In 457/56 eligibility to the highest office was extended by law to the three upper property classes (cf. Aristotle, Constitution of Athens, 26, 2), so that only the lowest property class, the Thetes, remained officially excluded. But Aristotle (*ibid.*, 7, 4) suggests that even this restriction was not observed in practice, so that a Thes could become archon if, at the time when the lots were drawn for that office, he simply failed to say that he was a Thes.

3. See Ugo Coli, pp. 3 ff.

4. See Xenophon, *Hellenica*, I, 7.

5. Many kings in antiquity, though by no means all of them, claimed to be of divine or semi-divine origin, and anthropologists in recent times have made much of the assumed origin of kingship from religious ideas and religious functions. In fact, wherever we encounter kingship in history it is surrounded by a certain character of sacredness which tyranny in the technical sense is lacking. Most kings in history, furthermore, have had definite religious functions. But this does certainly not mean that kings in general originally had purely or even preponderantly religious functions, and that their military, judicial, and administrative functions developed from these religious functions. Concerning the origin of chieftainship as one of the most primitive forms of monarchy arising from the functions of military leader and judge rather than from religious functions among American Indians, see the most illuminating book by K. N. Llewellyn and E. A. Hoebel, *The Cheyenne Way* (University of Oklahoma Press, 1941). It may perhaps also be pointed out that where in antiquity divine or semi-divine origin is claimed by kings, emphasis is always laid on the benefits bestowed on the human community by the divine or semi-divine monarch or by his divine or semi-divine ancestors, and that these benefits are usually mostly in the military field or in the field of the establishment of law and order and the administration of justice.

6. There is a third type of monarchy, distinguished by its origin from both kingship and tyranny, which may be called Caesarism. In this kind of monarchy the monarch rules not so much through the support of a political party as through the support of the army. This kind of monarchy cannot arise in primitive conditions where the people and the army are more or less identical. It can come into being only where the people and the army for some reason have become separated from one another, as was the case at the time of Caesar, but also to some extent at the time of Napoleon. Obviously this type of monarchy has certain characteristics in common with tyranny in the technical sense, but it is hardly ever quite so oppressive.

7. Not only can a king become one element in a mixed constitution where he has to share the active powers of government with other governmental agencies, but he can even be deprived of nearly all positive governmental functions and powers and still retain his usefulness as a symbol of the unity of the political community, while a tyrant in the technical sense loses everything when he loses his active political power. An interesting historical illustration of this fact is provided by the Greek tyrants who entered the Achaean League, which had, in a way, a mixed constitution. As shown above (see pp. 6 f.) most of these tyrants entered upon a political career within the League, but in order to do so they had to cease not only to be tyrants but to be monarchs,

while the Spartan kings remained kings for centuries within a community with a mixed constitution, and for some time even within the Achaean League.

8. It does not matter in this context whether the tradition concerning these archons is historically correct or not. The important issue at this point is merely that for the Greeks an archon ruling for a lifetime was not the same thing as a king, and exactly because he was only a functionary of the people.

9. An interesting illustration of this is the siege of La Rochelle in 1627–28; all through the siege the citizens and their leaders continued to recognize the king of France as their legitimate sovereign, though at the same time they felt compelled to defend their religious liberties against him.

10. See G. W. Botsford, pp. 25 ff.

11. Livy II, 1, 10–11.

12. See P. Willems, *Le Sénat de la république Romaine*, I (Louvain, 1885), 35 ff. This is still the most detailed and conclusive discussion of the question.

13. This ratification of a law voted upon and accepted by the people is the original technical meaning of the term (*patrum*) *auctoritas*. Concerning the meaning of the term *auctoritas senatus* in later times, when the *patrum auctoritas* in the original and technical sense had become practically ineffective, see the text, pp. 232 f.

14. See Chapter VII, p. 174.

15. See K. von Fritz, "Emergency Powers in the Roman Republic," in *Annual Report of the American Historical Association* (1942), Vol. III, pp. 226–27.

16. Concerning the political importance of this system see the text, pp. 234 ff.

17. *Leges XII Tabularum*, VIII, 21: "patronus si clienti fraudem fecerit sacer esto."

18. *Leges XII Tabularum*, XI, 1. To contest the historicity of this law merely because, according to the tradition, it had to be revoked a few years later, and because it was of course no longer valid in the later period of the Republic, is completely unwarranted.

19. See Livy III, 55, 10: "tribunos vetere iureiurando plebis, cum primum eam potestatem creavit, sacrosanctos esse." That this meant that the plebeians swore not to tolerate any violation of the sacrosanctitas of their tribunes is proved by the parallel passage in Livy II, 2, 5: "ius iurandum populi recitat neminem regnare passuros." Against this tradition it has been said that such an oath would not make sense as a foundation of a lasting institution, since the oath would not be binding on future generations. This seems, however,

too legalistic an interpretation of the event and of its meaning. Clearly the main value of the oath in any case was that it was the expression of an attitude of the plebeians. Hence the oath or its meaning would be respected by the patricians as long as they could assume that the same attitude would prevail among the plebeians, whether the oath was religiously binding or not. In actual fact tradition tells us that the oath was later replaced by one of the Valerio-Horatian laws. See also K. von Fritz, *Leges sacratae*, pp. 893 ff.

20. See Livy III, 9, 1–5.

21. Livy IV, 1; see also note 18 above.

22. Concerning this whole question see K. von Fritz, *Reorganisation*, pp. 23 ff.

23. See *ibid.*, pp. 8 ff., and our text, pp. 258 f.

24. Concerning the reasons for the restoration of the consulship and the creation of the new praetorship and the two curule aedileships, see the text, pp. 179 ff.

25. See text, Chapter VII, pp. 181 f.

26. Livy (II, 18, 4) says that it is not certain in which year a dictator was appointed for the first time nor who this was, but places the event in the first decade of the Republic. Some modern scholars have tried to prove that before 450 B.C. the Romans had a one-man presidency instead of the two-man consulate, and that the dictatorship was simply a temporary restoration of this one-man presidency in times of emergency. But this and similar theories which are necessarily conjectural need not be discussed here.

27. See, for instance, Livy VI, 38 ff., for the dictatorships of Furius Camillus and P. Manlius, which preceded the admission of plebeians to the consulship in 366 B.C.; Livy VII, 39, 17 ff., for the dictatorship of M. Valerius Corvus, and Livy VIII, 12, 14 ff., for the *dictatura popularis* of Q. Publilius Philo, who introduced the law quoted above. In all three cases the details of the stories of these dictators as told by Livy are confused and partly contradictory. This is the natural result of the fact that the documented history of that period contained only the barest facts concerning the constitutional innovations resulting from the struggle, and the names of the magistrates introducing the corresponding laws, all the rest of the story being made up from oral traditions and on the analogy of later events. Yet it is highly significant that the oral tradition was so full of stories in which dictators appeared as mediators between the plebeians and the Senate. For these stories cannot have been invented on the basis of later analogies. See also K. von Fritz, *Reorganisation*, pp. 23 ff.

28. See the text, pp. 257 ff.

29. Livy XXII, 8, 5 ff.
30. *Ibid.*, XXII, 25, 10 ff.

CHAPTER IX: THE SOCIAL, ECONOMIC, AND NATIONAL
BACKGROUND OF THE DISTRIBUTION OF POWER
IN THE ROMAN REPUBLIC

1. See the text, pp. 194 f.
2. This does not, of course, mean that the anecdote concerning the influence of Fabius' daughter on the political ambitions of her plebeian husband is also historical. See K. von Fritz, *Reorganisation*, pp. 4 ff.
3. According to the *Fasti Capitolini*, Licinius Calvus was consul in 364 and Licinius Stolo in 361 B.C. According to Livy, Licinius Stolo was consul in 364 and Licinius Calvus in 361. F. Münzer, pp. 155 ff., has shown that the version of the *Fasti Capitolini* is probably correct and that Livy is likely to have followed the Roman annalist Licinius Macer, who may have exchanged the names in order to give the history of the period a different turn.
4. There were only thirteen plebeian consuls in these twenty years because there were two patrician consuls in each of the years 355, 354, 353, 351, 349, 345, and 343 B.C. The magister equitum of the one plebeian dictator of the period, C. Marcius Rutilus (dictator in 356 and consul in 357, 344, and 342), was also a plebeian and identical with the plebeian consul of 358, C. Plautius Proculus.
5. According to Livy (VII, 42, 2), the law or plebiscite passed in 342 was to the effect that both consuls could be plebeians. But since two plebeian consuls were elected for the first time in 172 B.C., more than a century and a half later, this can hardly be correct. In actual fact, 342 B.C. is the year after which one of the consuls was always a plebeian. It is therefore most likely that this was the actual content of the law (and probably a preceding plebiscite) passed in 342. Livy's error was probably caused by a misunderstanding of the meaning of the agreement between plebeians and patricians concerning the consulate which had been reached at the end of the year 367 B.C. See K. von Fritz, *Reorganisation*, pp. 27 ff.
6. Plebiscites at that time did not yet have the force of laws (see the text, p. 203 f.), but could of course have a considerable influence on elections. For since the plebeians had undoubtedly the majority even in the upper classes of the Comitia Centuriata, they had merely to vote down any candidate whose election would have been contrary to the rule established by the

plebiscite. This is the probable reason why what was demanded by the Genucian plebiscite of 342 was actually observed for a decade, but then was gradually forgotten.

7. The observation of the two rules mentioned did, of course, not necessitate the appearance of nine new gentes supplying consuls for the Republic. For the Genucian plebiscite prohibited merely the re-election of the same individual within ten years, and not the election of a member of the same family. Apart from this, some of the consuls of the previous decades would have become again eligible within the ten-year period. That ten new families nevertheless appear may perhaps indicate that the purpose of the Genucian plebiscite was not merely to prevent individuals from becoming too powerful by holding the same office again and again, but also to prevent certain families from acquiring a monopoly of the highest positions in the state.

8. This does not, of course, mean that all the consuls of these years were *homines novi* in the sense in which this term was used in later times, i.e., to mean men who had no senatorial ancestors. On the contrary, everything indicates that most of them came from families which had gained access to the Senate before, but not to the consulate. Concerning *homines novi* see the text, p. 229, and notes 28–29.

9. The so-called Chronographer of the year 354 A.D. (*Chronographi Minores*, I, 13 ff.) has for the year 333 B.C. the note "hoc anno dictatores, non fuerunt (consules)." The report of Livy on this year is obscure and confused. According to him (Livy VIII, 17), the "new consuls" (which from the context would seem to mean the consuls of the year 334 B.C., T. Veturius and Sp. Postumius), appointed P. Cornelius Rufinus dictator and M. Antonius his magister equitum. Then some flaw was discovered in the performance of the rites by which they had been appointed. The dictator and his master of horse, therefore, abdicated, and when a plague broke out it was decided that the auspicia of the consuls had also been affected by the faulty procedure in the appointment of the dictator. So the consuls abdicated also, and after an interregnum new consuls were elected: A. Cornelius and Cn. Domitius.

According to the fasti these are, however, the consuls of 332 B.C., and if one assumes that all that Livy tells happened in one year, as his account would seem to suggest, two years are missing in his story. The special problem created by this confusion cannot be discussed in detail within the framework of the present study. I have, however, taken the liberty of including M. Antonius in the list of plebeian consuls of the decade, since, whatever his exact position may have been, he appears to have belonged to the supreme magistrates of that period. See Attilio Degrassi, "Fasti Consulares et Triumphales," in *Inscriptiones Italiae* (Rome, 1947), Vol. XIII, Part 1, pp. 107, 410 ff.

10. In the later Republic the plebeian branches of patrician families were often the descendants of freedmen who had been given the name of their former masters when they became Roman citizens. But this is certainly not the origin of the plebeian branches of patrician families in the first two centuries of the Republic. What the actual relation of the plebeian Claudii Marcelli to the patrician Claudii and of the plebeian Veturii Calvini to the patrician Veturii was, ancient tradition does not tell. But the stories of the migration of the numerous family of the Claudii from Regillae to Rome make it appear likely that not the whole family was admitted to the patriciate. It is then likely that the Veturii Calvini also had the same origin as the patrician Veturii but belonged to a branch which had failed "to make the grade" some one hundred and fifty to two hundred years before, when the patriciate became exclusive. The suggestion of F. Münzer (p. 123) that Veturius Calvinus was a patrician who became a plebeian in order to be eligible as a plebeian consul and so to increase the power of the patricians, appears most improbable and has no foundation in the ancient tradition.

11. K. J. Beloch, *Römische Geschichte bis zum Beginn der punischen Kriege* (Leipzig, 1926), pp. 247 ff.

12. Since some of the gentes appearing among the consular tribunes in the past were no longer very prominent in the late Republic, and since the name of the Domitii who became very prominent in the late Republic does not appear among the lists of consular tribunes, it appears certain that these names were not inserted when the younger annalists rewrote the history of the early Republic, partly to enhance the glory of some families, partly in order to make it suit their ideas of the struggle between patricians and plebeians.

13. C. Maenius won extraordinary military glory in his consulate so that a statue was erected to him in the Forum. Nevertheless, he does not appear again in the fasti until eighteen years later, when he was appointed dictator in a great emergency, and his family does not appear in any prominent position during the next hundred years.

14. F. Münzer (pp. 37 ff.) has tried to show that P. Decius was associated with the family of the Plautii and probably owed his elevation to the consulship to his plebeian predecessor, C. Plautius, who would then have presented him as a candidate in the elections. This is quite possible. Yet even so the connection of Decius Mus with such an old family may have been due to the personal distinction which he had earned.

15. See the text, pp. 255 ff.

16. See the text, pp. 250 ff.

17. See Livy XXII, 25, 18–19: "loco non solum humili sed etiam sordido ortus." This, however, does not mean that Varro was not wealthy enough to support himself in his high station. On the contrary, Livy says expressly that Varro's father was a butcher, but left his son enough money "ad spem liberalioris fortunae." This is always the prerequisite for a political career.

Some modern scholars have contended that a consul at that time could not possibly have been the son of a butcher, and that this must have been an invention of his enemies. In fact we do not know enough about this particular period, in which a new political and social development that was just about to gain some momentum was cut short by the Second Punic War, to make such a statement with confidence. But even if the statement should be correct the tradition preserved by Livy would still show that Varro's social origin was considered inferior in his time.

18. Livy XXII, 26, 1–2.

19. *Ibid.*, XXII, 25.

20. *Ibid.*, XXII, 34, 4.

21. See the text, pp. 166 ff.

22. It is quite irrelevant in this context whether Hasdrubal in 215 B.C. was sent to reinforce Hannibal in Italy, as Livy (XXIII, 27, 9) says, or whether he was sent to defend Spain against the Romans, as De Sanctis and others believe, since in any case his defeat in Spain by the Scipios prevented the Carthaginians from sending large reinforcements to Hannibal. The opinion that Hannibal "did not need reinforcements at that time" is so obviously wrong that it hardly needs to be refuted. When in 212/11 both the elder Scipios were defeated and killed in Spain, the Romans had already recovered sufficiently from their defeat of 216 so that the event was no longer decisive, especially since within less than a year it was followed by the first success in Spain of P. Scipio's son, the later Africanus.

23. See K. von Fritz, *Reorganisation*, pp. 3 ff. and 11.

24. See F. Münzer, *Adelsparteien*, pp. 124 ff., and especially Scullard, *Politics*, pp. 53 ff., who has tried to show that in the years around the outbreak of the Second Punic War the Fabii and the Cornelii Scipiones belonged to opposite factions within the aristocracy, and that the Scipiones were more friendly to the popular leaders like Flaminius than the Fabii were. This is in all likelihood correct. There were of course all sorts of cross-currents, and the old noble families formed by no means an absolutely solid block. But attention to the day-to-day developments in Roman politics must not be allowed to obscure the larger issues; and there can be hardly any doubt that

the military exploits of the Scipios, even though they were more popularly inclined and even though on various occasions they came into conflict with the more reactionary leaders of the Senate, did contribute to the increasing prestige of the old aristocracy in general.

25. See the text, p. 169.

26. See especially the Rogatio Marcia de Liguribus of 172 B.C., which supported the Senate against consuls who acted against the advice of that body (Livy, XLII, 21); the Lex Voconia of 169 B.C. (Cicero, *Pro Balbo*, 21 and Gellius, *Noctes Atticae*, XVII, 6), which was most fervently promoted by the elder Cato; the Lex Calpurnia of 149 B.C., whose initiator, L. Calpurnius Piso Frugi, is shown by the fragments of his historical work to have been a dyed-in-the-wool conservative, and the Lex Villia of 180 B.C. (Livy XL, 44), which supplemented earlier laws that had been initiated by the Senate. Of the Lex Aelia de Coloniis Deducendis of 194 B.C., Livy (XXXIV, 53) says expressly that it was brought before the people by Q. Aelius Tubero "ex senatus consulto," and it is therefore likely that the Lex Atinia de Coloniis Deducendis of 197 was also introduced on the initiative or with the approval of the Senate. Of the Lex Sempronia of 193, Livy (XXXV, 7) says likewise that it was initiated "ex auctoritate patrum."

27. For details see M. Gelzer, *Nobilität*, and A. Afzelius.

28. These are the *homines novi* among the consuls expressly mentioned as such in the ancient tradition, and it is not likely that there were more in the period from the beginning of the second century B.C. to the end of the Republic, though it cannot strictly be proved that there were not more. M. Gelzer, *Nobilität* (pp. 40 f.) points out that ancient tradition mentions only fifteen *homines novi* who attained the consulship from 366 B.C. to the end of the Republic. This is correct but somewhat misleading, since the tradition concerning the period from 366 to the consulship of Terentius Varro in 216 B.C. is here treated in the same way as the tradition concerning the last hundred and fifty years of the Republic. The tradition concerning the fourth century and the earlier part of the third century B.C. was not of such a nature that the ancient historians or Cicero could have known in every case whether a consul was a *homo novus* or not, and specifically in regard to those decades which were described in the lost books XI to XX of Livy, the preservation of the knowledge that a given consul was a *homo novus* is entirely fortuitous, as can easily be seen from the fact that a passage in Cicero's *Pro Murena* is the only source of our knowledge that M. Curius Dentatus, consul in 290, 275, and 274 B.C., was a *homo novus*. That most of the consuls of that early period also had senatorial ancestors cannot be doubted, but there is no serious reason to assume that the number of *homines*

novi who reached the consulate in the fourth and third centuries B.C. was only five.

29. The term *homo novus* is used for all senators and holders of curule magistracies who had no senatorial ancestors, though the quality of being a *homo novus* is of course especially emphasized in men who attained the consulship. That a great many people who had no senatorial ancestry reached the curule aedileship is emphasized by Cicero, *Pro Plancio*, 25, 60.

30. See the text, p. 192.

31. See the text, pp. 247 ff.

32. For details see M. Gelzer, *Nobilität*, pp. 32 ff., especially p. 36. See also Cicero, *Philippicae*, I, 1, 2.

33. The only extant ancient discussion of the *pedarii*, i.e. those senators who did not participate in the debate but were merely called upon to vote on definite resolutions, is found in Gellius, *Noctes Atticae*, III, 18. But what he quotes from Gavius Bassus and from Varro shows clearly that at the time of these authors, i.e., the time of Cicero, the institution was so obsolete that even the meaning of the term *pedarius* was contested. Nevertheless, Mommsen is undoubtedly right in his contention that the first explanation of the word given by Gellius, namely "qui in senatu sententiam non dicunt sed in alienam sententiam pedibus eunt," is correct, and if this is so there seems to have been a time in which not all senators had the right to participate in the debate.

34. The problems have been recently discussed in a number of very careful studies. The most important of these are: B. Jenny, *Der römische Ritterstand während der Republik* (Dissertation, Zürich, 1936); H. Hill, *The Roman Middle Class in the Republican Period* (Oxford, 1952); and A. Alföldi, *Der frührömische Reiteradel und seine Ehrenabzeichen* (Baden-Baden, 1952). An extensive bibliography of the earlier literature on the problem can be found in Hill's book, pp. 200–207.

It is particularly interesting within our context to note that this aristocracy below the senatorial aristocracy derived its origin from a military function, service in the cavalry. Down to the end of the Republic it was in some way connected with this function. But, as Hill (p. 47) has shown, as early as the time of Polybius "non-senatorial members of the equestrian centuries, ex-members of those centuries, and non-members who were qualified by their wealth for membership gradually formed a fairly homogeneous Middle Class which, by the time of Cicero, bore the title of *equester ordo*." One would merely have to add that the term "middle class," as used here by Hill, does not mean what we usually mean by it in this country, but a lower aristocracy with a very definite feeling of their standing above the middle

NOTES TO PAGES 230–38

class in the ordinary sense of the word. It might also be added that the formation of this class was certainly completed by the time of the Gracchi.

So there is here another aristocracy larger than the number of those who, in virtue of belonging to this aristocracy, have certain special political and military functions.

35. See the text, pp. 225 and 250 ff.

36. Aristotle, *Politics*, V, 1, 2, 1301a, 25 ff.; see also *Nicomachean Ethics*, V, 3, 6, 1131a, 25 f.

37. In the late Republic the equestrian census was 400,000 sesterces. (*Schol. Juven.*, 3, 155; Horace, *Epistles*, I, 1, 57.) Concerning the date when this amount was first fixed by law, see Hill, pp. 111 and 160.

38. See the text, pp. 161 ff.

39. See the text, p. 174.

40. See the text, p. 171.

41. See the text, p. 208.

42. See Caesar, *De bello civili*, I, 6, 4, where we learn that a tribune of the plebs interceded against part of a specific senatus consultum only a few days after an emergency decree of the Senate had been passed, and that nevertheless this particular intercession was considered valid and was heeded.

43. See especially Plato, *Politicus*, 291c f., 293a f., and *Laws*, IV, 722b–c.

44. Plato, *Politicus*, 294a f.

45. Livy, I, 43; the same figures are given by Dionysius Halicarnassensis IV, 16 ff. See also *Papyri from Oxyrynchus*, XVII, 2088. Concerning the somewhat different figures given by Cicero in his *De re publica* see the text, Chapter VI, p. 130, with note 27.

46. See Pliny, *Naturalis historia*, XXXIII, 43; Gellius (*Noctes Atticae*, VI [VII], 13) mentions 125,000 *asses* as the census of the first class, referring at the same time to the Lex Voconia of the year 169 B.C.

47. See the text, p. 204.

48. Concerning the connection of the curiae with the patrician gentes see the text, pp. 194 ff.

49. Livy I, 43, 13; Dionysius Halicarnassensis IV, 14; *Papyri from Oxyrynchus*, XVII, 2088.

50. Ernst Meyer (pp. 60 f.) has tried to prove the existence of Comitia Tributa in the fifth century B.C. by the following two arguments: (1) The Comitia Centuriata are mentioned in the Twelve Tables as the Comitiatus Maximus. This implies the existence of at least two other official assemblies, i.e., of the Comitia Tributa in addition to the Comitia Curiata. (2) After the addition of the tribus Clustumina in the late fifth century, care was taken

always to have an odd number of tribus, which, it would seem, was done in order to avoid a tie in the vote. Hence there must have been a legislative assembly voting by tribus. However, it is easy to see that both facts presuppose only the existence of the Concilium Plebis, in which the vote was taken by tribus, and not of Comitia Tributa distinguished from it. In fact, the designation of the Comitia Centuriata as Comitiatus Maximus can be more easily explained on the assumption that the third assembly was the Concilium Plebis. For that the Comitia Centuriata should be considered "bigger" either in size or in importance than the Comitia Curiata, which had lost all real importance, and consequently were hardly attended by many people (later the curiae were simply represented by the lictors, since nobody came to them any more) is very understandable. But there is no reason why the Comitia Centuriata should have been bigger or greater than the Comitia Tributa if the latter were a patrician-plebeian legislative assembly. But they were of course rightly called "bigger" than the Concilium Plebis, which was attended by the plebeians only and which could pass resolutions but not make laws. The possible objection that the plebeian assembly was a *concilium* and not a *comitiatus*, and that the term Comitiatus Maximus implies reference to a third and minor *comitiatus*, presupposes a meticulousness in terminology which is not characteristic of the Twelve Tables.

It should perhaps also be mentioned that E. Meyer in a later passage of his excellent book (p. 185) expresses some doubt as to the existence of Comitia Tributa different from the Concilium Plebis.

51. A certain distinction may have remained, inasmuch as the plebeian tribunes and the plebeian aediles were probably always elected by the plebeians to the exclusion of the patricians. This electoral assembly may then have continued to be called Concilium Plebis. But it is certainly significant that in regard to the period before 287 there is constant confusion in the ancient authors concerning Concilia Plebis and Comitia Tributa, and that shortly after 287 B.C., in which year the Concilium Plebis acquired the right to make laws, we hear no longer of laws made by the Concilium Plebis, but practically all laws appear to have been made by the Comitia Tributa.

52. The most extensive reference to the new order in extant ancient literature is found in Livy (I, 43, 12), who says: "nec mirari oportet hunc ordinem qui nunc est post expletas quinque et triginta tribus duplicato earum numero centuriis iuniorum seniorumque ad institutam ab Servio Tullio summam non convenire," and, following a reference to the creation of the urban tribus by Servius Tullius, continues "neque eae tribus ad centuriarum distributionem numerumque quicquam pertinuere," implying, of course,

that in his time, or rather in the late Republic, this was the case. The reference to the new order in Dionysius Halicarnassensis IV, 21, 3, is even briefer and less clear. Cicero's deviation from the description of the original (Servian) form of the centuriate order given by Livy and Dionysius Halicarnassensis is in all likelihood due to a confusion of the old order with the order prevailing at his own time (see text, p. 130 and Chapter VI, note 27). But since Cicero does not intend to describe this latter order, but that attributed to Servius, all inferences in regard to the later order that can be drawn from the relevant passage in his *De re publica*, II, 22, 39, are inevitably very uncertain. There are numerous references to votes of the popular assemblies in Cicero's orations. But all of them presuppose a knowledge of the divisions and the procedure and do not describe them.

The most recent and detailed discussions of the problem will be found in the works of P. Fraccaro, "La riforma dell' ordinamento centuriato," in *Studi in onore di P. Bonfante*, I (Milan, 1930), 103 ff., and Arnaldo Momigliano, "Studi sugli ordinamenti centuriati," in *Studia et Documenta Historiae et Juris*, IV (1938), pp. 509 ff.; see also H. Hill, *The Roman Middle Class*, pp. 38 ff.

53. See Dionysius Halicarnassensis IV, 14, 1; Livy I, 43, 13 and II, 21, 7. Livy gives the year 495 B.C. as the year in which the number of the tribus was increased to twenty-one. But it has been rightly pointed out that the twenty-first tribus, the Clustumina, could hardly have been added before the territory which it represented was conquered by the Romans, and that this does not seem to have been the case before about 428 B.C. The suggestion of E. Pais (*Storia di Roma*, Vol. I, Part 1, p. 320) that a passage in Livy (IX, 46, 14) proves that the urban tribus were created as late as 304 (i.e., under the censorship of Q. Fabius and P. Decius), has rightly been almost universally rejected.

54. See Diodorus XX, 36, 4; Livy IX, 46, 11–12. On an earlier occasion (II, 56, 3) Livy says that through the election of the tribunes of the plebs by "comitia tributa" (obviously he means by this a concilium plebis voting by tribus), the clients of the patricians were excluded from the vote. The story in connection with which Livy makes this remark has little claim to historicity, nor is it clear whether Livy means that the clients were excluded as clients or because of some incidental inability. But it is clear that the whole history of the struggle of the plebeians against the patricians, and of the role played by the Concilia Plebis in this struggle, presupposes that the clients had no part in the Concilium Plebis in the period in which clientship in the original sense was still a widespread and living institution. For the

clients would hardly have voted against the wishes of their patrons. It is then most likely that the clients were actually excluded because they were not considered independent owners of land.

55. See text, pp. 5 ff.

56. See text, p. 238.

57. Cicero, *Oratio post reditum in senatu habita*, 10, 25. A most lucid discussion of what we can find out concerning the distribution of voting power in the various popular assemblies in Rome in the different periods, and the influence which could be exercised on various groups of voters, can be found in Scullard, *Politics*, 20 ff.

58. The fundamental work on this subject is still J. Marquardt's *Römische Staatsverwaltung*. For more recent discussions of various aspects of the subject see especially H. Rudolph, *Stadt und Land*, and A. N. Sherwin-White, *Citizenship*. For the question of treaties with allied and conquered nations and the problem of *deditio* see E. Täubler, *Imperium Romanum* (Leipzig, 1912) and A. Heuss, "Die völkerrechtlichen Grundlagen der römischen Aussenpolitik," *Klio*, Beiheft XXXI (1933), and "Abschluss und Beurkundung des griechischen und römischen Staatsvertrags," *Klio* (1934). A more complete bibliography will be found on pp. 298 ff. of Sherwin-White's *Citizenship*.

59. Mason Hammond, *City State and World State in Greek and Roman Political Theory until Augustus* (Harvard University Press, 1951).

60. See *ibid.*, pp. 79-80: "Polybius found that it [the Roman constitution] represented . . . the achievement of the balanced form of mixed constitution in which control rested with the wise aristocrats. Thus on the one hand the Romans were regarded as destined for world rule . . . on the other hand the development of the Roman government toward a form capable of imperial responsibilities was stunted because thinking Romans were convinced that their city-state form of government had realized the ideal mixed constitution advocated in orthodox Greek political thought."

61. See J. A. O. Larsen, "Representation and Democracy in Hellenistic Federalism," *Classical Philology*, XL (1945), 65 ff.

62. For a more detailed discussion of this process see K. von Fritz, *Totalitarismus*, pp. 63 ff.

63. In actual fact the secret ballot was introduced in four steps, first by a Lex Gabinia in 139 B.C. for elections, then by a Lex Cassia of 137 for *iudicia populi*, except for cases of *perduellio*, then by a Lex Papiria of 131 for voting on proposed laws, finally in 107 by a Lex Coelia for cases of *perduellio* also. Before these laws were passed the citizens had voted "voce"; afterwards they voted "tabellis." But Cicero was of the opinion that this

should not make the ballot secret but that the voters should show their votes to the best and most responsible citizens (*De legibus*, III, 33–39). In fact, though at the time of Marius devices were created to prevent anyone from approaching the voter when he went to the urn, influencing of the voters during the voting process did not stop even then. Concerning this whole aspect of political life see especially F. B. Marsh, *A History of the Roman World*, pp. 21 ff., and *Modern Problems in the Ancient World* (Texas University Press, 1943), pp. 81 f. See also H. H. Scullard, *Roman Politics 220 to 150 B.C.* (Oxford University Press, 1951), pp. 12 f.

64. The factional struggles and changing alliances within the Roman aristocracy, which can be only touched upon within the present context, have in recent times been made the subject of a number of very careful and detailed studies. See particularly F. Münzer, *Römische Adelsparteien;* Lily Ross Taylor, *Party Politics in the Age of Caesar* (University of California Press, 1949); H. H. Scullard, *Roman Politics;* and R. Syme, *The Roman Revolution* (Oxford University Press, 1939).

65. A good illustration of this is, of course, the well-known anecdote told in slightly different versions by Cicero, *De officiis*, II, 25, 89, and various other ancient authors. According to Cicero, Cato, when asked what was the thing that contributed most to making a farmer prosperous, said "To be successful in raising cattle." What then was the second best? "To be moderately successful with cattle," and third? "To have poor cattle," and fourth? "To grow grain."

66. See the text, 225.

67. See K. von Fritz, *Totalitarismus*, pp. 63 ff.

Chapter X: The Causes of the Downfall of the Roman Republic

1. Montesquieu, *Sur les causes de la grandeur des Romains et de leur décadence*, Chapter 9.

2. *Ibid.*

3. See the text, Chapter IX, pp. 242 ff. and note 59.

4. See Plutarch, *Cato Maior*, 27, and our text, Chapter IV, pp. 92–93.

5. The most important law of this kind was the law against *ambitus* which, according to Livy (*Epitome*, 47), was passed in 159 B.C. It is obviously this law which Polybius has in mind when he says (VI, 56, 4) that in Rome it is a capital crime to buy votes by "gifts," i.e., by money. There had been an earlier second-century law against *ambitus*, the Lex Baebia of

181 B.C. (see Livy XL, 19, 11); and a small fragment (preserved by Nonius, 470) of a speech which the elder Cato some years later made to prevent its revocation seems to indicate that, at least implicitly, this earlier law was also directed against bribery in elections. But what Livy tells about the elections of the preceding years (see Livy XXXVII, 47, 6 and XXXVII, 57, 12 ff.; XXXVIII, 35, 1; XXXIX, 32, 10 ff.; XXXIX, 41, 1; and *passim*) shows that at that time direct bribery by money was not yet the main issue, but rather undue pressure on the voters by influential people, especially magistrates in office, unfairness of the presiding magistrate in presenting the candidates and in handling the voting procedure, tricks by which a candidate was prevented from presenting himself at the election, and so on. The same is of course true to an even higher degree of earlier measures against *ambitus* like the Poetelian plebiscite of 358 (Livy VII, 15) or the edict of the dictator C. Maenius in 314 B.C. (Livy IX, 26, 6 ff.).

This difference between the earlier and the later measures against *ambitus* is very significant. That the buying of votes by direct gifts or money did not play any important role before the middle of the second century B.C. does not mean of course that before then "influence" did not play an enormous role in Roman elections. The opposite is the case. But while influence, pressure, tricks, and even unfair manipulations of the voting procedure had been known long before, the law which made the buying of votes with money a capital crime shows clearly that this was something new, and that at first it was considered an enormity. Yet the harsh law could not be enforced, and some time later the practice which had at first been considered worthy of the death penalty became so common that no laws of any kind prevailed against it.

6. The first *quaestio perpetua* was created through the Lex Calpurnia de Rebus Repetundis in the year 149 B.C. (see Cicero, *Brutus*, 27, 106).

7. See Appian, *De bellis civilibus*, I, 15, 3. In the preceding chapter Appian says that "the wealthy" had objected to the re-election of Ti. Gracchus on the ground that it was illegal for a man to hold the same office in two consecutive years. This seems to have been true of all curule magistracies, though it is known for certain only of the censorship and the consulship, for which iteration had been altogether prohibited by law since 264 and 151 B.C. respectively. But it is doubtful whether such a law existed for plebeian tribunes, or whether it had merely become a well-established custom to observe the same rules for tribunes of the plebs as for curule magistrates after the tribuneship had become an aristocratic office like the others. The decisive factor was undoubtedly the intercession of the other tribunes, but

this intercession may very well have been justified by the claim that Tiberius with his second candidacy was violating the *mos maiorum*.

8. This emergency decree—if it is historical, the first ever to be passed by the Roman Senate—is mentioned explicitly only by Valerius Maximus III, 17, though it may be hinted at by Plutarch, *Tiberius Gracchus*, 18. For this reason, and also because the consul refused to act accordingly, the historicity of this first *senatus consultum ultimum* is questioned by many modern scholars. However, it is difficult to account for the fact that the men who had slain Tiberius were not tried, unless the Senate had formally expressed its opinion that the state was in danger, and both Plutarch and Appian indicate that the request addressed to the consul by Scipio Nasica to take action against Tiberius, upon which the consul answered that he would not kill a Roman citizen without trial, was preceded by similar requests of the majority of the Senate. At any rate there can hardly be any doubt that a large section, probably the majority of the Senate, expressed the opinion that the state was in danger and that extraordinary measures must be taken to cope with this situation. But this is essentially the meaning of an emergency decree of the Senate (see the text, Chapter VIII, pp. 215 ff.).

9. H. Last, in his excellent chapters on the period of the Gracchi in the *Cambridge Ancient History* (IX, p. 26), has tried to show that even under the changed conditions of the second century B.C. tribunician intercession still had a very important function which was beneficial to the state. For, he argues, without tribunician intercession the Senate would have had no check whatever on legislation introduced by any magistrate in a popular assembly after it had lost the auctoritas in its original form (see text, p. 174). However, though it is true that at a time when the plebeian tribunes had become accustomed to feeling above all as members of the senatorial aristocracy, the Senate could, and actually did, use tribunician intercession for this purpose, and though such intercession was undoubtedly sometimes beneficial, it is not difficult to see that what Last is really pleading for is that the auctoritas patrum in the original sense, the power of the Senate to withhold ratification of a law passed by an assembly of the people, should never have been abolished, since it placed a wholesome check on ill-considered legislation. Tribunician intercession was certainly a very poor and dangerous substitute for this right of the Senate, for it replaced the right of the Senate as a body with the right of ten individual tribunes, and since the tribunes were in no way obliged to obey the Senate, this meant that in fact any minority group in the Senate, if it could win the support of any one of these ten tribunes, could exercise a right which in the old time only the majority of

the Senate or of its patrician members had been entitled to exercise. Tiberius Gracchus was absolutely right in his conviction that such a use of tribunician intercession was totally contrary to the meaning and purpose of this institution.

10. According to Appian, *De bellis civilibus*, I, 12, 5, Tiberius asked the people "whether a tribune opposing the will of the people could retain his office."

11. Though Tiberius contemplated also the introduction of supplementary legislation for his second term of office, all ancient authors agree that fear for his life was the main cause for his seeking re-election, and there is no reason to doubt that the threats against his life actually played an important role in his insistence that he be admitted as a candidate in spite of the intercession of his colleagues.

12. This Scipio Nasica (Serapio) was the son of the Scipio Nasica (Corculum) who is said to have had the famous dispute with the elder Cato concerning the desirability of the preservation or destruction of Carthage (see the text, p. 92).

13. See Plutarch, *Tiberius Gracchus*, 19.

14. Until recently it had been generally assumed that the sudden rise of the Roman census figures from 318,823 in 131/30 B.C. to 394,736 in 125/24 B.C. represented the approximate number of families settled on newly created farms in Italy according to the agrarian laws of Tiberius Gracchus, which would mean that some seventy-six thousand farms had been newly created. In fact, there can be no doubt that there must have been some special reason for the increase in the census figures, for the increase between 136/35 and 131/30 was only 890, and between 125/24 and 115/14, i.e. in twice the time only 600, an enormous difference from the increase of 76,000 in the five years from 130 to 125. Recently, however, the accuracy of this inference has been questioned, partly on chronological grounds (the increase should have begun before 130, since the commission began its work in 133 B.C.), and partly on other grounds. The chronological argument has not much force if one considers that considerable preparations were necessary before the actual settlement of peasants could begin. Some other arguments which cannot be discussed here have perhaps more weight. But it is hardly possible to escape the conclusion that the extraordinary increase in the census figures between 130 and 125 must have had something to do either directly or indirectly with the implementation of Tiberius' agrarian law, which had come to an end in 125 B.C. In addition, the legislation of C. Gracchus appears to indicate that the public land possessed by private Roman citizens which was scheduled to be distributed by the agrarian

law had actually been distributed by that time. For details see Marsh, 46 ff., and Scullard's notes, *ibid.*, 407 f.

15. See Festus, p. 286, s.v. *res publica;* Cicero *De officiis,* III, 11, 47.

16. See Appian, *De bellis civilibus,* I, 34, 4: ὡς κοινωνοὺς τῆς ἡγεμονίας ἀντὶ ὑπηκόων ἐσομένους.

17. *Ibid.,* and Valerius Maximus IX, 5, 1.

18. Tiberius Gracchus had realized that the new farmers would need some money to start their farms and had proposed, and probably carried, a law providing that part of the large treasure willed to the Roman state by the Pergamene king Attalus III was to be used for that purpose. At any rate, it is clear that such money was made available.

19. The Romans had of course made use of foreign auxiliary troops ever since they had concluded alliances with nations or cities outside of Italy, but not until many years later did they draft provincials to serve in the Roman legions.

20. The chronology of the legislation of Caius Gracchus and many details concerning its content are anything but clear in the ancient tradition. The most convincing reconstruction offered so far, it seems to me, is that attempted by H. Last in the chapters which he devoted to this question in the *Cambridge Ancient History* (IX, 49 ff.). But there are many details in regard to which it will probably never be possible to arrive at a really well-founded conclusion. Most of these questions, however, fortunately are of no great importance for our subject.

21. The law was undoubtedly more specific, but ancient tradition about it is so vaguely expressed that it is hardly possible to determine exactly what its provisions were. Plutarch (*Gaius Gracchus,* 4) says that the law was directed against a magistrate who exiled or executed a Roman citizen without trial (ἄκριτον). But Tiberius' adherents appear to have been tried by a senatorial court under the chairmanship of Popilius Laenas. Cicero (*Pro Rabirio ad quirites* 4, 12) says: "C. Gracchus legem tulit ne de capite civium Romanorum iniussu vestro iudicaretur, hic popularis [sc. Labienus] a IIviris iniussu vestro non iudicari de cive Romano sed indicta causa civem Romanum capitis condemnari coegit." This has been taken to mean that decisions of law courts were also to be subject to the *provocatio ad populum* if capital punishment was involved. But the wording does not seem to favor this explanation. Whatever the exact meaning of the law may have been, however, its political purpose is quite clear.

22. Plutarch, *Gaius Gracchus,* 4: τὸν μὲν (sc. νόμον εἰσεφερε) εἴ τινος ἄρχοντος ἀφῃρῆτο .τὴν ἀρχὴν ὁ δῆμος οὐκ ἐῶντα τούτῳ δευτέρας ἀρχῆς μετουσίαν εἶναι.

23. I do not mention in this context the Lex Sempronia concerning the law courts, though some scholars place it in C. Gracchus' first tribuneship and consider it as part of his preparatory legislation. As pointed out above (Chapter VII, note 31), Appian (*De bellis civilibus*, I, 22), Tacitus (*Annales*, XII, 60), and Diodorus (XXXVII, 9) attribute to C. Gracchus a bill transferring the law courts from the senators to the equites. But Plutarch (*Gaius Gracchus*, 5) says that C. Gracchus' law provided that the members of the law courts were to be drawn *not only* from the Senate *but also* from a selected number of three hundred equites. Appian (*De bellis civilibus*, I, 35) attributes this latter law to the younger Livius Drusus, and Velleius Paterculus (II, 13) says that the younger Livius Drusus tried to give the law courts back to the senators but was opposed by the Senate itself. In the *Epitome* of Livy (LX) the version is that C. Gracchus introduced a bill to increase the number of the senators from three hundred to nine hundred. Finally the Lex Acilia de Repetundis, introduced and carried on the instigation of C. Gracchus but officially sponsored by his fellow tribune Acilius Glabrio, excluded senators from juries in trials *de repetundis*. The problems presented by these varied and partly conflicting ancient testimonies have so far defied a completely satisfactory explanation. All that can be said with some confidence is that C. Gracchus in all likelihood introduced some legislation concerning the composition of the law courts during his first tribuneship; but the exclusion of senators from the law courts was probably a second step, effected during Caius' second tribuneship by his fellow tribune Acilius Glabrio. Later the different measures were obviously confused. For a very thorough discussion of the problem see H. Last in *Cambridge Ancient History*, IX, 52 ff. and 892 ff. See also Scullard's note in Marsh, 409-10.

24. See Plutarch, *Gaius Gracchus*, 5.

25. *Ibid.*, 9.

26. See *ibid.*, 10; *Corpus Inscriptionum Latinarum*, I, 198 and 200; see also *Fontes juris Romani anteiustiniani*, Pars Prima iterum ed. S. Riccobono (Florence, 1941), pp. 84 ff. and 102 ff.; Livy, *Periocha*, 60; Velleius I, 15; Appian, *De bellis civilibus* I, 24. The date of Rubrius' tribunate is contested, some scholars placing it in the year 124/23 instead of 123/22; see E. Kornemann in *Klio*, Beiheft I, pp. 46 ff., and Eduard Meyer, *Kleine Schriften*, 413. But the bill can hardly be dated before the agrarian laws of Livius Drusus, if what Plutarch says about the latter is correct. See H. M. Last, *Cambridge Ancient History*, IX, 891 f.

27. Velleius II, 7, 5.

28. See Appian, *De bellis civilibus*, I, 24, 4; Plutarch, *Gaius Gracchus*, 11.

29. Concerning the Lex Acilia see above, note 23.

30. See Plutarch, *Gaius Gracchus*, 13–18; Appian, *De bellis civilibus*, I, 25–26.

31. For details see K. von Fritz in *Transactions of the American Philological Association*, LXXIV (1943), 146 ff.

32. See Plutarch, *Marius*, 4.

33. *Ibid.* According to Plutarch, Cotta induced the Senate "to fight" Marius' bill. Since the Senate had no right to invalidate a plebiscite it is not quite clear what this means, and unfortunately Plutarch does not make it clear either whether the action of Cotta and the Senate took place before or after Marius' bill had been passed by the people. In the first case the Senate might have tried to prevent it from being passed by inducing other tribunes to intercede, though since its experience with Tiberius Gracchus the Senate appears to have been reluctant to use this device against tribunes. Or it may simply have been a vote of censure (i.e., an expression of the opinion of the Senate that the law was contrary to the interests of the state), in which case Marius may have justified his action against the consul by arguing that by asking for a vote of censure he was showing disrespect to the assembly of the plebs and to its constitutionally elected tribune.

34. See Plutarch, *Marius*, 8; Sallust, *Jugurtha*, 78.

35. There appear to have been two different bills, one for the settlement of veterans and proletarians in Cisalpine Gaul, the other for the establishment of colonies overseas; but the two bills obviously formed part of one plan. See Cicero, *Pro Sesto*, 37, 101; Appian, *De bellis civilibus*, I, 29–31; Cicero, *Pro Balbo*, 21, 48–49; (Aurelius Victor), *De viris illustribus*, 73.

36. Cicero, *Pro Balbo*, 21, 48: "ut in singulas colonias ternos civis Romanos facere posset." This is so small a number that the provision could hardly have caused strong resentment among the city proletariat in Rome, as Appian (I, 29) affirms. Obviously, if the figure in the Cicero manuscripts is correct, the law must have contained other provisions concerning the participation of Italians without full Roman citizenship in the settlements.

37. Appian, *De bellis civilibus*, I, 29; see also the preceding note.

38. This law is mentioned only by (Cicero), *Ad Herennium*, I, 21, without date, and a number of scholars (F. W. Robinson, "Marius, Saturninus, and Glaucia," in *Jenaer historische Arbeiten*, III [Bonn, 1912], 63 ff.; Last, in *Cambridge Ancient History*, IX, 165; Passerini, and others) have tried to prove that it must belong in Saturninus' first tribuneship in 103 B.C. The arguments (mostly based on numismatic evidence) set forth for this assumption, however, are not convincing; and it does not appear likely that a bill which must have brought Saturninus in conflict with Marius should

have belonged to his first tribunate. See also T. R. Broughton, *The Magistrates of the Roman Republic*, I (New York, 1951), 578, notes 3 and 5.

39. Plutarch, *Marius*, 29: τῷ νόμῳ πειθαρχήσειν εἴπερ ἔστι νόμος.

40. Appian I, 36; cf. (Aurelius Victor), *De viris illustribus*, 4: "Latinis civitatem, plebi agros, equitibus curiam, senatui iudicia permisit."

41. See Cicero, *De domo*, 16, 41: "iudicavit senatus M. Drusi legibus, quae contra legem Caeciliam et Didiam latae essent, populum non teneri"; and *ibid.*, 20, 53: "quae est sententia Caeciliae legis et Didiae nisi haec ne populo necesse sit in coniunctis rebus compluribus aut id quod nolit accipere aut id quod velit repudiare?"

42. See Velleius Paterculus II, 29, 1: "ex agro Piceno qui totus paternis eius clientelis refertus erat contraxit exercitum" (sc. in 83 B.C.).

43. The tradition concerning the enrollment of the new citizens is contradictory and confused. According to Appian (I, 49, 4) ten new tribus were added to the thirty-five which remained reserved for the old citizens, while Velleius (II, 20, 2) says that the new citizens were to be distributed over eight (of the existing?) tribus. All ancient authors, however, agree that the arrangement was made in such a way as to restrict the influence of the new citizens.

44. According to Appian, *De bellis civilibus*, I, 55, 5, the consuls announced a long series of religious holidays during which no public business could be transacted. The announcement of such holidays (*feriae conceptivae* or *imperativae*), for instance to atone for some offense against the gods or to avert bad omens, was within the competence of the consuls. But it was of course a flagrant abuse of this competence to use it in order to prevent a vote on a bill introduced in a popular assembly.

45. Appian, *De bellis civilibus*, I, 59. The wording of this passage suggests that the old "Servian" order of the Comitia Centuriata was restored. See the text, pp. 130 and 238, with note 52.

46. For these and the following events see Appian, *De bellis civilibus*, I, 64 ff.

47. See K. von Fritz, *Leges sacratae*.

48. See the text, pp. 211 ff.

49. Livy, *Epitome*, 61; cf. Cicero, *De oratore*, II, 25, 106 and II, 30, 132.

50. Cicero, *Oratio in Catilinam quarta*.

51. See the text, pp. 228 ff.

52. In Livy, *Epitome*, 89, it is stated in clear terms that the tribunes of the plebs lost the *ius rogandi*. The arguments that have been set forth against this tradition are not conclusive, as H. M. Last has shown in *Cambridge An-*

NOTES TO PAGES 284-87

cient History, IX, 896. But even if the statement in the epitome of the work of Livy should be inexact and the legislative initiative of the tribunes was merely made subject to the auctoritas of the Senate, in the strict sense that they could introduce bills only *ex auctoritate senatus*, the practical result was not very different.

53. Cicero (*Actio secunda in Verrem*, I, 60, 155) says that the tribune of the year 75 B.C., Q. Opimius, was put on trial and punished by a very heavy fine "quod contra legem Corneliam intercessisset," i.e. because he had used or tried to use his power of intercession in violation of the Lex Cornelia, i.e., Sulla's constitution. Unfortunately we do not know in what cases tribunician intercession was prohibited by Sulla's laws.

54. The Lex Villia Annalis of 180 B.C. appears to have fixed the *ordo magistratuum* or *cursus honorum*, prescribing the sequence quaestor, praetor, consul; and, according to Livy (XL, 44, 2), it also prescribed a minimum age for each of these magistracies. But the details of the law are uncertain.

55. Such a demand had been made by the Genucian plebiscite of the year 342 B.C. But this plebiscite had obviously never become a law and was not observed in the elections beyond the year 330 B.C. (see text, Chapter IX, pp. 222 f., and note 6). In the middle of the second century a law seems to have been passed forbidding re-election to the consulate altogether. Cf. Livy, *Epitome*, 56, and the reference to a speech by Cato "ne quis iterum consul fiat" in Festus, p. 242 M. See also above, note 7.

56. See Cicero, *In L. Pisonem*, 21, 50.

57. Cicero, *Ad familiares*, III, 6, 3.

58. See text, Chapter VII, pp. 171 ff.

59. See Cicero, *De provinciis consularibus*, 3.

60. Cicero, *In L. Pisonem*, 21, 50; for other provisions of the Lex Cornelia maiestatis see Tacitus, *Annales*, I, 72; Cicero, *Ad familiares*, III, 11, 2; *Pro Cluentio*, 35, 97; *Actio secunda in Verrem*, II, 1, 12.

61. The term "written constitution" is perhaps slightly misleading, since Sulla's legislation did not supersede all previously existing laws that we would call constitutional, except in so far as they were expressly abolished. Yet since it marks the most important step, and in a way is the only attempt ever made, in the whole history of the Roman constitution (with the possible exception of the Valerio-Horatian laws, whose scope, however, was unquestionably much more limited), to create a whole body of formulated and written constitutional law at one stroke, the term used is perhaps not quite inappropriate in the context.

62. Since the main events of the period after Sulla, as far as they have to be mentioned in our context, are on the whole well known and well at-

tested, I do not give the testimonies in the notes as I have done in regard to the less well attested and much more controversial events of the preceding period. A most careful and complete list of the testimonies can be found in M. Gelzer's *Pompeius*.

63. See text, p. 279 and note 42.

64. See Eduard Meyer, *Caesars Monarchie und das Principat des Pompeius*, 3d edition (Stuttgart, 1922), and for a somewhat different view of Pompey's character, attitude, and aspirations, see M. Gelzer's *Pompeius*. See also K. von Fritz, "Pompey's Policy Before and After the Outbreak of the Civil War of 49 B.C.," *Transactions of the American Philological Association*, LXXIII (1942), 145 ff.

65. See, for instance, W. E. Heitland, *The Roman Republic* (Cambridge, 1923), II, 323.

66. For details see K. von Fritz, *Totalitarismus*, pp. 63 ff.

67. See the text, pp. 247 ff., 279, and 288.

68. See *Res gestae divi Augusti*, XXXIV, VI, 21–23: "potestatis autem nihil amplius habui quam qui fuerunt mihi quoque in magistratu collegae." It is most significant how the word "potestas" in this sentence has become ambiguous. All through the period of the Republic it designates the civil power which a magistrate has in virtue of his office. This was of course a very real power, though limited by law. It is of course perfectly true that whenever Augustus saw fit to assume the consulship he had formally the same functions and powers as his colleague in the consulate. But it is no less true that no consul would have dared to make use of the principle *in re pari maior causa prohibentis* against Augustus, and that generally speaking, whether Augustus at some given moment was consul or not, any conflict between him and a consul would have shown at once that the consul had his *potestas* only through the consent of Augustus.

69. Tacitus, *Annales*, XIII, 4, especially the last sentence: "teneret antiqua munia senatus, consulum tribunalibus Italia et publicae provinciae assisterent: illi patrum aditum praeberent, se mandatis exercitibus consulturum."

70. See K. von Fritz, *Totalitarismus*, pp. 69 ff.

CHAPTER XI: CONCLUSIONS

1. See text, Chapter VII.
2. Hobbes, *Leviathan*, Chapter 19.
3. *Ibid.*, Chapter 26.
4. *Ibid.*, Chapter 19.

5. *Ibid.*, Chapter 29.

6. *Ibid.*, Chapter 19: "as of old time in Sparta, where the kings had the privilege to lead their armies but the sovereignty was in the ephori."

7. *Ibid.*, Chapter 17.

8. *Ibid.*, Chapter 20.

9. There is another piece of specious reasoning in Hobbes' Chapter 18: "This great authority being indivisible and inseparably annexed to the sovereignty there is little ground for the opinion of them that say of sovereign kings though they be *singulis majores*, of greater power than every one of their subjects, yet they be *universis minores*, of less power than them all together. For if by all together they mean not the collective body as one person, then all together, and every one, signify the same and the speech is absurd. But if by all together they understand them as one person (which person the sovereign bears) then the power of all together is the same with the sovereign's power and so again the speech is absurd." But the king is not *singulis major*, except by being obeyed by the people, or by his soldiers, or by his executive organs, etc., and the question, if we are not to lose ourselves in purely abstract arguments that have no relation to reality, is exactly why and by whom and under what conditions and with what limitations, if any, he is obeyed.

10. See the text, pp. 187 ff.

11. Hobbes, *Leviathan*, Chapter 19.

12. Aristotle, *Politics*, 1292a, 29 ff.; 1293a, 38 ff.; 1294b, 8 ff.; and *passim*.

13. Hobbes, *Leviathan*, Chapter 19.

14. On this point see K. von Fritz, "Conservative Reaction and One-Man Rule in Ancient Greece," *Political Science Quarterly*, LVI (1941), 51 ff.

15. See, for instance, Arrianus, *Alexandri anabasis*, III, 23, 4; VI, 2, 1; VII, 24, 4, mostly from Ptolemy I; and Plutarch, *Eumenes*, 3–5, from Hieronymus of Cardia. It is also noteworthy that in some of the stories told in the passages mentioned a sovereign gives a high-ranking subject of a defeated enemy sovereign a position of great trust because of the latter's loyalty to his former master. This shows how loyalty is considered an objective quality, as something given to the sovereign as sovereign, i.e., as the incorporation of the legal order, not to him as to an individual person.

16. See Livy II, 18, 8; II, 30, 4 ff.; VI, 38 ff.; and *passim*. The details of the stories told by Livy on these occasions and, in the earliest cases, even the dictatorships themselves, are of course, of doubtful historicity. But what matters in our context is the general idea of the function of dictators in

the conflict between plebeians and patricians. This idea, which as Livy shows, was widely accepted in later times, must at least be based on some kind of oral tradition.

17. In the ninth chapter of his treatise on the constitution of Athens Aristotle enumerates the democratic features of the constitution of Solon and designates as the most important of them the fact that the courts established by him consisted of large juries on which citizens of any class selected by the lot could serve. "For," he adds, "when the people have the right to vote in the courts, they are the masters of the state."

Yet, if one considers this observation in the light of the history of Athens, it does not contradict what has been said above in the text, but rather confirms it. It is certainly true that the jury courts constituted the most democratic feature of the semi-oligarchic, semi-democratic constitution of Solon. But they never constituted a revolutionary element either under this or any of the later Athenian constitutions.

18. See, for instance, Livy II, 41 ff.

19. See Aristotle, *Politics*, II, 1266a, 39 ff., and our text, pp. 78 f.

20. Herodotus VII, 101 ff.

21. For a discussion of this totally different problem in the light of ancient history see K. von Fritz, *Totalitarismus*.

APPENDIX I: EXCERPTS FROM POLYBIUS' "HISTORY" CONCERNED WITH HIS POLITICAL THEORY

1. This term is found for the first time in Polybius and had not been used by Plato and Aristotle.

2. The Greek word translated in this book "rule of violence" and "anarchy" is χειροκρατία, which, literally translated, means "rule of the hand" or "rule of the fist," and must be distinguished from ὀχλοκρατία, i.e. ochlocracy or mob rule.

3. In the Greek text it is not quite clear to which part of the sentence the words "because of its adherence to tradition" were meant to be related grammatically. Since in the Greek they are inserted near the word ἐλαττουμένων ("being oppressed"), it is possible to argue that they must be connected with this word, so that the meaning would be "if one element is in danger of being oppressed because of its adherence to (or reverence for) tradition." But it is difficult to believe that this is what Polybius had in mind, since it would make his statement less general than it must have been intended to be, judging from the context. It is the purpose of a mixed constitu-

tion to prevent any of the components of the state from being oppressed by any of the others, regardless of the cause of the oppression. On the other hand, since a system of checks and balances establishes a tradition of preventing oppression, it may very well be said that a governmental agency which by its very nature will have a special reverence for tradition is particularly fit to prevent oppression.

4. I did not include in my translation a number of fragments of the sixth book of Polybius which in the edition of Polybius' history by Büttner-Wobst precede the following fragment, because they did not appear to be relevant to the subject of my book. The most extensive of these fragments tells at length how the Romans used to kiss their wives in order to find out whether they had consumed wine, which they were not supposed to do.

5. Though in regard to the main point, at least, the correct interpretation of the first part of this sentence was given more than seventy years ago by Eduard Meyer in an article in *Rheinisches Museum*, XXXVII (1882), 622 ff., it is still misunderstood by many editors, who, as Meyer rightly said, "against all reason" change the figure given in the text, and also by many translators and commentators. Since the passage is of crucial importance both for the reconstruction of Polybius' account of the development of the Roman Republic and for a full understanding of his analysis of the Roman constitution at the time of its highest perfection, it appears necessary to discuss the question briefly. The Greek text, as we find it in the excerpts *De sententiis* (see our text, p. 32) runs as follows: ὅτι ἀπὸ τῆς Ξέρξου διαβάσεως εἰς τὴν Ἑλλάδα καὶ τριάκοντα ἔτεσιν ὕστερον ἀπὸ τούτων τῶν καιρῶν ἀεὶ τῶν κατὰ μέρος προδιευκρινουμένων ἦν (sc. τὸ τῶν Ῥωμαίων πολίτευμα) καὶ κάλλιστον καὶ τέλειον ἐν τοῖς Ἀννιβαϊκοῖς καιροῖς ἀφ'ὧν ἡμεῖς εἰς ταῦτα τὴν ἐκτροπὴν ἐποιησάμεθα. διόπερ καὶ τὸν ὑπὲρ τῆς συστάσεως αὐτοῦ λόγον ἀποδεδωκότες πειρασόμεθα νῦν ἤδη διασαφεῖν ὁποῖόν τι κατ' ἐκείνους ὑπῆρχε τοὺς καιρούς. This sentence is undoubtedly very awkward, and many editors of the text have therefore assumed that there was a lacuna in the beginning, which they then tried to fill in in various ways. However, any attempt to arrive at a correct interpretation of the text should start from two fundamental considerations: (1) that we have here an extract from the work of Polybius, and that the original syntax of the statement may have been obscured by abbreviation; (2) that Polybius, speaking of a famous event of Greek history in a purely Roman context, obviously wished to synchronize an important event of Greek history with an equally important event of Roman history. It is then absurd to assume that the two events could have been separated by a period of three hundred years or more, as many editors who changed the figures in the text have assumed. At the same time

it can then hardly be a coincidence that 30 years after the crossing of Xerxes into Europe is the date of the *decemviri legibus scribundis* who published the laws of the Twelve Tables, and that according to the tradition this event (after an interval of another year in which the last two of the Twelve Tables were compiled and published) was followed by the second secession of the plebs and subsequently by the Valerio-Horatian laws. If these laws are accepted as historical, they may very well be said to have laid the foundation of a system of checks and balances between the patricians and the plebeians. Neither the figure 30 nor its relation to the date of the crossing of Xerxes should therefore be essentially changed, however awkward the expression in the Greek text of the manuscripts may be. It is just barely possible that a small figure before the figure 30 has fallen out in the text, since, as Meyer pointed out, it is likely that Polybius dated the Valerio-Horatian laws in the year 447 B.C. But this detail is of very small importance.

A second problem is presented by the words ἀεὶ τῶν κατὰ μέρος προδιευκρινουμένων ἦν καὶ κάλλιστον καὶ τέλειον ἐν τοῖς Ἀννιβαϊκοῖς. If what has been said about the synchronism is correct, these words cannot mean "it was always one of those polities which were an object of special study," as some modern commentators have understood, since the Roman constitution certainly was not an object of special study all through the period from 450 B.C. down to the Hannibalic War. The word διευκρινεῖσθαι, however, has two meanings: "to elucidate" and "to arrange well." Accepting the second meaning, one might understand: "it was always one of those constitutions that were well arranged in detail and it was most excellent and perfect at the time of the Hannibalic War." There remain, however, two difficulties. The προ in προδιευκρινουμένων is not accounted for, and the κατὰ μέρος does not make very much sense. For the point would be that the constitution was well arranged, not that it was well arranged in detail. Apart from this the position ἀπὸ κοινοῦ of the word ἦν would be somewhat awkward, though this is not a decisive point, considering Polybius' sloppy and somewhat awkward style. If all these difficulties are taken together, it appears preferable to take the first words as a genitive absolute and to translate as above in the text. The present tense of the participle προδιευκρινουμένων would then indicate the long process in which the detail of the political structure became more and more well arranged and the προ would mean that this long process preceded the state of perfection reached at the time of the Hannibalic War. In other words—and this is of fundamental importance—Polybius, according to this interpretation, distinguishes two high points in the development of the Roman constitution: (1) the time of the Twelve Tables and of the Valerio-Horatian Laws, when, as the result of a long process and a semirevolution concluding it, the Roman constitution for the first time became a mixed constitution in the full sense of the word; and (2) the time of the Hannibalic War, when as the result of a long process of further adjustments in details (κατὰ μέρος), this mixed constitution had reached the point of its greatest perfection. When, in the following sentence, Polybius says that he has given account of the σύστασις of this order, i.e. the way in which it first came into being, he clearly refers to the first of the processes mentioned, not to the process of greater perfection in detail. All this is in perfect agreement with the results of the analysis in our sixth chapter of the traces of Polybius' account of the development of the Roman constitution.

6. The expressions used by Polybius in this sentence are rather vague. "Common affairs" may simply mean "public affairs." But then it is difficult to see what the contrast would be, especially since the word appears to be emphasized. So it *may* mean affairs that are the common concern of the Senate and the people, in the sense that the acts of the Senate must be confirmed by the assembly of the people in order to become valid, as, for instance, agreements with foreign nations. This interpretation is to some extent supported by the fact that such affairs are not mentioned in the remaining part of the enumeration of various ways in which the Senate is "checked" by the people.

7. This passage of the third book was inserted by Polybius on the occasion of the appointment as dictator of the great Q. Fabius Maximus (Cunctator), in order to explain the meaning of the Latin word "dictator" to his Greek readers. Its last sentence obviously refers to the sixth book. In the extant parts of that book no reference to the office of a dictator is found. The question therefore arises in the lost parts of which section or sections (concerning these sections see the text, pp. 123 ff.) he dealt with the matter "more accurately" or more in detail.

The matter *may* have been discussed (1) in Polybius' survey of the early development of the Roman constitution at the point when the dictatorship was first introduced shortly after the abolition of kingship, (2) in Polybius' analysis of the Roman constitution at the time of the Hannibalic War and shortly thereafter, and (3) in connection with his description of Roman military institutions. In Chapter VI (pp. 133 ff.) it has been shown that a passage in Cicero's De re publica, in which the institution of dictatorship is discussed, is probably derived from Polybius. What Cicero says in that passage appears, however, to disagree completely with what Polybius says in the passage in the third book which is translated above. For in that passage Polybius finds the main difference between the dictator and the consuls in the former's greater independence of the Senate, pointing out at the same time that the power of the tribunes of the plebs is the only one that is not affected by the appointment of a dictator. Cicero, on the contrary, in the passage mentioned (II, 56) says that when a dictator was first appointed the direction of public affairs nevertheless remained firmly in the hands of the "first men of the state," i.e., the ruling aristocracy represented by the Senate, while the people had to give way.

This apparent contradiction, however, can be easily explained by pointing out that the two passages refer to different phases in the development of the Roman constitution. According to Cicero the institution of the dictatorship was introduced some time before the tribunes of the plebs acquired any official status in the public order at all, and we know that it continued to be exempt both from tribunician intercession and from the *provocatio ad populum* for a long time after the Valerio-Horatian Laws had given legal sanction to the most important political powers of the plebeian tribunes. In this time, and especially before the Valerio-Horatian Laws, a dictator, no less than the consuls, was not only a functionary of the community, but above all an agent of the ruling patrician aristocracy, by which he would be controlled even though he did not legally have to obey the orders of the Senate. In the time of the Hannibalic War, on the contrary, the dictator had become subject both to the *provocatio ad populum* and to tribunician intercession. On the other hand, since all the executive power was vested in him, he was much freer than the consuls from that indirect control over the latter which the Senate had acquired in virtue of the fact that the executive functions were divided among the two consuls and a number of other functionaries of the state (see the text, Chapter VII).

Thus the greater "accuracy" of Polybius' account of the dictatorship in the sixth book which he promises in his short explanation of the nature of that institution in the third book may for a large part have consisted in his pointing out the difference between the position of the dictator in the early and in the later Republic. Whether he did this in the section on the early development of the Roman constitution, in which, as the Cicero passage indicates, he must almost certainly have dealt with the dictatorship, or whether he also inserted a discussion of this institution into his analysis of the Roman constitution "in its prime," i.e. at the time of the Hannibalic War, cannot be decided with certainty. The latter assumption would seem to presuppose that Polybius supplemented his analysis of the checks and balances in the Roman constitution by a discussion of emergency institutions, as has been done above in Chapter VIII. But if there was such a discussion no trace of it has been preserved.

8. "Without a master" is a literal translation of the Greek word

ἀδέσποτον. Since the word κυβερνήτης, which in the following sentences has been translated by "pilot," means also "captain," one may wonder how a boat that has a captain can be called a boat without a master. But δεσπότης means a master with real authority, a master who is obeyed without question. In this sense then a boat that has a captain can be called a boat without a master if the captain has no authority over his crew.

9. The Greek expression is τῆς πολιτικῆς χώρας. This means obviously the land owned by or assigned to the full Spartan citizens, in contrast to the land owned by the Perioeci. According to the tradition, that part of the country which belonged to the full Spartan citizens was divided into lots containing an approximately equal acreage of arable and grain-producing land. These lots could not be sold; but it appears to have been possible for several lots to become the property of one man (or woman) through inheritance, which is at variance with Polybius' statement. See the text, Chapter V, pp. 108 and 113, with notes, and Appendix III.

10. What Polybius means is that the victory in a naval battle did not so much depend on the nautical skill (and bravery) of the crews of the ships as on the fighting skill and bravery of the (land) soldiers stationed on the ships. This was not always so in the long history of ancient naval warfare and naval tactics. In fact one can observe that there were alternating periods in which naval battles tended to be turned into land battles (so that, as Polybius says, the military qualities of the land soldiers stationed on the ships would be the decisive factor), and periods in which the skill of the crews in maneuvering the ships was decisive. In the first case the ships would approach one another until the soldiers of one boat could jump on the deck of the other boat and fight it out as if they were fighting on land. In the second case each ship would try to sink the other by ramming it, i.e. by driving its bow, which was fortified by bronze or iron, into the side of the other boat.

Thucydides (I, 49, 1), in describing the battle of Sybota, the first naval battle of the Peloponnesian War, says that the Corinthian and Corcyrian warships were still equipped ἀπειρότερον (i.e., in a way indicating less experience and skill), and in the old-fashioned manner, namely with heavy-armed soldiers, archers, and light-armed javelin-throwers fighting from the decks, implying that in the further course of the war these old-fashioned tactics were largely replaced by the modern ramming tactics which required more experience and skill. But the description of the battle of Salamis by Aeschylus, who had participated in it, shows (*Persae*, 408 ff.) that the ramming tactics had been used that early, with great success. It is however perhaps significant that Herodotus, who wrote shortly before the Peloponnesian

War, in describing the same battle, does not mention ramming at all, except in one case, in which one Persian ship, fleeing from a Greek one, rammed and sank another Persian ship that blocked its way.

Later the Carthaginians used the ramming tactics with even greater skill than the Greeks. But early in the First Punic War the Romans invented a new device, the so-called corvus or raven, which made it possible for them to drag an enemy toward themselves, to hold it, and to let their soldiers board it so that the sea battle would again be turned into a land battle as in the times of old (see Polybius I, 22).

APPENDIX II: POLYBIUS' CONCEPT OF TYCHE AND THE PROBLEM OF THE DEVELOPMENT OF HIS THOUGHT

1. The following analysis of Polybius' concept of Τύχη, and the section in Konrat Ziegler's article "Polybios" in Pauly-Wissowa dealing with the same problem, were written at about the same time and without our having been in communication with each other in that period. When later, however, we exchanged our manuscripts (see Preface), it turned out that we had arrived at very similar results. In the main points, in fact, they were nearly identical. Since, however, my arguments are for the most part different from his, and since Ziegler naturally did not emphasize what is most important in the context of this book, namely the close analogy between the problem of Polybius' use of the concept of Τύχη and the problem of the apparent contradictions in his theory of the rationally constructed versus the naturally developed mixed constitution, it appeared justifiable to publish the following analysis also. The fact that we arrived at nearly the same conclusions independently may perhaps be considered an argument in favor of the validity of these conclusions.

2. Polybius I, 86, 7.

3. *Ibid.*, II, 4, 3.

4. *Ibid.*, XXXVIII, 18, 8.

5. *Ibid.*, XXIII, 10, 12; see also XI, 5, 8 and XXIX, 19, 1.

6. *Ibid.*, XXIX, 22, 2 ff. For a compensation in the opposite direction see XV, 20, 8.

7. *Ibid.*, XXXVI, 13, 2; see also XV, 20, 5 and XXIII, 10, 2.

8. *Ibid.*, XXXII, 4, 3.

9. *Ibid.*, XXXIX, 8, 2.

10. *Ibid.*, I, 63, 9.

11. *Ibid.*, XXXI, 30, 2–3.

12. *Ibid.*, II, 7, 1; see also X, 5, 9.

13. *Ibid.*, XXXVI, 17, 1 ff.

14. *Ibid.*, I, 4, 1, and I, 4, 4.

15. *Ibid.*, I, 63, 9.

16. *Ibid.*, II, 38, 4–5.

17. See Cuntz, pp. 43 ff.

18. See von Scala, pp. 159 ff., and for still another slightly different version of the genetic explanation of the discrepancies in Polybius' views of Tyche, see Laqueur, pp. 254 ff.

19. See *supra*, notes 2–9.

20. For the approximate date of the composition of the last books of Polybius' Histories see the text, p. 36.

21. See Polybius I, 4, 1; I, 4, 4; I, 13, 12; I, 35, 2; II, 2, 10; II, 4, 3; II, 7, 1; II, 35, 5; II, 37, 6.

22. For earlier attempts to solve the problem in this way rather than by way of a "genetic" theory see Hercod, pp. 163 ff., Siegfried, pp. 106 ff., and Mioni, pp. 140 ff.

23. See the text, p. 390.

24. See the passages cited in notes 10–13 above.

25. Polybius XXXVI, 17, 13.

26. *Ibid.*, III, 6, 5 ff.

27. *Ibid.*, XXIX, 21: Polybius does not expressly refer to Rome when reflecting on the downfall of the great Persian power and, later, of the still greater Macedonian power, but the implication is obvious.

28. *Ibid.*, XXXVI, 17, 1 ff.; see the text, pp. 389 f.

29. A late product of this long controversy is Plutarch's little treatise *De Alexandri magni fortuna sive virtute*.

30. Polybius II, 38, 4 ff.

31. See the text, pp. 40 f.

32. Aristotle, *Physics*, II, 5, 196b, 10 ff.

33. Polybius XXXVI, 17, 1 ff.

34. See, for instance, Polybius I, 84, 9; XXIII, 10, 2; XXIX, 21, 1 ff.; XXXIX, 8, 1–2.

35. *Ibid.*, VI, 56, 6 ff.

36. See, for instance, V, 10, 9 ff.

37. In regard to Tyche see the quotation from a philosophical treatise of the peripatetic Demetrius of Phaleron in XXIX, 2 ff.

APPENDIX III: POLYBIUS' CRITICISM OF THE IDEALIZATION OF CRETAN POLITICAL AND SOCIAL INSTITUTIONS

1. Polybius VI, 45, 1.
2. Diogenes Laertius II, 6, 57.
3. See Jacoby III B, 460 (pp. 397 f.).
4. See Ollier, I, 400.
5. Plato, *Laws*, IV, 712e.
6. Strabo X, 4, 16 ff. (p. C 480 ff.); see also Jacoby, II A, 70 F 149.
7. For a very detailed analysis of the evidence see van Effenterre, pp. 77 ff.
8. The existence of the same institution under the same name in Sparta is attested by Plutarch, *Lycurgus*, 16.
9. See S. Luria in *Philologus*, LXXXII (1927), 113 ff.
10. For instance, by Hasebroek, pp. 253 ff.
11. Herodotus I, 65; see also Aristotle, *Politics*, II, 1271b, 23.
12. See, for instance, Ehrenberg, pp. 12 ff., who has, in addition, tried to explain how the tradition that Lycurgus imported the new constitution from Crete may have originated.
13. Aristotle, *Politics*, II, 1270b, 31 ff.
14. Xenophon, *Constitution of the Lacedaemonians*, 14; *Hellenica*, III, 4.

List of Books and Articles Frequently
Cited in the Notes

THIS LIST of books is not intended to represent or to replace a bibliography. A bibliography on all the problems which are discussed or touched upon in the present book would fill a volume of considerable size, and therefore cannot be given. A careful and up-to-date bibliography specifically on Polybius, though not on other problems discussed in this book, will be found in E. Mioni, *Polibio* (Padua, 1949), pp. 155–64. See also the article by Konrat Ziegler on Polybius in Pauly-Wissowa.

References in the notes to books contained in the following list have been made simply by the name of the author, or, where two or more works of the same author are included in the list, by the name of the author plus the most significant word of the title; for instance, Gelzer, *Nobilität*, or Gelzer, *Pompeius*.

Afzelius, A., Den Romerske Nobilitets Omfang. 1935.

Altheim, F., Literatur and Gesellschaft im ausgehenden Altertum. Halle (Saale), 1950.

Beloch, K. J., Römische Geschichte bis zum Beginn der Punischen Kriege. Leipzig, 1922.

Botsford, G. W., The Roman Assemblies. New York, 1909.

Chrimes, K. M. T., Ancient Sparta: A Reexamination of the Evidence. Manchester, 1949.

Coli, Ugo, Regnum. Rome, 1951.

Cuntz, O., Polybius und sein Werk. Leipzig, 1902.

Ehrenberg, V., Neugründer des Staates. Munich, 1925.

Gelzer, M., Die Nobilität der römischen Republik. Leipzig, 1912.

Gelzer, M., Pompeius. 2d ed. Munich, 1948.

Gsell, St., Histoire ancienne de l'Afrique du Nord. Paris, 1918.

Hasebroek, J., Griechische Wirtschafts- und Gesellschaftsgeschichte bis zur Perserzeit. Tübingen, 1931.

Heitland, W. E., The Roman Republic. 3 vols. Cambridge, 1923.

Hercod, R., La conception de l'histoire dans Polybe. Lausanne, 1902.

Jacoby, F., Die Fragmente der griechischen Historiker. Vols. I to II D, Berlin and Leipzig, 1923 to 1930; Vol. III A & B. Leyden, 1943 and 1950.

Kahrstedt, U., Griechisches Staatsrecht. Vol. I. Göttingen, 1922.

Kapp, E. and von Fritz, K., Aristotle's Constitution of Athens and Related Documents, with Introduction and Notes. New York, 1950.

Laqueur, R., Polybius. Leipzig. 1913.

Marsh, F. B., A History of the Roman World from 146 to 30 B.C. 2d ed. by H. Scullard. London, 1952.

Meltzer, O. Geschichte der Karthager. Vol. II. Berlin, 1896.

Meyer, Ernst, Römischer Staat und Staatsgedanke. Zürich, 1920.

Michell, H., Sparta. Cambridge (England), 1950.

Mioni, E., Polibio. Padua, 1949.

Münzer, F., Römische Adelsparteien und Adelsfamilien. Stuttgart, 1920.

Pauly-Wissowa, Real-Encyclopaedie der classischen Altertumswissenschaft.

Pöschl, Victor, Römischer Staat und griechisches Staatsdenken bei Cicero. Berlin, 1936.

Rech, R., Mos Maiorum: Wesen und Wirken der Tradition in Rom. Dissert. Marburg, 1936.

Rudolph, H., Stadt und Staat im römischen Italien. Leipzig, 1935.

Ryffel, H., ΜΕΤΑΒΟΛΗ ΠΟΛΙΤΕΙΩΝ: Der Wandel der Staatsverfassungen. Bern, 1945.

Scullard, H., Roman Politics from 220 to 150 B.C. Oxford, 1951.

Sherwin-White, A. N., The Roman Citizenship. Oxford, 1939.

Siegfried, W., Studien zur geschichtlichen Anschauung des Polybius. Leipzig, 1928.

Taeger, F., Die Archaeologie des Polybius. Stuttgart, 1890.

Täubler, E., Imperium Romanum. Leipzig, 1913.

Taylor, Lily Ross, Party Politics in the Age of Caesar. University of California Press, 1949.

van Effenterre, H., La Crète et le monde grec de Platon à Polybe. Paris, 1948.

Vogt, J., Rom und Karthago, Ein Gemeinschaftswerk. Tübingen, 1943.

von Fritz, Kurt, "Leges Sacratae and Plebei Scita," *Studies Presented to D. M. Robinson on his Seventieth Birthday*. Vol. II, pp. 893–905. St. Louis (Missouri), 1953.

—— "The Reorganisation of the Roman Government in 366 B.C. and the So-called Licinio-Sextian Laws," *Historia*, I (1951), 1–44.

—— "Totalitarismus und Demokratie im alten Griechenland und Rom,"
  Antike und Abendland, III (1948), 47–74.
von Scala, R., Die Studien des Polybius. Stuttgart, 1890.
Walbank, F. W., "Polybius and the Roman Constitution," *Classical Quarterly* (1943), 73–89.

Index

Achaean League, 3 ff.; voting rights, 5 f.; democratic character of, 7; decline of, 9; reconstitution of, 10; alliance with Macedon, 13, 15 ff.; defeat by Cleomenes, 16; alliance with Rome against Macedonia, 19; war with Rome, 19; relations with Rome, 19 ff.; policy of conquest, 20; Rome receives military support from, 22; revived independence of, 27; defeat by Rome, 27 f.

Acilius Glabrio, M'., 173, 270, 439, 460

Aediles curules, 180, 206 f.

Aelius Paetus, P. (consul 337), 222

Aelius Tubero, Q., 449

Aemilius Lepidus, M. (consul 78), 287 f.

Aemilius Paullus, 25

Aetolian League, alliance with the Achaean League, 12 ff.

Africa, North, establishment of a Roman colony, 269, 270

Agelae, 101

Alcman, 400

Alexander the Great, causes of his success, 394 f.

Alliances, 241 f.

Ambitus, laws against, 455 f.

Anarchy, origin of, 363

Ancus Marcius, 128 f., 140 f., 222

Andreia, see Syssitia

Antigonus Doson, 12, 13

Antonius, M., 223, 446

Antonius Merenda, Q., 223

Antonius Merenda, T., 223

Apella, 101, 312, 423

Appius Centho, see Claudius C.f. Centho, Ap.

Appius Claudius, see Claudius Ap.f. Pulcher, Ap.

Aratus of Sicyon, 3, 9 ff.; influence on Polybius, 11; motives of, 14 f., 18

Archon, 21, 22

Archons, functionaries of the people, 443

Archonship, requirements for, 441

Archytas, 83

Aristaenus, 19

Aristocracy, 192 f., 321, 358; transition to oligarchy, 60; origin of, 194 f., 362; development of, 220 ff.; corruption of, 253 f.; uncontrolled power and factional strife, 298 f.; position in a mixed constitution, 338 f.; military, 450

Aristocracy, see also Oligarchy

Aristotle, 230 f.; political theories, 45 ff.; *Nicomachean Ethics*, 47 ff.; *Politics*, 47 ff., 81 ff., 98, 110, 412, 422; emphasis on the good life, 51; Plato misinterpreted by, 66 f.; opinion of Lycurgan constitution, 107, evaluation of Sparta's weaknesses, 110; comparison of Carthage and Sparta, 117 f.; description of the institutions of Carthage, 118 f.; middle-of-the-road theory, 344

Army (Roman), 198 f.; difficulties in recruiting, 264 f.; proletarians enrolled in, 275; change in the recruiting system, 296; effects of changes in, 300; loyalty to the emperors, 305; separation from the civilian population, 337

Assembly, popular, 320

Asteropus, 424

Athenian fleet, condemnation of its commanders without trial, 341 f.

Spirit, importance in political systems, 351 f.

State, origin of, 45 ff.; development of, 52; influenced by moral concepts, 52 f.

State (word), Polybius' terms for, 50 f.; origin of the term, 412

Statesmen, conduct of, 24

Stobaeus, *Florilegia*, 82 f.

Stoic philosophy, Polybius' relation to, 55 ff.

Stolo, Licinius, *see* Licinius Stolo

Strabo, Pompeius, *see* Pompeius Strabo

Strategos, 4

Strikes, 212, 214

Strohm, H., theories concerning constitutions, 415

Subjected nations, 241 f.

Sulla, L. Cornelius, *see* Cornelius Sulla, L.

Sulpicius Rufus, P. (tribunus plebis 88), 279 f.

Sybota, battle of, 471

Synkletos, 4 f.

Synodos, 4 f., 9

Syssitia (andreia), 101, 106, 400

Tacitus, 189

Taeger, F., interpretation of Polybius, 419

Tarquinius, L., 129, 140 f., 365 f.

Tarquinius Superbus, 130 ff., 140, 141, 143, 148, 335

Tarquin kings, 148

Tatius, Titus, *see* Titus Tatius

Terentius Varro, C., *see* Varro, C. Terentius

Thebes, destruction of, 28; constitution, 91; successful leadership of, 373 f.

Themistocles, 374

Thrasybulus, anecdote about, 70

Thucydides, quoted, 417; history of the Peloponnesian War interpreted by Schwartz, 427

Tiberius (emperor), 295, 304

Tiberius Sempronius Gracchus, *see* Gracchus, Tiberius Sempronius

Timocracy, Plato's theories of, 64

Timocracy, *see also* Aristocracy

Timocracy (word), Plato's use of, 398 f.

Titus Tatius, 127, 137

Trajan, 296

Transalpine Gaul, governorship of, 291

Treasury (Roman), Polybius' account of, 158 f.

Triarius, Valerius, *see* Valerius Triarius

Tribunes, 103 f., 205 f.; role played in the contest between Fulvius and the Senate, 169; inviolability of, 200; right of intercession, 210, 212, 258, 284, 302, 303, 326, 329 ff., 340, 457 f.; negative power of, 216 f., 272; Polybius' fallacy regarding, 332; position of, 335; *see also* Consular tribunes

Tribuni plebis, 134

Tribus, 236 ff.; number of, 453

Triumvirate, first, 291

Tubero, Q. Aelius, *see* Aelius Tubero, Q.

Tullius, Servius, *see* Servius Tullius

Tullus Hostilius, 128, 144

Twelve Tables, laws of, 199 f., 202, 220 f.

Tyche, Polybius' concept of, 388 ff.; Aristotle's definition of, 395

Tyranny, 317, 358; caused by misuse of power, 60; Plato's opinion of, 66; contrasted with kingship by Cicero, 131; origin of, 362

Tyrant (word), Plato's use of the term, 425

Tyrants, 188 f.

United States, democracy in the, 185

Valerio-Horatian laws, 133, 136, 175, 201, 202, 326, 335, 468

Valerius Corvus, M., 444

Valerius Laevinus, 168

Valerius Publicola, P., 132

Valerius Triarius, 289

Varro, C. Terentius, 225 ff., 448

Varro, M. Terentius, 289, 450

Velleius Paterculus, 269

Vespasian, 296

Veterans (Roman), lack of allegiance to the Senate, 334

Veturia gens, 223

Veturii, 447

ROMAN HISTORY

An Arno Press Collection

Accame, Silvio. Il Dominio Romano in Grecia Dalla Guerra Acaica Ad
Augusto. 1946

Berchem, Denis van. Les Distributions De Blé Et D'Argent À La Plèbe
Romaine Sous L'Empire. 1939

Bouché-Leclercq, A[uguste]. Histoire De La Divination Dans
L'Antiquité. Four Volumes in Two. 1879/1880/1882

Cagnat, René [Louis Victor]. L'Armée Romaine D'Afrique Et
L'Occupation Militaire De L'Afrique Sous Les Empereurs. Two Parts
in One. 1913

Chilver, G[uy] E[dward] F[arquhar]. Cisalpine Gaul: Social and
Economic History From 49 B.C. To The Death of Trajan. 1941

Crook, John [A]. Consilium Principis; Imperial Councils and Counsellors
From Augustus To Diocletian. 1955

Cuntz, Otto. Die Geographie Des Ptolemaeus: Galliae, Germania, Raetia,
Noricum, Pannoniae, Illyricum, Italia. 1923

Déléage, André. La Capitation Du Bas-Empire. 1945

Delehaye, Hippolyte. Les Légendes Grecques Des Saints Militaires. 1909

Dessau, Hermann. Geschichte Der Römischen Kaiserzeit. Three Parts
in Two. 1924/1926/1930

Doer, Bruno. Die Römische Namengebung: Ein Historischer Versuch.
1937

Fritz, Kurt von. The Theory of the Mixed Constitution in Antiquity;
A Critical Analysis of Polybius' Political Ideas. 1954

[Fronto, Marcus Cornelius]. M. Cornelii Frontonis Epistulae,
Adnotatione Critica Instructae. Edited by Michael Petrus Iosephus
van den Hout. 1954

Grosse, Robert. Römische Militärgeschichte Von Gallienus Bis Zum
Beginn Der Byzantinischen Themenverfassung. 1920

Hardy, E[rnest] G[eorge]. Roman Laws and Charters And Three
Spanish Charters and Other Documents. Translated With
Introductions and Notes. 1912/1912

Hasebroek, Johannes. Untersuchungen Zur Geschichte Des Kaisers
Septimius Severus. 1921

Hatzfeld, Jean. Les Trafiquants Italiens Dans L'Orient Hellénique. 1919

Hirschfeld, Otto. Kleine Schriften. 1913

Holleaux, Maurice. ΣΤΡΑΤΗΓΟΣ ΤΠΑΤΟΣ: Étude Sur La Traduction En Grec
Du Titre Consulaire. 1918

Hüttl, Willy. Antoninus Pius. Two Volumes in One. 1936/1933

Laet, Siegfried J. De. **Portorium**: Étude Sur L'Organisation Douanière Chez Les Romains, Surtout À L'Epoque Du Haut-Empire. 1949

Magie, David. **Roman Rule in Asia Minor to the End of the Third Century After Christ.** Two Volumes. 1950

Marquardt, Joachim. **Römische Staatsverwaltung.** Three Volumes. 1881/1884/1885

Meltzer, Otto and Ulrich Kahrstedt. **Geschichte Der Karthager.** Three Volumes. 1879/1896/1913

[Nicephorus (Patriarch of Constantinople). Edited by Carl Gotthard de Boor]. **Nicephori Archiepiscopi Constantinopolitani Opuscula Historica.** Edited by Carolus de Boor. 1880

Nissen, Heinrich. **Kritische Untersuchungen Über Die Quellen Der Vierten Und Fünften Dekade Des Livius.** 1863

Oost, Stewart Irvin. **Roman Policy in Epirus and Acarnania in the Age of the Roman Conquest of Greece.** 1954

Paribeni, Roberto. **Optimus Princeps:** Saggio Sulla Storia E Sui Tempi Dell' Imperatore Traiano. Two Volumes in One. 1926/1927

Ramsay, W[illiam] M[itchell]. **The Cities and Bishoprics of Phrygia:** Being An Essay of the Local History of Phrygia From the Earliest Times to the Turkish Conquest. Two Parts in One. 1895/1897

Rosenberg, Arthur. **Untersuchungen Zur Römischen Zenturienverfassung.** 1911

Sands, P[ercy] C[ooper]. **The Client Princes of the Roman Empire Under the Republic.** 1908

Schulten, Adolf. **Geschichte Von Numantia.** 1933

Schulten, Adolf. **Sertorius.** 1926

Scriptores Originum Constantinopolitanarum. Edited by Theodorus Preger. Two Parts in One. 1901/1907

Smith, R[ichard] E[dwin]. **The Failure of the Roman Republic.** 1955

Studies in Cassius Dio and Herodian: H. A. Andersen and E. Hohl. 1975

Studies in the Social War: A. Kiene, E. Marcks, I. Haug and A. Voirol. 1975

Sundwall, Johannes. **Abhandlungen zur Geschichte Des Ausgehenden Römertums.** 1919

Sydenham, Edward A[llen]. **The Coinage of the Roman Republic.** Revised with Indexes by G. C. Haines, Edited by L. Forrer and C. A. Hersh. 1952

Taylor, Lily Ross. **The Divinity of the Roman Emperor.** 1931

Two Studies on Roman Expansion: A. Afzelius. 1975

Two Studies on the Roman Lower Classes: M. E. Park and M. Maxey. 1975

Willems, P[ierre]. **Le Sénat De La République Romaine,** Sa Composition Et Ses Attributions. Three Volumes in Two. 1885/1883/1885